MW01492577

To Bonnie
Merry Christmas,
God be with you always

Kenny

A SPIRITUAL APOLOGETIC

BEYOND BELIEVING:
BE-LIVING
IN A
WONDERFUL
WORLD
GONE WONKY

BRIAN SHOEMAKER

WESTBOW
PRESS®
A DIVISION OF THOMAS NELSON
& ZONDERVAN

WestBow Press books may be ordered through booksellers or by contacting:

WestBow Press
A Division of Thomas Nelson & Zondervan
1663 Liberty Drive
Bloomington, IN 47403
www.westbowpress.com
1 (866) 928-1240

ISBN: 978-1-9736-8782-5 (sc)
ISBN: 978-1-9736-8781-8 (hc)
ISBN: 978-1-9736-8783-2 (e)

Library of Congress Control Number: 2020904372

Print information available on the last page.

WestBow Press rev. date: 03/18/2020

FOREWORD

My own faith journey has been a long and winding road. I have been taught, helped and guided by many persons along the way. I was fortunate to grow up in a culture that valued faith to enable me to grow in my Christian walk.

Now, as an Anglican priest, I have been charged to help others in their journeys. There are so many in our world who are struggling to make sense of the challenges they face in a world that is constantly changing. It is difficult to find good teachers who can show us the way to a legitimate and profound faith.

I first met the author of this book, Rev. Dr. Brian Shoemaker, in 2016 when he came to visit us at St. Stephen Anglican Church in Louisville, Kentucky. I immediately recognized his passion to teach the gospel of love and reconciliation. Brian truly has a heart for those struggling with unbelief—atheists, agnostics, and nominal believers. He has personally experienced the grief of not being able to make sense of a "system" of Christianity that has become so nullified to the point that perhaps even the early Church would not have recognized it.

In this book, Brian Shoemaker asks relevant questions.

I believe Brian has made great strides toward offering answers that people are seeking today, answers that may lead to a legitimate faith. He tackles tough, ultimate questions about how one may believe in a loving God in the midst of a crazy culture. He directly addresses how our understanding of God in a contemporary culture is often contrasted to that of the God of scripture and the early church. In so doing, he leads the reader toward a fresh experience of faith—perhaps even a deeper understanding of the Presence of God in our lives, or as he describes it, more than believing – it is about BE-Living!

I hope that through the reading of this book one may experience the embrace or re-embrace of the joy of the Christian faith!

Father Jim Curry, Rector
St. Stephen Anglican Church
Louisville, Kentucky

Brian Shoemaker's work reflects not only the heart he has for God and his level of faith, but also the passion he has for a well-informed apologetic for the person of Jesus. This book will prepare open minds and hearts for a well-grounded understanding of the Christian faith.

Rev. Patti Napier, Senior Pastor
Carmel United Methodist Church
Indianapolis, Indiana

This book really is astonishing in its range of thought, its use of literary and poetic resources, and its spiritual insight. I think it is a great text and I loved reading it... so much rich material...a kaleidoscope of spiritual writing. It really is a substantial work! It is an imaginative, insightful record of a personal journey into God, giving an exciting new window into Christian belief.

The Reverend Professor Keith Ward
Author, "God: A Guide for the Perplexed"
Regius Professor of Divinity Emeritus
A Canon of Christ Church, Oxford
Professor of the Philosophy of Religion at Roehampton University
A Fellow of the British Academy, England

This is a most impressive document. It is a cover-all apologetic. I found it interesting and engaging. The breadth and depth is amazing! Dr. Brian Lee Shoemaker offers us a volume that addresses our distresses and answers our essential questions with remarkable breadth and depth.

The Rev. Dr. Kendrick L. Norris
Alumnus, C.G. Jung Institute of New York
Former Senior Pastor
First Congregational Church
New Haven, Connecticut

I have known Brian Shoemaker since 1976. He has faced difficult times and has emerged stronger in his faith. He has a good balance of intellectual prowess and personal compassion—not to mention a great sense of humor. He has concentrated on refining his education to be the best he can be for the glory of God.

Bart Irwin, PhD
Executive Director
Family Health Care Clinic
Louisville, Kentucky

This book is born from Dr. Shoemaker's own personal journey of seeking answers to profoundly important questions with which every thinking Christian wrestles. Drawing upon an impressive depth and breadth of experience gained from decades of mentoring and pastoring, his book addresses the real concerns and real questions that many struggling Christians face. True to form, Dr. Shoemaker combines intellectual rigor, keen insight, humor, and genuine pastoral concern in a practical apologetic that speaks directly to the experience of the twenty-first century Christian.

Meredith McBride Cutrer, PhD
University College
Dublin, Ireland

Dr. Brian Shoemaker presents a work both scholarly and remarkably accessible. In a world where "pop" Christian literature too often is condescending, even judgmental, Shoemaker offers his readers room to stretch, breathe, and even disagree. Comfortable in his own brokenness, he invites us all to join him on a journey toward legitimate revelation, rather than to rely on our own limited preconceptions and assumptions about God. This work strikes to the heart of "a world gone wonky."

Rev. Doug Couch
Pastor
Evangelical Lutheran Church of America
Danville, Kentucky

A beloved seminary professor impressed upon us that theology is simply "thinking about God." Consequently, good or bad thinking leads to good or bad theology. Brian Shoemaker helps us to think about God with wisdom, insight, and humor. Possessing the mind of a philosopher and the spirit of an artist, he has given us a magnum opus in 300 pages! If, as Phillips Brooks insisted, preaching is "divine truth through human personality," then the author brings us the Good News with warmth, intelligence, and compassion. Between the Invocation and the Benediction you will find a banquet of solid teaching and genuine worship. I must confess; this is the book I wish I had written!

Dr. Kenneth L. Fought
Retired Elder, UMC
Minister of Spiritual Care
Knoxville, Tennessee

Dr. Shoemaker's wisdom, "knowledge guided by understanding,"
combined with the depth of his experience as a Christian
apologist, reveals truth in a world full of wonky, suffering and sorrow.
Doc's book, will help you to see, both spiritually and
systematically, the grace & glory of God even amidst in the wonky.

Layton Howerton
Recording Artist and Songwriter
Host of "Highlights" on Family Radio
Columbia Falls, Montana

DEDICATION

This book is dedicated to:
Rhonda "Leah"... my once-in-a-lifetime love;
to
Keith Ward ... the most brilliant and empathetic professor
I have ever known;
and to
Jim Curry... the utmost portrait of a loving shepherd.

This book is also dedicated to my parents, *Estel, Jr.* and *Marilyn*, my son, *Andrew James-Vincent*, my sister, *Lori*, and my brother, *Rick*. With this book, I also give a nod to my nieces, *Jennifer and Sarah*, and my nephews, *Daniel, Jared, Travis, and Eli*, with warm affection and respect.

I also need to mention those in my extended family who I will always remember for sharing memorable moments of their lives with me: my grandparents, *Leland and Gladys Norris & Imogene Shoemaker*, my aunts, *"Thelma" Joyce, Olive Reeves, Carman Flor, Grace Norris Bailey* and *Jean Norris Crago*, and my uncle, *Donald Norris*. At one time or another, these loving persons helped an introverted little boy feel special.

Deepest gratitude to those persons who remain, for me, sparkling glimpses of God's tender mercy and grace: *J. M. Boswell, Wayne E. Ward, Mike Sawalich, Bart Duncan Irwin, Tony & Karen Rice, J. E. Hail, Doug Couch, Cindy Mescke Dillman, Larry & Kitty Keaton, Marsha Sparks, Shirley Schureck, Martha Blevins, Jim Fleming, Charles & Alice Weppler, Floyd "Grandpa" Sease, Bernie Brown, and Axie Reasor.*

I must also mention those persons who encouraged the faith journey of my youth: *Rosemary Sheets, Vic Simcox, Bob Harrington, James Robison, Tom Shill, Gary Bates & the New Happiness Singers, Ida "Granny" York, G. Willard Reeves, Tony Campolo,* and *Richard Cunningham.*

Finally, this book is dedicated to *all* my former students—especially those who encouraged its completion along the way: *Bryan Kloos, Adam Waggener, Austin Foster, Chase Carter, Camden Sloss, Matt Lay, Matthew Wine, Lindsay Thoman, Drew Turner, Ty Michael, Tyler Chelf, Natalia Bosch, Daniel Rhodes, Bradley Kurnick, Sarah Rhodes, Ashley Carlisle, and Zach "Bonecrusher" Page.* A posthumous acknowledgment to *Michael W.,* who left us before the world could realize his remarkable intellect.

A special acknowledgement is given to my typist, *Nikki Moore,* friend, former parishioner, and mother of rock star, *Edgar Red.*

CONTENTS

BEYOND BELIEVING: BE-LIVING IN A
WONDERFUL WORLD-GONE-WONKY

DIAGRAM: HOW CAN I BELIEVE IN GOD?
A SPIRITUAL APOLOGETIC

HUMAN ATTRIBUTES
Consciousness
Spiritual Personhood: Fruit of the Spirit
Laughter and Playfulness
Appreciation for Beauty
Music: Compositions in the Cosmos
Art and Aesthetic Motion
Altruism and Mercy
Creativity: Sub-creators
Improvisation and Novelty
Silence: Listening for the Inner Voice

Strength: Personal Strengths

RELIGIOUS EXPERIENCE: REVELATION / REFLECTION
"Mysterious and Universal Phenomenon of the Soul"

"Ecstasy: Supra-Rational Entering the Holy of Holies"

Soul: Innermost Being

RATIONAL EVIDENCE
The Moral Imperative – "Our Sense of Oughtness"
The Teleological Argument – "Creation by Design"
The Cosmological Argument – "Reason for the Cosmos"

Mind: Reason

"UNKNOWN" and "FASCINATING" QUESTIONS
Tolstoy: "Why am I living?"
"What is the cause for my existence and that of everyone else?"
"What purpose has my existence or any other?"
"What does the division which I feel within me into good and evil
signify, and for what purpose is it there?"
"How must I live?"
"What is death? How can I save myself?"
Einstein: "What is the meaning of human life...the life of any creature?"

Heart: Intuition

INVOCATION

"In the hour of greatest agony we are alone. It is such a sense of solitude which prompts the heart to seek the companionship of God … [for God promised], 'If they cry out to Me, I will surely hear their cry.'(Exodus 22:23/ KJV)."[1]

"The whole work of man in this life is to find God."[2]

Paul Tillich wrote "there can be no depth without the way to depth… discovered by the greatest geniuses through profound suffering and incredible labor."[3] The depth of meaning of which Tillich referred is not easily acquired through mere theological imagination, philosophical conversation, or scholarly achievements alone, if at all. There is a depth of meaning that must be experienced through communion with God's presence, as God creatively manifests Himself to vulnerable persons. Through our vulnerability we may be guided to this awareness, to sacred space in real time.

The effects of the wonky in our wonderful world may jolt us to the core of our being, shaking the very foundations of our existence. Crisis and chaos may awaken us to how askew our lives can become without a sense of meaning or purpose. Like the jumper cables that spark new life to a dormant battery, so too, may a jolt of wonky jolt us from the depths of our being, and perhaps awaken us to seek more than the latest fad, status quo, or the impulsive gratification of bio-chemical urges. Unlike the gospel of our contemporary culture, living well does not mean existing for the sake of wealth, fame, or sexual conquest. Real life is not measured by the whimsey and fickleness of human fantasies and delusions.

---

[1] Abraham Joshua Heschel, *Man's Quest for God:* Studies in Prayer and Symbolism (Santa Fe, NM: Aurora Press, 1954), 18-19

[2] Thomas Merton, *The Bread of Life* (NY: Farrar, Straus & Giroux, 1956), 97

[3] *The Depth of Existence,* from *The Shaking of the Foundations* (NY: Charles Scribner's Sons, 1948), 55

During seasons of "death, plucking up, killing, breaking down, weeping, mourning, throwing away, refraining from embracing, loss, tearing apart, silence, hatred, and war" (Ecclesiastes 3:1-8/NIV), the core of our being yearns for contentment, fulfillment, and a calm directive that will navigate us through the midst our estrangement from God. In tumultuous times, we hunger for spiritual manna, not materialistic mammon, for humanity seems to be designed for the nourishment of what Jesus metaphorically called "the bread of life that comes from heaven and gives life to the world." (John 6:33/NIV).

Jesus taught his disciples, "one's life does not consist in the abundance of possessions" (Luke 12:15/NRSV). "Man does not live by bread alone, but by every word that proceeds from the mouth of God" (Matthew 4:4/NRSV). To live well or "in abundance" (John 10:10/NRSV), means that one gains a new perspective for being as one enters into *sacred space,* or a deeper awareness of the presence of God. In this sanctuary-within-the-self we discern our exquisite capacity of a holy communion between infinite persons with an infinite Presence. This phenomenon does not come easily. It requires a vulnerability to God that throughout biblical and church history is exemplified by persons who suffered from the effects of the wonky of human behavior and positioned themselves to experience this exquisite moment of encounter. This phenomenological experience is what some call "conversion," "being born again," "saved," or simply as a threshold to spiritual transformation. The context of such an experience may differ, resulting in the verbiage of a various sectarian expressions. But the exquisite moment of encounter yields similar results: persons grow--*learning to love God and all that God loves, and striving to be the person God designed that person to be.*

This book originated a decade ago after grappling with the effects and challenges of my own wonderful world *--gone horribly wonky.* While I was decisively religious, I found myself in an unfathomable fallout of doubt and estrangement. All that I had once believed in demanded revision or rejection. My religious *training* was superseded by a deeper yearning: more heavenly manna, less earthly mammon and religious fluff. Some answers upon which I had once relied, were no longer sufficient to engage the crisis in my life. I was alone, but for the modicum of hope that kept me breathing.

What emerged from my season of despair was a rekindled awareness of God's presence, a mysterious communion with God and this book, a revised "spiritual" apologetic. Taken as a holistic experience that continues to this hour, this phenomenal experience is what I call *BE-Living: learning to love (or intimately know) God with heart, mind, soul, and strength, to love all that God loves, and to grow to be the person God designed me to be.*

While I hope the reader will find this offering challenging and perhaps even enlightening. One's own exquisite moment will be respective his or her openness and vulnerability to God. Tthere is no formula that requires God to act according to our specifications, schedules, or formulas. "God has mercy on whomever He chooses." (Romans 9:18/NRSV). All we can do is to "prepare the way of the Lord." Through our humility, reverence, and vulnerability we may position ourselves toward guidance into the deeper awareness of the sovereign God of the cosmos.

In all of humanity there is a striving to know the fullness of reality. Intuitive questions, empirical data, and insight concerning our existence enables persons to understand the fullness of life as sometimes wonderful and, at other times, wonky. For a multitude this means a search for an essential, guiding Presence that may offer answers to our deepest and most profound questions. New Testament scholar, William Barclay wrote that God has made us so that "instinctively" we long for God. There is in humanity that which makes us "grope in the darkness after God."[4]

If this is true, nothing less than the legitimate presence of God, above all other ascents to knowledge or gratification, will be enough to fulfill our *groping*. No matter how much you labor on it, sucking on gristle, won't nourish your belly. Neither can anything less than God's presence nourish the soul. It is nourishment we seek. Filling our mouths with materialistic fluff may gratify our bio-chemical urge for the moment, but it will never satisfy the inner, spiritual hunger pangs for which we often crave...or *grope*.

Encountering the presence of God is not easily dissected, even by the most learned philosophy, theology, or intellectual disciplines. How could even our most devoted "god-talk" encapsulate the sovereign God of the cosmos?

---

[4] *Acts of the Apostles* (Edinburgh: St. Andres Press, 1953), 143

To experience the magnificence of God certainly requires the totality of ourselves, intuition, reason, insight and personhood, or "heart, mind, soul, and strength."

This phenomenon may be of the type described by atheist and French philosopher, Andrea Comte-Sponville as *"enstasy"*—the experience of *interiority*, an immanence, a unity, an immersion or an inside-ness. "A mystery? Yes. A revelation? If you like." [5] Perhaps God sparks within the core of us a threshold to "enstasy" when we are most in despair, or at the end of our delusional thinking? Perhaps it is only as we reach the end of our *autonomy*, we discover this threshold to "enstasy" and may enter into the phenomenon of God's presence?

I sincerely hope this book provides some encouragement to trek your own course toward a greater awareness of God. Perhaps you are in a position to discover your own *spiritual apologetic* for believing at all? Keep in mind as you continue, no one can "pigeonhole God."[6] *No formula or directive can possibly do that—especially mine!* But God may be made known to those who truly seek to know Him. (Jeremiah 29:13/NIV).

The underlying principle of this book is that God manifests Himself to those who seek Him holistically. It counters the idea of *relativism*—that we project who we want God to be and fashion a theology around that premise. The apologetic I am describing is not relativism, it is *relationalism*. God manifests His presence not to fit our own projections of Him, but in relation to, or respective of, our capacity or vulnerability to be apprehended *by* Him in real time.

While the following pages offer the reader a *spiritual apologetic* from a moment in my own faith journey, and there may be similarities to other such phenomena in the lives of others, I truly believe that God reveals His presence to each person uniquely respective of he or she is capable of receiving that encounter. This is my story. It begins on an intuitive level, climbs toward empirical evidence for a simple belief in the existence of God, and moves into the realm of revelation. Your story will undoubtedly be unique, respective of the person God has designed you to be.

---

[5] *The Little Book of Atheist Spirituality* (New York: Viking, 2007), 155
[6] Gustavo Guiterrez, The God of Life (Maryknoll, New York: Orbis, 1991), 163

Where is God?

May 3, 1962. During a meeting in Washington DC of the Committee on Space Research of the International Council of Scientific Unions for its International Space Symposium, Russian cosmonaut Gerhman Titov was being interviewed along with American astronaut John Glenn. Both presented papers regarding their respective flights into space. During the interview, Titov was asked if his Soviet policy of atheism had been challenged at all by his flight into space. The Soviet responded, "Only now there is proof for the Communist position. I went into space and didn't see God, so that must mean God does not exist."

The reporter then turned attention to Glenn. "Did you see God in space, Colonel Glenn?" Glenn responded, "I didn't expect to…. The God I believe in isn't so small that I thought I would run into Him just a little bit above the atmosphere."

One of my boyhood heroes is John Glenn. Not only did he devote his life in service to his country but exhibited extraordinary bravery as a NASA astronaut. He experienced a perspective of the cosmos that only a handful of individuals ever do. From that perspective, in his Memoirs, he wrote, "'How can anybody prove there's a God? I can't. There's no mathematical formula or chemical composition that adds up to God, like there's no formula for love, or hope, or honesty…I can't look around this world and believe that it came out of chance encounters of cosmic debris. But you know, God doesn't have to be believed in to exist."[7]

A prayer of invocation:

> May today I learn peace, a contentment, O God, from you, from within.
> May I trust you in preparing your way in this sojourn I tread.
> May I not forget the infinite and limited possibilities that are born of this faith.

---

[7] John Glenn, *A Memoir* (NY: Bantam, 1999), 288, 317

May I use those capacities I have received to discern truth from falsehood, and
be guided by the legitimate promptings of your presence.
May I find contentment simply knowing I am of your design.

"Let your presence settle in my bones, and allow my soul the freedom to sing, dance, praise, and love." (St. Teresa)

Teach me to love and know you, O God,
With my entire Being: "heart, mind, soul, and strength."
Amen.

INTRODUCTION

Our Wonderful World Gone Wonky

Humanity owns a significant and essential purpose for being: learning. We are not "all that," but we are an essential continuum of all that is growing and emerging in creation. We are profoundly influential in what makes this world both wonderful -- and wonky! We are not only significant in this world, we are essential to a continuing creation, influencing it either for good or evil, order or chaos. Humanity has a unique and qualified place in the cosmos. We have the latitude to exercise an empathetic care for, or the exploitation and trafficking of, our world, our neighborhoods, even ourselves. We have the freedom to be a blessing or a curse to creation.

The Psalmist reminds us that we are "fearfully and wonderfully made!" (Psalm 139:14/NIV). The word, "fearfully," suggests the root meaning, "awe" or "reverence." We might say that even though we are not divine, God is somehow in awe *of* us and all He has created as interconnected and "good:" the atmosphere, the vegetation, the seas and terrain, the mountain peaks and the lowlands, the diversity of creatures-- all were created in preparation for the sustaining of a "very good" humanity in the continuum of an emerging and good creation. In the biblical context, all life is wonderful!

The biblical narratives unfold with a creative process designed to support life, a progressive universe and an ecosystem in which humanity may adapt. God offers a provisional eye over all creation, including watch care for "wildflowers of the field" and the "sparrows of the air." (Matthew 6:26-34/NIV). The traditional gospel song does remind us, *"His eye is on the sparrow and I know He watches me."* There is through the biblical narratives a sense of Presence *with, or within* creation from the beginning, the emergence of life that continues becoming more defined and refined with the progressive unfolding of creation. This emergent unfolding occurs within both the turbulent and tranquil moments for the maturing of humanity-in-creation. The suffering of humanity in the flow of history, may actually be a part of this maturation process that brings to us a deeper sense of spiritual truth in an ever-emerging world. God is not disconnected to creation.

According to composer, Civilia Martin, the beloved song, "His Eye is on the Sparrow" was written after she and her husband contracted a friendship with a Mr. and Mrs. Doolittle, whom she described as "true saints of God." The couple had suffered for years with terrible maladies: Mrs. Doolittle was bedridden for over twenty years, and her husband was wheelchair bound. Still, the saintly couple, despite their physical misfortunes, lived faith-filled lives, and were a inspiration and hope to all who crossed their path. Civilia Martin recorded in her 1905 journal:

> One day while we were visiting with the Doolittles, my husband commented on their bright hopefulness and asked them for the secret of it. Mrs. Doolittle's reply was simple: "His eye is on the sparrow, and I know He watches me."

Why should I feel discouraged? Why should the shadows come? Why does my heart feel lonely, when God's eye is on the sparrow, surely I too must be within His purview as well. Even in the midst of the wonky of our existence, there is a momentum toward what is good—both because there is a sense of accountability for what is not good, and because there is a sensibility to strive toward the wondrous possibility that we are indeed not alone in our existence. We are guided, not stalked, and we are cared for, not patronizingly tolerated. For truly, *"His eye is on the sparrow and I know he watches me."* While I don't know *how* that happens, I trust such a phenomenon is real.

What is God envisioning from this good creation set in motion from the epicenter of Eden? How does that vision include my own timely and good existence? Six times the narrative in Genesis says that God found His creation "good." After man was created, He found it "very good." Being is better than nothingness, order superior to chaos, and man's existence, with all its difficulties, is intended to be a blessing to an ever-emerging world. While humanity is "never called perfect; it will in fact be man's task to assist the Creator in perfecting His creation, to become His co-worker."[8] Being co-workers with God in an emerging world is bound to be

---

[8] W Gunther Plaut, *The Torah: Genesis: A Modern Commentary* (NY: Union of American Hebrew Congregations, 1981), 22

a blessing and a curse, both wonderful and wonky. Biblically speaking, we were intended, in our goodness, to express our lives as conscious, enabled, creative and free-thinking extensions of God's handiwork in our world. With that expectation comes responsibility and accountability. As Adam and Eve were raised up to tend the garden, with an inter-connectedness to God's Presence, to one another in community, and to their environment, we too were created for such a purpose: to learn to tend to the goodness of the garden: to love/know God, to love all that God loves, and to grow to be the persons God designed us to be. Obviously, in the story of the young, probably adolescent couple, they had a lot to learn.

Because we are of Divine origin, we are inspired with a sense of personal and communal autonomy and accountability. Thus, we are at best, *qualitatively autonomous!* We have the latitude in our consciousness to choose a pattern of behavior that regards either our own true spiritual insight and personhood or one that could regulate us to a level of impulsive, animalistic instinct.

Humanity exists in a spectrum of behavioral patterns. Such patterns may range from a religiously, in fear of a judgmental, tyrannical Deity, to a reckless libertinism which allows for the freedom of choice without regard to personal, community, or Divine accountability. We may choose the way of wantonness lusted for by the flesh, or to the sojourn of meaning and the maturity of personhood, the latter being guided by the inner core of our being. For many of us, our restlessness occurs when we try to exist in indecisiveness, in the in-between of instinct and insight.

In our qualified (or limited) autonomy we are proffered a biblical admonition: "Trust in the Lord in all thy ways and lean not unto your own understanding, seek his will in all that you do, and God will guide thy paths." (Proverbs 3:5-6/ KJV). This is what is meant by *qualitative autonomy*: we are free to choose our own quest for existence. Only in our regard to the presence of God in our lives may our quest be for the highest good. Our autonomy is qualified by loving God and all that God loves. In this qualified autonomy we find our sojourn in communion with God's purpose and intention for creation. In our human liberation to learn, we are not invited to live as libertines.

While this intended goodness is a positive potential in our lives, it is not an automatic "given" in a world wherein humanity disconnects from God for the purpose of their *unqualified autonomy*. Therein is the potential for the anti-good. The result of which is a world-gone-wonky: systems and cultures accepting of irresponsible and unjust behavior, and persons mired in misadventures and the misuse of human freedom. Erupting chaos interrupts the continuum of a good creation when human autonomy is not tempered by our recognition and reliance on God's sovereignty and guidance. This is how the world goes wonky!

Obviously, our world has gone wonky—crooked, off-center, remarkably askew. Unqualified autonomy has led us from progressive communities to segregated centers of egoism. "The lust of the eye, the lust of the flesh and the pride of life" (I John 2:16/NASV), when loosed without temperance, or without a sense of our own interconnectedness to a grander scheme of existence, creates a chaotic imbalance in the ongoing momentum toward reaching our highest good in the continuum of creation.

Henry Nouwen described the practice of unqualified autonomy as "absurd living."[9] The inclination for wonkiness is a potential for humanity because we are created with the latitude to learn. While wonky is not an inevitability, we see its effect when we choose to be estranged from the God who provides for us "the good, the true, and the beautiful in humanity itself."[10] While we KNOW there is a given good, we also are cognizant that we must learn to strengthen that good in order to diminish the wonky!

We live in a world wherein "absurd living" is not invincible, nor is "the good, the true, and the beautiful" inevitable. Where there is a given latitude-for-learning in a wonderful world with human autonomy for creative expression, there is also the potential for estrangement and brokenness.

> *Broken bottles, broken plates,*
> *Broken switches, broken gates,*
> *Broken dishes, broken parts,*
> *Streets are filled with broken hearts*
> *Broken words never meant to be spoken,*
> *Everything is broken*

---

[9] *Spiritual Direction* (NY: HarperCollins, 2006), 17
[10] Albert Einstein, *Ideas and Opinions* (NY: Modern Library, 1994), 52

Take a deep breath, feel like you're chokin',
Everything is broken. (Bob Dylan, "Everything is Broken" from
the album, *Oh Mercy, Columbia: 1989)*

Anglican scholar, John Macquarrie, defined this brokenness as a pathological disorder in human life, "a radical alienation deep within our existence," and on account of it, "we fall down on one side or the other from that narrow precipitous-path along which we have to walk."[11] Brokenness results when, in our collective and qualified autonomy, societies and cultures choose to live outside good and divinely-inspired boundaries; refusing to recognize God's sovereignty over our limited autonomy.

Unqualified Human Autonomy and the Potential for the Non-good

My tenure as a Christian pastor, and then as a Christian educator for decades, has convinced me that we are traumatized persons, battered and broken. Sometimes due to the consequences of our own misuse of freedom, sometimes due to the ebb and flow of the behavior of others -- we are not only broken, *we suffer.* The consequential effects of the misuse of freedom or our own egoism remains steadfast. None are immune from the effects of personal, political, social, or continental drifts. No human being is immune from the effects of *unqualified autonomy*: the misuse of freedom and disregard for our mysterious accountability before God, one another, and the fullness of creation. Kentucky novelist, Wendell Berry put it this way:

> *We don't know how to deal with mystery. All we want to do is to draw a little circle around what we are conscious of and try to control that -- and, of course, the results are disastrous. While we can control up to a point, we are blind to the effect of our control... our influence (our autonomy) enters the world-at-large.* [12]

Perhaps the following poetic excerpt from *The Paradox of Our Age,* first preached by Pastor Bob Moorehead of Seattle, Washington, best describes a wonderful world-gone-wonky. From the perspective of the pulpit: "we've

---

[11] John Macquarrie, *How is Theology Possible?* from *On Being a Theologian* (London: SCM Press, 1999), 47

[12] *Conversations with Wendell Berry,* Edited by Morris Allen Grubbs (Jackson: University Press, 2007), 39-40

learned how to make a living, but not a life. We conquered outer space but not inner space. We've cleaned up the air, but polluted the soul.[13] Similarly, note the seasoned observation of the Dalai Lama: "it's a time when there is much in the window, but nothing in the room."[14]

Our wonderful world has suffered from metropolitan centers, "ruled by structures of evil, symbolized as demonic powers...producing anxiety in all its forms."[15] Such "forms" include "unjust economic relations, oppressive political relations, biased race relations, patriarchal gender relations, hierarchical power relations, and the use of violence to maintain them all."[16] The wonky in our world that may, when unattended, become wickedness, is widespread. No one is immune from the effects of unqualified autonomy!

Within the latitude of our freedom there is, in turn, the recompense of our actions, various and natural consequences. From what some might blame as our own cooperation with demonic influences, schemes and devises, to what others would describe as our practice of what is anti-good or sin, humanity participates in its own lostness and may even promote human and cosmic suffering: "the slings and arrows of outrageous fortune."[17]

Sometimes the effects of this "outrageous fortune" can feel like being "plunged into the mire of the deep waters...where the waves overwhelm me, and my eyes have failed, while I await my God." (Psalm 69:1-3/KJV). Sometimes the only time we can truly enter through the threshold of God's presence is when, as the result of our suffering, after all other possibilities of human inquiry have been exhausted, we become vulnerable to God's interdiction.

Through the darkest season of my life, I have discovered that the turmoil in our ever-emerging creation can be positively engaged through an ever-expanding vulnerability to, and awareness of, a sovereign and mindful God. Suffering in a world of autonomous persons and societies is not only possible, it is inevitable. However, while suffering is inevitable, it may also

---

[13] Excerpt from *Words Aptly Spoken*: Sermons & Papers (1995)

[14] *TheArtofWisdom.com*

[15] Paul Tillich, *Systematic Theology II* (Chicago: University Press, 1963,) 27

[16] Walter Wink, *The Powers That Be* (NY: Doubleday, 1998), 39

[17] William Shakespeare, *Hamlet Act III, Scene I*

be an instrument through which we may learn our need for God. Through mishaps and mendacities, and the consequences of human misbehavior, we may learn that our autonomy is limited and qualified, and we are in need of what Freud noted as "that sense of eternity, of something limitless, something with no borders...at one with the All."[18]

The tension between primal instinct and spiritual insight: the ignoble and the noble

By the nature of our being, there is tension between our primal nature that ensures our physical survival and insightful notions that move us toward a nobler personhood. When we refuse to recognize this modality, the tension which results is often a source of guilt and suffering. Instinctive behavior motivates an unhealthy lust for absolute autonomy, while inspirational notions spark a sense of a healthy vulnerability to a Mindfulness greater than our own. How we strive toward personal and interpersonal well-being must regard our true selves as both fleshly primal and spiritually pristine -- responsive to, and responsible before, a sovereign God. Thomas Merton described this essential modality of the human being as the grappling between our primal nature: self-will or "automatism;" distinguishable from our spiritual nurturing or *"genuine liberty in obedience to God."*[19] Perhaps the grappling lessens in understanding the process of our becoming God's design for humanity in an ever-emerging and wonderful world?

How we *BE-Live* our own personhood before a sovereign God is the theme of this book. Beyond believing in something that will satisfy (or justify) our survival instincts, this book is about *BE-Living* in a Presence that will sustain and transform us into the persons God has designed us to be! It is not a book about the flesh in conflict with the spirit, but rather how the good creation of the flesh can adapt and be guided by the presence of a loving God.

This book is about trusting in the experience of Presence, rather than in our own devising. While "some trust in chariots and some in horses, we trust in the name of the LORD our God." (Psalm 20:7/KJV). When we admit our autonomy is qualified, we may become positioned to prepare

---

[18] Sigmund Freud as quoted by Andrea Comte-Sponville, in *The Little Book of Atheist Spirituality* (NY: Viking, 2007), 155

[19] *New Seeds of Contemplation* (Boston: Shambala, 2007,) 199

the way of the Lord in our lives. In our vulnerability, we may learn how to experience a Presence in a way that is personally transformational, profound, and existentially progressive. In short, through all the wonky in a wonderful world, we may learn how to do more than believe in something, we may BE-Live the lives God designed for us to live.

The Story of Job: God meets us in our vulnerability

> *"Where could I go?*
> *Where could I go but to the Lord?*
> *Seeking a refuge for my soul*
> *Needing a friend to help me in the end*
> *Where could I go but to the Lord?"* (1940 by James Coats, a songwriter from Jones County, Mississippi. His inspiration for the song came some years earlier while Mr. Coats was at the bedside of one of his dying neighbors, an African-American gentleman named Joe Keyes).

"Where can I go from your spirit? If I say, 'surely the darkness shall cover me and the light around me become night,' even the darkness is not dark for you." (Psalm 139:7-12/NRSV).

Job suffered from his wonderful world gone horribly wonky! Job sought God's presence, but in vain. Through all the theological discourses with his learned friends, all he found was a continual ignorance and the foreboding silence of God. Job, *a* good man, had lost everything he had achieved. The god in which he had trusted had become confounding. *Why?* What would cause such terrible things to happen to such a good man?

He could not theologize his plight. He could not find solace in the "hearsay religion" of his friends. Yet, through his suffering, he gained "new insight, superseded by an immediate encounter with the divine."[20] Job complained: "God stays away from me." (Job 19:25/NRSV). But he is certain that will God somehow redeem his suffering. He continued: "and if my skin then all turns to shreds, my eye will see him in my skinless flesh." Job hoped this divine presence would free him from the silence of God, and revitalize him."[21]

---

[20] J Gerald Janzen: Job (Atlanta: John Knox, 1985), 253
[21] Martin Buber: *Letters* (NY: Schacken Books, 1991), 633-634

Job did not claim to have found a rational or satisfying explanation for suffering. Still, despite everything, the good man remained resolutely disposed to look for and find a way of theologizing his situation. The good man remained deeply religious. He took seriously the reality of suffering and did not deny the difficulty in understanding it. His faithful fortitude prompted him to challenge the popular theology of his closest friends. He is guided into a sacred space wherein he may discover ways of talking about God, not only with his learned friends, but through "a surrender to God's presence and unmerited love."[22] His popular religion was superseded by a relational renaissance, or "rebirth;" a revival of learning and wisdom after a terrible period of spiritual stagnation.

The intensity of our suffering may awaken us to such a relational renaissance, a new and holy dimension, a presence that could elude even the most scientific analysis. With the cessation of his reasonable and religious rhetoric, in "being still" (Psalm 46:10/NASB), Job came to know the Presence of God in a way that he had not experienced before. Likewise, there is a stilling pause that arises within us when we learn, often through the wonkiness of our circumstances, that in our comprehension of God, our reason is limited, and our religiosity insufficient. It is in our capacity for intuition, reason, and insight that we come to the awareness that our human autonomy is limited: "God is serenely and supremely in charge."[23] Struggles in this existence awaken us to that startling reality.

One of the recurring themes of the biblical narratives is that when God's people are in the throes of wonky, "His mercies never come to an end." (Lamentations 3:22-23/NRSV), "He gives power to the faint and strengthens the powerless." (Isaiah 40:28-29/NRSV). Truly, although "there is no darkness in God" (I John 1:5/NIV), God does abide in the darkness, our ignorance, *with* us. Holocaust survivor and novelist, Elie Wiesel wrote, "God accompanies his children into exile. What happens to us touches God."[24] God abides near those who become confounded by the wonky in a wonderful world. Jewish

[22] Gustavo Gutierrez, *I Will Not Restrain My Tongue*, taken from Essential Writings, edited by James B. Nickoloff (Minneapolis: Fortress Press, 1996), 312

[23] Walter Bruggemann, Theology of the Old Testament (Minneapolis: Abingdon Press, 1997), 153

[24] Elie Wiesel, *Memoirs: All Rivers Run to the Sea* (NY: Alfred A Knopf, 1995), 103

poet and holocaust survivor, Abraham Sutzkever, offered the following spiritual rationale in his poem, *Resurrection:*

> *I searched for the Shofar of Messiah*
> *In specks of grass, in scorched cities*
> *To awaken my friends. And thus spake*
> *My soul of bones;*
> *See, I glow*
> *Inside you*
> *Why look for me outside.*[25]

Job discovered a sacred place, a path to higher thoughts and a deeper awareness of God's presence. He confessed, "how small a whisper do we hear him...the thunder of God's power, who can understand?" (Job 9:9-10/NRSV). It was only after his suffering, and subsequent calling out to the God he perceived had abandoned him, that the good man became an insightful and godly man. Job not only believed in God, he *experienced* God: "My ears had heard of you but now my eyes have seen you." (Job 42:5/NRSV).

In a world-gone-wonky, God arises from the midst of the mire and reveals to those who "prepare the way," the wonder and awe of His Presence! Martin Luther King believed humanity to be are in "a season of suffering." Recognizing suffering for a righteous cause is a learning curve, enabling humanity to grow to its fullest stature. Like Job, humanity has the capacity to use the ordeals of our era as "the opportunity to transform ourselves"[26] toward being who God has designed us to be.

For many honest theists, the reality of suffering is an apologetic up-hill climb when in debate with atheists or agnostics who cannot come to terms with the possibility of the existence of a benevolent God. The harshest suffering can seem to outweigh the beauty of an Eternal Good. Yet, there is a deeper consciousness that may arise in the midst of suffering that one may receive by no other means. God may even seem to be distant and silent during our seasons of suffering. Still, an awakening to insight from "a realm of complete

---

[25] Moscow, 1945, taken from *Art from the Ashes*, edited by Lawrence Langer (Oxford: University Press, 1995), 574

[26] *Papers*, Volume Seven: *To Save the Soul of America*, January 1961-August 1962 (University of California Press, 2014), 231

barbarity and degradation might be a revelation."[27] In God's silence, we may become more vulnerable to his presence and the discovery of insight. We may find God in the exhaustion of our own resources; in the exhale of our last attempt to breathe.

As she experienced the hardships and inner turmoil of her own in the sickness and poverty laden streets of Calcutta, in her *Private Writings,* Mother Teresa wrote, it is profoundly painful to be lonely for God. Yet, as one is faithful in the resolve toward His presence—"the greater the pain and darker the darkness, the sweeter will be my smile at God."[28] Truly, in times of utter despair, where can I go but to the Lord God and to the provision of His presence to which He guides?

As the intellect is challenged by the process of learning, so is insight gained by the arduous process of growing. From the war in Vietnam, Naval chaplain-turned-social activist, Robert McAfee Brown, explained how he could navigate belief among the wonky of a sometimes wicked and brutal world:

> *God was to be found in the midst of all the evil—not apart from it. What is it like for God to be situated in the midst? So God is in the foxhole, in the Jeep. God is in the bomber screeching down in flames. God is in the dying soldier on the beachhead. God is a vulnerable God, sharing the human predicament with us.*[29]

Perhaps the anguish in which we live is a pensive prelude -- an opportunistic threshold to the awe we might experience when anguish prompts us to seek Higher Knowledge? Perhaps a REAL Presence can be apprehended respectively through the effects of a world-gone-wonky? Some might concur it is not only through wonky alone wherein we are prompted to seeking after "Higher Knowledge," but it is in arising from the effects of the wonky that we discover a deeper awareness of the Sovereign God. Pastoral psychologist, Wayne E. Oates wrote:

---

[27] Frederick Schleiermacher, *The Christian Faith,* (Philadelphia: Fortress Press, 1976), 52

[28] *Come Be My Light*: The Private Writings (New York: Doubleday, 2007,) 222

[29] *Reflections Over the Long Haul*: A Memoir (Louisville: Westminster John Knox Press, 2005), 41

Only when some overwhelming crisis hits do we become 'shaken up' in our internal structure of our personality. The peace that passes human machinations in the discovery of the Living God, his grace is all sufficient to meet that crisis.[30]

How is it the good man, Job, could arise to a greater awareness of the Presence of God? His experience of the god of his dogmatically learned friends, their articulation of a theological discourse, was superseded by the Presence of what Rudolf Otto called *"the mysterium tremendum:"* that which is beyond conception, something absolutely and urgently positive "arousing in our hearts."[31] From his season of suffering, a good man became a more noble one: God *"turned the captivity of Job, when he prayed for his friends."* (Job 42:10/ESV).

An experience of the "Wholly Other"[32] is only apprehended "when we are reduced to nothing."[33] When I embrace that i am nothing, then i may become vulnerable to the presence of the "I AM God." This phenomenon of the human quest is what Martin Buber called a "portal" of a new and greater awareness of God, along with a deeper understanding of our own being.[34] Metaphorically descriptive, God's *face* must be "revealed" as "a presence of strength and meaning."[35] This presence is our source for intuition, reason, and insight.

God oriented all things relative-to-humanity as "very good" for the sake of our physical and spiritual well-being, a divinely-inspired *homeostasis*, through which to become the persons God designed us to be. Humanity participates in the continuum of God's good creation. Within this continuum of good, we have the capacity to lend blessing or curse, wonderful or wonky, to the world. As there are instincts for physical survival, there is also insight for spiritual well-being. Within that modality for being is an ever-emerging

---

[30] *My Theological Journey*, taken from *How I Have Changed My Mind*: Essays by Retired Professor of the SBTS, edited by John DW Watts (Louisville: Reviews and Expositor, 1993), 31

[31] Rudolf Otto, *Idea of the Holy*, Oxford: University Press, 1958), 13

[32] Ibid, 25

[33] *St. John of the Cross*, Collected Works, 172

[34] Martin Buber, *I and Thou* (NY: Simon and Schuster, 1970), 160-161

[35] Ibid., 158-159

experience of both wonky and wonder. The momentum of our orientation is toward the "very good."

Our being in a world of wonder is purposeful. Even the wonky of our existence has the potential to teach us the nobler purpose of our being. If humanity can embrace the continuum of a good creation and understand our place in that momentum, we might better envision a holier worldview in which to invest *our lives*. Carl Jung wrote, "as far as we can discern, the sole purpose of human existence is to kindle a light in the darkness of mere being." We must be cautious that in this process of discernment that we are not "robbed of transcendence by the short-sightedness of the super intellectuals."[36]

In the human experience, we find ourselves in a profound process of change, adaptation, and transformation. If God is the consummate Creator, then we, created in the image of God, are designed to be extensions of God's creative momentum which began in the epicenter of "Eden." We are not only being created, we are also creating. God continues to create through all that was created good! Being from being must regard our commission to "tend the garden and keep it flourishing." (Genesis 2:15/NIV). We have the capacity to choose-- to "tend" or to "exploit" the good in creation as well as, in ourselves and others.

In his classic work, *Hymn of the Universe*, Pierre Theilhard De Chardin eloquently concurs with this perspective of a good creation in which we are purposed to become instruments of God's handiwork:

> *It seems that a comprehensive plan is indeed being slowly carried out around us. A process is at work in the universe...the new earth is being formed and purified and is taking on definition and clarity. [Furthermore] Human suffering holds hidden within it, in the extreme intensity, the ascensional force of the world. The mysterious work of creation could be manifested to our eyes.*[37]

Quite simply, we are designed for the tending of the good. Humanity has the capacity to learn to love God, all that God loves, and grow toward being

---

[36] Carl Jung, *Memories, Dreams, and Reflections* (NY: Vintage Press,1962)
[37] *Hymn of the Universe* (New York: Harper and Row, 1961), 92-94

the persons God designed us to be. In this, we become essential extensions of the continuing hand of God's creative purposes for the world. Not only is creation viewed as good, as coming out of the goodness of God, but it is viewed as well as "theophany or a disclosing of the heart of God's being." Creating through our innate goodness is a purpose of life. It gives "rise to being, just as evil leads to non-being and is a denial of life's sacredness."[38] Much of the suffering in the world stems from the denial; however, even in the effect of that denial, one may come to a deeper understanding of the good God intends for a world-gone-wonky.

As we become what God intends for us to be, we become God's instruments of grace and godliness. The obstacle toward this progression of godliness, is our determination for unqualified human autonomy, and its effects. When we recognize our autonomy is qualified before a Sovereign God, and limited by our life-TIME, we may participate more fully in an unfolding cosmos guided by the Presence of an ever-emerging God. British philosopher, Keith Ward observed, the highest potentialities of the universe will, after all, be brought to its fullness. "God will ensure that the goal of creation is realized, a goal of great value."[39] Is this a goal that gives all life meaning and purpose for being?

God intends for humanity to be guided toward the positive potentialities of humanity that will continue the unfolding of a good creation. We are created to use our autonomy responsively to God and responsibly before God. The activity of God toward redemption and reconciliation does not prohibit, but does endeavor to qualify the freedoms in the context of human will and autonomy. Elie Weisel observed that the responsible exercise of human freedom is a purpose for humanity:

> Man is free, for God wants him to be free to choose every moment of our life. WE are free to choose between life and death, good and evil, laughter and tears, free to choose compassion over cruelty, beauty over ugliness, morality over immorality, and we are free

---

[38] J Phillip Newell, *Christ of the Celts: The Healing of Creation* (Glasgow: Wild Goose Publications, 2008), 59

[39] Keith Ward, *God, Chance & Necessity* (Oxford: One World, 2001), 199

to choose between freedom and the absence of freedom. It is up to
us to shape and nourish it.[40]

In His genius, God may use our wonky ways (or even the chaos in our communities) to guide all things toward ultimate goodness. Through the consequences of our wonky ways, God awakens us, sometimes harshly, to a pattern of a living discourse that may reveal to us redemptive truths: "destruction and ruin are followed by rebuilding and life."[41]

In a first century discourse, Christian mystic, Origen, depicted one's season of suffering as a goldsmith crafting a useful piece of artwork.

> *He brings it often to the fire; he strikes if often with a hammer; he*
> *burnishes it often; so it may BECOME more purified and brought*
> *to the shape and the beauty intended by the artisan… vessels of*
> *honor…into holy fruitfulness.*[42]

The Course of this Book

Beginning with a review of the classical ideas for simple belief in God, this book becomes a spiritual apologetic for Be-Living in the actualization of God's presence. It is an accumulation of both intellectual and insightful acumen, a wealth of observations, from generations of honorable persons who have sojourned through a wonky world of their own and discovered higher knowledge and deeper truth. It is also a compendium of discernment by many who have sought to discover the depths and mysteries of how one lives in response to the phenomenon, not only of believing in God, but BE-Living in awareness of His presence. My own journey through their writings and testimonials have both challenged and enabled my own faith journey from the wonky to the wonderful!

Chapter one begins the content with the foundation for the book: Jesus taught that God may be known through a holistic experience of "heart, mind, soul, and strength." The chapter offers the reader how this teaching

---

[40] Elie Wiesel, *And the Sea is Never Full: Memoirs* (Alfred A. Knopf, 1999), 147

[41] Gustavo Gutierrez, *The God of Life*, Maryknoll (New York: Orbis, 1991), 41

[42] Homily XXVIII

is essential to have an intimate knowledge of God, through a wholistic experience *with* God.

Chapter two introduces the apologetic discourse itself. With the guiding admonition of the disciple, Peter to "always be ready to make a defense to everyone who asks you to give an account of the hope that is in you, yet with gentleness and reverence" (I Peter 3:15/NASV). The book proceeds to offer the reader a commentary on how one comes to *"love" or "intimately know"* God with "heart" (intuition with fascinating questions); "mind" (reasonable and empirical evidence of God), which is a reminder of the classical arguments for the existence of God: the cosmological, the teleological, the moral imperative, and the argument from religious experience; "soul" (the religious experience or revelation in the inner core of our being); and "strength," (our essential and designed personhood and human attributes). The chapter concludes with a unique perspective of what is meant by biblical insight toward higher knowledge or how the Bible is a resource for insight, with narratives that serve as a "prompts."

Chapter three offers an apologetic for conceptualizing the character and nature of God. How can we know the character and nature of the "one God?" Is it possible to know God through the momentum of good in creation, even in the "very goodness" of humanity in our inclination toward what makes us well? This chapter outlines what that "very goodness" in humanity is like and how in observing those qualities (or strengths) may unveil for us some attributes of the One who created us "in His image."

Chapter Four is celebrates a selection of biblical narratives that serve as *prompts* toward a deeper awareness of God and how humanity may grow toward the persons God has designed us to be. In short, these prompts teach us to not only believe in something, but to BE-Live in the Presence of God—the ultimate some-One. As if climbing the rungs of a spiritual ladder of ascent, we are intended to fulfill the purpose of learning and growing to become the persons of God's intention. Biblical narratives are not just writings to be proven critically and historically accurate, but mysteriously discerned through the guidance of God's Spirit for the purpose of BE-Living.

The final chapter is an apologetic for the identity of Jesus as the ultimate prompt for the redemption and reconciliation of humanity with God. This chapter moves in a momentum that addresses perspectives of Jesus in other world religions, in a materialistic and atheistic culture, and through the eyes of the gospel writers. The uniqueness of Jesus as revealed through his personhood, his message, his miracles, as a mediator, with a portrait of a sacred humanity, offer the reader a path into the unquenchable momentum of life and a future hope.

Finally, the conclusion of the book is a irony. While the Epilogue concludes this book, it also invites the reader to an introduction to a personal journey, a new invocation of his or her own to follow. This invocation returns the reader toward the admonition of Jesus to love or know God holistically, with "heart, mind, soul, and strength." The illustration of this comes through a rendering of Psalm 46, illustrated by the music and instruction of gospel music icon, Andrae Crouch to love and know God, we must "modulate," or discover a change in the tonality of our lives.

CHAPTER 1

God: An Experience of Heart, Mind, Soul, and Strength

(Deuteronomy 6:5; Mark 12:30; Luke 10:27)

God can only be *known* by learning of and loving Him. It is the contention of this spiritual apologetic that the knowledge of God can only be discerned through a coalescence of the heart (intuition), mind (reason), soul (innermost center of the self), and strengths (human attributes). This coalescing or holistic approach to learning is activated by our vulnerability to God. It is in our sense of being intentionally vulnerable and responsive to God and living responsibly before God, that we experience the phenomenon of God's presence. This learning is a holistic ascent of our human capacity within the whims of God's pleasure to guide us to those moments wherein He may be –"made known"- in meeting us where we are.

"Epiphelations" (a rendering of the words epiphany and revelation conceived by my precious wife, Rhonda), cannot be manufactured or manipulated by the human will, or by simply believing in something. "Knowing" or learning to love God is a process of the interaction between humanity and the presence of God who enables humanity to believe that God exists, and BE-Live in the deeper awareness of His presence. Thomas Merton articulated this phenomenon poetically:

> *Tis not the skill of human art,*
> *Which gives me power my God to know;*
> *The sacred lessons of the heart*
> *Come not from instruments below.*
>
> *Love is my master. When it breaks,*
> *The morning light, with rising ray,*

To Thee, O God! My spirit wakes,
And Love instructs it all the day.

And when the gleams of day retire,
And midnight spreads it dark control,
Love's secret whispers still inspire
Their holy lessons in the soul.[43]

A senior high school student approached me after class. He shared with me that after all his years "raised in a Christian school," he was now a "convinced atheist." He could not reconcile scientific explanations of "creation" with the "six-days-of-creation," be it literal or a myth. Nor could he negotiate his way through the idea of a "loving and benevolent" God with such a "malevolent" world. To him, the universe was chaotic and without purpose. It seemed to have come into being randomly and by chance. "So," the student began, *"how can I believe in God?"*

My programmed response would assert taking him back through the proscribed curriculum: "the classical arguments for the existence of God" in the writings of Thomas Aquinas. But my student was searching for a formula more satisfying than rational arguments or physical evidence. In recognition of his plea, I simply replied, "I don't know how you can believe in God. Perhaps it is the god that you have been programmed to believe in that you reject? Maybe you have just not been convinced by the 'reasonable' arguments that have been presented to you. I don't know. All I can tell you is how I have come to believe in God, how God has been *revealed* to me."

So, this is my story. It may have some similarities to yours. Or, maybe not. Honestly, I don't know how God speaks respective to others. While there are similarities, I can only share the ways God has been *revealed* to me. I share those ways with some trepidation, for any religious experience that downsizes God to one's own personal experience can become idolatry. Moreover, only through symbolic language can I describe this phenomenon in my life, and I do so with a deep sense of awe, wonder, and reverence.

---

[43] Madam Guyon, taken from *Union with God* (Jacksonville, Florida: Seedsowers, 1999), 83

A Personal Ascent:

<u>**What I Think I Have Learned about God...so Far**</u>

I have learned to believe in the God who "exceeds God... beyond religious ideology."[44] A God who does not exceed our impressions of God is not God. God bound by language, limited by sectarian definitions, known by familiar names, is not God but becomes an idol or a projection of our own wishful thinking. The sovereign God of the cosmos cannot be so readily defined. I have become cautious that, in religious systems, one's god may become one's own projected idol or merely an icon of an exclusive religio-cultural conviction, rather than—well--God! God is not bound by any perceptions of Him--even mine! God cannot be confined in the encryptions of any ecclesiology or theology. The prophet Malachi proclaimed to the people of God, "Great is the Lord beyond the borders of Israel!" (Malachi 1:5/NIV). That is, the activity of God in the cosmos is not bound within the restrictions of any scientific, religious, or sectarian formulas.

Latin theologian, Gustavo Gutierrez wrote that no place or historical event is capable of containing or conjuring God. Implicit in the biblical narrative is the idea that God cannot be manipulated. God cannot be "enclosed in time. God is utterly free."[45] Scottish theologian, John Baillie, concurred: "the infinite riches of the divine Personality who is revealed to us cannot be exhaustively enclosed in any number of abstract nouns or conceptualizations."[46] I learned many years ago that to experience wonder, I must relinquish my tourist mentality of theology and follow the path of exploration into the realm of mystery. Too many speak about God as a tourist only hesitates to take a snapshots of things more wonderful to contain in a photograph. This *spiritual apologetic* was ignited as:

> *I lingered along a lonesome path,*
> *whereon wonder arose from the soft pristine*
> *wherein my old breath was taken*

---

[44] Dorothy Soelle, *Theology for Skeptics* (Minneapolis: Fortress Press, 1995), 38

[45] Gustavo Gutierrez, *Hermeneutical Principle*, taken from *Essential Writings*, edited by James B. Nickoloff (Maryknoll, NY: Orbis, 1996), 134

[46] John Baille, *The Idea of Revelation in Recent Thought* (NY: Columbia University Press, 1956), 27

and a fresh inhale of serene—did my soul receive. (Brian Shoemaker, 2010)

With this in mind, I humbly offer the following dram of discernment. I have learned to believe in an incomprehensible God who reveals His presence to humanity respective of both His love and our capacity for comprehending that love. God is not a deity whose anger must be appeased or His empathy for humanity manipulated by our good deeds or sanctimonious rites. God is neither defined nor regulated by the projections and personality traits of human design, anthropomorphisms or philosophical formulas. Although God may use such metaphors to aid us in our attempt to know Him, God is not bound by our limited and myopic projections or feelings *about* Him.

I have learned to believe in a God that I cannot figure out—even with the most astute theology and sincerest sectarian dogma. God is the God of my own contrived god! God is greater than anyone could sufficiently define by reason alone, through ego-centric projections, or by designs of wish fulfillment. "This knowledge is too wonderful for me to fathom." (Psalm 139:6/KJV). The apostle Paul wrote "The wisdom of God *in its rich variety* might now be made known." (Ephesians 3:10/NRSV; emphasis added).

I surrender to the God of abounding and creative grace. As the One who is not simply "the guardian of a rigid moral order," but the Sovereign Love of the cosmos and for all creation, no one can justify any notion that would "pigeonhole God"[47] or put conditions on His mercy. I don't believe in a God whose grace is bound by our estimation of persons outside our own sectarian formulas, faith traditions or standards of behavior.

While I can experience what Professor John Templeton called a "religious sense," a discerning inner mind, a nagging desire to know and enter that Creative Spirit, the Reality of that presence, while unconfined to my comprehension, is not beyond my apprehension! This strangely universal "religious sense" is an understanding that behind the awesome phenomena of nature and the continuum of good are unseen but not unnoticeable forces at work. Upon reflection, the experience is more "a sense of wonder and awe than fear."[48]

---

[47] Gustavo Gutierrez, *The God of Life* (Maryknoll, NY: Orbis, 1991), 162-163.

[48] John M. Templeton and Robert L. Hermann, *The God Who Would Be Known: Revelations of the Divine in Contemporary Science* (San Francisco: Harper and Row, 1989), 5-6

How could such a phenomenon of presence be encapsulated by the perceptions and preconceptions of our thinking? Abraham Isaac Kook *(1865-1935)* was the "chief rabbi" of Palestine prior to the establishment of the State of Israel. He was noted to be a major Talmudic scholar in his day. In his lesson on the character and nature of God, he surmised the foundation of religious faith as rooted in the recognition of the majestic greatness of the Infinite. Whatever one may say of good, mercy, justice, beauty, contentment and well-being, the greater reality for whom the soul aspires, is above all these. It is "only a tiny and dull spark of the hidden light to which the soul aspires when it utters the word, 'God.'"[49]

There is more to be gained from interaction *with* God than there is from speculation *about* God. Definition of God tend to express some idolatry when expressed definitively. All we can use to comprehend Him are symbols, poetry, and explanatory aids. There is an unmistakable difference between religious "chatter" and an understanding that goes to the core of our being as "that which will waft us up out of the grit and safely distances us from the anguish in the suffering of daily life."[50]

Although theology and rational inquiry serve as a check and balance between reality and superstition, we are more in need of the supra-rational experience of phenomena than empirical abstractions or religious speculations. Dialogue with God is more invigorating than conjecture about God. There is a marked distinction between genuine God-consciousness, or the mindful discernment of God's presence, and God-talk. The former is reaching one's soul-driven transfixion. The latter is the wandering through an endless maze of both scientific and theological conundrums.

Much of the wonky in this world is due to bad religion or bad science. The manner in which atheists and theists interpret God or deify their own disciplines is lame, or a distortion, in comparison to what could be considered a more legitimate purview of God. Physicist Steven Weinberg cited an example of such potential idiosyncrasy in the discipline of science:

---

[49] Kook, *The Pangs of Cleansing*, taken from *Essays, The Classics of Western Spirituality* (New York: Paulist Press, 1978), 261-262

[50] Ann Belford Ulanov & Barry Ulanov, taken from *Reaching to the Unknown: Religion and the Psyche Clinical Handbook of Pastoral Counseling*, Vol II, edited by Robert J. Wicks and Richard D. Parsons (NY: Integration Books, 1993), 9

> *Of course, science has made its own contribution to the world's sorrows, generally by giving us the means of killing each other, although the is not the motive. Where the authority of science has been invoked to justify horrors, it really has been in terms of perversions of science, like Nazi "racism" and "eugenics."*[51]

"Perversions" in both bad religion and bad science tend to limit the incomprehensibility and magnificence of God by limited presumptions and egocentric thinking. Such thinking has been and continues to be the source of much irresponsible behavior or the *wonky* in our world. Forbid that God should be so confined to easy-phrased frivolity or anthropomorphic perceptions.

Could the Origin of all wonder be subject or confined to any religious dogma or scientific dictum? It would be illogical to think so. Perhaps God truly IS the God of our respective gods in religion or icons of science?

I have learned to believe in a God who would be known through holistic *discernment*. Biblically, God introduced himself in relation to the vulnerabilities of those who sought Him. (I Chronicles 28:9; Psalm 119: 10; Isaiah 55:6; Hebrews 11:6/NRSV). This is far from relativism, in which a god is created by the imagination or projections of an individual. God is always God! In biblical history, God's manifestations are always timely and seasonal, fashioned to the faith level of persons, particularly persons-in-crisis.

Dr. Austin Farrer was Dean of Oxford's Magdalene College at the time of C. S. Lewis. Lewis described Farrer at that time as "one of the most learned theologians alive." In his book, *A Faith of Our Own*, Farrer offered an essential component toward *knowing* God:

> *It is to God himself that I must go, it is God that I must implore to give me care for God. All are called and indeed commanded, to love God with all their heart, mind, soul, and strength…Let us advance step by step, seeing what we can see.*[52]

---

[51] Steven Weinberg, *Dreams of a Final Theory* (NY: Pantheon Books, 1992), 258-259
[52] Austin Farrer, *A Faith of Our Own* (Cleveland: World Publishing, 1960), 54

Therese of Lisieux reminds us: "how different are the ways that the Lord leads souls."[53] I believe in a God not bound by dogma or sectarian formulas. A God that I can explain would not be a god of much potency. God transcends our speech about God, but only when we do not "lock God into prisons of symbols,"[54] and manifests Himself to persons respective of the capacity of those persons in their vulnerability to Him, not by simply embracing an imposed dogma or indoctrination.

This is NOT to say that I have no appreciation for doctrine or theological orderliness. I do! I respect how individuals throughout church history have articulated their experience of the phenomenon of God -- in their context. This book does not intend to demean the importance of good theology or the proper interpretation of Biblical narratives. Good theology undergirds a healthy spirituality and guards against superstitious nonsense. It is admirable to tame our brains toward those things that promote a deepening awareness of God: "whatever is true, noble, right, pure, lovely, admirable -- if anything is excellent or praiseworthy." (Philippians 4:22/NIV). But we cannot be so egoistic as to conceive our God talk, within our limited context, to encapsulate the eternal potential, depths and mysteries of God. If we could do that, then WE ourselves would be God.

Moreover, if we are to know God intimately and accurately, we must regard the influence of holy dialogue within a concentric community of faith. Variances of healthy insight may offer persons clearer vision of an all-encompassing God. However right a man's ideas, they are bound to go wrong if "he nourished them by himself."[55] One must remain constant in seeking what is true, but we need be graceful enough to consider the validity of the sacred journeys of others along the way. It is in and through community we are challenged and encouraged to learn and to grow as humans—*being*!

If we are to grow "in grace and the knowledge of the Lord" (II Peter 3:18/NIV), then we cannot exist within the confines of our own biases, or exclusive system of belief, without challenge or affirmation. Just as with

---

[53] *The Story of a Soul* (Brewster, MASS: Paraclete Press, 2007), 229

[54] Dorothy Soelle, *Theology for Skeptics* (Minneapolis: Fortress Press, 1995), 27

[55] Charles Williams, *The Descent of the Dove: A Short History of the Holy Spirit in the Church* (Vancouver: Regent College Publishing, 1939), 38-39

the four gospel writers in their respective opinions regarding the identity of Jesus, no one denomination can be so exclusive as to disregard the reasonable and sincere erudition of others in the community of faith when discussing the character and nature of God.

A Momentary Pause

Who or What is God? Discernment in the Wonder!

God is His own respective existence! God is more than anyone's formulation or perceptions. "'For my thoughts are not your thoughts, nor are your ways my ways,' says the LORD." (Isaiah 55:8-9/NRSV). God is the one whose presence and provision excels above all we can apprehend by reason alone. God has no humanity-imposed boundary or brink. Many atheists simply cannot believe in a God who so bound by the downsizing of God through limited human projections.

In his autobiography, Charles Darwin relates the adaptation of his *"slow maturing and agnostic mind,"* that eventually lost a sense of wonder and awe. He calculated a conception of the existence of God concocted by his own reason and observations, unaided by other possible ways of knowing. This exclusivity followed the extreme difficulty of conceiving a consummative creation: an immense, awe-inspiring universe, a remarkable ecosystem and a humanity with the capacity for creating what is good. Moreover, Darwin could not well explain the phenomenon he observed in humanity and sensed within himself. This phenomenon he described as

> *the sense of sublimity; and however difficult it may be to explain the genesis of this sense, it can hardly be advanced as an argument for the existence of God any more than the powerful though vague and similar feelings excited by music. The mystery of the beginning of all things is insoluble by us; and I for one must be content to remain an Agnostic.*[56]

Darwin admittedly lost his sense of "wonder and awe" in his observations of the world as dominated by the survival instincts of the *red tooth and claw* behavior of animals. Much later, the 20th century, Darwinist, Richard

---

[56] Charles Darwin, *Autobiography* (NY: W. W. Norton & Company, 1958), 85-96

Dawkins, used the reference to *red in tooth and claw'* in his book, *The Selfish Gene,* to summarize the behavior of *all living things* which arise out of the evolutionary theory of "natural selection" and the survival of the fittest.

But is what Darwin called "the mystery of the beginning of all things" truly "insoluble by us?" If so, why would one regard the need for scientific inquiry at all? Could Darwin's agnosticism have to do more with losing his sense of "wonder and awe," as superseded by his purview of the world as nothing but "red tooth and claw?"

French philosopher and atheist Andre Comte-Sponville, while similar to Darwin in his naturalistic view of the world, also recognized what he called a "dazzling" presence. He was aware of the extraordinary presence of peace, simplicity, serenity, delight, silence, harmony, "a perfect chord," beauty and truth that ignited within humanity, an "oceanic feeling, an altered state of consciousness." The atheist-philosopher answered his fascinating question: "why would you need God?" with the response, "the universe suffices." For atheists like Comte-Sponville, projections of God have so downsized that it has become impossible for him to believe in anything greater than the universe.

While Comte-Sponville comprehends a continual wonder and awe in life, his assessment of God is notably connected to his rejection of any religious phenomenon "accompanied by dogmatism, obscurantism, fundamentalism and sometimes fanaticism and superstition," yet remarks that he "owes much of what I am or what I try to be to the Christian religion."[57] Thus, rather than the question, "why would you need God?" perhaps, the better question is "why INDEED do we need God?"

Such myopic or negatively biased projections regarding the fullness of creation do not offer a holistic view of existence. In fact, the phenomenon of God's revelation to those who "actively seek Him" (I Chronicles 28:9/ NASB), serves to constantly save us from delusions, our false images of who he is and what he is like. In the very act of his silence, or "hiddenness, God is slowly weaning us from fashioning Him in our own image."[58] He lingers

---

[57] Sonville-Comte, *Atheist Spirituality*, Ibid. p. ix-x, 157
[58] Richard Foster, *Prayer: Finding the Heart's True Home* (New York: HarperCollins, 2002), 20

in the shadows of our discontent, until we are prompted by the wonky in our world to seek Him in the light of our sorrows.

Perhaps God is more than a projection of one's own limited observations of the world? Moreover, perhaps God is *living,* and moving within the continuum of what is both being and becoming?). If so, then God is ever *active, creative, and communicative, communing* with those who are open and vulnerable to His presence. God's presence challenges our projections and perspectives. Rudolf Otto believed "a God comprehended is not God."[59] Humanity is in need of that Presence in order to experience the revelatory and prophetic truth that guides teaches us to be humans—*being!*

In his book, *God: A Guide for the Perplexed,* Keith Ward concurred with Otto. Our knowledge of God advances by realizing that the Source of all being is profoundly greater than anything we can think of, beyond our highest thoughts or wishful thinking. We can only "represent God to ourselves by using symbols…of a father, a rock, a judge, a shepherd, or a warrior."[60] We must defer to such symbols, yet also realize that any symbol will not suffice in describing the magnificence of God. Moreover, such symbols may be satisfactory for one individual in the moment of his or her awareness of God's presence in his or her context. Such encounters with God tend to be pronounce in the moment, but also fluid in the momentum of God's continuing creative activity in our lives and in all creation.

While, in order to redeem His creation, God may adapt to the whims of a free-thinking humanity, God does not change His essential being. But our perceptions of Him tend to grow as we mature awareness of His presence. In other words, our symbols of God may change, but they are still only symbols we devise in order to articulate the One who is incomprehensible. In my own experience, I have grown to see the judgment of God as more as a means of reconciliation than punishment. Both are only symbols of how God ultimately redeems all of creation to Himself. Jewish rabbi, Maimonides, wrote that "all our God talk is metaphorical." According to him, God is *beyond* human thinking.[61] Christian theologian, Reinhold Niebuhr, stated

---

[59] *Idea of the Holy* (Oxford: University, 1958), 105
[60] Ward, Oxford: Oneworld, 2002, 47
[61] *Guide for the Perplexed*, Book I: 51-53, 1168

that God "does not fully disclose Himself, and His thoughts are too high to be comprehended by human thought."[62]

How then can such an incomprehensible God be known?

The Sovereign God of our concepts of god is of such magnitude that any construct we have of Him is only a small glimpse or symbol of God's essential Being. We must be ever alert to God as phenomena. and not merely reduce that experience of Him to a mere philosophical construct. If God *does* "fit any of our categories [we may] end up with an idol more congenial to us."[63]

We must be cautious! Our own projections of the ethereal, metaphysical, or religion can hide from us, the face of God. While theology and religious conviction may be a tool through which to articulate what is beyond our rhetoric or verbiage, "dogma, when its claim of origin remains uncontested, has become the most exalted form of invulnerability against revelation." [64]

Einstein observed how commonplace are the anthropomorphic characterizations of God. He also remarked that, in general, only individuals of "exceptional endowments, and exceptionally high-minded communities, rise to any considerable extent above this level."[65] This statement may allude to the fact that revelatory experiences of God supersede the most casual or imaginative speculations. Intuition, reason, and insight must coalesce in any attempt to comprehend an incomprehensible God.

For many, like the student-turned-atheist, the challenge was not the possibility of the existence of *A* god, but the difficulty in believing in the god of their upbringing or the god of the projected god of others whose lives articulate the foibles of a bad or faulty religion. For that student, there was little personal inquiry toward a higher notion of God; God was either the one of his upbringing or there was no God at all.

---

[62] *Essential Reinhold Niebuhr* (New Haven: Yale University Press, 1986), 240

[63] Walter Bruggemann, *Awed to Heaven, Rooted in Earth* (Minneapolis: Fortress, 2003), 35

[64] Martin Buber, *Between Man & Man*, taken from *Dialogue* (England: McMillan, 1947), 17-19

[65] *"Religion and Science,"* from *Ideas and Opinions* (Modern Library, 1944), 41

Perhaps this higher notion of God defines and requires *revelation?* German theologian, Emil Brunner contended: "Wherever there is religion, there is the claim to revelation," and through the respective ways in which these revelations take place, "mysterious and secret knowledge is given to men."[66] If God is to be known, His presence must be holistically discerned, apprehended in our fullest capabilities of perception: *intuition, reason, soul, and through our uniquenesses as persons.* A sovereign God of the cosmos could not be measured by natural imagination, religious dogma, or scientific conjectures alone! There is certainly more to the reality of God that could possibly meet the eye.

At times, through this holistic capacity for divine apprehension, humanity may experience the phenomena of God. Perhaps such a phenomenon may occur due to the travail we experience in a world gone wonky? Perhaps it is in recognition of the wonder in the world, that we discover the Greater Reality wooing us to Himself?

Often it is in and through the effects of a misguided freedom, our will to an unqualified autonomy or its effects, that we suffer hardship. But it is also through such times of struggle that humanity *naturally* searches for a lifeline for our survival. Perhaps it is only through such times that we even holistically seek a more refined awareness of a more legitimate God of everything?

> *God of the rivers and the waterfalls*
> *God of thunder and lightening*
> *God of the plains and the mountains*
> *Of rainbows and prairies*
> *God of birth and death*
> *Of love and hope*
>
> *And it came to pass on a cloudy night*
> *That I found myself lost in the dark*
> *And the wind blew cold and I was afraid*
> *And if love were lost how would I live*

---

[66] Emil Brunner, *Revelation and Reason* (Wake Forest: Chanticleer Publishing, 1946), 20

You were like some mist in the fading light
And my broken dreams wept in the night
Where was all the love we had known before
In this sea of tears would I reach the shore

God of sun and moon
God of ocean tides
You, who drive the sun
You of perfect light
Teach me how to sing
God of everything. (Judy Collins, "Singing Lessons"
Wildflower Company/ASCAP, 1998)

CHAPTER 2

An Apologetic Discourse

In observation of the cosmos, religious devotees are not bound to the *"God in the gaps"* idea in conceptual thinking about God. God is not a default when we are ignorant about the *how's* regarding the emergence of life. When religionists cannot understand the technical thinking of naturalistic conjecture about how the cosmos came to be, many tend to simplistically remark, "who knows? God did it." Thus, the contention of atheists toward some theists is they suffer from adipose brains, yielding in their ignorance to a blind, rather than informed faith.

Michael Ruse aptly described the "god in the gaps" argument as "that which supposes that God might slip in a directed quantum event as it suits His purpose." He continued to defend his anti-theist argument with his presupposition that if religionists cannot think of an explanation of how things work, they merely "fit God into the spaces where their understanding fails."[67] He then concludes his assessment of the inadequacies of theism by asking questions, such as: if God gets *credit* for producing intelligence, why should he not also get *blamed* for producing the "wrong quantum event" such as "bad mutations, earthquakes, floods, even Hitler and Auschwitz?"[68]

While such maladies and atrocities are concluded *wrong* or *bad*, in comparison to the overwhelming goodness of the created order, simply denying the existence of God and rejecting any divine intervention in the process of creation is similar to implying that science has (or eventually will have) an all-encompassing "theory of everything" through which to explain all that is, both good and bad. Both the notion of the "god in the gaps" and the "theory of everything" are comparable ascents of faith. While bad religion may default to the "God in the gaps" when science is intimidating, likewise,

---

[67] *Can a Darwinian Be a Christian: The Relationship Between Science and Religion* (Cambridge: University Press, 2001), 91-92

[68] Michael Ruse, Ibid.

the "theory of everything" may become for bad science a safe refuge from anything with a hint of the supernatural.

Martin Rees, former Director of the Institute of Astronomy at Cambridge University, in his recent book, *On the Future: Prospects for Humanity*,[69] described himself *as* a practicing but unbelieving Christian who irregularly participates in his Anglican Church. He argued that with the "god in the gaps" mentality, anything can be 'explained' by invoking supernatural intervention: "*God did it*." This was often the justification for many of the heinous events justified by professing theists in human history. Like many theists and atheists alike, Rees struggles in the tension between the world as it is and the world we'd like to live in and share with the rest of creation. Moreover, he argued that just because something has a scientific explanation does not preclude that everything can be explained through an anti-theistic scientific inquiry, outside the possible influence of a mindful, Intelligent Entity. Therein, lies the struggle.

Rees concedes, that while he does not believe in God, unlike Darwin, he does grasp the wonder and mystery of life. Rees and other significant scientists in history have held a variety of religious attitudes, if not a solid belief in God. There are traditional believers as well as hardline atheists among them. Not everything within the realm of scientific inquiry is readily observable for empirical explanations alone. Rees concluded, "If we learn anything from the pursuit of science, it is that even something as basic as an atom is quite hard to understand." If even the tiniest atom is hard to understand, how could God be so classified into the limitedness of the human intellect? Even with the remarkable advances in science and information, wonder and mystery remain.

As progressive as naturalists and humanists like to think of themselves, science must also admit to "great gaps in knowledge"[70] yet to be filled. Just as bad religion resigns to filling that void with a *"god in the gaps"* argument, so does the scientific mentality seek to answer "intuitive questions" with their own, *final theory for everything, "*a system of interlocking equations that

---

[69] Martin Rees, *On the Future* (Princeton: University Press, 2018), 199-204
[70] E. O. Wilson, Consilience: The Unity of Knowledge (New York: Alfred A. Knopf, 1998), 263

describe all that can be learned of the forces of the physical universe."[71] Both arguments are faith ascents, or knowledge based on both suppositions and wishful thinking rather than brute fact and insight.

Biologist and renowned conservationist, Edward O. Wilson, was partly right and partly wrong when he estimated that while science presumably has taken us very far from the personal God who once presided over Western civilization, "it has done little to satisfy our instinctual hunger so poignantly expressed by the Psalmist: *'man lives his days like a shadow. Now, Lord, what Is my comfort? My hope is in thee.'"*[72] While science may have brought humanity to a better understanding of *how* life works, the discipline is not equipped to answer the fascinatingly ultimate questions of *why* life works. Perhaps the "satisfying of our instinctual hunger" cannot be found in science alone, but requires an ascent into religion?

The challenge for Wilson regards the very notion of a personal God as incompatible with the grandeur of science. However, science is not so equipped to answer the intuitive question of "WHY?" things have come to be-- and are becoming what they have yet-to-be? Wilson even called for the "secularization of religion itself." At the same time he admitted that ethics and religion were still "too complex for present day science to explain with legitimacy or depth." He contends that both science and religion face the most humbling of challenges. Science must contend with ethical behavior and religion must somehow find the way to incorporate the discoveries of science in order to retain credibility. In both disciplines, "blind faith will not suffice."[73]

Perhaps a better grasp of the reality of God is evidenced by the wonder and mystery itself? Rather than to acquiesce to the "god in the gaps" mentality, we could instead consider the **"God in the gasps"** phenomenon. In observation of the cosmos, and in contemplation of the wonders of life, we are ignited to a sense of awe, or what Albert Einstein called the universal "cosmic religious feeling."[74]

---

[71] Ibid.

[72] Psalm 144:4; Isaiah 55:6; Ephesians 5:16; James 4:14

[73] Wilson, Ibid.

[74] Einstein, "The Religious Spirit of Science" Mein Weltbild (1934), 18.

Does the evidence of a divine Mindfulness reside in this universal phenomenon of wonder? Is the ultimate question not so much "how" things were created, but "why" the wonder came to be and, amidst the odds, are continuing to inspire humanity toward what is discernably good?

> When no one listens
> To the quiet trees
> When no one notices
> The sun in the pool
>
> Where no one feels
> The first drop of rain
> Or sees the last star
>
> Or hails the first morning
> Of a giant world
> Where peace begins
> And rages end
>
> Closer and clearer
> Than any wordy master,
> Thou inward Stranger
> Whom I have never seen,
>
> Deeper and cleaner
> Than the clamorous ocean,
> Seize up my silence
> Hold me in Thy hand![75]

Albert Einstein recognized the validity or rational recognition of "the mysterious" in the context of our common human existence. He wrote that the most beautiful experience a man can have is the sense of the "mysterious". It is the "underlying principle of religion as well as all serious endeavors in art and science…this is 'religiousness.'"[76]

---

[75] Thomas Merton, *The Stranger*, from *Collected Poems* (New York: New Directions, 1977), 189-190

[76] Albert Einstein, from *"What I Believe,"* Forum and Century 84 (1930), 193-194

Well-known for his PBS series, *COSMOS,* former professor of astronomy and space sciences at Cornell University, Carl Sagan, described this inner experience of wonder as the "religious sensibility" in looking up on a clear star-studded night. "Every culture has felt a sense of awe and wonder looking at the sky."[77]

Perhaps Einstein's "religious sense" and Sagan's "sense of awe" should be regarded as more than just a jolt of curiosity or a biochemical eruption? *WHY* is humanity capable of such awe and wonder? Is there something more to be discerned in that experience? Perhaps theists and atheists ought to supersede *the* "God in the gaps" theory that science often uses to critique bad religion with a "God in the gasps" postulation?

> *Oh, this is such a world of wonder,*
> *You have no idea.*
> *The poets try to tell you, and the artists,*
> *Composers, and the saints;*
> *But you're immersed in game shows, and in disco,*
> *In marketing, and in making it,*
> *While all around you wonder hums.*[78]

In his poem *The Celestial Surgeon (1885),* Robert Louis Stevenson was a bit more terse, even retaliatory, in his poetic critique of those who refused to recognize the wonder in creation:

> *If beams from happy human eyes*
> *Have moved me not; if morning skies*
> *Books. And my food, and summer rain*
> *Knocked on my sullen heart in vain:*
> *Lord, then most pointed pleasure take*
> *And stab my spirit broad awake.*

Essayist and poet, Paul Laurence Dunbar (1872-1906), inferred that such wonder is not an experience of randomness, but one through which persons are directed toward an awareness of a more profound Presence. Even the

---

[77] Carl Sagan, *The Varieties of Scientific Experiences: A Personal View of the Search for God,* edited by Ann Druyan (NY: Penguin, 2006), 2

[78] Steve Allen, *Wonders,* taken from *Reflections* (NY: Prometheus Books, 1994), 83

fluttering of a sparrow can become a guide for wonder when one takes the time to notice. Perhaps this is one manner through which God woos us to Himself, rather than to stalk us for himself with raw, scientific data?

> A little bird, with plumage brown,
> Beside my window flutters down,
> A moment chirps its little strain,
> Ten taps upon my window-pane
> And chirps again, and hops along,
> To call my notice to its song;
> But I work on, nor heed its lay
> Till, in neglect, it flies away.

SECTION 1:
Believing in God

In this section of this book, I propose a personal apologetic for why I have come to believe in God as "Ultimate Ground of Being" *(Tillich)*, "Wholly Other" *(Otto)*, or the "Thou" of our existence *(Buber)*. I have come to believe in a God who manifests a presence through momentous and historic glimpses, wherein His intentions for creation are revealed, documented through the high use of symbols, metaphors, poetry, parables and raw personal experiences.

This discourse discusses the possibility of the very existence of God. How can we think rationally about or discern God's legitimate presence in regard to the fullness of reality? How one may gain an understanding of such a fullness of Being may require how "intuition, emotion, and intellect all interrelate"[79] in the discernment of this reality.

Indeed, there are finer truths and refined perceptions within which "a reconciliation of a deeper religion and a more subtle science will be found."[80]

---

[79] Ed Mitchell, *The Way of the Explorer: An Apollo Astronaut's Journey Through the Material and Mystical Worlds* (NY: Putnam's, 1996), 5

[80] Alfred North Whitehead, *Science and the Modern World: The Lowell Lectures, 1925,* (Pelican Mentor Books), 184

The "God of the gasps" cannot be defined or articulated by either discursive speculation or a blind faith; by bad science or bad religion. Whatever the conception we have of this "God in the gasps," our ideas can only be imaginative projections, forming some image of "a reality that is beyond all images."[81] An informed faith must conceptualize a holistic articulation of God if that presence is to be apprehended within the confines of human existence. A truly scientific "theory of *everything*" would not readily dismiss the possibility of God as well.

Physicist and theologian, John Polkinghorne asserted that the Creator has not filled the cosmos with items stamped '*made by God.*' There is only the evidence that awakens humanity to the awareness of God's presence. The renowned physicist-turned-Anglican-priest contends that the presence of God is "veiled" because, the presence of the Infinite would overwhelm finite creatures, "depriving them of the possibility of truly being themselves and freely accepting God," and offering to persons, "the space to be themselves."[82]

This freedom toward BE-Living as one's true self is *"individuality,"*[83] in what Einstein observed as the good, the true, and the beautiful in creation, "realized in his discovery and creative demonstration of his humanity itself."[84] This realization is a purpose for a humanity, created in the image of God, and thus, regards how God manifests Himself to the respective nexus of our being as individuals. This is to say that in God's genius, He offers glimpses of His presence uniquely designed to manifest His being to His creation in the context of one's individuality and perception.

Admittedly, my own "god-talk" is metaphorical. Reinhold Niebuhr warned, "God does not fully disclose Himself." His mindfulness is too high to be comprehended by human thought. Niebuhr went on to conclude that our quest for God must become balanced between: "merely poetic appreciations of mystery and the philosophies of religion." This perspective assumes rightly that humanity is capable of "apprehending clues to divine mystery"

[81] Keith Ward, *Is Religion Dangerous?* (Cambridge: Eerdmans, 2006), 16

[82] John Polkinghorne & Nicholas Beale, *Questions of Truth* (Louisville: Westminster John Knox Press, 2009), 11

[83] Wayne E. Oates, *The Psychology of Religion* (Waco, Texas: Word, 1982), 54

[84] *"The Need for Ethical Culture,"* January 5, 1951, Einstein Archives 28-904

and accepting the disclosure of the purposes of "God for which he has made us."[85]

We must be aware of our dependence upon the One we seek for such an awe-inspiring manifestation of God's presence. Our knowledge of God advances by realizing that the Source of all being is infinitely greater in every respect than anything we can project or imagine. God is beyond our most impressive religious and scientific thoughts. We can only poetically represent God to ourselves "by using symbols of a father, a rock, a judge, a shepherd, or a warrior."[86]

"God in the Gasps": The Universal Phenomenon of Wonder

At the beginning of the 19th century, academia mounted major scientific theories in the measurement, mechanisms, and mathematical character of the eccentricities and symmetry of the cosmos and our ecosystem for life. A prominent scientist during the time was Professor Michael Faraday, who's proposed a myriad of ideas to sort out fact from fantasy, the wonder from the wonky. Faraday's experiments were a blend of his own spiritual and scientific acumen. Only through the coalescing of these two disciplines did Faraday believe he could accurately determine the fullness of reality, explore the mysteries of life, and perhaps even gain a glimpse into the character and nature of God.

In his book, *The Electric Life of Michael Faraday,* biographer Alan Hershfeld, described Faraday's explorations as more than objective observations about nature. They were a sincere attempt to discern God's "invisible qualities" through the remarkable design of the world and humanity. Faraday believed that through phenomena, he would witness God's "divine signature" in all things. Michael Faraday, the elder statesman of science in the nineteenth century, wrote that nothing in this world was "too wonderful to be true." Creation by a divine hand, reveals the character of God, everywhere to be seen, investigated, and understood. His religious devotion motivated and informed his scientific inquiry. Described by Hershfeld as an "intuitive experimentalist" and an explorer of scientific theories about space, light, and electrical force, Faraday suggested that the wonder of the world could

---

[85] Niebuhr, Ibid., 391
[86] Keith Ward, *God: A Guide for the Perplexed* (Oxford: Oneworld, 1986), 240

be best experienced by challenging both "pseudoscience" *(bad science) and* "spiritualism" (bad religion) through the compliance of both legitimate scientific inquiry and an informed faith.

The intellectual ascent of theistic scientists like Michael Faraday not only moved scientific inquiry forward for the sake of education, but also inspired a way forward toward insight and enlightenment of a humanity in cooperation with God and the goodness of a creation in process of creating a more wonderful world. For Faraday, science and religion were not in competition, but were created to complement the exploration of a wonderful world.

> *I hear babies cry,*
> *I watch them grow,*
> *They'll learn much more,*
> *Than I'll ever know.*
> *And I think to myself,*
> *What a wonderful world."*[87]

As our lifespan fades into the common threshold of death, we learn how truly wonderful the loveliest and simplest things in our world tend to be. This is articulated in reflections of a wonderful world by humorist, Jonathan Winters. Such reflections included:

> *rainbows after a thundershower, authentic winks from beautiful women, warm handshakes from complete strangers, the sounds of laughter, 'thank yous' and phrases like 'I'll never forget you,' 'You've made my day,' the expressions of kitties and puppies, sunsets and sunrises. You say they're always the same? Wrong! ...the least expensive and perhaps the most rewarding of all: our memories!*[88]

---

[87] From *"What a Wonderful World" Written by: Robert Thiele, George Douglas, George David Weiss*
Lyrics © BMG Rights Management, CARLIN AMERICA INC, CONCORD MUSIC PUBLISHING LLC, Round Hill Music Big Loud Songs, 1968
[88] Jonathan Winters, *Winters Tales: Stories and Observations for the Unusual* (NY: Random House, 1987), 208-209

There is purpose in the recognition of the purist attributes of human existence. This wonderful world can be experienced in the more complex discoveries of human inquiry. Winner of the 1965 Nobel Prize in physics for his work in quantum electrodynamics, Richard Feynman wrote that all sorts of things are "infinitely more marvelous than the imaginings of poets and dreamers of the past." In his discourse, *The Value of Science*, the renowned scientist added his own rather subjective expression of appreciation for the "wonderfulness" of the world: "I stand at the seashore, alone, and start to think…

> *Deep in the sea*
> *All molecules repeat*
> *The pattern of one another*
> *Till complex new ones are formed.*
> *They make others like themselves*
> *And a new dance starts.*
>
> *Atoms with consciousness;*
> *Matter with curiosity.*
> *Stands at the sea,*
> *Wonders at wondering…*

Feynman concludes that the same thrill, awe and mystery, comes repeatedly as one observes such wonders and questions emerge deeply. With more empirical knowledge comes a deeper, more wonderful mystery, "luring one on to penetrate more wonderful questions and mysteries—a grand adventure! …a particular type of religious experience."[89]

SECTION 2:
How Can We Know A Good God in a World Gone Wonky…and sometimes Wicked?

Jesus said to the religious elite, "you have heard it said, but now I say to you…" (Matthew 5/NIV). With his teaching, a new and challenging experience of

---

[89] Richard Feynman, "*The Value of Science*," from *What Do You Care What Other People Think? Further Adventures of a Curious Character* (NY: W W Norton and Company, 1988), 242-243

God emerged. The teachings of Jesus continues to influence the world yet today. The God-consciousness of Jesus, devastatingly impactful, wooed his disciples to follow him and his detractors to renounce him. Jesus offered to the world the visual of a divine phenomenon: the "God in the gasps" defined more clearly as a God of love and community accountability.

Jesus did not promote a new religion. His teachings were not intended to be anything more than a practical application of Judaism, with its emphasis on "loving God with heart, mind, soul, and strength" (Deuteronomy 6:5/NIV). Jesus inaugurated a *movement* of God's articulated presence, a momentum toward the experience of a moment-to-moment God-consciousness, a supernatural embrace, and the discernment of a progressive watch care over and continuum of creation.

Moreover, Jesus revealed that to know God, one must *learn* to **<u>love God with heart, mind, soul, and strength.</u>** The experience of God is not just a philosophical abstraction or theological conviction but a holistic and spiritual phenomenon! This phenomenon is a consummate awakening, not easily explained, but observed in the activity and admonitions of Jesus. In the pages to follow, I will describe to the reader this holistic approach to phenomenon as a spiritual apologetic based on our innate capacity for intimacy with God through an integration of *"heart (intuition), mind (reason), soul (core personhood), and strength (human attributes)."*

In his letter to the church in Rome, the apostle Paul wrote, "What can be known about God is plain to them, because God has shown it to them… understood and seen through the things he has made." (Romans 1:19-20/NRSV). What are those "things He has made," the evidence, that enable us to discern the existence of God?

The *God of the gasps* would certainly not be grasped by human reason alone. Knowing God with the "heart" implies an awareness of ultimacy through a gut *intellect*, asking fascinating questions with an intuitive hope toward answers to those questions. This is the idea undergirding the notion of the prophet, "You will seek Me and find Me, when you search for Me with all your heart." (Jeremiah 29:13/NRSV). It is from an intuitive hope to know a consummate reality that prompts us to higher reason and deeper insight.

Humanity has a capacity for the experience of God that is not dependent upon our observations alone. Insight from the inner core of our being, or the "soul," enables us to experience God's existence similar to that of Helen Keller's moment of "mental awakening." Keller's maladies of physical blindness and deafness did not hinder her from experiencing higher knowledge, nor limit her quest to find answers to her own fascinating questions. She wrote:

> Suddenly, I knew not how or where or why my brain felt the impact of another mind, and I awoke to language, to knowledge, to love, lifted from nothingness to human life. The world to which I awoke was still mysterious. A sudden flash of intuition revealed an infinite wonder to me. I perceived the realness of my soul. In that new consciousness shone the presence of God. The deafness and blindness, then, were of no real account. They were to be relegated to the outer circle of my life.[90]

Keller's story lends credibility to the admonition for humanity to "live by faith (an inner knowing) and not by sight (reason alone)." (II Corinthians 5:7/NIV). From an intuitive prompting came her capacity to exercise a trust in the Good beyond our circumstances or the *red tooth and claw* of natural selection. Keller ascended to an understanding of the fullness of reality not by reason alone, but through *insight*, described as: *"what no eye has seen, nor ear heard, but God has revealed to us through the Spirit, even the depths of God... teaching spiritual things to those who are spiritual."* (I Corinthians 2: 6-13/NIV).

This is not the exercise of blind faith. Acquisition of *insight* can be dangerous if it is exercised exclusively within the impulsive whims or self-indulgences of a person without a rational critique, accountability, or legitimate safeguards. Christian mystic, Mechthild of Magdeburg, referred to these *safeguards* as "discernment."[91] Humanity has the innate capacity not only of primal instinct for survival, but also of discerning insight for spiritual well-being and the experience of God.

---

[90] Helen Keller, *Light in My Darkness* (West Chester, PA: Chrysalis Books, 1998), 19-25

[91] *The Flowing Light of the Godhead*, Book VI: 4

SECTION 3:

Intuition: The Articulation of Unknown, Ultimate and Fascinating Questions

"Intuition, speaking to us, giving us insight and knowledge to help us...perceive facts outside the range of the usual five senses and independent of any reasoning process." (Mona Lisa Schultz, M.D., PhD. from Awakening Intuition: Using Your Mind-Body Network for Insight and Healing (New York: Harmony Books, 1998. p. 19)

Just as we may act on instinct that requires only raw data of self-concern on a primitive level, humanity also has the capacity for wisdom and insight through the condition of "human consciousness and envisaging through intuition."[92] Just as there is mental knowledge to be gained for the intellect, humanity may also cultivate mindful awakening for the soul. This process toward insight begins with intuitive questions about the consummate reality and our comprehensive capacity for the awareness of its fullness.

Astronomer Martin Rees contends there are questions that continue to perplex us. Although many questions have been answered, new questions will be posed in the future we can't conceive of today. We should nonetheless be sufficiently "open-minded" about the possibility that despite our efforts, "some fundamental truths about nature could be too complex for unaided human brains to fully grasp or perhaps any universe complicated enough to allow our emergence is for just that reason too complicated for our minds to understand."[93]

Perhaps scientific inquiry alone, *unaided* by any other possible entities of knowledge is insufficient in understanding the complexities of life? Perhaps an experience of a deeper insight is required for such understanding? I contend this deeper insight may be acquired by all persons on respective grounds of acquisition. Both the formally and non-formally educated have the remarkable capacity toward intuitive questions and the potential for insight. Intuition, as defined by Jung, lends itself more to the process of knowing non-prejudiced facts. From the launching of intuition evolves a process of rational inquiry and insight "at the end of which one has seen something nobody else

---

[92] C. G. Jung, *"Questions and Answers at Oxford,"* from *Interviews and Encounters* (Princeton University Press, 1977), 104-105

[93] *On the Future: Prospects for Humanity* (Princeton: University Press, 2018), 199; 193

would have seen."[94] Here is the threshold of a mysterious capacity toward knowing the fullness of reality unique to all humanity.

Intuition is an inner knowing not limited by our five senses. Plato said that most of us live in a dimly lit cave amid "shadowy derivative reflections," but it is possible to exit the cave and see what is "in clear light…ultimate reality."[95] Aristotle referred to intuitive thinking as "the source of scientific knowledge."[96] One might go so far as to say, that without intuition there is no reason for rational exploration. From the fuel of intuition, humanity is launched toward insight.

Formally defined: intuition is a person's capacity to obtain or have "direct knowledge and/or immediate insight, without observation or reason… not preceded by inference.'"[97] It's the gut feeling prompting one toward exploration into possibilities despite nay-saying opposition to the contrary. Intuition regards the truth of a proposition as 1) evident, 2) needs no justification to be explored and 3) is affirmed once all the facts are known. Of such dynamics "mathematical truth must be learned, but it is justified first by an appeal to intuition."[98]

Srinivasa Ramanujan:

The Intuitive Thinking of a Genius Mathematician

In the summer of 1913, the twenty-two-year old Ramanujan, a self-taught prodigy in mathematics, entered King's College at Cambridge to the astonishment of his professors around him. One individual at the time remarked, Srinivasa Ramanujan was a mathematician so great that his name "transcends jealousies, the one superlative great mathematician whom India has produced in the last thousand years."[99]

---

[94] Jung, *The Houston Films*, Ibid., 313

[95] Huston Smith, *Tales of Wonder* (NY: HarperCollins, 2009), 154

[96] Aristotle, *Metaphysics*

[97] *The Encyclopedia of Philosophy*, Volume 4 (NY: Macmillan, 1967), 204

[98] Greg Koukl, *Intuition: A Special Way of Knowing*, taken from site: bethinking.org

[99] Robert Kanigel, *The Man Who Knew Infinity* (London: Washington Square Press, 1991), 3

According to biographer, Robert Kanigel, His "leaps of intuition" confounded mathematicians even today, 70 years after his death. His papers are still plumbed for their secrets. His theorems are being applied in areas of polymer chemistry, computers, even cancer, "between the pristine proofs of Western mathematical tradition and the mysterious powers of intuition."[100]

Ramanujan's supervising professor, G. H. Hardy, was described as _the mathematician_ of his day, and an anti-theist, who "judged God as his personal enemy."[101] This distinguished senior professor described his student's mysterious knowledge as "arrived at by a process of mingled argument, intuition, and induction, of which he was entirely unable to give any coherent account."[102] Ramanujan attributed to the Hindu god, Namagiri his ability to navigate through the shoals of mathematical texts. He never discounted the unseen realm of an ethereal cosmos. In Ramanujan, "the mathematical and the metaphysical lay side by side inextricably intertwined." The result of this "intertwining" of intuition and the subsequent intellectual pursuit of "proofs" was what some called, the ranting of a madman, but was actually a "highly evolved vision of the cosmos."[103]

Just as there is "instinct" for the sake of human survival, there is the human capacity of "intuition" for the sake of spiritual awareness. Paul Tillich defined intuition as "knowledge by participation in a life-process. it is not irrational, and neither does it by-pass a full consciousness of experimentally verified knowledge."[104] According to Aristotle, "certain intuitions must anchor all other knowledge, lest there would be infinite regress."[105]

In short, without our capacity for intuition, attaining knowledge would be an impossibility. We would never reach the point of knowing anything to be true. Intuition, like empathy, is our participation in a process of understanding what is not necessarily measurable, or lends itself to scientific scrutiny, but is legitimate just the same. Examples of this definition would be like the lingering of an artist before an empty canvas. The painting unfolds

---

[100] Kanigel, Ibid.

[101] Ibid., p. 11

[102] Ibid., p. 216

[103] Ibid., 32-33; 65-66

[104] Paul Tillich, _Systematic Theology, Volume I_ (Chicago: University Press, 1963), 103

[105] _Metaphysics_, 1006a

on the canvas with the intuitive strokes of the artist's brush. His hand flows systematically from a sense of what is real for the canvas to emerge "from nothing to something."[106]

For the theist, intuition regards the reality of *hope*. John Polkinghorne writes: "human beings possess a significant intuition that in the end all shall be well."[107] More than a strategy for self-preservation, there is in humanity a gut knowledge with an accompanying passion for inquiry-- for access to a deeper dimension of reality not "readily perceptible in the generality of daily life."[108] This hope is a confident expectation that life is of value and meant to be lived in an ever- emergent and comprehensive understanding of its fullness.

Eric Clapton:

The Intuition of a Genius Musician

This *deeper dimension* of existence is intuitively discerned. When we cannot find our way through the resources of our own reason or religiosity, we tend to become more vulnerable to deeper sensibilities, guided by intuitive impulses of inquiry and hope. Note the experience of musician, Eric Clapton, from his autobiography:

> *Though I had certainly looked at religion, I have always been resistant to doctrine, and any spirituality I had experienced thus far in my life had been much more abstract and not aligned with any recognized religion.*

In March 1991, his infant son, Connor, fell through an open window of his mother's apartment at the Mayfair Regent Hotel in New York. The boy fell 49 floors to his death. It was in the midst of this horrific tragedy that Clapton needed more than reason to cope with his despair. Although Clapton was not one for religious experiences, he described the same "spiritual presence" that had once helped free him from drug use many years before was manifested again.

---

[106] Templeton and Hermann, *The God Who Would be Known* (NY: Templeton Foundation, 1989), 20-21

[107] John Polkinghorne, *The God of Hope and the End of the World* (London: Society for Promoting Christian Knowledge, 2002), 31-32

[108] Ibid.

I recounted the story of how, during my last stay...I had fallen on my knees and asked for help to stay sober. I told the meeting that the compulsion was taken away at that moment, and as far as I was concerned this was the physical evidence that my prayers had been answered. Having had that experience, I knew I could get through this.[109]

Clapton discovered a spiritual presence that could not only sustain him but offer him hope. He concluded, "I really believe it's about spiritual application, no matter how poverty-stricken I feel my application may be."[110] An intuition of hope provided for him a vulnerability to a Presence he had only known through crisis, and now again, discerned as real. This experience may be what physicist-turned theologian, John Polkinghorne called "an experience of the veiled divine presence."[111]

Intuition is a threshold toward a deepening awareness of a mystery, with some attempt at "ideation, which is often lost in rational abstraction."[112] Intuition is a spark that ignites a common, inner quest for understanding through a progressive process that begins with the inquiry of intuitive or ultimate questions that may determine our being or non-being. 'Being' means the fullness of human reality, the structure, meaning, and the aim of existence. Humanity is ultimately concerned about his "being, meaning, and the totality of his true self."[113]

Intuition ignites questions of ultimate concern and the conditions under which such "contact with the Cosmic Life may be obtained."[114] St. John of the Cross taught that answers to intuitive questions must emerge from "loving attention to the tranquil intellect." He believed from intuition of hope, gradually the divine peace with the wonder of divine love, will be "infused into the soul...to behold God.[115]

---

[109] Eric Clapton Autobiography (New York: Broadway Books, 2007), 14; 244-245

[110] Ibid., 256

[111] John Polkinghorne, *The God of Hope and the End of the World* (London: Society for Promoting Christian Knowledge, 2002), 34

[112] Eric C. Rust, *Religion, Revelation, and Reason* (Macon, GA: Mercer University, 1981), 27

[113] Tillich, Ibid., 14

[114] Evelyn Underhill, *Mysticism* (Scarborough, Ontario: Meridian, 1974), 64

[115] *St. John of the Cross, The Ascent of Mt. Carmel*, Book Two, Chapter 15: 5

Seeking answers to his most intuitive questions prompted the famous phrase of St. Augustine, "Thou hast made us for Thyself, O God...our hearts are restless, O God, until they find their rest in Thee."[116] Perhaps it was also in his restlessness for answers that Pilate inquired of Jesus, "What is truth?" (John 18:38/NIV). Intuition nags us with the quest for the answers to such questions. In other words, as we tend to our intuitive questions, we are "invited to a training of latent faculties, languid consciousness, a turning of attention to new levels of the world." In this process toward comprehensive knowledge, we may become aware of insight which the "spiritual Artist is always trying to disclose."[117]

The "Unknown and Fascinating Questions" of Leo Tolstoy and Albert Einstein

The stirring of intuition includes what Tolstoy called asking "unknown questions," or the profound exploration of the fullness of life through common inquiry. His questions included:

> "Why am I living?" "What is the cause for my existence and that of everyone else?" What purpose has my existence or any other?" "What does the division which I feel within me into good and evil signify, and for what purpose is it there?" "How must I live?" "What is death—how can I save myself?"[118]

Such questions imply there are answers to our need to understand meaning and purpose. We innately seek deeper insight than merely answers to questions exclusively for the survival of the species. Even with our technological discoveries and sophistication, we remain strangely restless and unfulfilled, or as some would determine-- lost, in need of redemption.

Intuitive or "fascinating questions...a category of questions not within the compass of scientific inquiry or the criterion of testability,"[119] may guide humanity to the "whys" of existence, or an ascent toward higher knowledge.

---

[116] Confessions, Book 1:1

[117] Evelyn Underhill, *Practical Mysticism* (Columbus, Ohio: Ariel Press, 1986), 30

[118] Tolstoy, *Living Thoughts* (London: Cassell and Company Ltd, 1948), 4

[119] Stephen Jay Gould, *The Structure of Evolutionary Theory* (Harvard: Belknap Press, 2002), Introduction

At least, the questions, intuitively asked, are "a way of orienting ourselves toward ultimate concern."[120]

Albert Einstein asked what he called, "fascinating" questions. These questions included: what is the meaning of human life, or the life of any creature? Could there being meaning to life simply in the capacity to ask such fascinating questions? He concluded, the one who regards his own life and that of his fellow human being as meaningless is not merely unhappy but "hardly fit for life."[121] For Einstein, answering such questions offer a purpose for being.

Even the basic question, *"who am I?"* presupposes in the quest for identity, which is in itself, a purpose for being. The question seeks a wider context of personhood and acknowledges "the polarity and tension that lies at the core of all human existence."[122] Why do I ask "why?" Why am I conscious of my ability to do so? Why are naturalistic explanations alone insufficient to respond to these questions? Why am I restless until I can find answers to ultimate questions?

Perhaps that intuitive restlessness for answers to "unknown" *or* "fascinating questions" are themselves designed to lead humanity toward empirical evidence for a more comprehensive reality? Through the rational observation of *how* things exist, one might discover some evidence for *why* life happens. Science is an ingenious discipline for answering the "how" questions: "How did the universe evolve to the observable order and form that we see?" But it is woefully inadequate in addressing the "why" questions: "Why is there anything at all?" "Why is there such a remarkable ecosystem that supports life?" These are questions of ultimacy, common in all persons, which require the inquiry of religion or philosophy.

Former Harvard professor of paleontology and evolutionary biology, Stephen Jay Gould wrote that whereas science tries to theorize and explain the factual character of the natural world, religion operates in the equally important, but in a distinctive "realm of human purposes, meanings, and

---

[120] John Haught, *Science and Religion: In Conversation, Annual Journal of Physics*, Volume 64, Issue 12 (1996), 1532-1533

[121] *"The Meaning of Life"* from Ideas and Opinions (NY: Modern Library, 1994), 12

[122] John Macquarrie, *On Being a Theologian* (London: SCM Press, 1990), 34; 47

values—subjects that the factual domain of science might illuminate, but can never resolve."[123] (Emphasis added).

It is significant that Gould recognized the categories of *"purpose, meaning, and values"* as conundrums to the scientific community. Such realities as these are not easily scrutinized through a scientific lens alone. Perhaps a more holistic approach to knowing the fullness of reality is required for the scrutiny of not only "how" life works, but "why" life *is* at all. Through intuitive hope articulated through "unknown" (Tolstoy) or "fascinating" (Einstein) questions, we may be guided to empirical observations, seeking rational evidence for a more comprehensive reality. In so doing, one may come to discover purpose, meaning, and values distinctive to humans-*being*-as designed by a Higher Intellect, or God.

SECTION 4:
Intuitive Questions and Empirical Evidence for the Existence of God

> *Humans throughout history have had a passionate drive to understand the origin of the universe. There is, perhaps, no single question that so transcends cultural and temporal divides, inspiring the imagination. At a deep level, there is a collective longing for an explanation of why there is a universe, and for the rationale—the principle—that drives its evolution…some of these questions can be answered scientifically. (emphasis added)."* [124]

Human exploration regards an ultimate explanation of *everything observable*, what Richard Swinburne called, "the object or objects on which everything else depends for its existence or properties."[125] This explanation of which theist Richard Swinburne mentioned, is similar to that of atheistic physicist Steven Weinberg in his book, *Dreams of a Final Theory,* wherein he ponders the answer to his own ultimate questions: *1)* "Why is the universe built to

---

[123] Steven Jay Gould, *Rock of Ages: Science and Religion in the Fullness of Life* (NY: Ballantine Books, 2002), 4

[124] Brian Greene, *The Elegant Universe* (NY: Random House, 1999), 345

[125] Richard Swinburne, *Is There a God?* (Oxford: University Press, 1996), 39

follow certain laws and not others?" and 2) "Will we find an interested God in the final laws of nature?"[126]

Is there evidence for believing in a God who has brought all things into actualization by some divine momentum or whim? Is the intelligibility of the universe, the elegance, consistency, and novelty, strong enough evidence to "postulate an eternal and necessary being...rationally?"[127] There is arguably an intuitive spark toward our desire to *know* the answers to these "unknown," but disputed questions. In our contemporary culture the universal sense of wonder at the orderliness of natural law, seems to be the "guiding principle" of a scientist's life and work insofar as he succeeds in keeping himself from "the shackles of selfish desire."[128]

In this section, I will mention briefly some of the major or *classical* arguments for the existence of God, or a benevolent Mindfulness. Although each argument alone can be debated *ad nauseum,* when they are systematized as a progressive step-by-step rationale, together, they become a reasonable argument for the existence of God.

According to Thomas Aquinas, the universe must have an uncaused, changeless, and necessary cause, a prime mover of all that is moving. If we are to have an absolute explanation of its existence. This theorem assumes the universe to be "intelligible;" every event has to have a cause, there is "a reason for everything."[129] Swinburne maintains, if there is a God who is essentially eternally omnipotent, omniscient, then He will be "the ultimate brute fact" which "explains everything else--anything else."[130]

Some would ask, if everything has to have a cause, then "what caused God?" By definition God would not be God if God had been *created* like every other *thing.* If that were to so, logically, the creator of God would be a higher God. That higher God would be the actual God. So goes cyclically hypothetical

[126] Steven Weinberg, *Final Theory* (New York: Pantheon Books, 1992), 2242-2245

[127] Keith Ward, *The Evidence for God: The Case for the Existence of the Spiritual Dimension* (London: Darton, Longman & Todd, 2014), 70

[128] Albert Einstein, *"The Religion Spirit of Science,"* from *Ideas and Opinions,* Ibid., 43-44

[129] Ward, Ibid., 69

[130] Richard Swinburne, *Is there a God?* (Oxford: University Press, 1996), 19

arguments in the brains of humanity who would endeavor to either create their own projections of God, or to become gods themselves.

Still, there is empirical evidence for the existence of God based on its intellectual merits, rather than a dependence upon either a "god in the gaps" religion or a lame "theory of everything" science that in the words of noted American physicist, Paul Davies, "reduces God to the level of a conjurer, a trickster, or an illusionist." (Davies' view of God is more abstract, if not agnostic. He describes God as "grander than this meddler which is the image you get if you just want God to intervene from time to time." [131])

The Cosmological Argument: "Reason for the Cosmos"

Two similar theories of this argument have been offered by three philosophical perspectives: from Islamic philosopher, Avicenna[132] and Catholic theologian, Thomas Aquinas.[133]

The Cosmological Argument according to Avicenna:

1. The universe has a cause;
2. If the universe has a cause, then an uncaused, personal Creator of the universe exists, who *sans* the universe is beginningless, changeless, immaterial, timeless, spaceless and enormously powerful;

Therefore:

3. An uncaused, personal Creator of the universe exists, who *sans* the universe is beginningless, changeless, immaterial, timeless, spaceless and enormously powerful.

Avicenna articulated the concept of God as a "Necessary Being" for all things to have come into existence as they have. He wrote: Whatever has being must either have a reason for its being, or have no reason for it. If it has reason, then it is contingent through interconnected beings ending in

---

[131] Paul Davies, *"Interview: Traveling Through Time: A Conversation"* from Science and Theology News (August 16, 2008), 8

[132] c. 98-1037

[133] c. 1225-1274

a "necessary Being."[134] By definition, a god with a beginning must have another source of being; therefore, god would not be God in that case. God, is the necessary Being, the *primary mover* or *first cause* of all that has come into being and is continually becoming.

The Cosmological Arguments of Thomas Aquinas:

1. Everything that exists has a cause of its existence.
2. The universe exists.

Therefore:

3. The universe has a cause of its existence.
4. If the universe has a cause of its existence, then that cause is God.

Therefore:

5. God exists.

In his exhaustive *Summa Theologia,* Aquinas offers five *demonstrations* through which one might support the above assertion. Those five demonstrations of the existence of God:

1. *The argument from* motion. God is the prime or first mover, "put in motion by no other;"[135]

2. *The argument from efficient causality.* There is an order of efficient causes. God is necessarily the first efficient cause;"[136]

3. *The argument from* contingency. Every necessary thing has its necessity caused by another. God of Himself is His own necessity, and not receiving it from another, but causing in others their necessity.[137]

---

[134] Avicenna, *On Theology,* 25
[135] ST, Part IQ.2, Article 3
[136] ST, 1.2.3
[137] Ibid.

4. *The argument from goodness.* The maximum in any genus is the "cause of all in that genus; as fire, which is the maximum heat, is the cause of all hot things." Therefore, there must also be something which is to all beings the cause of their goodness, and this highest Goodness "we call God;"[138]

and

5. *The argument from final causality.* The governance of the world, as humanity and all creation directed by God, is endowed with knowledge and intelligence; as "the arrow is shot to its mark by the archer." God exists by whom all natural things are directed to their end.[139]

Is there sufficient reason to surmise the possible existence of God through the empirical evidence articulated by Avicenna and Aquinas? Of course their arguments are predicated on the idea that the cosmos had a *beginning.* Their explanation of a "beginning" is one brought about by a divine *First Cause* or *Prime Mover* who ignited and then guided the development of the cosmos and the ecosystems of sustainable life.

Note that the intuitive question is not so much concerned with the *how* of all things, but the *why* of all things that came to be. It is the latter question religion seeks to answer. If religion is undergirding by honesty and integrity, it should never be threatened to add empirical knowledge to its system of thought and perspective. An informed inquiry can dispel resignation to an inherited, superficial or blind faith.

Evidence for "In the beginning:"

<u>**God as a "First Cause" or "Prime Mover"**</u>

"Everything seems an echo of something else."[140]

---

[138] Ibid.

[139] Ibid.

[140] Robert Penn Warren, *A Way to Love God,* from The Collection of Poems edited by John Burt (Baton Rouge: Louisiana State University Press, 1998), 325

The arguments above are predicated with confidence that "in the beginning God created the heavens and the earth" (Genesis 1:1/NASB), the cosmos and the ecosystems that support life. God, in his divine mindfulness was intentional, in a methodology either *immediate* or *in process* to create all that is and is becoming. In some way incognizant to humanity, from the First Cause or Prime Mover, all things came to be from what was naught. Is there a connection between a biblical "beginning" and the empirical evidence for a "Big Bang?" Is a divinely creative initiative comparable to a scientifically theorized happenstance?

The Big Bang theory is a scholarly, scientific postulation set forth to explain what happened at the very beginning of our universe. Reasoned discoveries in astronomy and physics have shown evidence that our universe did in fact have a beginning. Prior to that moment little to nothing is confirmed knowledge. But during and after that happenstance, there was something: our universe and the movement toward a life-supporting ecosystem.

Apparently the "Big Bang" inflated, expanded and cooled, going from very small and very hot, to the size and temperature of our current universe. This expansion continues and cools to the present day and all creation continues within it: living on a unique planet, with a life-supporting ecosystem, circling a sun, with stars clustered together with billions and billions of other stars in a galaxy pirouetting through the universe, all of which is inside of an ever-expanding universe that began as an infinitesimal singularity or luck of some celestial roulette wheel, which appeared, by the estimation of some, "out of nowhere for reasons unknown." The big bang theory is an effort to explain what happened during and after that moment.

> Our universe is thought to have begun as an infinitesimally small, infinitely hot, infinitely dense, something - a singularity. Where did it come from? We don't know. Why did it appear? We don't know. This is the Big Bang theory.[141]

Modern cosmology posits evidence of a "beginning" as more than possible. But was it of a Mindful origin? To repeat the intuitive, fascinating, or unknown questions: "Where did it come from?" "Why did it appear?" Must

---

[141] http://big-bang-theory.com/

we wait for scientific theory of everything for an answer? These questions are not only intellectually interesting, they seem to be somewhat universally intuitive as well.

The Big Bang Theory and the "In the Beginning?" of Genesis 1:

<u>**A Supra-Rational Possibility?**</u>

Today, astrophysicists at NASA, combine mathematical models with observations to develop workable theories of how the universe came to be. Spacecraft such as the Hubble Telescope and the Spitzer Telescope continue measuring the expansion of the Universe. "One of the goals has long been to decide whether the universe will expand forever, or whether it will someday stop, turn around, and collapse from a Big Bang to a "Big Crunch?"[142] From a mysterious singularity to the expanse of the universe, is there momentum, a continuum of creation or is there a devolution toward chaos?

In his benchmark best seller, *A Brief History of Time,* astrophysicist Stephen Hawking asserted that "…distant galaxies are moving…" suggesting there was a time, called "the big bang," when the universe was" infinitesimally small and infinitely dense."[143] In other words, there happened from a single point in the universe, "the development of complicated and intelligent beings."[144] But just as there is little raw data explaining what was happening before the Big Bang, so is there little-to-no-knowledge to unfold the location of that "single point in the universe."

Does the pre-scientific purview of Genesis actually preclude the contemporary and scientific suggestion of a happenstance *roll-of-the-dice* in the emergence of creation? The statements above suggest a "beginning," but do not necessitate a God from which all things came to be. However, they do lend legitimacy to the idea that *something emerging from something*, even order from chaos, rather than something came from nothing, or meaningful being from a purposelessness void. What is the *singularity* from which or Whom all things came to be?

[142] http://science.nasa.gov/astrophysics/focus-areas/what-powered-the-big-bang/
[143] Steven Hawking, *A Brief History of Time* (NY: Bantam Dell Books, 1988), 8
[144] Steven Hawking, *The Theory of Everything: The Origin and Fate of the Universe* (Beverly Hills: New Millennium Press, 2002,) 35, 157

Was a "beginning" ignited by chance, necessity, or by an intentional and creative God? Moreover, the result of this "beginning" did not remain in a perpetual state of chaos but developed into both a sustainable ecosystem and a purposeful, communal society. How can we negotiate a theory of what might have precipitated such a mysterious (or miraculous) event? Any legitimate theory, religious or scientific, may proceed not only through intuitive questions, but also lend itself to faith ascents, as well as, through the study of empirical evidence.

In a recent interview, Hawking asserted that precipitating events before the Big Bang are simply not within the scope of being well-defined, because there's no way one could measure what happened at them. "Since events before the Big Bang have no observational consequences, one may as well cut them out of the theory, and say that time began at the Big Bang."[145] This is a scientific asserted statement of faith!

While nothing is known about events prior to the beginning of the cosmos as we know it, a theistic worldview would include one wherein the activity of a consummate, ever-creating God creates galaxy after galaxy, forming new matter, continually manifesting an artistic Presence and a portrait of Mindfulness portrayed in the cosmos. This would certainly be possible as one configures scientific theory with the biblical notion that from out of chaos emerged a created order and a life-supporting ecosystem, with "complex, intelligent beings" who have the capacity to learn and discern, and to grow as humans—being and becoming.

Jewish philosopher Maimonides denoted that every occurrence must have an immediate cause, and that cause must also have a cause, and so forth until we arrive at "the First Cause of all: God and His will."[146] As we observe the radiant beauty and the continual vitality of *how* life works, it is not unreason to assume the answer to the intuitive question of *why* life works as the purpose of God.

As in the emergence, processes, and progress of the creation of the cosmos, we may likewise experience an unfolding of God's mindfulness for our own

---

[145] https://www.livescience.com/61914-stephen-hawking-neil-degrasse-tyson-beginning-of-time.html
[146] Maimonides, *Guide for the Perplexed, Book II*, 48

existence as human beings, in our own peculiar ecosystems or movement from chaos to order. Moreover, we ourselves, are contingent agents of cause and effect, conscious extensions from a First Cause and Prime Mover. We have a capacity for cause and effect and can be agents of either chaos or order. Perhaps that is what is meant by our being "created in the image of God?" (Genesis 1:27/NIV).

The Teleological Argument:

The Impression of Design

Physicist Richard Feynman wrote that there is, to some degree, an amount of faith and imagination required for scientists to ascend to the heights of human inquiry and discovery. Feynman's "unknown" or "fascinating" question regards a teleological inquiry: *why does the stuff of the universe and ecosystem look to be designed?* Moreover, if things were not so readily observable, there would be no need or purpose for science to take notice or strive toward a "theory of everything" yet to be discovered.

Regarding the origin of the cosmos, he asked: *from where does "the stuff of life" and earth originate?* This stuff of life that Feynman affirmed as having of the look of design includes: "repeating patterns, a wonderful world, the physiology of human beings, electricity, the forces of attraction, human reasoning ability, testing and observation, virtue."[147] If such things cannot be subjected to scientific testing, does this mean that does not exist or of no relevance? Not unlike religion, scientific theory is a body of statements of varying degrees of faith. None is absolutely certain without the complement of one with the other.

Perhaps there is a limit to comprehensibility in aspects of the universe that remain scientifically "unexplained?" Columbia University Professor of Physics and Mathematics, Brian Greene observed even a "theory of everything" would not be the end of the human exploration of the fullness of reality. Perhaps the wonders of life and the universe are just reflections of microscopic particles engaged in "a pointless dance fully choreographed by

---

[147] Richard Feynman, *The Meaning of it All: Thoughts of a Citizen Scientist* (Reading, MASS: Perseus Books, 1998), 10; 26-27

the laws of physics."[148] Or perhaps, there is a more mindful Choreographer at work?

The cosmos and our own ecosystem seem to reflect both a well-choreographed routine, but also offers the capacity for a wondrous, improvisational dance. Such choreography requires both a rudimentary knowledge of *how* things work, and perhaps, a deeper understanding of *why* things move at all; a discernment which guides the dancer into the synchrony of the movement designed by the choreographer, with his or her own creative expressions included.

The Teleological Argument for the existence of God simply founded on perceptions of "design" alone is not all that makes it rationally compelling. The argument is remarkably captivating also in that perceptions of design in the choreography of life, one has the capacity to experience what NASA Apollo 14 astronaut, Ed Mitchell, called "an overwhelming sense of universal 'connectedness…an ecstasy of unity… an intelligent process at work."[149]

The Teleological syllogism is as follows:

1. Every design has a designer
2. The universe manifests a design
3. Consequently, the universe has a Designer
4. That Designer is God.

Expressed in a less sectarian way:

1. Some things in nature are apparently designed-like or perceived to look intentionally created
2. Design-like properties are not producible by (unguided) natural or chance happenstance and must be a product of intentional design.

Therefore,

3. Things in nature are resultant of an intentional design or "creation."
4. Thus, an Intelligent Designer as required for creation must exist.

---

[148] Brian Greene, *The Elegant Universe: Superstrings, Hidden Dimensions, and the Quest for the Ultimate Theory* (Vintage Books, 2000), 17, 367
[149] Edgar Mitchell, *The Way of the Explorer*, Ibid., 3-4

In short, the Teleological Argument lends rational support for an "Intelligent Designer" guiding the complexity in the cosmos and the biological structures into a natural ecosystem that supports life. Arguably, mere chance or directionless evolution cannot fully account for all the life forms and fanciful happenstances in the progression and adaptation of life on Earth. The evidence from *how* life works may be a clue as to "why" life *IS*. The following dynamics comprise significant components to the teleological argument for an Intelligent Designer:

1. The Anthropic Principle: an observation of the fortuitously specific details in the "design" that sustains life.

2. Information Theory and DNA: the wonder of individualistic genetic codes.

Both dynamics above constitute values of constants and parameters that make life not only possible, but magnificently and mysteriously progressive, both breath-taking and breath-giving! Such magnificent details in the design add more credence to the reality of the "God in the gasps."

The Anthropic Principle

Even if the above is interpreted as happenstance-by-chance, the Teleological Argument is a rational one on two levels. First, the argument DOES posit rational evidence that there is an undeniable appearance of design that COULD point to the possibility of an Intelligent, if not Mindful *Designer*. Second, the anthropic principle is universally personal in denoting the conditions essential for the livability of all life on Earth. In considering the following conditions, one may sense a direction toward purpose and meaning, a reason for being, beyond mere survival *instincts,* or the dreaded "red tooth and claw" of Social Darwinism.

Here are some examples of how the Anthropic Principle directly affects the livability of our planet:

The availability of water. Every known life form depends on water in the continual process of respiration, the continuum of existence. The important properties of water include its solvency, the buffering of temperature, as a metabolite, and to insure a healthy living environment.

Earth's atmosphere. The gases that make up the Earth's atmosphere include Nitrogen (78%), and Oxygen (21%); also Argon (.93%) and Carbon dioxide (.04%). If there were too much of just one of these gases, our planet would suffer a runaway greenhouse effect. On the other hand, if there were not enough of these gases, life on this planet would be devastated by cosmic radiation.

Earth's reflectivity or "albedo" (the total amount of light reflected off the planet versus the total amount of light absorbed). If Earth's albedo were much greater than it is now, we would experience runaway freezing. If it were much less than it is, we would experience a runaway greenhouse effect.

Earth's magnetic field. If it were much weaker, our planet would be devastated by cosmic radiation. If it were much stronger, we would be devastated by severe electromagnetic storms.

Earth's place in the solar system. If we were much further from the sun, our planet's water would freeze. If we were much closer, it would boil. The population of Earth enjoys a place of honor in the solar system when one considers such allowances for life on Earth. If our solar system were too close to the center of our galaxy, or to any of the spiral arms at its edge, or any cluster of stars, our planet would be devastated by cosmic radiation. Daily adjustments occur as the Earth is rotates. Rotation is so precise, enough for one place of the earth to go dark, and that would be night. When the earth rotates back facing the sun, that part of the earth gets daylight. Annual changes in seasons are due to the revolution of the Earth. Caused by the earth having an axial tilt of about 23.44°, this value remains about the same relative to a stationary orbital plane throughout the cycles of an amazing precession.

The Rhythm of Life: "the circadian rotation for our well-being." Chronobiologists agree that survival instincts in our genetic coding and protein pathways regulate our lifetime, promoting what is most healthy for our well-being. When our "body clock" is out of sync with light and darkness, we tend to disrupt or disengage from established *"rhythms of life."*

According to professor of molecular neuroscience Russell G. Foster, what happens in our bodies, our physiology and biochemistry, is rhythmic. Daily "circadian rhythms" (circa, about; diem: a day) are orchestrated by a central clock to keep our bodily systems working in harmony. "Like the conductor of an orchestra, the clock keeps the ensemble of the human body beating to a collective time, on time and in order. If we did not separate our bodily events by time we would be in a fine mess."[150] In the observation of constants with the appearance of design, there is a noticeable degree of both intention and improvisation within the cosmos and ecosystem. Against the odds: *life works!*

Theologian John Haught suggests that within the created order, God offers novelty, freedom hope, and "liberation from the lifelessness of perfect design." Ours is a world of gradual emergence from initial chaos and monotony, exploration, and a search for the more intensely deeper and more profound experiences of being," wherein God "invites creatures to participate in the ongoing creation of the universe."[151]

Similarly, Paul Davies wrote: "we seem to be constructed from an overwhelmingly vast tapestry of biological possibilities," as well as healthy consistencies. As one observes the totality of all this is, there seems to be complexity with specificity, or, a "*haecceity;*" that regards "the question of meaning about how to come to terms with the specificity of our individual existence."[152] This "haecceity" is the fruit of the intuitive questions that launch us into a search for empirical evidence for a greater Reality. British astronomer Fred Hoyle remarked, "apparently random quirks have become part of a deep-laid scheme."[153] Such a scheme could be concluded to be well-composed design by a consummate artist.

Finally, Stephen Hawking affirmed how conditions to support life CAN be rationally implied to be of a precise *design* through the laws of science,

[150] Russell G. Foster and Leon Kreitzman, *Rhythms of Life: The Biological Clocks that Control the Daily Lives of Every Living Thing* (New Haven: Yale University Press, 2004), I; 2-3; 32-33

[151] *God and the New Atheism: A Critical Response to Dawkins, Harris, and Hitchens* (Louisville: Westminster John Knox Press, 2008), 107

[152] Paul Davies, *The Faith of Scientists,* ed. Nancy K. Frankenberry (Princeton: University Press, 2008), 436

[153] "*Religion and Scientists,*" as quoted by John D. Barrow and Frank J. Tipler, *The Anthropic Cosmological Principle (*Oxford: Clarendon Press, 1988), 22

based on precise integers such as the size of the charge of the electron and the ratio of the masses of the proton and the electron. Hawking asserted, that the values of these numbers seem to have been "very finely adjusted to make possible the development of life." Moreover, it would be very difficult to explain why the universe should have begun in just this way, "except as the act of a God who intended to create beings like us."[154]

However, in an interview with NBC, Hawking asserted his non-belief in God or an Intelligent Designer. For the renowned physicist, such a concept would be beyond the grasp of the human mind, and, since for Hawking there is no aspect of reality beyond the reach of human reason, such a God could not exist. This is, of course, a statement of faith that would need more empirical evidence! Hawking, does, however continue to offer humanity some choice in the matter:

> The choices seem to be clear from a rational point of view. Either life as we know it, with all its dynamics toward _purpose and meaning,_ has evolved by chance or there is a Presence underlying it all—a profound "ground of Being." One of the "unknown" questions for empirical reflection would regard which of the choices is indeed more rational—particularly if that answer was concurrently informed or aided by intuition? (emphasis added)."[155]

In his concluding statement, perhaps Hawking was correct that in some ways, empirical reflection needs the aid of other concurrent information-- even intuition, or perhaps other resources of knowledge that are not viable within the context of human intellect alone, but require a more wholistic experience of ascent. Moreover, perhaps there is within the human "design" a capacity for such an ascent?

Information Theory and DNA:

The Working Code of Individual Persons

Deoxyribonucleic acid or DNA is a molecule that carries genetic instructions used in the growth, development, functioning and reproduction of all known

---

[154] Hawking, _A Brief History of Time, Ibid., 125-127_
[155] http://www.nbcnews.com/science/space/im-atheist-stephen-hawking-god-space-travel-n210076

living organisms. DNA stores biological information respective to each of those living organisms. Unique to a theory of all things *created* by design is the concept of individuality and diversity within the boundaries of a created *order of kinds or* "species." This is for what Information Theory may lend some support: the biblical notion of the uniqueness of *personhood.*[156]

In other words, each living organism was uniquely designed, created, or formed, "each after its own kind." (Genesis 1/KJV). To the ancient Hebrew tribes, God was not an abstract force, He was a living entity—all which implied an intimacy with a community of individuals. Individuality was the deepest expression of creation, and "God the Creator could himself be spoken of only in such terms."[157] God was an indescribable, yet personable entity respective of God's unique existence within a *progressive* community. The community of faith began in the hearts of individuals who encountered the presence of God. From that respective phenomenon there emerged a worshipful family, then a tribe, a nation, and movement toward an inclusive, beloved community wherein all uniquely-designed persons are welcome.

Stephen C. Meyer, a Cambridge professor of the philosophy of science and author of *Signature in the Cell: DNA and the Evidence for Intelligent Design*, asserts that the DNA in every cell of every creature reveals ample evidence of having been *deliberately designed by God.* In an interview, Meyer explained "what is DNA?" and why its pointing to an Intelligent Designer is our most logical conclusion:

> *The molecule of heredity is a beautiful structure, highly organized, but it's a particular kind of organization or order that played a role in the origin of life. If the human person is designed, then you can have an understanding that there is a definite human nature, and therefore moral laws that advance human flourishing.*[158]

---

[156] Walter Brueggemann, *Theology of the Old Testament,* (Minneapolis: Fortress Press, 1997), 451-454

[157] *The Torah: A Modern Commentary,* ed. W. Gunther Plaut (New York: Union of American Hebrew Congregation, 1981), 21

[158] From: *How DNA Proves God Made All Creatures Great and Small,* an Interview with Terence P. Jeffrey, July 10, 2009. http://cnsnews.com/news/article/how-dna-proves-god-made-all-creatures-great-and-small

Information Theory, and specifically the remarkably creative function of DNA, either points to the rational validity of an Intelligent Designer with an intentional specificity AND randomness in mind, or it is merely the effects of evolutionary chance. Which is most enthrallingly reasonable or challenge the limits of scientific inquiry? Many scientists are also religiously-inclined either by choice or by the raw data they observe. Among those scientists who are not religious in a conventional sense, such as physicist, some confess to a passive notion that there is 'something' yet to be discovered in an ultimate sense, perhaps some meaning behind existence. Is the universe a purposeless accident that can be assessed by empirical evidence? Is ultimate reality even assessable through reason alone? Davies wrote:

> Much of the discussion involves new advances at the frontiers of science have led to interesting and exciting ideas about God, creation, and the nature of reality. this method of investigating the world is worth pursing as ...*rational inquiry to its limits*. (emphasis added)."[159]

In conclusion, even if one disputes the above arguments as religious bunk, they cannot be discounted as being either irrational. Moreover, in the possibilities proposed, there is a further evidence for a Divine Intelligence undergirding all of creation in existence, and in the purpose of living well as the persons in whom we have been designed.

One of the highlights to the Anthropic Principle, or the *design in the details* argument, regards the place of *constants* in creation. The fact that there are constants to be observed and measured indicates an intentionality to creation, to provide borders and boundaries that are to be respected if life is to be lived well or in its fullness. Conceptual constraints for living well cannot readily be explained by a *creation-by-chance* worldview.

Secondly, there are notable common human traits exercised for the physical survival of individuals; as well as, behavioral *variances* in design, personality, and giftedness that serve a communal purpose. Diversity within a framework of community, with a regard for the contribution of persons to that community, offers a nurturing environment to persons. Everyone

---

[159] Paul Davies, *The Mind of God: The Scientific Basis for a Rational World* (NY: Simon and Schuster, 1993), 14-17

is *meant* to be accounted for and accountable to be their true selves in the bio-diversity of life.

Our true selves are the essential "details in the design" for a healthy community, not just for the survival of an exclusive tribe, but for the preservation and nurturing of all of creation itself. From the evidence of behavioral constants, along with variances and the interconnectedness of diverse persons, one could conclude there is a Mindful Intelligence discerned through life in the context of community. Perhaps this is why It is not the highest good that persons be alone?

New questions emerge from empirical evidence: What are then the *behavioral constants* of human beings—the non-negotiables that promote life? What variances might be celebrated for the sake of the fullest experience of being? What attributes must we value, nurture, and cherish that promote purpose and meaning? Is there a continuum of a created order that regulates human behavior rather than an animalistic impulses that ignite deconstructive chaos?

All of these questions resonate with the self in an intuitive and reasonable way. They come into focus as we consider the empirical evidence for a Divine Presence with a nature and character respective of God. Answers must be surmised both by *heart (intuition)* and *mind (empirical or rational evidence)*, by way of "contemporary scientific theism,"[160] or an informed faith, unfettered by either religious superstition or pseudo-scientific rhetoric.

SECTION 5:
Morality: Our Inclination Toward Oughtness

"He has told you O mortal, what is good... do justice, love kindness, and to walk humbly with your God." (Micah 6:8/NRSV).

---

[160] John Hick, *An Interpretation of Religion* (New Haven: Yale University Press, 1989), 81

"We all may not always be so good as Mother Teresa who wanted to succor the poor of India because it was the right thing to do, but each and every one of us knows the tug of moral obligation."[161]

"Now, we know that, even with moral values <u>granted</u>, human beings are weak; they must be reminded of the moral values in order that they may be able to follow their <u>consciences</u>. It is not simply a matter of having a <u>right conscience</u>; it is also a question of maintaining strength to do what <u>you know is right</u>. (emphasis added)."[162] Such are the scholarly impressions of physicist, Richard Feynman, himself an avowed atheist. His regard for the inner knowledge that prompts morality is remarkably astute and his verbiage in the above statement somewhat prophetic for the scientific mind.

This prophetic proclamation articulated by the prophet, Micah, insinuated that "moral values" leading to *justice, kindness, and humility* before God, is self-evident or *"written on the hearts of humanity" (Jeremiah 31:33; Romans 2:5/NIV)*. This knowledge, essential to well-being of the self and community, was not only for the survival of the species, but also for the nurturing of community. If life was simply about the survival of the most fitful person or tribe, the moral code we sense as <u>good</u> would certainly change befitting a selective or survivalist code. *(See: "The Nine Satanic Statements of the Church of Satan of America,"* an anti-theist system of behavior based on Social Darwinian principles in the philosophical thought of Satanist, Anton LaVey in his Satanic Bible.[163])

An innate standard of human behavior, beyond one's concern for personal survival, considers chivalry, nobility, or the highest good for communal life. While science can help to decide whether we should or should not do certain things, science can only help us see what might happen if we do or do not do them. The question as to whether we want something to happen depends on conscious choices we make regarding not just what is beneficial for the self, but for the sake of sustaining the "ultimate ethical good."[164]

---

[161] Michael Ruse, *Can a Darwinian be a Christian? The Relationship Between Science and Religion* (Cambridge: University Press, 2001), 191

[162] Richard P. Feynman, *"The Relation of Science and Religion,"* from *The Pleasure of Finding Things Out* (Cambridge: Perseus Books, 1999), 252

[163] Anton LaVey, The Satanic Bible (NY: Avon Books, 1969), 25

[164] *Perfectly Reasonable Deviations from the Beaten Track: Letters of Richard P. Feynman,* ed. Michelle Feynman (NY: Perseus Books, 2005), 149

This sense of an "ultimate good" leads us to other questions. Why does 'good' exist? From where does this distinction of good and non-good originate? Is the practice of 'good' a purpose for being? In his address to the Ethical Culture Society in New York City in January 1951, during the Cold War, and not long after the insidiousness of World War II, Albert Einstein said:

> An ethical configuration of our common life is of overriding importance. Here no science can save us. I believe, indeed, that overemphasis on the purely intellectual attitude, often directed solely to the practical and factual, in our education, has led directly to the impairment of ethical values. The cultivation of this most important spring of moral action is that which is left of religion when it has been purified of the elements of superstition. In this sense, religion forms an important part of education. Without an 'ethical culture' there is no salvation for humanity.[165]

There is an observable standard of morality that fuels not only co-habitation, but community; one which informs autonomous choices. More than egocentric decisions made for the sake of one's own comfort or survival, moral choices consider their effect on the stranger, as well as, one's own concentric circle of concern. Humanity is inclined to value moral choices as good and immoral behavior as destructive. Those details may differ, the categories of good and evil are innate *givens,* with a common inclination toward what is objectively *good.*

The absence of good exploits human autonomy toward an abeyance of what we *know* to be nurturing for ourselves and for our community. We are prone to mistakes for the sake of growing toward well-being, but we can also behave contrary to what we know to be essentially good. Mistakes are mendable. Living mendaciously contrary to good often leads to tragic consequences for ourselves and others. We have the capacity to choose. But while good is not inevitable, neither is the "non-good" invincible! Living the good, or that which promotes well-being is a purpose for living. If life is a positive good, then "life is the purpose of life."[166]

---

[165] *Ideas and Opinions,* 58

[166] Stephen Lackner *Peaceable Nature*: An Optimistic View of Nature (San Francisco: Harper & Row, 1984), x

According to the Christian scripture, Jesus of Nazareth engaged the "non-good" while alone in the wilderness. (Matthew 4:1-11; Mark 1:12-13; Luke 4:1-13/NASB). With each temptation, Jesus referred to innate or higher standard of behavior from which he found his ability to conquer *demonic* influences that would compromise his identity—his true self.

Similarly in his letter to the church at Ephesus, Paul warned of *demonically-organized* influences of "non-good" he called, "the wiles of the devil," that could distract a community from pursuing what is "good," and could also stifle their knowing or "love for God" and for one another. Does this sense of "good" originate from a Mindful God? Can this "goodness" lead us to the threshold of God's Presence --to actually LOVE God and all that God loves?

The Syllogism for the Moral Argument for the Existence of God:

1. There are <u>objective</u> moral laws.
2. Moral laws come from a moral lawgiver.
3. Therefore, a moral lawgiver exists.

The theoretical evidence for God based on an imperative of morality that is common to all human beings has its roots in the respective works of Immanuel Kant (1724-1804) and Rashdall Hastings (1858-1924). Both of whom define ethical behavior as imperative to human existence.

Immanuel Kant argued that the supreme principle of morality is a standard of rationality that he dubbed the "Categorical Imperative." Kant characterized the Imperative as "an objective, rationally necessary and unconditional principle that we must always follow despite any natural desires or inclinations we may have to the contrary.[167] While Kant did not believe in #2 or #3 of the syllogism above, he did believe that there was indeed a scheme of morality that infiltrated the thinking and behavior of all humanity.

Kant's thinking is that morality originates from the development of human reasoning without a higher authority from which to draw or derive one's ethical behavior. Even so, one is seemingly guided with a momentum toward

---

[167] Immanuel Kant "Critique of Pure Reason" excerpt from *Stanford Encyclopedia of Philosophy, 104*

a greater goodness: *justice, kindness, humility, and the quest for and to love.* In his *Critique of Practical Reason,* Kant discussed our moral imperative as one's "duty." He suggested that God could exist due to humanity's capacity for the *"highest good."* He wrote that the "highest good" in the world is possible only insofar as a supreme cause of nature in keeping with the moral disposition is assumed. In any event, it was our "duty" to promote the "highest good."

Perhaps Kant's "highest good" is better defined as *love?* If good is an indicator of a *highest* good, could love, which is irrational-yet-observable, indicate a the existence of an *ultimate love?* Could all things have originated and continue to be created for this "highest good" through an "Ultimate Love?"

Hastings Rashdall, an Anglican theologian and historian at Oxford University, added a more specified dynamic to Kant's philosophy of morality. In his famous two-volume work, *Theory of Good and Evil,* Rashdall wrote that when we have admitted that the self is as real as or more real than any 'thing' of which physical science can fully explain to us. Such as how the self chooses certain events that recognize the reality of duty, of ideals, of "a good which includes right conduct"[168] as distinctive from that behavior with is destructive to the self and to community.

The *given* for both Kant and Rashdall is the observable nature of morality excelling to its potential for love. There is a moral code to live by. There are nurturing initiatives to make well oneself as well as one's community. The categories of good and evil exist. They are defined within the margins of what is good both for personal and tribal survival; but also for the well-being of one's own personhood and persons-in community, and for the stewardship of creation at large.

If we are merely a product of chance evolution, why would we bother about goodness, a moral code, or love? Why not create a hedonistic code for survival rather than a moral code that embraces the well-being of all humanity...and non-human life as well? If survival is our optimal goal for existence, then any action for the sake of saving one's life would be acceptable under such a worldview. A godless cosmos would not offer any accountability for the behavior of the species and it would not matter.

---

[168] Hastings Rashdall, *The Theory of Good and Evil,* II, Book III: 1 (Oxford: Clarendon Press, 1907), 4

Whether one holds to the idea of Kant that this knowledge of morality is *learned*, or of Rashdall that it is somehow *assumed*, it is certain that without a sense of accountability, there really is NO legitimate moral code or standard through which a community might strive toward well-being or love. We may be able, perhaps, to give some meaning to our sense of moral duty without the reference to God, but not to its essential meaning or purpose. If the existence of God is not a postulate of all morality, it is a postulate of a sound morality or "a moral obligation which means moral objectivity."[169] In other words, humanity seems designed not only for morality, but toward a progressively good morality with the sense of duty to fulfill that standard of behavior for personal and community well-being.

If there is no objective morality for which humanity can review his/her actions, then anything is permissible. If there is no higher good or ultimate love from which we might be ultimately accountable, we are then pawns in our own insatiable, unqualified autonomy, morality by our own perverse codes, and a humanity behaving as reprehensive god-like creatures in our own purposeless existence of self-preservation.

Can humanity truly be empathetically moral without the benefit of an objective moral code—without sensitivity to the teachings of good religion? At this point in human history, as the Judeo-Christian ethic has permeated our worldview, that would be a difficult question for atheist and anti-theists to answer *rationally*. They can only speculate what might have emerged in a world without the moral codes of Judaism (the Ten Commandments: designed for *tribal-limitation*) and the teachings of Jesus in Christianity (the Beatitudes: designed for *personal-transformation*).

Philosopher Keith Ward asserts that morality leads inevitably to some form of religious devotion, perhaps in the form of "belief in the sovereignty of reason, the reality of the intelligible world, and the nature of the phenomenal world as a temporal appearance of intelligible reality."[170] Morality does not seem to just happen by chance or merely because of the instinct toward self-preservation.

---

[169] Ibid.

[170] Keith Ward, *Morality, Autonomy, and God* (London: Oneworld, 2013), 126

The "rule" of right and wrong, good or evil, must be a real thing, not made up by simply for the sake of our own preservation. There is in humanity a sense of obligation or *duty* to something of a higher cause than the self. Something of a higher knowledge expects mature persons to behave in a certain way, "directing the universe…urging me to do right and making me feel responsible and uncomfortable when I do wrong."[171]

Why do we conscious beings have an aptitude or inner voice acting as a guide to the rightness or wrongness of one's behavior and for the flourishing of one's personhood? From where comes this innate ability for distinguishing right from wrong, to make moral judgements and evaluate healthy values? What undergirds humanity's preference for *nobility* from a common humanity and our distaste for rabble? There is an urgency in the direction of my choices and behavior, a "yes" and "no" in what promotes my well-being personally and in community. There are irresponsible choices I have the freedom to choose, but "the evil approaches us in a whirlwind, the good as direction."[172]

Richard Swinburne, Emeritus Professor of Philosophy at Oriel College in Oxford, argues that the existence of God is not a prerequisite for morality, but the existence of God as the source of morality does impact what moral truths are legitimate for the well-being of humanity-in-creation. As created in God's image (or as a "reflection" of the character and nature of God), humanity is intentionally *good*. Thus, all humanity has some sensibility for living out a *goodness* or a practical code of ethics in time and space, with or without a profession of belief in the existence of a Creator.

Like the other arguments for God's existence, the argument from morality can be articulated in a propositional form set forth by Swinburne. In it he proposes through an equation of probability that God provides a better explanation of moral knowledge than what is rationally coherent in a naturalistic universe of chance:

1. *Humans possess objective moral knowledge.*
2. *Probably, if God does not exist, humans would not possess objective moral knowledge.*

---

[171] C. S. Lewis, *Mere Christianity* (San Francisco: Harper, 2003), 34
[172] Martin Buber, *"The Education of Character,"* from *Between Man & Man* (NY: McMillan, 1947), 114

3.   *Probably, God exists.*

The problem of a morality without God is evident. Objective values may get muddied in the subjective acting out of survival "instincts" or personal mores in a manner outside of what is truly *good*. The idea that "God meant this code of morality for *all*, but I am the *exception*" is certainly possible if we begin to compromise or manipulate objective moral values with those we deem *more* acceptable for our more *exceptional selves*. Good is truly not good, if it is only beneficial for my exclusive interests or that of my tribe.

When the origin for our moral code is God, there is a sense that our ethical behavior is not intended merely for personal *survival*, but also for the well-being of persons-in-*community*. We may be good for our own benefit, but unless we are cognizant of God's intention of our ethical behavior which undergirds our subjection to it, we are not aware that God's intention for us to be not only to be good, but to be *loving*.

As conscious beings we have the capacity to conceive of the dynamics of a good creation, toward "basic regularities in virtue."[173] Thus, the idea of a morality influences our human capacity for discernment, a greater intrinsic intelligibility than the urges of purely materialistic forces, animalistic urges and self-preserving impulses. This intelligibility may include the notion of a universal morality, categories of right and wrong, good and bad, as innate in the DNA of humanity. Whether we are born with this sense of morality or whether we learn how to thrive within its length and breadth, it is still a recognition of the reality of a given-good and a progressive *highest good,* or an Ultimate Love for whom humanity is inclined to strive.

Community Oughtness:

Common Sensibilities and Justice

"And I will make justice the line, and righteousness the plummet; hail will sweep away the refuge of lies, and waters will overwhelm the shelter." (Isaiah 28:17/KJV).

Would moral codes, love and justice be essential to a humanity who emerged by chance or without Divine accountability? How can one explain humanity's

---

[173] John Hick, *Interpretation of Religion*, Ibid., 80

capacity for love or our essential sense of justice as an expression of that love if not for the mindfulness of God?

In the 1982 film, *The Verdict*, Frank Galvin is a down-on-his luck lawyer, an ambulance chaser. Due to unjust and wonky circumstances beyond his control, he is reduced to soliciting clients at funerals, shamefully marketing himself to family members, posing as a friend of their deceased loved one, hoping for hire.

Then a case of a moral injustice arises. Medical negligence causes an innocent young mother to become comatose. As a result, the sister of the young mother hires Galvin. He files a lawsuit against the presiding surgeons and the powerful religio-politically ruled system that camouflaged the physician's negligence and malpractice.

At first, the lackluster lawyer demurred at the challenge, hoping for a compromising settlement, (and his subsequent commission) rather than to challenge the gargantuan system. Galvin's friend and former associate, Mickey Morrissey, reminds him of his moral obligations as a lawyer to take this type of case. Reluctantly at first, he takes the case seriously. It brings him back into practicing law for the sake of justice, rather than personal gain.

Galvin is approached by the opposition with a tawdry sum to settle out of court. It would have been a simple course of action, just to take a small settlement and let it go at that. But after seeing the suffering of the innocent victim, Gavin decides to *do the right thing*. He does not accept the minimal settlement and decides to fight the evil system for the sake of justice and the well-being of the one who could not speak for herself.

The revitalized lawyer ascended to a higher purview of his profession and exercised a transforming initiative toward a higher good: justice! Awakening to the treachery of a wonky religio-political system of self-interest and greed, Galvin finds his soul's eye. In his closing remarks to the jury, he spoke for *the* "lesser." Through a seeming innate empathy for the disenfranchised, Galvin spoke to the jury of the highest good, love and justice:

> You know, so much of the time we're just lost. We say, 'Please,
> God, tell us what is right; tell us what is true.' And there is no

*justice: the rich win, the poor are powerless. We become tired of
hearing people lie. And after a time, we become dead... a little
dead. We doubt ourselves, we doubt our beliefs. We doubt our
institutions. And we doubt the law.*

*But today you are the law. You ARE the law. Not some book...not
the lawyers...not a marble statue...or the trappings of the court.
See those are just <u>symbols of our desire to be just.</u>*

*In my religion, they say, "Act as if ye had faith... and faith will be
given to you." IF... if we are to have faith in justice, we need only
to believe in ourselves. And ACT with justice.*

See, <u>I believe there is justice in our hearts</u>. (emphasis added).[174]

In summary, the moral imperative through which humanity is guided
toward well-being, begins with an sense of a given good. While this is in
itself not necessarily evidence for God, how humanity moves within that
imperative or paradigm of goodness is somewhat revealing of something
greater than the goodness itself. From that common goodness, there is a
higher good, altruism, justice, stewardship, and love that has been noted as
such in lives of remarkable persons in history. This higher good has served as
an example of extraordinary purpose for being to people of the given-good.

The innate striving for the higher good, or love does serve as evidence for
the possibility of a mindful or benevolent force in the cosmos. Certainly
there is momentum of the given good that moves humanity toward a higher
good, or love. But that momentum does not stop with the highest good, or
love. There is an ascension on the climb to an Ultimate Love, unconditional
empathy and the sacrifice of self for the well-being of all of creation.

While the inclination of humanity toward the given good and the highest
good, or love may provide some foundation undergirding a believe in God,
the notion of the presence of an Ultimate Love ignites within the core of our
being an intuitive hope that cannot be dismissed or denounced by atheistic

---

[174] Excerpt from *"The Verdict" film (1982)* David Mamet, Screenwriter, Scripts.com.
STANDS4 LLC, 2019. Web. 18 Oct. 2019. <https://www.scripts.com/script/the_
verdict_380.

rationales. Hope in Ultimate Love is the life breath through which humanity finds its being. This then is deeper evidence for the existence of God—or Ultimate Love.

Summary of the Classical Arguments with My Atheist Pen Pal:

<u>Morality and Empathy</u>

In the late 1990s, H. McClelland was considered to be one of the most militantly atheistic voices and activists in the Miami Valley region of Ohio. He was so active in causes that would definitively separate church and state, he became a scourge to the mission of many conservative evangelical churches in the Dayton area. Not only did his "Letters to the Editor" of the Dayton Daily News appear regularly, but he was also a frequent presence on campuses and government property protesting the latest issues that would in any way support any hint of state-sponsored religious activity. He was especially agitated by nativity scenes and posting the ten commandments in the public square.

My encounter with McClelland began in the Fall of 1994, while I was the pastor of a small, conservative evangelical church in Beavercreek, Ohio. Although we never crossed paths, our debates-via-US mail were to continue for nearly a year. I began that interaction after a very opinionated and somewhat hostile parishioner of mine came to me with a copy of one of McClelland's letters to the editor in her hand. She had torn it out of the Sunday newspaper and brought to church.

"You have to answer this bird!" she demanded. "He is trying to remove the ten commandments from the courthouse in Xenia. He always does this. Says terrible things about God and religion. He is an atheist! One day he is going split hell right open!"

I decided not to write a letter to the newspaper, but to find the critics home address and send a letter directly to him. It was before email or Facebook. My first letter, I felt, was quite astute, having 8 hand-written pages! I used a pamphlet I had saved from local Christian bookstore that outlined the cosmological, teleological and moral arguments for the existence of God.

It was several weeks later that I received an 18 page personal letter from McClelland in reply to my discourse.

His letter included startling expletives and insults regarding my mental stability and the sexuality of Jesus. I tried to keep my temper in check as I scribbled a retort to this retort. I sent the third re-write for a reply.

His next letter was over 30 pages, then 54, then exceeded 60 pages, all hand written with little cartoon images of Jesus as a satanic character, and other random commentary on the moral shortcomings of Jesus, the Pope, Billy Graham, and others. With the third letter, he included several tracts published by American Atheists, the organization founded by Madelyn Murray O'Hair.

This correspondence concluded after I sent to him the book, Mere Christianity, by C. S. Lewis. In this book, Lewis delineates the classical arguments for the existence of God, focusing on the Moral Argument. I felt these arguments would be much more influential to one like McClelland, who demanded more rational evidence of the existence of God. For several weeks, there was no response.

His final letter in the scope and sequence of our debate was short and to the point. It read: "Neither you nor I will change our minds. This is the last letter I will send to you. I have enjoyed our debates, but I have many others ignorant believers to write to. Good luck, H. McClelland"

Months later, I learned that McClelland's father died after a lengthy illness. Not long before the passing of his father, my dad died of pancreatic cancer. I understood how painful it was to experience the death of a parent. This is a sense of flying without a net for the rest of your life, in losing your dad, or as, Herb McClelland called him, your "pop."

It was in that context, with that empathy, that I sent Herb a sympathy card. It had no religious overtones, I simply added a few words of sincere understanding. It was not long after that McClelland sent me a final letter. The following is an excerpt from that letter:

September 25, 1995

Dear Brian,

It was heart-warming to receive a sympathy card from one of my Christian critics, and I want you to know that out of all the cards I received from family and friends, yours was perhaps the most meaningful to me personally. It made me feel a bit guilty for being so harsh on you in my various letters.

Again, thank you for your kind words of sympathy, Brian. If there IS a god, may he bless you!

Herb

In a situation of ultimacy such as the death of our fathers, there was an intimacy of demeanor, a "higher good," empathy, or love, that superseded our most rational (or irrational) debate. While our letters bantered back and forth the classical arguments for the existence of God, it was not until we had become vulnerable in recognition of our own mortality and the intuitive questions we had in common, on that level of inquiry, could we communicate, or become more susceptible to those questions, reasonable ideas, and, perhaps, a mystical, or religious experience one might call revelation in the soul.

Not only did I, somewhat insightfully, sense a need to reach out to him during his time of grief; likewise, McClellan responded with a similar need to offer some word of a more reflective nature. While I regret that I never heard from McClelland again., I am somewhat content in periodically hoping for his holistic awareness and well-being, with the hope of his words, *"if there is a god..."*

SECTION 6:
<u>The Marvel of the Sacred and Mysterious</u>

I, too, believe there is a mystery! In fact, I believe there is not much else! True, many things can be explained—but not all things, not even the complete set of explicable things. As a result, all our explanations are shrouded in inexplicability. Nothing could be more mysterious than the existence of the world, nature, being![175]

Thus far, I have only briefly outlined the classical arguments for the existence of God. My own "reasons" for believing in God may have begun with intuitive questions and an ascent into empirical evidence, but my own journey moved from the rational to the supra-rational or the experience, not of magic, but of mystery. In this I relate the following dynamics to my own belief in God:

1. The obtaining of a variety of cosmic circumstances as pre-conditions of an orderly universe producing a growing and life-sustaining ecosystem;

2. The universal recognition of moral values, good and the highest good, love and ultimate love;

3. The fact that the processes of human existence are measurable by and to some extent meaningful in the well-being of persons in community.

In summarizing the work of F. R. Tennet in 1930, John Hick in his extensive work, *An Interpretation of Religion,* concluded his "reasons" for believing in God with one more essential dynamic:

4. the phenomenon of "the human capacity for a distinctively religious experience."[176]

As reasonable as humanity is, even with the advancements we have made in this generation in science and religious thought, we still seem to be profoundly lost in a maze of materialism: the hokum, the hype, and the hysteria of the flesh. Although humanity is thoroughly entertained and technologically advanced, we seem to have become also a lonely, restless

---

[175] Andrea Comte-Sponville, *Atheist Spirituality, 104*
[176] Ibid., 81

"civilization with a limitless multiplication of unnecessary necessities."[177] The sensationalism of our culture has left us desensitized to what it truly means to be humans—being.

> *A civilization which has destroyed the simplicity and repose of life, its poetry, its soft romantic dreams and visions, and replaced them with a money fever, sordid ideals, vulgar ambitions, and the sleep which does not refresh. It has created a thousand useless luxuries and turned them into necessities, and satisfied nothing. It has dethroned God and set up a shekel in his place!*[178]

Emil Brunner was correct when he asserted, that our capacity for reason may also be the cause of our restlessness and discontent, due to the fact that reason is "derived from God and has been made for God."[179] The further away we move from a disposition of a qualified autonomy before a sovereign God, the more lost we become. Our lostness happens when we would rather enmesh ourselves in trivial inquiry, materialistic gain, or cyclical intellectual ascents than to become vulnerable to the God for whom we have been designed.

Perhaps humanity has become so comfortably accustomed to our stockpiles of superstitions, theories, formulas, policies, and by-laws that we have become what T. S. Elliot called: "Hollow men-- shape without form, shade without color, we exist between the idea and the reality, and thus falls the shadow;"[180] "ever learning and never coming to the knowledge of the truth." (2 Timothy 3:7/NIV).

An obsessive acquisition of more and more fluff that satisfies less and less can only result in restlessness, loneliness, and estrangement—feeling lost, from our true selves and as persons in community. Our culture has exchanged the garden oasis for concrete walls of graffiti, and holy

---

[177] Mark Twain, *More Maxims of Mark*, compiled by Merle Johnson, privately printed November 1927, 6

[178] Hal Holbrook, *Mark Twain Tonight,* Writings and Speeches of Twain, arranged, edited, and performed by Mr. Holbrook at various times and respective venues from 1954-1967 and from 2006-2017.

[179] Eric Rust, *Revelation and Reason, Macon, GA: Mercer University, 1981,)* 56

[180] *Hollow Men*, from: *Collected Poems*: 1909-1962, (Harcourt, Brace, Jonanovich, 1991)

sanctuaries for the Hollywood soundstage. After years of the ingenious advancements in technology, we are now more prone to send a *text* to one another as acquaintances than to commune with one another as friends. Film makers have become quite sophisticated in imaginative ways to depict human brutality and exploit innocent victims. Scientific progress not only researches cures for the most hideous of diseases, but it has also invested incredible resources in the development of bio-chemical weapons of mass destruction, that tend to poison both our environment and persons, but also to traumatize our fragile minds.

We are still a lost and estranged humanity. In our *pseudoscience* and *sanctimony*, we are lost in a maze of materialism, "selfies" and insomnia. We have an innate longing for a greater reality, yet in our contemporary giddiness we continue to idolize what has been created without reference to, or reverence for, the God of our being. "For although they knew God, they neither glorified Him as God nor gave thanks to Him, but they became futile in their thinking and darkened their hearts. Although they claimed to be wise, they became fools." (Romans 1:21-22/NASB).

For J.R.R. Tolkien, humanity has lost its passion for the discovery of a treasure "long forgotten." What matters is a recovery, a regaining of a clear view. We need to "clean our windows, so that the things clearly seen may be freed from the drab-blur of familiarity."[181] London pulpiteer Leslie Weatherhead put this human malady of foolishness in perspective:

> Some seek mental peace in holidaying as often as possible, in hobbies, in alcohol, in pills, in nightclubs, or watching television, in frantic efforts never to be alone, never to be quiet, always to be entertained. The hectic pace of life, anxiety about security, about health, business worries, a feverish quest for unsatisfying goals, the noise, rush and speed of modern traffic and always the background fear of war add up to more than the unaided nerves can stand.[182]

---

[181] J.R.R. Tolkien, *Mr. Baggins*, Part One, John D. Ratliff (ed.), *The History of the Hobbit* (London: HarperCollins, 2007), xi

[182] Leslie Weatherhead, *"Peace of Mind,"* from *Time for God* (New York: Abingdon Press, 1967), 44

When we settle for intuitive and empirical evidence alone for the existence of God, we may remain in a gloomy place that leaves us in restless misery. For C. S. Lewis, this "gloomy place" was called the "shadowlands," a place in contrast to the "real land," wherein is the peace humanity seeks, "a mountain higher than you can see in this world, where the heart leaps and a wild hope rises within."[183]

This "real land" of which Lewis speaks is sacred space, the innermost sanctuary of personhood, wherein one may encounter and commune with God. Here, we may discover a more redemptive path, where "childish things are put away" (I Corinthians 12:31; 13:11/NIV), and "old things pass away as all things become new." (II Corinthians 5:17/NIV). Among those "things" that "become new" are what humanity cannot seem to change in themselves. Here is where our personhood experiences re-creation, "new as if he had been freshly created by the hands of God."[184] In this sacred space, humanity yields to the reality that *our human autonomy is qualified* by the sovereignty of God. We learn to live responsive to God's presence, and responsibly in our place in community.

In yielding to the sovereignty of God, we may discover the emergence another dynamic in the evidence for the existence of God: *revelation*, the supra-rational experience of the awakening of insight. This dynamic phenomenon, not comprehended by reason alone, is an awakening to a knowledge that transcends and/or expands what is intellectually critiqued as rationally possible.

The revelatory or *religious experience* not only crosses cultural, geographical, and generational boundaries, but it is one area in which there are no statistical dis-proofs. The only rebuff for the skeptic is to opt for the argument that such phenomenon is simply unexplainable. To the skeptic, anything deemed as supernatural and "the devices of human understanding are not the same

---

[183] C. S. Lewis, from *The Last Battle* in *The Chronicles of Narnia* (NY: HarperCollins, 1956)

[184] William Barclay, *Letters to the Corinthians* (Philadelphia: Westminster Press, 1956), 232-233

subject."[185] Perhaps there is more in the capacity for human understanding and the fullness of reality that the skeptic has yet to comprehend?

A Momentary Pause:

Could intuition and empirical data prompt a legitimate supra-rational experience that may provide us with enough evidence to comprehend a *"world-other-than-human?" (Sheldrake)*, even what could be defined as "holy?"

As we observe the emerging and elegant universe, and as we strive for the highest good of our existence, could we be awakened to the experience of a God creating and adapting all of creation toward a consummation of all things? Could we perceive of a God who metaphorically "rested" on a seventh day of creation, but continued after, and continues now, to create through a mysterious connectedness to what He has already created? Perhaps God guides all things with His intention for a future consummation with the extended assistance of the qualified autonomy and giftedness of humanity?

Here our common adherence to a simple code of ethics for the sake of human survival becomes transposed to a deeper awareness of purpose. More than "it is the right thing to do" for the sake of human survival, this revelation of God's design for life ignites *"magnanimity; a greatness of heart, not a goody-two-shoes namby-pambiness."*[186] More than a given good, humanity has a capacity for nobility and virtuous living with an inclination toward the highest good and ultimate love.

In *Rock of Ages: Religion in the Fullness of Life,* biologist Stephen Jay Gould, concluded the universe, for all we know by reason alone, may have purpose and meaning. *Ultimates* may be set by a "rational and transcendent power legitimately called God." But, he contends, the resolvable subject matter of the sciences "falls into another realm below the purview of such philosophical and <u>probably</u> unknowable generalities. (emphasis added)."[187] Gould's use of

---

[185] Wendell Berry, *Life is a Miracle: An Essay Against Modern Superstition* (Washington DC: Counterpoint, 2000), 97

[186] Wayne E. Oates, *"Christian Life and Personal Maturity,"* from *The Writings of Wayne E. Oates,* ed. Thomas W. Chapman (Louisville: Westminster/John Knox, 1992), 148

[187] Stephen Jay Gould, *Rock of Ages* (NY: Ballantine, 1999), 199

the word "probably" offers a fair notion there may be knowledge unattainable through what is exclusively rational.

Whatever ultimate concerns one deems legitimate as reflected in "fascinating questions," it is obvious the purpose of both science and religion is to reach beyond the boundaries of the *known* for the sake of whatever revelation might emerge from our inquiries. Humanity seeks a boundlessness of knowing whether by reasonable curiosity or through the wooing of the human soul. The supra-rational or religious experience regards a transcendence from the commonplace and challenges humanity to consider the possibilities that, in the moment, might not be within the scope of intellectual inquiry alone.

The noted German sociologist of the early twentieth century, Georg Simmel, offered a unique perspective from his observations of human "religiosity" and the quest for a unified purview of God. He described this quest as "the mists rising from the murky depths of the soul," some greater momentum or a more profound relationship to the Ultimate. This he described as a "subjective relationship. Belief in its purest form… active in the soul."[188]

Discerning the presence of the supra-rational requires a holistic experience, not only intuitive questions and empirical evidence, but also of one's *respective soul* and *strength*. Oxford professor of Christian theology, Alister McGrath, asserts that every life of faith is completely original and is grounded in the unique identity of each believer. He wrote: "Every rutter reflects the personal experience of a unique individual. …to come to focus on our own personal journey of faith.[189]

This is the religious or "supra-rational" experience I propose. A person may experience God through one's unique capacity and vulnerability to that possibility in a *real time* moment While intuitive and reasonable evidence may lend general support toward this sojourn, it is only God who gives credibility to His presence in a way befitting the uniqueness of individuals "who seek after (Him) with all their being. Wherein He will answer…

---

[188] Simmel, *"Religion and the Contradictions of Life"* (1904) and *"The Personality of God "*(2011), from *Essays on Religion*, edited and translated by Horst Jurgen Helle (New Haven: Yale University Press, 1997), 36-62

[189] Alistair McGrath, *The Journey: A Pilgrim in the Lands of the Spirit* (NY: Doubleday, 1999,) 35

and tell great and wondrous things we do not know."(Jeremiah 29:13; 33:3/ NRSV). This supra-rational interaction is described by Professor Ward as "a transcendent spiritual reality."[190]

SECTION 7:
Religious Experience: The Mysteriously Universal Phenomenon of the Soul

"We can express God himself in no clearer terms, nor in terms expressing more Dignity, than in saying we cannot express him."[191]

"People have had this sort of experience on every continent, in widely diverging intellectual and spiritual contexts, only making the resemblance among their descriptions all-the-more striking. It is neither dogma nor an act of faith, it is an experience."[192]

In his book, *Out of My Life and Thought,* physician and Lutheran theologian, Albert Schweitzer observed that humanity is not as overtly materialistic as it may seem. While there is a will-to-power and egotism to be reckoned with, there is also an innate idealism to consider, something often held deep within the core of one's personhood. He wrote:

> The nature of the living Being without me I can understand only
> through the living Being which is within me. To unbind what is
> bound, to bring the underground waters to the surface: mankind
> is waiting and longing for such as can do that.[193]

In other words, our discerning minds have a greater capacity than our intellectual brains. We are vulnerable to awareness of a consciousness

---

[190] Keith Ward, *Divine Action: Examining God's Role in an Open and Emergent Universe* (London: Templeton Foundation Press, 1990), 176

[191] John Donne Sermons, VI, 16.511-513

[192] Andrea Comte-Sponville, *The Little Book of Atheist Spirituality* (New York: Viking, 2007), 153

[193] Albert Schweitzer, *Out of My Life and Thought* (New York: Holt, Rinehart and Winston, Inc., 1933), 114; 126-127

"beyond the human level."[194] Therein is the mystery, the sense of hope that moves us ever forward and upward toward supra-rational "meaning or purpose in life," with the instilling of values such as "gratitude, generosity, and forgiveness."[195] Such values science cannot create in a laboratory nor satisfactorily explain.

> *Where, then, is the gap through which eternity streams? The impulse to a spiritual view persists, and the evidence of that view's power among historical forces and among contemporary ideas persists, and the claim of reasoning men and women that they know God from experience persists.*[196]

The phenomenon of the religious experience is a mystery. Like a sudden, rushing breeze that seems to come from nowhere, yet influences the direction of a seafaring vessel, so is the happenstance of religious experience for the sojourner seeking a greater reality.

This *mystery*, does not imply hiddenness, but an "enveloping reality that cannot be manipulated and within which we define the character and meaning of our lives."[197] While meaning and purpose for being may be contrived by human imaginations, such notions are never without a deference to a grander vision of higher good. In the most contrived and potentially dangerous "realities" of human machinations, there is the safety net of a moral standard in which to fall. The moral *standard* is a part of the mystery that naturalistic propositions are challenged to explain.

Preeminent anti-theist-turned-theist, Anthony Flew, confessed in 2004 that our common dilemma regards "the crisis of the insufficiency of human thought to explain the dimensions of nature that point to a superior mind."[198]

---

[194] Rupert Sheldrake, *Science and Spiritual Practices* (Berkeley, California: Counterpoint, 2017), 3

[195] Ibid.

[196] Annie Dillard, *"The Book of Luke Readings and New Work"* Reader (NY: HarperCollins, 1994), 265-266

[197] Gustavo Gutierrez, *The Kingdom is at Hand*, from *Essential Writings*, (Maryknoll, NY: Orbis, 1996), 173

[198] *There is a God: How the World's Most Notorious Atheist Changed His Mind* (NY: HarperCollins, 2007), 88

Why is it that humanity recognizes "the insufficiency of human thought" when seeking to answer fascinating questions? Why does humanity own a capacity toward deeper sensibilities, a wooing toward the encounter with something sacred or holy? Is there validity in exploring the role of religious experience or the spiritual ascent to what is "ultimately Real."[199]

In the midst of an aggressively materialistic culture, there is still a mysterious admonition in the soul, an impartation to grow, to learn, or to experience Ultimate Love. Note the similarities between the religious experiences of liberal theologian, Frederick Schleiermacher's

> **Higher state of consciousness**...*a feeling that points to the presence of an absolute other, God. It is above all and essentially an intuition and a feeling...a desire to lose oneself in the infinite, rather than to preserve one's own finite self.*[200]

and Cistercian monk, Thomas Merton's

> **Paradox that lies at the very heart of human existence**...*that must be apprehended before any lasting happiness is possible in the soul of man.*[201]

According to a 2010 study by the Pew Foundation expounded upon the phenomenon of human religiosity, worldwide, more than eight-in-ten people identify with a religious group. A comprehensive demographic study of more than 230 countries and territories conducted by the Pew Research Center's Forum on Religion & Public Life estimates that there are 5.8 billion religiously affiliated adults and children around the globe, representing 84% of the world's population of 6.9 billion.[202] This is not to concede that just because billions of people are *religious* there is undeniably a God. It may be

---

[199] John Hick, *The Fifth Dimension: An Exploration of the Spiritual Realm* (Oxford: Oneworld, 1999), 170

[200] Frederick Schleiermacher, *On Religion: Speeches to its Cultural Despisers*, edited by R. Crouter, (Cambridge, 1988)

[201] Thomas Merton, *Seven Story Mountain*, (NY: Harcourt, Brace, & Company,1948), 169

[202] *http://www.pewforum.org/2012/12/18/global-religious-landscape-exec/*

concluded in light of this universal phenomenon there is a an awareness of something *Holy* to be reckoned with, if not revealed.

Although the numbers are impressive in themselves, it is more the *type* of religious experience I am referencing that makes the possibility of a legitimate encounter with God even more plausible. This evidence cannot be rebuffed as insignificant, reduced to the category of an illusion or a hoax, ignorance or the result of mass hysteria. There seems to be *natural prompts* within the context of human existence that enable persons to articulate intuitive questions, motivate rational inquiry and seek a deeper awareness of Ultimate Love.

Consider the religious (or revelatory) experience of the author of the *Vampire Chronicles*, Anne Rice. She believed the prompt of the creation around her was talking to her of God. "The purple evening sky, to the canopy of oak branches that sheltered our front steps, to the flowers blooming beyond garden fences. The world around me was filled to the brim with God."[203]

Religious or supra-rational experiences happen to the formally and informally educated through a common recognition of the wonder of life. Such revelation is not bound to any exclusive geography, generation, status, or caste. If God were of such a nature to interact with humanity, then this possibility would be available to all persons, religious sect notwithstanding, whether *formally educated or illiterate*—within a context respective of that person's capacity to comprehend our "ultimate concern" *and* "ground of being."[204] Expressions of such encounters would reflect the idiosyncrasies of the person, whether liturgical and tranquil, or lighthearted and raucous, there are those revelatory moments meant to bring focus to the presence abiding with persons—*respectively*--in the context of their personhood, not by the exclusivity of their own chosen sect.

I have heard very pious believers regard the uniqueness of *their* faith encounter as superior to all other experiences distinctive or different from their own. Such expressions of strict sectarianism tend to develop from a formula of belief wherein one envisions for himself an exclusive relationship

---

[203] Anne Rice, *Called Out of Darkness: a Spiritual Confession* (NY: Alfred A. Knopf, 2008), 174

[204] Paul Tillich, *Systematic Theology I* (Chicago: University Press, 1967), 10-11

with God. All others not in their fold merely perform empty rites and rituals, and at best, are only searching for God. True believers have found God through a salvific experience formulated *by* their own imaginations and exclusively *for* their own needs. Such prejudicial peccadillos are indicative of a sanctimonious myopia—with the manipulation of their own very lame or impotent Deity. Such perspectives produce a shallow sacredology rather than a truly sacred ascetism. In such cases, the blur of religious sight needs the clarity of spiritual vision!

"Lord, that I might receive my sight!" (Luke 18:41/NIV).

The phenomenon of our common need for a legitimate revelatory moment permeates human existence! Whether it is articulated in devotion to Darwinism, traditional faiths, or through an unquestionable reliance upon things satanic, humanity strives toward a common quest for higher knowledge or revelation. But, ultimately, it is not merely higher knowledge we seek for the contentment of our being, it is the tender presence of God for Whom we yearn. We have an innate inclination for intellectual instruction *and* transformational insight. We can see the importance of deepening our science prowess and religion devotion from "gaining as wide a knowledge as possible of the world."[205]

Often, we are not aware of this phenomenal possibility until, in the foreboding consequences of the wonkiness in our world, we come to the limits of our own rumination. It is here wherein one may become vulnerable to a wooing Presence, guiding us inward to an encounter between God and our true selves-- the persons we were designed to be! Therein we discover the God through whom we can make sense of things, and embark upon a path of salvation, our personhood in community, and a more hopeful existence: *BE-Living.*

Paul Tillich believed there is no exclusive religion which does not in some way offer a relatedness to its devotee. In every religion there is an "experience" to be reckoned with, or a revelation of some truth. All legitimate religious experiences claim some connection to a Greater Reality or a bearer of

---

[205] Keith Ward, *Are Faith and Reason Incompatible?* (London: Darton, Longman & Todd Ltd., 2012), 16

revelation. Furthermore, he explained that of such experiences, God may lead one toward insight and spiritual awakening.

> Through stars and stones, trees and animals, growth and catastrophe...tools and houses, sculpture and melody, poems and prose, laws and customs; through parts of the body and functions of the mind, family relations and voluntary communities, historical leaders and national elevation; through time and space, being and nonbeing, ideals and virtues, <u>the holy can encounter us.</u> (emphasis added).[206]

In this quest for revelation, religion is a phenomenon that cannot be minimized as simply an outmoded attempt to vanquish the fear of dying. It is not merely a family tradition to be passed down from generation to generation, a belief system or set of values we simply inherit from our genealogy. Rather, there is an undeniable and universal curiosity wooing us to discover not only the *reason* for our "sense of awe, personal littleness, and dependence,"[207] but also to discern the truth that will explain our restlessness and secure for us a peace that surpasses human reason alone.

Section 8:
Holistic Centering and the Transfixion of Our Being

There is an observable, universal longing for release from our mundane existence, or closed universe. We seem to be striving for a sacred space, a holy and insightful sanctuary away from the malaise of superstition, pseudoscience, and political sanctimony.

Religious experiences come to us in various modes of apprehension. We know no words to express what we see or hear or taste or smell or touch.

---

[206] Paul Tillich, *"The Personal Character of the Experience of the Holy,"* from *Biblical Religion and the Search for the Ultimate Reality* (Chicago: University of Chicago Press, 1964), 22-28

[207] Evelyn Underhill, *The Ways of the Spirit* (NY: Crossroad, 1996), 136

We live on *"the borders of the unfathomable,"*[208] and rely upon both scientific verbiage and religious rituals to communicate experiences of wonder.

Although humanist psychiatrist Carl Jung was not a member of any religious sect, he did confess that the soul, or the "psyche" did exist. He was open to the possibility that "religious awe" could indicate an "inner core" of knowing within the realm of human experience. Through our rational thinking, we experience the obvious. Through the sensibilities of intuition, rational inquiry and spiritual ascent, we may come to regard mystery and wonder as thresholds to revelation. Consider Carl Jung's fascinating questions:

> *What if there was a living agency beyond our everyday world—something even more purposeful than electrons? What if what science calls the "psyche" is not just a question-mark arbitrarily confined with the skull, but rather a door that opens upon the world from a world beyond, allowing the unknown and mysterious powers to act upon man and carry him on the wings of night to a more personal destiny?*[209]

It is in the deepest core of our being, the *"psyche,"* or the *soul* that humanity may come to the awareness of and into communion with God. During moments of extreme vulnerability, nothing can easily "extinguish that sense of God in the soul."[210]

> *God doth instill into the soul a fire and a love and a sweetness not customary, wherein it doth greatly delight and rejoice; and it doth believe that this hath been wrought by God Himself...granted unto the soul through grace—whereby it doth perceive that the Divine Being hath entered into it, and hath made companionship with it.*[211]

---

[208] Ann and Barry Ulanov, *Religion and the Unconscious*, (Louisville: Westminster, John Knox Press, 1985), 10

[209] Carl Jung, *The Spirit in Man, Art, and Literature* (Princeton University Press, 1966), 94-95

[210] John Moses, ed., *One Equal Light*: An Anthology of the Writings of John Donne, *On Discerning God* (Norwich: Canterbury Press, 2003), 143

[211] Angela De Foligno, *The Book of Divine Consolation*, Treatise II: Chapter I

Metaphorically speaking, God *is manifest* to the psyche, the soul, or the "holy of holies," in the core of persons as "the temple of the Holy Spirit." (I Corinthians 6:19/NIV). It is here *God enters in,* providing for humanity a revelation of His presence that otherwise could not be apprehended by intuition, reason, or religious instruction alone. There is an exquisitely mystical and profoundly personal quality about this "phase of experience with God"[212] that intentionally stands distinctive of intuitive questions, empirical data, or devotion to religiosity.

More than the fundamental activity of the brain, the soul, is the *discerning experience* of the mind. More than the accumulation of information in the brain, the soul is the *centering place* for the discernment of insight in the mind. Both information and insight enhance one's potential for a legitimate spiritual experience: the wooing and fear of an awe-inspiring mystery—*revealed.*

From a naturalistic perspective, perhaps the soul might even be located deep within the untapped potentiality of the brain itself? Perhaps the discerning mind or soul is located in a sacred space in the brain? Noted neurologist, Dr. Kevin Nelson, research professor at the University of Kentucky in the area of mystical phenomena in the human experience, has concluded that both instinct and spiritual intuition are legitimate dynamics to human biology in the brain.

Originating deep in the brain, Nelson asserts that perhaps spiritual awakening erupts in "the borderlands between consciousness, unconsciousness, and dreaming," when our conscious states are not whole but vulnerable and "fragmented". The borderlands of spiritual awakening affect a very special expression of consciousness, the sense of our individual self or personhood. Nelson believes that one of the dominant features of spiritual experience is "the loss of self," often into what some people have called "an 'expanded' state of consciousness."[213]

The soul is a spiritual threshold to sacred space, of dialogue between the human and the Divine. It is in the soul, in the silence of wonder, where God

---

[212] Frederick Schleiermacher, *The Christian Faith*, (Philadelphia: Fortress Press, 1976), 262

[213] Kevin Nelson, *The Spiritual Doorway in the Brain: A Neurologists Search for the God Experience* (NY: Dutton, 2011), 58

authenticates His presence through the "noiseless invasion of Thy Spirit."[214] It is here we may actualize a momentary revelation of God's presence. Through a prismatic-like reflection of the fullness of God, we may discern a manifestation of His mindfulness, and learn from this reflection, how to BE-Live.

Such was the experience of Hadewijch (1179), a writer of both visionary allegory and analogue to explain what had been *revealed* to her soul: "my senses were drawn inwards with a great tempestuous clamor by an awe-inspiring spirit that from within drew me within myself...as a renewed mind."[215]

For the Christian mystic, while the evidence of God's existence was intuitively questioned and reasoned in the brain, revelation was discerned and apprehended in the soul. Within the soul is sacred space wherein God may be revealed as Ultimate Love. Hadewijch wrote: "reason cannot see God except in what he is not; love rests not except in what he is."[216]

John Hick, Professor of Philosophy of Religion, described the soul as simply, "the moral and spiritual personality."[217] In other words, the soul is a sacred space wherein both one's truest personhood originates and made known and the presence of God is, in some mysterious way, apprehended.

For Hadewjich and Hick, the soul is our core personhood wherein the presence of God is intimately welcomed and revelation made known. It is the place wherein my truest self is never forsaken, where God and the person God designed me to be meet in intimate communion; where interaction with the divine ignites insight and humanity is invited to ascend into Ultimate Love. From darkness of our limited intellect, we may ascent to the discernment of an enlightened soul, or "advance to the light of understanding."[218]

---

[214] Howard Thurman, *Our Little Lives*, taken from *Meditations of the Heart* (Boston: Beacon Press, 1981), 83

[215] A Beguine of the 13th Century

[216] *Greatness of the Soul*, Letter 18

[217] John Hick *Death and Eternal Life* (Louisville: Westminster/John Knox, 1976), 45

[218] Thomas Merton, *"The Problem of Unbelief"* from *The Ascent to Truth* (London: Burnst and Oates, 1951)

It is in the soul, wherein I not only experience God, but where God apprehends the *"real me,"*[219] my divinely-designed personhood. This is the place through which, after intuition, empirical evidence, and religious rituals have been exhausted, revelation of God's abiding presence is manifested to persons in His desire for communion with whom He has created good. Thus is the cry of the human soul:

> *Lord, you are my lover,*
> *My longing,*
> *My flowing stream,*
> *My sun,*
> *And I am your reflection.*[220]

Hildegard of Bingen, a twelfth-century German nun, wrote extensively on doctrinal and political matters of her day. Although she was often at odds with her ecclesiastical authorities, she managed to preach in public about spiritual reform within the church. Much of her writings are still preserved, not for the sake of doctrinal accuracy, but for the sake of spiritual reformation through revelation. In her "lament of the soul," she envisioned herself "a living breath, which God placed in dry mud."[221]

It is through the *soul* God exhales his breath (Genesis 2:7/KJV) into us and we become *living beings*. Through inhaling God's breath we awaken to God's presence (Ecclesiastes 12:7; Genesis 6:3/KJV). It is in God's presence we emerge from estrangement to our truest selves The soul is a sacred space wherein this transaction takes place, where we are apprehended by God and wherein God can be apprehended. To know anything about God, it must be God who *must be revealed* to humanity in ways that each individual may come to *discern*. Humanity can only command belief in their statements *about* God when it seems reasonable, but "the things that are of God no man knows, but the Spirit of God."[222]

---

[219] John Polkinghorne and Nicolas Beale, *Questions of Truth* (Louisville: Westminster/John Knox, 2009), 23

[220] Mechthild of Magdeburg, Germany, *Fliessende licht der Gottheit* (*Flowing light of the Godhead*, written between the 1250s to 1270s) Book One: Paragraph 24

[221] Hildegard, *Soul and Body*, Vision 4, 1

[222] Thomas Merton, *"The Problem of Unbelief"*, Ibid.

Whereas intuitive questions, empirical reason and religious devotion may work together toward a legitimate concept of God, it is through the centering of our core being, the psyche or the *soul*, our "holy of holies," wherein we may comprehend what is immeasurable, from where we may "grasp God, arise! and stride into God."[223]

A Momentary Pause

A *Modality*: the Flesh and the Soul in the Fullness of Being!

Judaism teaches that the body is not in competition with the soul. They are intended to be inseparable for the time we are active on the earth. The flesh, when guided by the soul, is essential to the "good works," and our creative influence in our world. The soul is the "animating force...the unique, everlasting, intangible part of a person"[224] through which we "live and move and have our being." (Acts 17:28/KJV).

The soul prompts discernment, like the "tempering of the air,"[225] guiding persons into Ultimate Love. Rabbi Kook believed *the soul* affects "an attachment...directing one to an upright path."[226] This is the sacred space most sensitive to the acquisition of revelation and the desire for "whatsoever things that are true, honorable, just, pure, lovely, are of good report; and gracious." (Philippians 4:8/NAB).

The soul it is not a seat of emotion, but a guiding impetus toward recognition of Ultimate Love. It is from the soul humanity thirsts for God and hungers to actualize our design as persons in community. It is through my revelatory moment of communion, presence with Presence, I become more aware of God and God, in turn, reveals to me what only God may make known.

> *As the deer pants for streams of water,*
> *so my soul pants for you, my God.*

---

[223] Meister Eckhart, Sermon 84, '*Puella surge*,' an exposition of Luke 8:54
[224] Rabbi Rachel Leila Miller, *Body and Soul: Indispensable Partners for Doing Life's Sacred* Work (August 2004)
[225] *The Creator and Creation*, Vision 4, Book 1, Paragraph 25
[226] Abraham Isaac Kook, *Essays: "The Pangs of Cleansing"* The Classics of Western Spirituality (Mahwah, NJ: Paulist Press, 1978)

My soul thirsts for God, for the living God.
When can I go and meet with God? (Psalm 42:1-2/NRSV)

It is logical to assume that if humanity indeed has a soul, and if that phenomenon is denied or ignored, the result would be a world left to our own misguided autonomy. The result would be naturalistic chaos: the effects of a world-gone-wonky! It is the soul that positions us to "prepare the way of the Lord," wherein one becomes vulnerable to a Divine encounter of God's own Spirit, the articulation of His word, and the discernment of His presence.

It is in the revelatory capacity of the soul that offers the most explicit evidence of God's existence. From his pulpit at St. Paul's Cathedral in London, John Donne proclaimed:

> *Poore intricated soule! Riddling, perplexed, labyrinthicall soule!*
> *Thou couldest not say, that thou believest not in God, if there were*
> *no God; Thou couldest not beleeve in God, if there were no God;*
> *If there were no God, thou couldest not speake, thou couldest not*
> *thinke, not a word, not a thought, no not against God.*[227]

Christian mystic, Bede Griffiths, explained humanity's spiritual dilemma:

> *We have become separated from the center of our being. We*
> *wander endlessly exploring the mouth of the cave being in a world*
> *of shadows...as sense of separation from reality. Where is the clue*
> *to the center?*[228]

SECTION 9:
Revelation and Ecstasy: An Experience of the Soul

The knowledge of God is "a mountain steep indeed and difficult to climb—the majority of people scarcely reach its base."[229]

---

[227] LXXX Sermons, (48) 1640, taken from *The Complete Poetry and Selected Prose*, edited by Charles M. Coffin (New York: Modern Library, 1952), 562-563

[228] *The Golden String* (Springfield, ILL: Templegate Publications, 1980), 184-185

[229] Gregory of Nysa, c. *335-395*, from *The Life of Moses, AD 390's*, Chapter 1:52

Although contemporary atheist Sam Harris denies any empirical evidence for the existence of God, he admits that the phenomenon of *spirituality* is not easily explained by scientific inquiry. In his book, *Waking Up*, he wrote that spirituality remains "the great hole in secularism, humanism, rationalism, atheism, and all the other defensive postures that reasonable men and women strike in the presence of unreasonable faith...visionary experience has no place within in the context of science."[230]

Harris' comment reeks of a "block universe" mentality, a closed-minded approach to the fullness of a reality yet to be discovered, especially by adventurous scientists *with vision*. Perhaps there is more to the human capacity toward understanding a consummate reality than Harris is willing to admit? Perhaps there are more holistic ways of knowing that fullness than mere atheistic conjecture?

Poet and essayist, Wendell Berry, observed that our human capacity reveals two distinct ways of knowing the fullness of reality, "the rational mind and the sympathetic mind." The rational mind is the "objective, analytical, and empirical, and precise, the official mind of science, industry, and government." The sympathetic mind is not unreasonable, but refuses to limit knowledge or reality to the scope of reason or 'factuality' or experimentation." The function of the sympathetic mind is to be considerate of whatever is present: "feeling, affection, familiarity, reference, faith, and loyalty."[231]

Our journey toward an "existence in the full, dynamic sense,"[232] truly becomes real when we cease to refuse to recognize the unchanging mysteries in the fullness of our existence and we have filled that space with "the higher intuition which comes from God."[233] This "higher intuition" of which Solzhenitsyn refers enables us to become vulnerable to revelation in the core

---

[230] Sam Harris, *Waking Up: Searching for Spirituality Without Religion* (New York: Simon and Schuster, 2014), 202-203

[231] *"Two Minds"* from *"The World-Ending Fire,"* The Essential Wendell Berry, edited by Paul Kingsworth (Berkley, CA: Counterpoint, 2017), 182-184

[232] John MacQuarrie, *Principles of Christian Theology* (London: SCM Press, 1977), 498-499

[233] Alexander Solzhenitsyn, *The Eternal Questions Remain,* from *Reader* (Wilmington, DE: ISI Books, 2016), 596; 578

of our being. Our vulnerability may begin through intuitive questions such as those of Solzhenitsyn:

> Is there an infinite outside us? Is this infinite, one, inherent, permanent, necessarily substantial, because it is infinite... necessarily intelligent...while there is an infinite outside of us, is there not an infinite within us? Does it think? Does it love? Does it will?[234]

Revelation as "Divine Self-Disclosure"[235]

If there is God, one might well expect him to make his presence known to humanity not merely through the "over-all pattern of the universe,"[236] but also in ways *creative* and respective to the context of the humanity He has designed. This is a logical assumption for a *God in the gasps!*

Christian philosopher, Eric Rust, defined a supra-rational, religious experience as God's self-disclosure, not as a set of propositions about God, but as an "active impartation of the Divine Presence made explicit in symbols which employ personal structures and follow personal patterns."[237] Aptly defined, revelation emerges from a discernment in the soul. The knowledge of God, proceeds as God manifests Himself as He wills. This interactivity between the phenomenon of His presence with the vulnerability of the human person is a "divine response to man's innate quest for God."[238]

This could be called the seeking of God through the eyes of the soul. Artist Vincent Van Gogh described this experience the world with "two currents of thought." First, the material, and second, through "the study of color," or the eagerness of a soul that envisions life "enlivened by a sunset radiance."[239] Reason explains the mechanics of the sunset in the brain. Revelation expresses the radiance and significance of it's meaning in the soul. This is legitimate spirituality: *a holistic experience of wonder.* There are realities so

---

[234] Victor Hugo Prayer 5:2:4

[235] John Baille, *The Idea of Revelation* (New York, Columbia University, 1956), 19

[236] Richard Swinburne, *The Existence of God* (Oxford: Clarendon Press, 1979), 225

[237] Rust, *Revelation and Reason*, Ibid., 56

[238] Macquarrie, *Ibid.* 53

[239] Vincent Van Gogh Arles, 1888

profound that they reach a degree superior to human thought alone; grander than our human acumen can casually understand.

Paul wrote to the church at Corinth: "The natural person does not accept the things of the Spirit of God, for they are folly to him, and he is not able to understand them because they are spiritually discerned." (I Corinthians 2:14/NRSV). In other words, God is not confined to human thought or conclusions drawn from the structure of the universe, nor through profound meditation on sacred things. For those vulnerable to His presence, "God is *known* through revelation alone."[240]

The God of which he can only speak, is one who *reveals* His presence to vulnerable persons, in and through eras in community histories and seasons in person's lives, wherein we are admonished to "be still and know the I AM God." (Psalm 46:10/Jewish Publication Society Version). Any projections or machination about God would pale in comparison to God's legitimate revelation of Himself. Moreover, our own thinking and projections may even distract us from a legitimate communion with God and the apprehension of His revelation.

How can we know if revelation is legitimately from *God?*

"He withdrew Himself from our eyes, so that we might return into our hearts and find Him there,"[241] confessed St. Augustine during a season of contrition and vulnerability.

In the New Testament, Jesus taught "what is impossible for humanity is possible with God" (Luke 18:27/NIV). Humanity can neither manufacture legitimate revelation from God anymore than we can ever manipulate God by our righteous acts or religious rituals. By the nature of revelation, God takes the initiative to reveal what only God will reveal. All one may do is to *prepare the way of the Lord* or intentionally position oneself in vulnerability to God's presence, entering into our "holy of holies," trusting God to "remove the veil from something which is hidden."[242] It is interesting that Tillich described revelation as the removing of a "veil." Just as the veil in the Temple

---

[240] Emil Brunner, *Revelation and Reason*, (Wake Forest: Chanticleer, 1946), 44
[241] *St. Augustine Confessions: 4.12*
[242] Tillich, *Systematic Theology Volume I*, Ibid., 109-111

had to be removed for the Hebrew priest to have interaction with God, so too does God mysteriously enable our aptitude to experience a revelatory moment, *healing our spiritual blindness or removing the materialistic scales from our eyes.*

One may discover the revelation of God as we enter into sacred space, where God is "incomprehensible to the created eye and inaccessible to the created brain."[243] Our quest is for spiritual insight is availed to the soul by Ultimate Love: the innovative, immutable, and immeasurable grace of God. The Spirit that continues to hover over our deepest darkness and ignorance with the enlightenment of His presence.

Thomas Merton was an irascible intellectual to be reckoned with while a student at Columbia University. He was noted in those days as a staunch atheist, (rejecting the Protestantism of his parents), and an endless critic of religion. In 1938, at twenty-three years old, he experienced what he called the "conversion of his intellect," followed by a "happy execution and rebirth." In his famous autobiography, *Seven Story Mountain,* Merton described his experience as a *soul* entering into the presence of God:

> *In the temple of God that I had just become...I had entered into the everlasting movement of that gravitation which is the very life and spirit of God: He called out to me from His own immense depths.*[244]

The revelatory experience is apprehended in the mystical, sacred space of the soul. God cannot be confined or 'comprehended' in any sectarian dogma, concept, opinion, or conviction. God cannot be defined by simple emotion or biochemical sensation. We cannot downsize God or the revelatory experience to our own formulas or expectations. A God we can regulate, manipulate, or postulate for our own purposes is no god at all. For many of us who try to do that, we must come to understand that *"God is greater than our god.*[245]

---

[243] Gregory of Nyssa, *Ibid.* 1:57

[244] Merton, *Seven Story Mountain* (New York: Harcourt, Brace and Company, 1948), 224-225

[245] Henri Nouwen, *Spiritual Formation: Following the Movements of the Spirit* (New York: HarperCollins, 2010), 4

A Momentary Pause:

"The light shines in darkness, and the darkness cannot overcome it." (John 1:5/ NRSV).

> *Like a foolish dreamer, trying to build a highway to the sky*
> *All my hopes would come tumbling down, and I never knew just why*
> *Until today, when you pulled away the clouds that hung like curtains*
> *on my eyes*
> *Well I've been blind all these wasted years and I thought I was so wise*
> *But then you took me by surprise*
>
> *Like waking up from the longest dream, how real it seemed*
> *I've been lost in a fantasy, that blinded me*
> *Until your love broke through.*[246]

Believing in God, begins with asking intuitive questions, followed by empirical reasoning, then, aided by "infused virtues, spiritual senses and mystical ecstasies, we are led to divine things."[247] Humanity is never fully content in offering reasonable conjectures to ultimate questions any more than man can find lasting fulfillment by consuming only bread and water. There is in the design of humanity, a spiritual appetite, the capacity for a fulfillment in nothing less than manna and wine!

SECTION 10:

Biblical Insight: The Classical Arguments for the Existence of God in the Biblical Rhetoric of Paul in Acts 17:22-31

"This Bible, this ubiquitous, persistent black chunk of a bestseller is a chink- often the only chink—through which winds howl." [248]

---

[246] Songwriters: Keith Gordon Green, Randy Stonehill, Todd Fishkind (© EMI Music Publishing, 1977)
[247] Bonaventure, *The Soul's Journey into God*, 5:1-2; 7:1-2
[248] Annie Dillard, *Reader* (NY: HarperCollins, 1994), 266

Various biblical narratives with their respective literary devices are used to prompt unknown or fascinating questions that may guide a process of personal inquiry toward the revelation of God's presence and insight. It is not only the history, but the histrionic discourses and stories disclosed in the sacred scripture that may ignite the truth of that text in the core of our being. The biblical narrative of the blind man conversing with Jesus resonates in my own soul: "Lord, that I may not only have my sight, but *insight*." [249]

Although the classical rationales for the existence of God were not systematically formulated until centuries after the birth of the church, there is some hint to their pre-scientific notions in the rhetoric of the Apostle Paul during his discourse with the free-thinking philosophers in Athens as recorded in Acts 17:22-31. Here we might see the beginnings of a rational apologetic or defense for the existence of God based on intuitive questions and pre-scientific reasoning. Through his reputedly "impassioned eloquence" and skill in "argumentation and classical rhetoric," [250] Paul actually outlined the empirical evidence for God's existence through the progressive "steps to his sermon." [251] The content of his rhetoric, is a precursor to the classical arguments for the existence of God as noted in the later writings of Thomas Aquinas: *the cosmological, teleological, moral imperative, and religious experience.*

In *Acts 17*, Paul entered Athens, a "city full of idols" *(17:16/NRSV)*, to a community already *"extremely religious"* (17:22/NRSV), searching for a god they had yet to know *(17:23/NRSV)*. It was the "God of their gods," whom Paul presented to them through an apologetic discourse. Paul began his discourse in noting their intuitive search for the Greater Reality: "Athenians, I see how *extremely religious you are.*"

The men of Athens asked fascinating questions and sought empirical evidence for reasonable answers. According to New Testament scholar, William Barclay, "all they wanted to do was to talk with mental acrobatics and the stimulus of a mental hike. They were lost in words." [252] These sages of Athens, tried to explain their intuitive sense of a Greater Reality by reason

[249] Leslie Weatherhead, *Time for God* (NY: Abingdon Press, 1967), 89

[250] Raymond Brown, *Introduction to the New Testament* (New York: Doubleday, 1997), 452; 412

[251] Barclay, *Acts of the Apostles* (Edinburgh: St Andrews Press, 1953), 143

[252] Ibid., 144

alone. They were so content with the debating of their own rational theorems and mental conjectures that they were not cognizant of the possibility of revelation. Perhaps even a revelation personified in Paul?

Through a steady movement of repeating their intuitive questions, and offering empirical evidence of God, Paul sought to ignite his erudite audience toward insight. Paul methodically guided the men-of-thought, not to a canonized 'natural theology,' but toward engaging their "inchoate longings...to their proper object...The Lord of heaven and earth."[253] The God they were seeking was not one Who could be contained by the limits of reasonable thought, described definitively by human words, or "contained in buildings or idols constructed by human hands." (Acts 7:48/NRSV). An awareness of this phenomenon required revelation.

The God Paul offered to them was the "Lord of all things, who cannot be circumscribed by any 'other gods'." (Acts 17:24/NRSV). God is transcendent. "The God who made the world and everything in it" (**the Cosmological Argument or *"first cause"***); "he himself gives to all mortals life and breath and all things. In him we live and move and have our being" (**the Teleological Argument: *"God as designer"***); and, "he commands all people everywhere to repent" (**the Moral Argument: *"God is the source of the standard of good for all humanity"***).

God is imminent. Through his ***religious experience*** or revelation, Paul superseded the empirical evidence for believing in God by sharing his experience of Ultimate Love: *Jesus!* Through a speech "portentous, succinct, and idealized," Paul exercised a kind of apologetic discourse that engaged the context of his surroundings: *"negotiating the religious and philosophical perceptions of the Greek world."*[254] What was the immediate result of Paul's initiative? According to the text "some scoffed; but others said, 'We will hear you again about this,' some joined him and became believers." (Acts 17:32-33/NRSV).

Curiously, all were captivated by the subject matter. Why? Because Paul addressed the common quest of humanity to find answers to their unknown

---

[253] Luke Timothy Johnson, *The Acts of the Apostles, Sacra Pagina* (Collegeville, MN: Liturgical Press, 1992), 319
[254] Johnson, Ibid., 318

and fascinating questions. He met them on the common ground of ultimate inquiry and used their language, quoted their sages, and sought to reach them in terms they would understand. Paul's discourse is "a profound exposition of reason and revelation"[255] that continues to speak to contemporary, inquiring minds. Remarkably, this enlightened discourse was through a pre-scientific mind, yet one enlightened nonetheless.

I Clement: Pre-scientific observations

An Apologetic Defense of God's Existence in the Early Church

The letter entitled, I Clement was sent from the church in Rome, addressed to a kindred congregation in Corinth. The purpose of the writing was to develop a *one-God theism* in debate with Greco-Roman polytheism. The identity of that writer is uncertain. Suffice to say that the author was quite knowledgeable in the area of the emerging apologetic practices of the early church.[256] According to biblical historian Laurence Welborn the composition of 1 Clement was written between A.D. 80 and 140.[257]

We can see from the following passage that as the early church began to become influential in the Roman empire, it had to formulate its own rational defense for a belief in God. As the following passages indicate the early church argued for the existence an Intelligent Designer through the *Teleological Argument* (**creation by design**).

The Teleological Argument of Creation by Design in I Clement, Chapter 20:

> 20:1 *The heavens, being* **put in motion** *by his appointment, are subject to him in peace;*
> 20:2 *night and day accomplish* **the course** *ordered by him, in nothing hindering one another;*

---

[255] John Polhill, *Acts: The New American Commentary* (Nashville: Broadman, 1992), 336-339

[256] J. B. Lightfoot and J. R. Harmer, *Introduction to I Clement,* taken from *The Apostolic Fathers,* ed. Michael W. Holmes (Grand Rapids; Baker Academic, 2007), 33-38

[257] *The First Epistle of Clement,* The Anchor Bible Dictionary, v. 1, 1060

*20:3 The sun and the moon and the dances of the stars according to his appointment, in harmony and without any violation of order, roll on **the courses** appointed to them;*

*20:4 The fruitful earth bringeth forth in due **season** according to his will, abundant nourishment for men and beasts;*

*20:9 The **seasons of spring and summer, autumn and winter**, in peace succeed one another. (Translated from the Greek text by Michael W. Holmes in The Apostolic Fathers Grand Rapids: Baker Academic Press, 2017).*

While the above text was written during a pre-scientific era in human history, the observations of the writer were remarkably perceptive, explaining in poetic verbiage his/her observations of seasons, a seemingly created order that would support life. Perhaps this empirical, pre-scientific observation by Clement was a precursor to a progressive revelation of a personable God?

Even if one comes to believe in God, how may one discover the character and nature of that God among the many concepts of god? Intuitive questions, the seeking of empirical evidence, and insight through revelation is a process through which to seek an answer. If humanity is a faint reflection of the Creator, we could discern some hint of God's attributes through an observation of the given goodness of what He has created—even the good things of humanity.

CHAPTER 3

"Created in God's Image" (Genesis 1:27/NASB):

Knowing God with Our Strengths: Human Attributes that Imply a Mindful and Personable God

> *We must learn the language of our audience. And let me say at the outset that it is no use laying down a priori what the 'plain man' does or does not understand. You have to find out by experience.*[258]

The following attributes are observable evidence for a personable God, in whose *image* humanity has been designed. These good idiosyncrasies are a common language of humanity. We have the capacity to articulate them in real time. In the observation of our *strengths* as uniquely designed persons, we may come to implications of God's character and nature. "For what may be known about God is plain because God has shown it to them." (Romans 1:19/NIV).

Perhaps, God does speak or reveal to humanity a semblance of His character in our own vernacular? Through our own positive attributes, God also reveals in Whose image we have been created. In considering the momentum of a good creation, our concept of God may raise Him to the notion of being the "living God," not a deity of some mythical dimension or an egocentric projection of our own.

The vastness of the cosmos, an ecosystem designed to support life, and the goodness of our own personhood, all may prompt insight toward the character and nature of the God. God is both ethereal in transcendence and existential within our existence. The personable God may be discerned in the innate goodness of a humanity cognizant of its qualified autonomy, and in deference to God's sovereignty over all of creation. Human beings are made in the image of God not in physical form, but because we can think with

---

[258] C. S. Lewis, *God in the Dock* (Grand Rapids: Eerdmans, 1970), 96

wisdom and intelligence, distinguish between good and evil, and because we can act for the sake of goodness, morality and justice. However partially and imperfectly, "we as humans share in these qualities"[259] as a reflection of a personable God.

The following dynamics are qualities of goodness celebrated in humanity. They are common to the thriving of persons as individuals and in community. Each promotes a sense of well-being. They are included in this section of the book as a reminder of the goodness of creation that often becomes minimized by the wonkiness of our unqualified autonomy. Does our inclination toward the goodness of the following dynamics enable us to believe in, and refine our understanding of God?

SECTION 1:
Consciousness and the Human Capacity for Discernment

"Consciousness is not a set of opinions, information, or values, but a total configuration of attitudes given any one individual which makes up his perception of reality, his world view."[260]

Consciousness is the quality of awareness of an external object or something within oneself. More than the recognition of physiological urges for self-preservation, this consciousness is both self-actualization, identity of the self-in-community and awareness of the fullness of reality. Whereas some would reduce humanity to evolutionary chance with primal urges for the sake of survival physical homeostasis and instinct, American psychologist, Abraham Maslow, concluded there are factors of ultimate concern common to most mature human beings. These factors include the integration of the essential self in community.

Why does humanity own a propensity toward *personal and social health*: the actualization of an autonomous (one who at times resists *enculturation*) and communal self (one who seeks *assimilation*)? How is it we are conscious

---

[259] Keith Ward, *The Mystery of Christ: Meditations and Prayers* (London: Society for Promoting Christian Knowledge), 6-7

[260] Wayne Oates, *Psychology of Religion*, (Waco, TX: Word, 1973), 129

of these inclinations and have the capacity to make these choices for the sake of both personal and communal well-being? Why is humanity able to exercise humility and respect, ethical behavior, appreciation and gratitude, peak experiences in life, the unselfish from the selfish, and even recognize and correct one's own imperfections? How could such desirable attributes happen *by chance?*

Maslow listed the following attributes unique to humanity as dynamics for goodness and well-being: "truth rather than dishonesty, unity among diversity, uniqueness rather than conformity, completeness, justice and order as a positive paradigm, simplicity rather than extravagance, playfulness, novelty, and improvisation, and the quest for meaningfulness."[261] Such dynamics are vital toward our being what Paul called "vessels of honor" (I Timothy 2:21/KJV) and what James called "instruments of peace." (James 3:18/KJV).

Humanity owns a consciousness for the purpose of becoming mature human beings, personally, and in community with others. In this consciousness, humanity has the capacity to learn through in a continuum of fascinating questions:

> *The Descriptive Question: What is consciousness?*
>
> *The Explanatory Question: How does consciousness of the relevant sort come to exist?*
>
> *The Functional Question: Why does consciousness of the relevant sort exist? How and why can we wonder why and how?*[262]

Finally, humanity not only has consciousness, but we also have the capacity to *elevate* consciousness from learning to mental awakening, epiphany, and revelation! This experience of joy-in-self-actualization in the expanded

---

[261] Abraham Maslow, *Motivation and Personality* (New York, NY: Harper, 1954) & *Toward a Psychology of Being: An Empirically Based Psychology and Philosophy which Includes Both the Depths and Heights of Human Nature* (Floyd, VA: Sublime Books, 2014)
[262] http://plato.stanford.edu/entries/consciousness/#CreCon article: *Consciousness,* dated Jan 14, 2014

awareness of one's fullness of being is very akin to the "highest and best that religion has offered through the ages."[263]

Consciousness, or self-actualization is a process of learning and discovery. Learning is our threshold for adapting to a fantasized, techno-sized, and mechanical world. It is more than trivial knowledge, data entry and scripture memorization. Legitimate learning "changes our character to ever new, more efficient, more intelligent, and also more beautiful forms."[264] Humanity is capable in its consciousness to explore the consummate reality and the fullness of living well.

SECTION 2:
A Holy Temperament: Profound Dispositions of a Spiritual Personhood

Humanity is uniquely created with personal autonomy and communal inclination. While in this freedom there is the potential for "non-good," there is also an inner groundswell toward the growth and development of one's character. The "fruit of the Spirit" (Galatian 5:22-23/KJV) are spiritual manifestations in the progressive development of the true self. They are profound dispositions the existence of which are difficult to explain without reference to a benevolent, mindful, or loving God.

In his important book, *Science and Spiritual Practices,* Cambridge biologist, Rupert Sheldrake, asserts regarding the human mind, there is a consciousness greater than what can be explained by science or mechanical thinking alone. There is a noticeable distinction between the bio-chemical formulae of the materialist's view of reality and "the experience of the wholistic human being in the phenomenon of love, joy, and peace. Such dynamics cannot well be explained by bio-chemical theories.[265]

In the development of these dispositions, one discovers more than a momentary gratification of the flesh, one discovers *contentment,* a *major chord*

[263] Wayne E. Oates, *The Psychology of Religion* Ibid., 138
[264] Stephan Lackner, *Peaceable Nature: An Optimistic View of Life on Earth* (San Francisco: Harper and Row, 1984), 152
[265] p. xix-xv

of our personal and communal identity, or the fulfilling fruitfulness of love, joy and peace. More than a moral code for survival, finding contentment through the *"fruit of the spirit"* guides humanity to more than a system of belief, it ignites the path toward BE-Living.

Whereas codes of moral law were developed to regulate the behavior of humans-in-tribes (i.e., the Decalogue), there are also revelatory moments wherein humanity learns insight, guiding us toward the transformation of our character and our contentment as persons-in-community (i.e., the Beatitudes of Jesus in the New Testament). Paul articulated insight in his letter to the Galatians. He metaphorically used the term *"fruit of the Spirit"* like a character-building stair steps ascending to "spiritual purification… qualities of spiritual energy that are recognized as the Divine Presence [Who] dwells in every human being."[266]

What emerges from *love, joy, and peace* are the communal attributes of *"patience, kindness, generosity, faithfulness, gentleness, and self-control;"* dynamics that transform tribal co-existence to what Martin Luther King, Jr. defined as "the beloved community." More than self-preservation or the survival of one's own tribe, the *fruit of the Spirit* stir in humanity a godliness beyond goodness: love beyond affection, joy beyond happiness, peace beyond the absence of violence, and grace, justice and stewardship beyond a survivalist morality.

The fruit of the Spirit are compelling, not due to the survival instinct of Social Darwinism, but because we are created in the image of Ultimate Love. We are inclined to find contentment in *love, joy, peace* and the godliness that follows: *patience, kindness, generosity, faithfulness, gentleness, and self-control.* Consequently, we learn to de-value the more instinctive urges of the flesh: *fornication, impurity, licentiousness, idolatry, sorcery, enmities, strife, jealousy, anger, quarrels, dissensions, factions, envy, drunkenness, carousing, and things like these."* (Galatians 5:19-21/NRSV).

As the *fruit of the Spirit* come to fruition, we become extensions of God's continuing activity of goodness in creation. The flesh and the soul are not intended to be in a duality, but a modality! Our natural existence is guided

---

[266] Thomas Keating, *Fruits and Gifts of the Spirit* (New York: Lantern Books, 2007), 11-21

by the spiritual stewardship of the soul. Humanity is as planted in a garden of community is intended for tending, not exploiting that garden for self-aggrandizement or tribal crusades. Growing *the fruit of the Spirit*, is "the work and the concern of the soul."[267] As the fruits of the Spirit grow, we are sensitized in our awareness of God and of others, toward "living responsively to God and responsibly before God."[268] We discern how to love God and all that God loves—and grow to be who God designed us to be: mature persons creating healthy communities, forming "a catalog of grace."[269] The following dispositions are poetically defined for a deeper understanding of our capacity for a more sacred or spiritual personhood:

LOVE: "AGAPE"

This love is an "unconquerable benevolence" of the human will, not of sordid or sanctimonious emotions. It enables us to "rejoice with those who rejoice and weep with those who weep." (Romans 12:15/NRSV). Sympathy for others is transcended to empathy toward persons.

This love, in Greek, AGAPE, is a self-giving love. We grow in this love to accept people as they are, not as we would manipulate them to be. We suffer with them our mutually congruent list of limitations, faults, mendacities and obsessions. From the insight of AGAPE, we may *live love* without bias or respective of the class or a *make-believe* caste of persons of some imagined social order. Through the momentum of agape, we come to realize that we are not "all that," but like all others, we are a unique design within the panorama of all that is!

In the midst of his own tumultuous times, Martin Luther King, Jr. proclaimed, AGAPE is something of the understanding, creative, redemptive goodwill for all men. "When you rise to love on this level, you begin to love men, not because they are likable, but because God loves them."[270] Through Ultimate

---

[267] Chrysostom, Homily on Galatians 5:22

[268] Interview with Wayne E. Oates, Southern Baptist Theological Seminary, Louisville, KY Spring), 1996

[269] Timothy George, *Galatians New American Commentary* (Nashville: Broadman and Holman, 1994), 399

[270] Martin Luther King, Jr. *"Loving Your Enemies"* from *A Knock at Midnight*: Inspiration Sermons, ed. Clayborne Carson and Peter Holloran (New York: Time

Love, we enter into a genuine conversation with God and others. This dialogue is not self-seeking, but one that is of a phenomenological design for the fulfillment of persons and the creation of the good community, wherein all are welcomed *home*.

JOY: "CHARA"

"CHARA" denotes the exuberance a life that is interdependent with the inner Presence of the Spirit, and not co-dependent upon outside circumstances. (Barclay refers to the later as a shallow happiness or a momentary "sensation from cheap thrills."[271]

This state of "CHARA", "enstasy", or revelatory euphoria, steadies us and prompts us to celebrate "an abiding sense of well-being,"[272] a conscious relationship with the God who loves us, liberates us from the false self. We live in hope, the confident awareness of God's Presence and in celebration of God's grace and mercy as a constant in our lives.

Joy is an exuberance of Life beyond life! For in this joy we find affirmation of our own personhood as we affirm the personhood of others. In a religious sense, this exuberance of being is an awakening from darkness into light; from confinement to a rusty cage of despair to being freed to soar toward a vastly endless dawn of possibilities. The Psalmist sang: *"weeping lasts for the night, but joy comes in the morning."* (Psalm 30:5/NASV).

The integration of heaven with an earthly existence is a source of joy to celebrate. Howard Thurman wrote a remarkable description of *joy* as expressed in the "traditional gospel spiritual." The upswing of the music from those who may not know happiness, experience joy regards "the profound conviction that God was not done with them, that God was not done with life." They are conscious that God had not "exhausted His resources in the vicissitudes of life." The awareness of the presence of God who [is] personal, intimate, and active was the central fact of life and the source of their joy.[273]

Warner Books, 1998), 48

[271] Ibid.

[272] Thomas Keating, *Fruits and Gifts of the Spirit* (NY: Lantern Books, 2007)

[273] *The Negro Spiritual Speaks of Life and Death*, taken from *A Strange Freedom: The Best of Howard Thurman on Religious Experience and Public Life*, edited by Walter Earl

<u>PEACE</u>: SHALOM and EIRENE

This "peace" does not refer to the absence of war or conflict, but it is rather a quality of contentment, at times that supersedes the turbulent effects of conflict and want. The Apostle Paul had this in mind when he wrote to the Philippian church, "I have <u>learned</u> to be content with whatever I have...in any and all circumstances...well-fed or hungry, having plenty and of being in need." (Philippians 4:11-12/NRSV).

Shalom or EIRENE is a "pervasive sense of contentment"[274] beyond a fleeting moment of self-reflection. This "peace" lingers and prompts one to learn the deeper awareness of God's presence, protection, and provision. This is the "peace of God which surpasses all understanding" (Philippians 4:7/ NRSV), or what Barclay described as "the tranquil serenity of heart which comes from the all-pervading consciousness that our times are in the hands of God."[275]

In ancient Jewish thinking, the Hebrew word, "shalom" did not only refer to the cessation of conflict, but also to the "overcoming of strife, quarrel, and social tension...the prevention of enmity...of harmony, on several levels, physical and spiritual...." This quality of peace is what Dr. Aviezer Ravitzky, of Hebrew University called "a meta-value," a blessing, or a manifestation of divine grace.[276]

In early Christian thought, EIRENE, or "peace from and with God...and with others" surpasses reasonable human calculations or predictions. Moreover, when the peace of God has come upon us, we comprehend the incomprehensible God. There will be no inner discord, nothing subject to quarreling, for peace is "the state of being already at rest, already secure... for all that is needful for you in this life God provides."[277] All shall indeed, become well.

Fluker and Catherine Tumber (Boston: Beacon Press, 1998), 69-70

[274] Keating, Ibid.

[275] Barclay, *Letters to Galatians and Ephesians,* 54-57

[276] Article defining *"Shalom"* from *MyJewishLearning.com*

[277] Marius Victorinus, *Homily on the Epistle to the Philippians 4.7,* from *Bibliotheca Scriptorum* (Leipzig: Teubner, 1824)

In our "holy of holies" experience, it is the "mysterium tremendum" in Whom we find ourselves in communion with peace! Z. Marwa Kisare, a Mennonite leader from Tanzania, testified of his experience of spiritual contentment as "a serenity born of harmony with God."[278] I experience peace as my life moves in sync within the momentum of God's creative activity on earth. For the mature person, passing the peace of God becomes a purpose for being.

A Momentary Pause:

The Revelation of God in the "Fruit of the Spirit" (Galatians 5:22-26)

Unlike animals who rely on instinct for survival, human beings have a remarkable capacity to cultivate the profound attributes of *love, joy, and peace*. Is this explainable through a complex theory in naturalistic thinking or social-Darwinism? Unlikely. Instincts for survival are in the natural DNA of the species. Whereas insight for the thriving of persons are in some way manifested in the soul.

We are mysteriously guided toward AGAPE, CHARA, and SHALOM as we seek *contentment*, through the cultivation of our personhood and growing in community. This indicates that humanity has the capacity and inclination toward a deeper way of life, beyond mere survival. There is a momentum in life through which we are capable, by design, to pursue the character and nature of the God in Who's image we have been created.

Empathy (not Hostility) Toward Others

Growing in empathy for others, redeems the flesh. In communion with God, we grow beyond superficial sympathy and express genuine empathy--even for those judged by our prejudices to be the least of humanity. Empathy regards the pain of others effecting our own being. The biblical admonition describes this spiritual attribute as *"rejoice with them that do rejoice, and weep with them that weep."* (Romans 12:15/KJV).

---

[278] *A Leader's Integrity* (1984) from *Readings from Mennonite Writings New and Old*, edited by J. Craig Haas (Intercourse, PA: Good Books, 1992), 233

St. Francis of Assisi simplified this phenomenon of empathy, or the care for others in a simple, but profound prayer that not only recognizes the lostness of humanity, but also the path through which our flesh may be redeemed and our lostness healed:

> *Lord, make me an instrument of Your peace...*
> *Grant that I may not so much seek*
> *To be consoled as to console;*
> *To be understood, as to understand;*
> *To be loved, as to love;*
> *For it is in giving that we receive,*
> *It is in pardoning that we are pardoned,*
> *And it is in dying that we are born to Eternal Life.*

Through the "fruit of the spirit" we become aware of how God intended for humanity to *BE-Live* in a world-gone-wonky. The distinctions between those who waste their lifetime in vainglorious gain and those who invest their life-breath in sacred ascents are clearly articulated in the steps of Jesus's pilgrimage of grace taught in the Beatitudes. This ascent requires one to transform from one's egocentric self into a "peacemaker" (Matthew 5:10/ NIV). True peacemakers are those who "preserve peace of mind and body for love of our Lord Jesus Christ, despite what they suffer in this world."[279]

Whereas the materialist might affirm an only the powerful and most cunning, the "just peacemaker"[280] will offer him/herself for the sake of the care of others or for the perpetuation of the noble cause: "to seek and to save the one who is lost." (Matthew 18:11; Luke 19:10/NIV). This may include the sacrifice of one's physical existence for the redemptive purposes of God by His "enabling presence." (Jude 1:24/NIV).

In a lecture given in 1987 at Harvard, Henri Nouwen described Jesus as "the prince of peace, the one who doesn't cling to his divine power or rule with great power. He is the source of all peace.[281] In the biblical narratives, Jesus is the one who taught by example to relinquish our fleshly lust for power,

---

[279] St. Francis, *The Admonitions* XV.
[280] Glenn Stassen, *Just Peacemaking* (Westminster John Knox Press, 1992)
[281] *"Adam's Story: The Peace That is Not of This World"* Seeds of Hope: A Henri Nouwen Reader, ed. Robert Durback (New York: Doubleday, 1997), 265

our obsessions with materialistic *want* and our addictions to intoxicating fads and folly. The vision of the peacemaker is for contentment, personally and in communion with others.

SECTION 3:
The Apostle Paul's "Fruit of the Spirit" in Contrast to Abraham Maslow's "Meta-Needs"

Somewhat parallel to the Apostle Paul's *fruit of the spirit*, are what Abraham Maslow called the special, "meta" *or* "hierarchy of needs;" dynamics of psychological well-being based on fulfilling innate human needs in priority, "culminating in self-actualization."

According to Maslow, in his 1943 paper, *"A Theory of Human Motivation"* humanity may find fulfillment (or contentment) in the pursuit of personal behavior and attributes quite similar to the admonition of Paul in the early first century. In order to become our fullest selves as designed by God, humanity may move in the momentum of goodness and wholeness. From the moral imperative to the higher good and the nobility of personhood, the *love, joy, and peace* we experience through the presence of God, reveals to humanity an empathy and honesty in community.

Paul's "works of the flesh: immorality, impurity, sensuality, idolatry, sorcery, enmity, strife, jealousy, fits of anger, rivalries, dissensions, divisions, envy, drunkenness, orgies, and things like these." (Galatians 5:19-21/ESV), are similar to the distinction between the dynamics of contentment or contention in Maslow's psychological assessment of mature persons.

Through his learned research, Maslow listed those behaviors that most fulfill the nobility and truest character of what it means to be a human in a state of BE-Living. There is a notable distinction and inclination toward the good as opposed to the non-good. Maslow's "meta-needs" include:

> *Truth, rather than dishonesty*
> *Goodness, rather than evil*
> *Beauty, rather than ugliness or vulgarity*
> *Aliveness, not deadness or the mechanization of life*
> *Uniqueness, not bland uniformity*

Simplicity, not unnecessary complexity
Playfulness, not grim, humorless, drudgery
Meaningfulness, rather than senselessness.

All of the above may be attained through the cultivation of the fruit of the Spirit. While the dynamics for well-being above are noble for humanity to achieve, they are unlikely to come to fruition through a philosophy of social Darwinism. More likely the hope for such transformative living lies not in one's materialistic achievements, but in one's positioning toward vulnerability to God's presence and growing to become the persons God designed us to be.

SECTION 4:
"Love God with...Strength:"

Knowing God Through Being Our Noblest Selves

"Verily, I say to you, unless one becomes as a little child, he cannot see the Kingdom of Heaven." (Matthew 18:3/NIV).

"...so be wise as serpents and innocent as doves." (Matthew 10:16/NIV).

Of the *pristine* (not the tribally-*primitive*) exuberance and innocence of children, Marian Wright-Edelman wrote: "Children come into the world resilient and full of joy and laughter with God's commission to live and learn and sing and dance and grow."[282] Perhaps as we consider the original innocence of children, we might come to a better understanding of those human attributes that best define how humanity reflects being "created in the image" of a mindful and loving God?

The following dynamics may offer to humanity some clue regarding the character and nature of a God in whose image we were created. The image of God is a concept and theological doctrine in Judaism, Christianity, and Sufism of Islam, which asserts that human beings are created in the character and nature, or the likeness of God. This is not an assertion of any kind of

---

[282] *Lanterns: A Memoir of Mentors* (Boston: Beacon Press, 1999), 133

physiology, but a term that implies attributes of goodness of character and being; original innocence.

When one considers the human inclination toward that goodness of character and being, one may logically assert such attributes are in some way distinctive of the Creator of humankind. While we are careful not to project our own idiosyncrasies to a formulation of God, we may gain some revelation of God through the celebration of the goodness in the discovery of our truest personhood in Him.

The following list of uniquely human attributes would be considered a reflection of the goodness of humanity. While there is the potential for the non-good, it is the good for which humanity strives, morality and justice, and the freedom to create within the boundaries of that goodness. Perhaps as we consider these attributes in humanity, we might also gain a better glimpse of the God from who's image humanity has been created?

Laughter: Humor, Playfulness and the Absurdities of Life

> "I am not religious in the dogmatic sense. There are things beyond reason. How can be comprehend a thousand-billionth part of a second? We live by more than what we think. Faith is an extension of the mind…in the realm of the unknown there is an infinite power for good."[283]

> "If I had no sense of humor, I should long ago have committed suicide."[284]

> "I was by God's side…delighting him…ever at play before God's face, at play everywhere in the world." (Proverbs 8:30-31/ The Jerusalem Bible).

"Humor is never artificial. It comes from an imperceptible touch of something permanent that one feels," said humorist Mark Twain, during

---

[283] Sir Charlie Chaplin, *My Autobiography* (New York: Simon and Schuster, 1964), 291
[284] Mahatma Gandhi, *All Men are Brothers: The Life and Thought of Mahatma Gandhi In His Own Words*, ed. Krishna Kripalani, Shantilal Harijvan Shah (Navajivan Press, 1960), 218

an interview with the Sydney Morning Herald, September 17, 1895. Although the real Samuel Clemens, noted by be either atheistic or agnostic, understood some humor to be a common quality in all humanity, ignited by an "imperceptible touch of something permanent that one feels." Could this be "imperceptible touch" be further evidence for humanity created by an intelligent and, perhaps, even *mirthful* God, creating "occasional islands of transient meaningfulness within an ocean of absurdity?[285]

Is there a purpose for human mirth and whimsey? Does this attribute of humanity offer a hint into the character and nature of God?

Humanity has the unique capacity to cope with the absurdities of life by way of humor. To laugh at the wonkiness of our dilemmas (in which our unqualified autonomy often takes us) is evidence of a more realistic level of being; conscious that life is inundated with absurdities. With our capacity for a whimsical response, humanity is distinctive from the rest of creation. "The man with the real <u>sense</u> of humor is the man who can put himself in the spectators place and laugh at his own misfortunes."[286]

The ability to laugh at the crucibles of existence is necessary for survival, perseverance, and healing. "There is a time to weep and a time to laugh."(Ecclesiastes 3:4/NASV). "It (laughter) will be healing to your flesh and refreshment and refreshment to your bones." (Proverbs 3:8/NASV).

At the end of his life, the children of famed comic actor, Harpo Marx, remarked about their father's legacy of humor and what it meant to a world-gone-wonky: "reviewing our triumphs and trials of day, Dad (Harpo) fielded the gripes and hang-ups with all the wit and wisdom of a second-grade dropout—which is to say, by reducing tragedy to absurdity. First thing you knew, he had you laughing at yourself and your problem faded away. He was a born healer."[287]

---

[285] John Polkinghorne, *The God of Hope and the End of the World* (London: SPCK Press, 2002), 26

[286] Bert Williams, minstrel show comedian, from *The Comic Side of Trouble* (American Magazine, January 1918), 33

[287] Bill Marx, *Ode to the Silent Harp*, from *Harpo Speaks* by Harpo Marx (New Jersey: Limelight Books, 2008), 478

Is laughter *designed* for persons to be able to take our pain, play with it, and thus, preserve our sanity in a wonderful world gone wonky? Why is it that humanity not only must experience the crucibles of life, but also have the capacity to cope with this suffering through comedy...*instinctively*? Could this phenomenon (unique in human behavior) be an indication of a God who not only allows the absurdities of our existence, but also provides for us the higher use of humor to engage it? We can laugh at of our own blunders, flaws, and pratfalls! Even in our *brokenness*, thorns may pierce the flesh, but wholesome and healing laughter may truly be "the real tonic of the soul."[288]

In his article, *The Science of Laughter*, psychiatrist Robert Provine studied laughter as a fundamental dynamic to everyday life that may have therapeutic qualities. Provine called laughter as a "'speaking in tongues' in which we are removed not by religious fervor but by an unconscious and instinctive behavior programmed by our genes. [It serves as] pain reduction and may temper intense pain."[289] Laughter binds us through the absurdity of play. It strips away the disguises of our false selves, and challenges the notion that we ourselves are immune from the wonky in our world.

Humorist Steve Allen defined laughter and the phenomenon of humor as:

> the sheer, gleeful, silly, having-a-good-time laughter, to which even sober adults occasionally succumb. There is a familiar theory about the origins of humor that holds that the funniest individuals, and the most amusing social groups, are those who have known a tragic history.[290]

In his more theological assessment of *humor*, Reinhold Niebuhr taught that laughter is an expression of and recompense for a divinely-ordained, human freedom. For Niebuhr, the gift of humor gives humanity the capacity to stand outside of life and review our lives with a positive perspective. We laugh at "the juxtaposition of things which do not fit together...a proud man slipping on the ice is a poetically just rebuke of his dignity." Humor is a proof

---

[288] Leslie Weatherhead, *Humor,* from *This is the Victory* (New York: Abingdon, 1951), 165

[289] *Psychology Today* (November 2000)

[290] *But Seriously: Steve Allen Speaks His Mind* (Amherst, NY: Prometheus Books, 1996), 98-100

of the capacity of the self to gain an objective vantage point from which it is able to look ourselves and the fullness of life itself. It is a "by-product of self-transcendence[291] and human consciousness.

Humor, laughter and comedy are indicators that God did not create a world that is to be lived strictly within the bounds of prosaic laws and regulations alone, but poetically experienced with novelty, absurdity, and *a sense of the ridiculous.*[292] Perhaps at times, God is not the judgmental tyrant, but is the jovial teacher—using humor a means toward our learning to be real?

This is the comic vision that is observable in the human design the prevalence of whimsy not only preserves our sanity, but reveals our mortal, foolish bungling, our fumbling fantasies, and our impossible dreams of grandeur. Comedy is a cosmic reminder of our total mortality, but also offers us "a greater appreciation for the muddiness of human nature—even in its noblest aspirations and righteous pretentions…and the problems of life that are ignored by those who would restrict themselves to major crises and important decisions."[293]

Humor and laughter as evidence for a whimsical God was articulated often by Red Skelton in the closing remarks of many of his comedic performances: "If by chance someday you're not feeling well and you should remember some silly thing I've said or done and it brings back a smile to your face or a chuckle to your heart, then my purpose as your clown has been fulfilled…I personally believe that each of us was put here for a purpose -- to build not to destroy. If I can make people smile, then I have served my purpose for God." Perhaps in the design of God for our lives, in the reality of terrible things that occur, God has included a coping mechanism that no other creature has: humor and capacity to simply laugh!

During a most turbulent time in the life of Great Britain, the *Blitz bombing* by the Nazis in World War II, then-pastor of the City Temple in London,

---

[291] Niebuhr, from *"Humour and Faith,"* The Essential Reinhold Niebuhr *(London: Yale University Press, 1986), 49-60

[292] Ed Wynn interview from *The Great Comedians Talk about Comedy,* by Larry Wilde (New York: Citadel Press, 1968), 376

[293] Conrad Myers, *The Spirituality of Comedy: Comic Heroism in a Tragic World* (London:Transaction Publishers, 1996), 96; 105

Leslie Weatherhead, affirmed the need for and the provision of humor for the homeostasis of humanity. He proclaimed: humor as "a real tonic of the soul and one of faith's finest allies. Those light touches which give perspective, which maintain buoyancy, which save us from taking anything, least of all ourselves, too seriously."[294]

This is not to postulate that everything painful is funny! Not at all. There are horrendous events in real time, hideous atrocities that come with the continuum of creation: natural disasters, genocide, injustice, and exploitation are never tipping points for laughter. Such things awaken us to our need for dialogue with God. Job said, "I will argue my ways before Him." (Job 13:15). In our dialogue with God, through lens of humor, we may often discover our "ways" as absurdly humorous when compared to the ways of God.

Those things, unlaughable, that keep us bound to despair may actually clarify our vision, awakening us to from sustaining level of coping to actual confrontation with the wonky and the wicked. With such a purview we may even laugh, assured "in His comforting of us, and joying in God that the fiend (the source of our despair) is overcome."[295] We may even laugh when we consider that even in our *worst of times*, "nothing can separate us from the love of God." (Romans 8:39/NRSV).

Perhaps the renowned clown, Red Skelton, was correct: God creates humor and purposes humorists to implement it in the world? According to biographer, Arthur Marx (son of Groucho), in his biography of Skelton, reputedly the comedian began to "bless" his audiences at the end of his performances with the famed closing line, "Good night and may God bless," after a series of jolting experiences in his own life.

On a flight from Rome to London as the airliner soared over snow-capped Mont Blanc in the Alps, two engines sputtered and died. Then a third engine caught fire and the plane started to go down. Understandably, panic began to break out among the passengers, among whom there were large numbers of children of various nationalities and religions, including Hindu, Jews, and Christians.

---

[294] Leslie Weatherhead, *This is the Victory* (NY: Abingdon Press, 1951), 155-156
[295] John Baille, *A Diary of Readings: Day 15* (New York: Charles Scribner's Sons, 1955)

"Suddenly Father Carney, in the seat next to Skelton, turned to his comedian friend and said, *"Okay, Red, you take care of your department, and I'll take care of mine."* The two men quickly unstrapped their seat belts and while Father Carney prepared to give the last rites to all who wished, Red Skelton, "America's Clown," started running up and down the aisles of the plane, clowning, joking, and miming even more frenetically with pathos and empathy.

> *Few of the children in Red's audience that day could understand a word he was saying, but the beauty of pantomime is that they didn't have to. He was able to make them laugh and forget the impending crash, despite the language barrier. 'None of us ever expected to get out of there alive,' recalled Red. 'It was the most wonderfully satisfying performance I ever gave.'*

Through his humor, those who were falling toward their demise found a moment of repose and refuge, some stability in the horror they were facing. The pilot was able to glide the plane to a "shaky landing." There were no injuries or loss of life. "For Red...their escape was not so much a result of good piloting (though that helped) as it was 'a miracle performed by the Guy Upstairs,' as he often referred to his Maker."[296]

In his biography about the great Vaudevillian and Television comedian Jimmy Durante, author Gene Fowler described the need for humor as performed by "the great clowns" as a "refuge" for a turbulent world. Fowler wrote:

> *The great clown stays on with us, as great clowns always stay in the hearts of men and women and children who seek in <u>the refuge of merriment</u> an hour of escape from the scowls of the long day. Out of his seeming artlessness there shines a surviving sanity in a world gone daft. It seems a glad summons to man's dimming hope, a call to hold fast. And <u>we feel something deep down</u>.[297]*
> [Emphasis Added].

---

[296] Arthur Marx, *Red Skelton: An Unauthorized Biography* (New York: E.P. Dutton, 1979), 159-161

[297] Gene Fowler, *Schnozzola: The Story of Jimmy Durante* (New York: Viking Press, 1951), 261

Finally, Leslie Weatherhead stated, that true humor, is not vulgar catharsis. It is only a momentary awareness or a deeper sense that there is joy in the heart of the universe. In this respect, "humor is divine."[298]

In the winter of 1965, Stan Laurel of the classic comedy team, Laurel and Hardy, died from a massive heart attack. His private funeral was attended by comedic friends Buster Keaton, Tim Conway, Patsey Kelly and Dick Van Dyke. It was mentioned during the proceedings that Stan had once remarked, "If any of you cry at my funeral, I'll never speak to you again." It was in the closing of the eulogy for Laurel when Van Dyke recited a poem lending credibility to the notion that our sense of humor is not by chance, but is evidence of a loving and mindful, and mirthful God:

> God bless all clowns,
> Who star in the world with laughter,
> God bless all the clowns.
> Alchemists most, who turn their hearts' pain,
> Into a dazzling jest to lift the heart.
> God bless all clowns.[299]

Appreciation for the Beautiful and the Lovely

"The final laws of nature are coherent and universal — beauty in those laws mirror something that is built into the structure of the universe at a very deep level."[300]

"Beauty…symmetry and elegance in form… all that harmonizes man with his Creator is in the diversified domain of the beautiful."[301]

Perceiving those things beautiful is an aesthetic experience. It is a complex experience with several dimensions. In religious experience, through beholding the beautiful, we perceive the holy or the sacred otherness

---

[298] Ibid., 9; 170-173

[299] Author unknown. Quoted by Dick Van Dyke in his autobiography, *My Lucky Life In and Out of Show Business: A Memoir* (New York: Crown/Archetype, 2011), 136-138

[300] Steven Weinberg, *Dreams of a Final Theory* (New York: Pantheon Books, 1992), 243

[301] George Caleb Bingham, *Art, the Ideal of Art, and the Utility of Art*, a lecture given to the University of Missouri (February 1879)

amidst our being. Appreciation for the beautiful is for some "our imperfect attempt to give an intellectual explication of the experience."[302] Beholding what cannot be held in our grasp, what is deemed as beautiful for the sake of its loveliness is itself an attribute distinctive of humanity, but evidence of a mindful designer. The beauty of the lovely moves me to a deeper mindfulness, "as a meadow delights the eyes and subtly infuses the soul with the glory of God."[303]

There is an indication of a higher consciousness in our appreciation of beauty for the sake of its loveliness alone. An appreciation for beauty has nothing to do with natural instinct or personal survival. An avowed atheist, physicist Steven Weinberg concluded that "nature seems more beautiful than is strictly necessary."[304]

With those *somethings* noted for their beauty, there is an inner surge of interconnectedness. A "something grander than I" mentality emerges. There is a distinguishable grandeur in the good of creation, even in the seemingly chaotic nonsense or wonky in our existence. Does our experience of the *beautiful* universe propose purpose and meaning? Or does what-appears-to be a beautiful and raw panorama just indicate chaotic nonsense for which we project value?

Oxford philosopher Richard Swinburne wrote "God paints with a big brush from a large paint box and he has no need to be stingy with the paint he uses to paint a beautiful universe."[305] Certainly atheists would tend to disagree. Many would see what is startlingly beautiful as only a natural and confounding projection of our own pathological need for a purposeful universe. On the other hand, perhaps their purposeless "chaotic" universe is a projection of *their* own atheistic disposition? What is beautiful is still noted as a panorama worthy of our attention, wonder, and awe. Admiring and subsequently pondering the beauty of the universe—as dark as it may seem to some—is a universal phenomenon.

---

[302] John Macquarrie, *Principles of Christian Theology* (London: Canterbury Press, 1977), 68

[303] St. John Damascene, *De image.* I, 27: para. 94

[304] Ibid., 250

[305] Richard Swinburne, *Is There a God?* (Oxford: University Press, 1996), 63

Through his own extraordinary observation of the cosmos, Edwin Hubble observed among stars, there is a definite relation between colors and spectral types. While the cause of the phenomena is unknown, the variation is well established; "the colors represent very precise measures."[306]

Such an observation depicts the order, movement, and improvisation of a consummate artist whose purposes may be simply the articulation of a cosmological wonder! Nothing can destroy our aesthetic appreciation of an "elegant universe." *(Brian Greene)*. Whether it be through the artful depiction of Van Gogh's *Starry Night*, or through the moody composition of Gustav Holst's *Planets,* there is something in the core of our being that recognizes and celebrates the raw beauty in the cosmos. Perhaps that wonderment is a purpose for a seemingly "pointless universe?" While "war and ugliness, horror and beastliness will pass. Beauty is one of the eternal values that abides."[307] Humanity not only leans toward the moral, but is mysteriously compelled toward the beautiful.

Moreover, once beauty has been *noticed,* humanity will work very hard to conserve its existence. The conservation of beauty for the sake of the ecstasy we find in its loveliness is in itself a purpose for being. There is no materialist reason for that ecstasy unless there is an experiential interconnectedness to its distinguishable loveliness. We are drawn to beauty and humbled by the presence of its grandeur—a grandeur often admittedly, greater than ourselves. Author John Haught explained that in order to experience beauty in nature, in others, in works of art, persons must allow themselves to be vulnerable to an aesthetic phenomenon. This aesthetic experience of being grasped by the beautiful is closely involved in the intuition of a Greater Reality, the ultimate beauty that "transcends the universe itself.[308]

There are still those who would not include the mere appreciation of beauty for the sake of its loveliness as evidence for a purposeful universe. For them, beauty is just a by-product of a pointless naturalistic happenstance. For example, physicist Richard Feynman thought that the great accumulation of understanding as to how the physical world behaves only convinces one that

---

[306] *The Realm of the Nebulae* (New Haven: Yale University Press, 2013), 52

[307] Leslie Weatherhead, *This is the Victory,* Ibid., 156

[308] John Haught, *What is God? How to Think about the Divine* (New York: Paulist Press, 1986), 69-70; 87

this behavior has a kind of *purposelessness* about it. It is a conclusion endorsed by Steven Weinberg in that "'the more the universe seems comprehensible the more it also seems pointless.'"[309]

However, physicist Paul Davies suggests there could be a purpose in the universe that science simply has yet to discover. Perhaps it is in the appreciation of the beauty of scientific inquiry itself there is meaning? He concluded that the beauty of doing science itself is an indication of purposefulness to the cosmos. Where is the evidence of a "cosmic purpose?"

> *Well, it is right under our noses in the very existence of science itself as a successful explanatory paradigm. Doing science means figuring out what is going on in the world—what the universe is 'up to', what it is 'about.' Science is a voyage of discovery, and as with all such voyages, you have to believe there is something meaningful out there to discover before you embark on it.*[310]

The comprehend-sensibility of the cosmos is more than a study for scientific inquiry, it provides meaning or purpose of being: that is, to appreciate and create beauty. Even science itself can be a threshold to an appreciation of beauty for the sake of what is esteemed not only as good, but awe-inspiring. For the composer of hymns, this sense of the beautiful as evidence of a consummate and divine artist who continues to create and recreate on a canvas as vast at the cosmos:

> *For the beauty of the earth*
> *For the glory of the skies,*
> *For the love which from our birth*
> *Over and around us lies.*
> *Lord of all, to Thee we raise,*
> *This our hymn of grateful praise.*[311]

---

[309] Quoted by physicist, cosmologist, and astrophysicist, Paul Davies, Arizona State University, from an address, *"Does the Universe have a Purpose: PERHAPS, A Templeton Conversation"*
http://www.templeton.org/purpose/essaydavies.html
[310] Ibid. (Used by permission of Professor Davies 10/09/2019)
[311] Folliott S. Pierpoint, *For the Beauty of the Earth* (1864)

Music: Compelling Compositions of the Cosmos

Love is still the commonest theme of our songs.[312]

Man is a harp of a thousand strings;
Touch the spiritual chord of his heart,
And lo! with what inspiration he sings,
Unaided by science, skilled in art,
'Tis the voice of God in his soul that sings,
And is more than a harp of a thousand strings.[313]

We live in a cosmos of both symmetrical and improvisational vibrations *wherein* "even color and light are forms of music that are simply perceived by a different sense organ, the eye. Science shows us that different creatures 'see' and 'hear' sights and sounds that are "beyond human perception."[314] Perhaps such a phenomenon is also only perceived by the most ethereal of auditory capabilities?

For the more earthy listener, composer Aaron Copland observed, that all melodies exist within the limits of some scale system. Where you listen to Mozart or Duke Ellington or Hank Williams, you can deepen your understanding of music only by being a more conscious and aware listener, to listen for the ambiances of the piece. We are persons not just listening, but experiencing for the intentional dynamics to the composition: "melody, rhythm, harmony, color and tone."[315]

Richard Feynman wonders if anyone can truly *read the music* in the cosmos? He refers to a kind of cosmic rhythm of life, from the tonalities in the universe to the fanciful activity of atoms in the human person, or what he described as a pattern or dance. "The atoms come into my brain, dance a dance, then go out—there are always new atoms, but always doing the same

---

[312] Charles Darwin, *The Descent of Man*, 1871

[313] Traditional Shaker hymn, circa 1893

[314] John Michael Talbott, *The Music of Creation* (NY: Putnam, 1999), 17

[315] *What to Listen for in Music* (New York: McGraw-Hill Company, 1957) 51; 19-25. Note: *NASA's Sounds in the Universe: https://www.youtube.com/watch?v=7-t_Bo54ftM&t=125s*. Note: *Music from the inner rungs of vintage trees: https://www.youtube.com/watch?v=JKZb6sIH-SE*

dance, remembering what the dance was yesterday.[316] All around us in the compositions of the cosmos, our ecosystem, and within our own being are rhythmic patterns of our existence.

Music is in conversation with humanity in a holistic way. Music reaches into the core of our being to prompt emotion, thought, and vision. It helps us to give expression to both our seasons of joy and of sorrow. It charms us, challenges us, ignites our passions, and soothes our most harrowing of days. It is a source of wonderment that science still has a difficult time explaining away as merely a chance of evolution. It seems to have a purpose for being.

Celtic theologian J. Phillip Newell of Iona Monastery in Scotland concurred, that physicists now speak of being able to detect throughout the universe the sound that comes from the beginning of time. "It vibrates through everything that has being...eternal rhythm."[317]

Perhaps what some would describe as purposeless chaos in the cosmos is actually a divine composition orchestrated by the mindfulness of an incomprehensible Composer? Perhaps the universe is an artist's canvas or a composer's cosmic ledger? Perhaps the panorama of the cosmos is actually the moment-to-moment continuum of God's creative momentum—like a living a hymn that fills the whole universe with a melody that continues whether we are listening or not. "the hymn of cosmic sounds and intimate whisperings... is the song of Presence."[318]

God music is all encompassing. It moves from measure-to-measure by the whims of a soft breeze or sometimes through the manifestation of a rushing, mighty wind. In his book, *The Elegant Universe,* theoretical physicist and mathematician, Brian Greene wrote that music provides metaphors for "questions of cosmic concern." With the discovery of superstring theory, musical metaphors suggest that the microscopic landscape is "suffused with tiny strings whose vibrational patterns orchestrate the evolution of the cosmos. The winds of change, gust through an aeolian universe.[319]

---

[316] Richard Feynman, *What do You Care: Further Adventures,* Ibid., 244

[317] J. Phillip Newell, *Christ of the Celts,* (Glasgow: Wild Goose, 2008), 52-53

[318] Ibid., 118

[319] Brian Greene, *The Elegant Universe* (New York: Vintage Books, 1999), 135

Biblically speaking, the winds of the Spirit continue to hover over creation with original overtures and melodies that few pause long enough to hear.

If our existence is merely a chance, chaotic, and or meaningless mess, then what of music? -- that strange melodious entity Shakespeare called "the moody food of us that trade in love?"[320] Whether it be rhythmic sounds within the natural order or inspired lyrics composed by the genius of humanity, the performing of, the listening to, or the dancing with music is in itself a purpose for being.

For musician Wynton Marsalis, music is "organized sound in time" meticulously composed but not always performed in verbatim to the score-as-written. There is the human performance and interpretation of music: *improvisation!* In the melodious composition of the cosmos we experience both precision of movement and the novelty of improvisation; structure--with freedom of will to move about within that structure for personal expression, interpretation and improvisation. Music adapts to the purposes for which it seems to have been "designed."

Marsalis described three keys to musical composition as: 1. to create something on the spur of the moment; 2. use whatever is available in creating that something; and 3. put your feelings and personality into whatever you create. "No two people create the same way."[321] There is a constancy to the myriad of melody in all of creation and its origin.

How does music originate? According to Marsalis, for the composer, "the creative process begins in a shrouded impenetrable darkness, a mystery to most people…in an unapproachable ivory tower…inspired to compose as if born to do so."[322] This would certainly reflect an image of God, the creator. From the mystery or darkness of the nothing comes a composition of exquisite melody. Perhaps human beings created in the image of God point to a Composer who continues to *create* life—both intentionally by way of composing the arrangement, but also through the means of the interpretation or improvisation of those who perform it? From the nothing,

---

[320] *Antony and Cleopatra* II, v.
[321] *Marsalis on Music* (New York: W.W. Norton & Company, 1995), 22; 159
[322] Ibid., 19

through the Composer's masterpiece on paper and with the interpretation of the musician, comes the fantasia of life!

There is in the musical score, the latitude for personal expression, interpretive movement within the composition. Renowned violin virtuoso, Isaac Stern described this unique capacity of humanity in the realm of musicianship as personal expression within an established composition or imaginative movement within the boundaries of the composer's intentional design. In his autobiography *My First 79 Years*, Stern wrote:

> *You must know the tonal, harmonic, and tempo relationships among the movements to make a work hold together throughout its entirety, from the first to the last note. The performer grasps the totality of the composition, he gauges the amount of sound and speed required by the work against his own skills with tonal and volume pressures and technical fleetness. It's clear that's the way it should be. Every artist also has a very personal and indefinable symbiosis with his instrument. As he plays, he hears the composition in his or her own very special personal voice...a distinctive interpretative strength.* [323]

As in performing music, every human being has a 'distinctive interpretative strength" in how one lives well within the context of God's composition. Stern's remark lends credence to the idea of music as an intentional "design" with natural symmetry and latitude for idiosyncratic expression.

Stern regards how the score moves from the overture to the outro. But, in the performance of the composition as written, the musician is free within that composition to improvise his or her own interpretations, or musical prowess, until the final note of the composer's masterpiece is played. Our only instruction, Stern believed is to make it "harmoniously beautiful!"

Music reaches the deepest regions of the soul and may even move us into sacred space as nothing else may. Liturgical musician, John Michael Talbott observed we all have been created in God's image, and as a result we inherently desire to create the music of the cosmos with our divine Composer, "the music of

---

[323] Isaac Stern, *My First 79 Years* (New York: Alfred A. Knopf, 1999), 67

God.[324] Martin Luther even believed that music in praise of God, or "musica est optimum," could actually become a *bridge* of connection between heaven and earth. He wrote, whenever human beings use their voices to sing God's praises "musica humana and musica caelestis [are] conjoined."[325]

At ninety years old, singer Tony Bennett in his autobiography, *Life is a Gift,* recognized that humanity has the capacity through music, to "go with truth and beauty and leave the rest behind."[326] Like a musical composition with the movements of adagio and allegro, cadence and cadenza, dissonance and drone, gradioso, legato, and modulation, rococo and the romantic, life works with the precise composition as it was written, but with the improvisation and interpretation of the performer of what has been intricately composed.

Author Anne Rice wrote "The music of a violin sound to me of God. An intense study of the lives of various composers spoke to me for the love of God."[327] Perhaps music is a vessel through which we may even come to an awareness of creation as a continuing composition performed though the participation and co-operation of ourselves as the musicians?

The entire cosmos moves in "elliptical orbits,"[328] "vibratory and sonic, and at the same time conscious."[329] If there is connection to the personability of God and His creation, then music would certainly be a manifestation of God's creative activity. Cambridge University biologist, Rupert Sheldrake concluded that if there is *a galactic mind*, then it might well hear the "repetitive rhythms of all these celestial movements as tones or qualities, as a kind of planetary, stellar, and galactic music." As everything in nature is rhythmic of vibratory, including our own physiology, the phases, cycles, and rhythms of being, perhaps music can link us to a musical mind far greater than our own, and "ultimately to the source of life itself."[330]

---

[324] John Michael Talbott, *Ibid.*; 68-69

[325] Quote from Jeremy Begbie, *Music, Modernity and God: Essays in Listening* (Oxford: University Press, 2013), 33

[326] Tony Bennett, *Life is a Gift* (New York: Harper, 2012), 210

[327] Anne Rice, Ibid., 174

[328] Johannes Kepler, *The Harmony of the World* (1619)

[329] Rupert Sheldrake, *Science and Spiritual Practices* (Berkeley, CA: Counterpoint, 2017), 125

[330] Ibid., 127-128

A Momentary Pause:

Tonality Throughout the Cosmos:

Kentucky folk storyteller, Jesse Stuart observed:

> *Thank God I have a Love that goes with me*
> *When **there is music in the wind at night;***
> *On mountains where boughs weave incessantly*
> *Between us and the moon and the pale starlight.*
> ***Immortal symphonies are played by the wind***
> *Of destiny that sweeps the upland cone.*
> ***Night wind in pines is a crying violin;***
> ***Night wind in oaks is a tenor saxophone.***
> ***Night wind in sassafras is a magic flute;***
> ***Through sourwood branches is a soft-toned guitar.***
> ***In sawbriar tendrils night wind is a lute,***
> *Beneath the floating cloud, the moon and star.*
> *We store a portion of **this symphony***
> *To live unwritten in our heart and brain;*
> *We live a night of love and poetry,*
> *A night of nights we hope will come again (emphasis added).[331]*

Art: Creatively Aesthetic Motion

"The mission of the artist...we have to touch and to please before our audience can be made to think."[332]

"Their musings, science and the arts, whisper: 'Follow us, explore, find out."[333]

Why is it that humanity can not only value what is beautiful for the sake of its loveliness alone, but can also create what is distinguishably beautiful as

---

[331] Jesse Stuart, *When There Is Music,* from *The World of Jesse Stuart: Selected Poems* (New York: McGraw-Hill, 1975), 86

[332] Marcel Marceau Speaks: Interview with William Fifield (NY: Caedmon Records, 1971)

[333] E. O. Wilson, *Consilience: The Unity of Knowledge,* (NY: Alfred A. Knopf, 1998), 233

well? With originality, novelty, through joy, grief, and resilience, humanity is profoundly wooed toward creating what is beautiful. We just can't seem to find our fill of artistic expressions of beauty and depictions of what is good. Where beauty and good are nowhere to be found, humanity is innately designed to create or recreate it.

Is this a sign of a humanity created in the image of a consummate or master Artist?

Why is it we tend toward creative expressions of our being, filtered through an appreciation of what is beautiful and agitated by what is not? Whether it be a painting on a canvas, the spectacle of panoramic view, meticulous architecture, or the preciseness of a mathematic equation, we are *moved* by the aestheticism in works of artistic expression.

Does our capacity for artistry indicate evidence for a master Artist, a God who reveals presence through the aesthetically creative momentum of life? In describing the mystical experience of St. Francis of Assisi, biographer Thomas of Celano wrote in every work of the artist, he (St. Francis) "remised the Artist;" whatever he found in the things made, he referred to the Maker. He followed the Beloved everywhere; he made for himself "a ladder by which to come even closer to His throne."[334]

Kentucky storyteller, Wendell Berry relates the arts as very much alive. We can speak of the arts only "within limits," but we can certainly see that they are "essential to our lives."[335] Carl Jung concurred in that the poet seems to be drifting off by an artistic impulse or a creative urge lives and grows in all humanity "like a tree in the earth from which it draws its nourishment. A creative process as a living thing implanted in the human psyche."[336]

Artistic expression for nothing but for the sake of the aesthetic nourishment in provides is purpose in an art seemingly without purpose. In the educating the spectator to the point of view of the artist, there is the emergence of a deeper awareness of the fullness of reality. Artistic expression tends to

---

[334] Thomas of Celano, *Second Life*, cxxxiv, 165

[335] *Conversations*, Ibid., 53

[336] Carl Jung, *The Spirit in Man*, Art and Literature (Princeton University Press, 1966), 74-75

"drag a resisting humanity forward and upward."[337] The common and, in extraordinary cases, uncommon tendency for humanity to be artistically creative is further evidence that a mindful Artist is continuing the work of creation with the purpose being the actualization of the aesthetically fulfilling coming into being. For 14th century painter, Cennino Connini, the "vestments" of the artist are love, fear of God, obedience, and perseverance.[338]

Dramatist, novelist, poet and essayist *Dorothy Sayers* wrote of aestheticism as "the vocation of the creative mind in man." The artist's knowledge of his own creative nature is often unconscious; yet, humanity innately pursues this mysterious way of art, a self-transcendence through the pattern of "the creative mind—the pattern of the being of God.[339] Of such is being in created in God's image.

There is evidence of the presence of a mindful Artist simply in one's appreciation for the noticeability of what has been created without the interference of humanity—the pristine as over and contrasted to the primitive. Perhaps such things offer to the poetic mind a solace and simplicity of being that was intended by God?

Humanity has the unique capacity to apprehend and articulate the awe and wonder of a poetically designed world if we are vulnerable enough to listen for the poet's promptings. Consider the *Poet's Mind (1830)* by Alfred Lord Tennyson:

> *Vex not thou the poet's mind*
> *With thy shallow wit:*
> *Vex not thou the poet's mind;*
> *For thou canst not fathom it.*
> *Clear and bright it should be ever,*
> *Flowing like a crystal river;*
> *Bright as light, and clear as wind.*

---

[337] Wassily Kandinsky, *Concerning the Spiritual in Art and Painting in Particular* (New York: Wittenborn & Shultz, 1947), 23-27

[338] *The Book of Art*

[339] Dorothy Sayers, *The Image of God*, from *Spiritual Writings* (London: Society for Promoting Christian Knowledge, 1993), 78-79

Altruism: Mercy and Stewardship

"...do not oppress the widow, the orphan, the alien, or the poor; and do not devise evil in your hearts against one another..." (Malachi 3:5/NRSV).

"... 'love one another and pray for those who persecute you...' (Matthew 5:44/NRSV).

> The quality of mercy is not strain'd,
> It droppeth as the gentle rain from heaven...
> It is an attribute to God himself...
> The deeds of mercy... [340]

If humanity can be reduced to mere "survival machines"[341] evolved by chance from a composition of flotsam or jetsom, "memes," or "shuffled chromosomes," what then of compassion, devotion to the welfare of others or mercy? How can the stewardship of community, or "walking in the light of creative altruism in the midst of the darkness of destructive selfishness,"[342] be explained without reference to a benevolent God?

In the words of *Cervantes' Don Quixote, why* does humanity have the capacity for nobility? Why do we marvel at those who offer themselves in the nobler cause to:

> *slay pride in giants, envy by generosity and nobleness of heart, anger by calmness of demeanor and equanimity, gluttony and sloth by the sparseness of our diet and length of our vigils, lust and lewdness by the loyalty we preserve to those whom we have made the mistresses of our thoughts, indolence by traversing the world in all directions seeking opportunities of making ourselves look more to that future glory that is everlasting in the ethereal regions of heaven than to the vanity of the fame?[343]*

Can the exercise of *mercy and benevolence* be explained through naturalistic theory with only its insistence upon natural selection or the "survival of the

---

[340] Shakespeare, *The Merchant of Venice* IV, i

[341] Richard Dawkins, *The Selfish Gene* (Oxford: University Press, 1976)

[342] Martin Luther King Jr., *"Three Dimensions of a Compete Life"* from *Strength to Love* (NY: Harper & Row, 1963), 72

[343] *Cervantes*, Don Quixote, Chapter VIII

fittest?" Is humanity simply reduced to a bio-chemical eruption of naturalistic urges? Perhaps there is more to being human? Perhaps the moral imperative is a *given* that measures and critiques our choices and serves as a launching point toward the highest good: love, and the actualization of the character and nature of God?

There is a noticeable distinction between behavior noble and ignoble. Humanity is keenly aware of the difference between the tender and the brutal. In the core of our being, we respond respectively to both. Why is humanity agitated by behavior that is violent and brutal? If Social Darwinism is the only paradigm for our behavior, why shouldn't brutality be the norm, rather than a negative behavior from which humanity needs to evolve?

Moreover, a strictly Darwinian point of view would rebuke tenderness as weakness or inconsistent with the progress of creatures existing for the sake of survival. Digressing to its most horrible expression, the "survival of the fittest" paradigm, with its tendency toward affirming even the brutality of the fittest, can lead to a lynch mob mentality, subjugating the poor, exploiting the weak, and unjustly crucifying the innocent.

What is the result of a culture that denies the practice of altruism? Note the anti-theistic credo of the Church of Satan of America by its founder, Anton Szandor LaVey, in *the Satanic Bible (1969)*. Taken to its exclusively naturalist conclusion, the following code was intentionally devised to agitate those who hold to the Judeo-Christian ethic. In this code, Satan is merely the metaphorical antithesis of the *good,* or militant anti-theism. This anti-theist code of morality includes:

1. *indulgence instead of abstinence!*
2. *vital existence instead of spiritual pipe dreams!*
3. *undefiled wisdom instead of hypocritical self-deceit!*
4. *kindness to those who deserve it instead of love wasted on ingrates!*
5. *vengeance instead of turning the other cheek!*
6. *responsibility to the responsible instead of concern for psychic vampires!*
7. *man as just another animal; because of his "divine spiritual and intellectual development," has become the most vicious animal of all!*
8. *the so-called sins, all lead to physical, mental, or emotional gratification!*

To the reasonable or morally *attuned* the above anti-theist rhetoric is alarmingly repugnant. The question must be asked to the skeptical atheist: if there is no purpose for being other than the survival of the powerful, then *why* is this satanic, anti-theistic creed morally agitating, even repugnant? Because we have in the core of our being not only an inherited moral code, but an innate altruism, the capacity for compassion and empathy for others.

Certainly not all naturalists or atheists are Satanists. But without God, there is no rationale or accountability for altruism. It is even conceivable that if there is no God, there would be no need for altruism. For in a naturalistic perspective, with the "survivalist" mentality, the above list could evolve into a *creedal* "moral code" of its own, for the sake of nothing but the irrational gratification of the *self* and the emergence of totalitarian centers of "principalities and powers, rulers of the darkness of the world, spiritual wickedness in high places." (Ephesians 6:12/NASB).

While philosopher of science, Michael Ruse, the author of many books of Darwinism and evolutionary biology, may oppose the notion of morality as rational evidence for an Intelligent Designer, he does recognize "the tug of moral obligation" as distinctively altruistic. But he explains this extraordinary phenomenon from an evolutionary point of view as merely referring to the actions performed by "organisms" towards others because there is an "expectation of return,"[344] for the sake of personal, biological reward.

Ruse observes in the chemistry of human beings "supreme moral principles of substantial ethics" which includes "giving according to people's needs and maximizing the benefits of life for all, with the social contract of cooperation." He asserts the morality of the *Ten Commandments* as right in line with a commonsense morality, and the *love commandment* (of Jesus) as the way for "direct reciprocation,"[345] a kind of ethical *tit-for-tat*.

But Ruse's myopic concept of reciprocation of which he insists qualifies the benevolence between persons is countered with the admonition of Jesus to do your alms "in secret." (Matthew 6:4/NIV).

---

[344] Ruse, *Can a Darwinian be a Christian?*, Ibid., 191-192
[345] Ibid., 197-199

While Professor Ruse must be affirmed in his observation of the distinctiveness of moral and ethical behavior, his purely naturalistic view is somewhat confined to a limited perspective of what is possible from a more supra-rational purview. Are what he termed as "supreme moral principles of substantial ethics" only a progressive expression of natural selection, and self or tribal preservation? Is there more to morality than merely a code written for the sake of one's own survival?

In his *Challenge to Neo-Darwinism,* Professor of Biology and Geology Stephen Jay Gould, himself an agnostic, believed that morality and the ascent to altruism is actually a given to human consciousness in the actualization of a maturing personhood. He believed that humanity could excel beyond our own self concerns, and consciously decide whether to enhance or to injure those with whom we reside. We can distinguish between what is enhancing and what is injurious. This is what Gould described as "higher level fitness; to act accordingly." Here, the strict Social Darwinian explanations for altruism offered by sociobiology is deemed by Gould to be inadequate. He wrote: "evolutionary adaptation does not specify how we must behave or what we must do."[346]

"You KNOW what is right: do justice, love kindness…" (Micah 6:8/ NIV).

Be careful not to practice your righteousness in front of others to be seen by them. (Matthew 6:1-4/NRSV)

Life is an obligation which friends often owe each other in the wilderness.[347]

While a simple moral code *may* have originated from a need to regulate the behavior of a tribal people, altruism is a matter of character development or even the transformation of our true selves or our *designed personhood.* Altruism is empathy-in-action, regardless of reward or recognition. It is not just sentimental or sympathetic thought. Nor is it just dying for a personal conviction or for the survival of one's own tribe. It is living in empathy for the needs or causes that are esteemed as greater than one's own survival. Generally, if not universally, in civilized cultures, living in empathy means to

---

[346] Gould, *The Richness of Life:* Essential Writings (New York: W. W. Norton and Company, 2006,) 234-235

[347] James Fennimore Cooper, *The Last of the Mohicans,* Chapter VIII: paragraph 7

Be kind to people, help children and the less fortunate, and try to do so in proportion to need, give priority to mothers, don't rape and/or use gratuitous violence toward women, keep your word, don't take what is not yours, try to moderate habits like boastfulness which are going to irritate others, and stick up for your country or your group.[348]

Human beings have the capacity to ascend from intuitive questions to empirical inquiry and from the rational to the supra-rational, revelatory experience. Similarly one may behave within the givenness of a moral imperative, but also ascend from *"common ethic demands"* (E. O. Wilson) to *"supreme principles"* (Michael Ruse) and even to the exercise of *"transforming initiatives"* (Glen Stassen) for the sake of the *"beloved community"* (Martin Luther King, Jr.) and the purpose of a just peace and the practice of Ultimate Love.

Becoming activists for the sake of community would describe what British cosmologist and astrophysicist, Martin Rees defined as *"effective altruism."* This includes the emergence of urgent improvements to people's lives through the intentional directing of available resources to persons, communities, and nations in need. For Rees, who noted himself to be a "practicing, but unbelieving Christian," the intention of effective altruism, "is the role of the world's religions—transnational communities that think long-term and care about the global community, especially the world's poor."[349] (With only a naturalistic code of behavior, why would anyone bother about an impoverished or hungry population outside one's own household? From the course of a strict evolutionary view of "natural selection," why not just "let *them* die?")

Moreover, from an exclusively naturalistic point of view, E. O. Wilson also observes the capacity of humanity for *"stewardship,"* which appears to arise from emotions "programmed in the very genes of human social behavior." Stewardship reflects a mindfulness, not only about the care of human beings, but for all of creation as well. Stewardship regards our respective place in

---

[348] Ruse, Ibid., 198
[349] Rees, *On the Future*, Ibid., 224

nature, received from an ethical perspective to *tend* creation and live in sync with our environment.

This instinctive behavior Wilson described as originating from a part of human nature, he calls "biophilia…to affiliate with other living systems, an innate tendency to be attracted to other life forms—not just that of my own tribe or habitat.[350] The qualitative sense of oughtness in the practice of mercy, altruism, and stewardship are not only learned behavior, they are innate qualities of human character. This kind of behavior certainly distinguishes humanity from other creatures in the world. Humanity may grow from merely a sense of oughtness to an experience of Ultimate Love. Such a phenomenon may indeed reflect even an ultimate expression of morality, the more profound nature of God, and the mystery of *mercy and grace.*

Imagination and Inspiration: *"the mystery which urges men to create"*[351]

The wonder of creativity has been "infused into the minds of men" said Venetian painter, Carlo Ridolfi.[352] This creative "urge" in the make-up of humanity may look well designed, composed, and inspired and as such will "incite devout feelings." It may be works of "a sacred and noble nature,"[353] that reflects an interconnectedness to an imaginative Creator. Merton taught that the exercise of a nobler creativity is a purpose for being:

> *There is no genuine creativity apart from God. The man who attempts to be a 'creator' outside of God and independent of him is forced to fall back on magic or wizardry. If man was first called to share in the creative work of his heavenly Father, he now became involved in the 'new creation,' the redemption of his own kind and the restoration of the cosmos.*[354]

God is the consummate Creator. What was God doing before *our* creation? Perhaps He was creating? It is arrogant to assume God was only devising

---

[350] Wilson, *The Future of Life* Ibid., 132; 139

[351] Georgio DeChirico (1913)

[352] *The Wonder of Art* (1648)

[353] Pietro Berrettini DeCortona, *Treatise on Painting and Sculpture* (1652)

[354] Thomas Merton, *Theology of Creativity*, taken from *Selected Essays*, ed. Patrick F. O'Connell (Maryknoll, NY: Orbis, 2013), 100-101

plans for life on Earth through an exclusive seven days of creation. Creation was (is) an eternal and continuing activity of God. Our universe is but one canvas among many. Creation qua creation is a manifestation of God's self-activity. Other universes, and life forms may be the product of that activity.

Furthermore, if the mark of our finite personality is to be endlessly creative, we might expect this to be an idiosyncrasy of God in His continuing activity of creation. Perhaps God involves our lives as expressions of this continuing activity in our world, in real time? That would certainly be a purpose for our being—and becoming.

God continues to create through a humanity created in His image. <u>We are not divine!</u> As human beings we are not able to create *ex-nihilo* ("out of nothing"). We may manipulate what has been created to develop what has yet to be. Advances in exploration and discovery, technology, medicine, artistic expression, and geo-politics are all expressions of a humanity who seeks to take the resources of what has already been created by God toward reaching its greatest good and *redemptive* crescendo.

Humanity is predisposed toward *designability*, to create within divinely established perimeters of purpose. What is the purpose for humanity? To become extensions of a continuing and divinely inspired handiwork toward the actualization of God's intention for creation. There is within the human personhood a motivating force of the consciousness of a creative Presence directing the movement of life. According to Tolstoy, humanity is "a compound of animal and divine life. And the nearer this compound approaches the divine, the more life there is." Humanity only suffers torment from "the glaring contradiction between what is and what should be."[355] In short, humanity is urged to be a creative mode toward the realization of the yet-to-be.

With our capacity to recognize the *incompleteness,* or the *not-yet* of our existence, we also have an amazingly innate sense of what ought to enhance to our existence and what ought to be excluded from it. Thus, nearly every one of the world's spiritual traditions teaches that there is "an

---

[355] Leo Tolstoy, *The Lion and the Honeycomb: The Religious Writings*, Edited by A. N. Wilson (San Francisco: Harper and Row, 1987), 78-105

intimate connection between God's act of creating the cosmos and human creativity."[356]

Striving toward the yet-to-be is a purpose for being. Living in harmony with God's creative activity enables us to live "a spiritually-grounded life,"[357] not as *a god*, but as our truest selves, the continuing handiwork of God. Humanity reflects the image of God in our exercise of creative imagination, we may envision God as "a great imaginative Artist, working in the same sort of way as a creative artist...the most natural thing in the world."[358]

J.R.R. Tolkien wrote to his *Inklings* chum, C. S. Lewis: "Man [is] sub-creator, the refracted light through whom is splintered from a single white to many hues."[359] Life works because as humanity, as sub-creators with God, learns as our existence unfolds, emerges, and grows. There are appointed lifetimes, seasons, and eras into which humanity may contribute to the progressive momentum of harmonious living with God and all that God loves.

Tolkien originated the concept of *Mythopoeia* (Greek for 'mythos-making,' first mentioned in *Fairy Stories, 1947)*, to position himself as opposed to rank materialism, or exclusive rationalism. Tolkien believed humanity was destined for nobler purposes, to become *"little makers,"* tending to creation, both with improvisation and within the structures of God's original composition.

> *I will not treat your dusty path and flat,*
> *Denoting this and that by this and that,*
> *Your world immutable wherein no part*
> *The little maker as with maker's art..."*[360]

From this perspective, life is ignited with meaning and purpose: to create! We become "sub-creators" *(Tolkien)* in the continuum of God's creative

---

[356] John Michael Talbot, *The Music of Creation* Ibid., 16

[357] Ibid.

[358] Dorothy L. Sayers, *"Creative Mind,"* from *Letters to a Diminished Church* (Thomas Nelson Publishing, 2004), 35-36

[359] *Letters of J. R. R. Tolkien* ed. Humphry Carpenter (NY: Houghton, Mifflin, Harcourt, 2013), September 19, 1931

[360] J.R.R. Tolkien, *Tree and Leaf,* 1988

activity in the cosmos, our environment and in community. Humanity has been given the capacity to contribute to this interconnectedness with all of creation. We must not see ourselves as the climax of creation, but as instruments of a continuum of all that is and is becoming. We become vessels for the purposes of God: the continuing "good creation." The momentum of our existence becomes "self-creative" in partnership with God and with the predisposition "to evolve into life and mind, biological creativity and creative novelty [toward] cosmic beauty."[361]

Martin Luther King Jr. prayed that the purpose of creative persons be revealed as vessels of honor in the world, promoting "the higher principle of love:"

> God grant that the resources that you have will be used to do that, the great resources of education, the resources of wealth, and that we will be able to move into this new world. A world in which men will throw down the sword and live by the higher principle of love, freedom and justice![362]

The "higher principle of love" is the guiding light from Light in our capacity as "sub-creators." Beyond a naturalistic or inherited moral code for the survival of *self*, humanity is *designed* with the inclination to create, enabled by an empathy for the wellness of all persons in community. We recognize the health of ecological systems and interpersonal connections as essential to our own well-being. Much is anticipated for a humanity who has been given *much!*

The provision of resources we have been given to invest creatively are not to be squandered for mere survival or self-aggrandizement. As sub-creators by design, we are urged into a continuum of good for the progress of life and the ultimate hope for the well-being of humanity. Creative mindfulness is at the core of our existence as humans—*being.* Whether it be articulated through artistry in stone, paint, music, or literature, this pattern seems to be common in all persons. The need to express one's individuality artistically can unfold through politics, agriculture, manufacturing, and athletics. In

---

[361] John F. Haught, *Science and Religion: from Conflict to Conversation* (NY: Paulist Press, 1995), 62

[362] A prayer of Martin Luther King, Jr. from *Thou, Dear God: Prayers that Open Hearts and Spirits*, ed. Lewis V. Baldwin (Boston: Beacon, 2012), 153

the continuum of creation toward the *yet-to-be*, all of humanity has an innate capacity to discover a purpose for being as "sub-creators" with God.

Novelty and Improvisation: The Enthralling Existence of Humanity

Although for some an observation of movement in the cosmos seems meaningless and without purpose, others may envision a purpose through the simple creative dynamic of improvisation for the sake of novelty both in the atmosphere as in our respective expressions of how we live our lives on the earth.

Biologist Stephen Jay Gould contended, "I also willingly confess a sound proliferation in viewing sharp transitions and changes of status as important parts of nature's panoply or the [emergent] 'novelty.'"[363] Can the existence of novelty be evidence for a purpose for being—even of Divine non-interference within the structure of a workable created order?

Humanity has the capacity for improvisational inconsistencies, "a mysterious, ever-changing freedom at the very heart of creativity."[364] Unlike any other creature, we have a freedom within the human experience that moves from the center of the orderliness required for the survival, to the outrageousness of the artful ad lib, or impulsive spontaneity, of which adds a lighthearted exploration, as well as, potential danger to the human experience.

In his book *Evenings with Horowitz: A Personal Portrait,* biographer David Dubal recounted the words of the renowned pianist: "I was always a good improviser. Some of my improvising are tremendous, some very poor... some good with startling things, then twenty minutes bad."[365] Like the ever-emerging cosmos, that seems to some as pointless or void of intent, improvisation is an expression of human autonomy. The bounds of orderliness tempers, or qualifies our autonomy, holding us accountable for the consequences of our freedom, and critiquing its outcome for good or bad.

---

[363] Stephen Jay Gould, *An Urchin in the Storm: Essays about Books and Ideas* (London: W W Norton and Company, 1987), 214

[364] Byron Javis, Liner notes for *Vladimir Horowitz: The Complete Masterworks Recordings*, Volume III, 8

[365] David Dubal, *Evenings with Horowitz* (NY: Birch Lane Press, 1991), 79-82

Perhaps a purpose for life is merely to improvise our capacity to be influential the actualization of a good creation? Moreover, could the cosmos actually be a seasonal, era-driven, ever-unfolding canvas upon which the consummate Artist of the cosmos creates through improvisation, while at the same time, move within an ordered structure and life-sustainable ecosystem? Does the human capacity for improvisation and novelty within healthy boundaries reflect such an attribute of God?

Horowitz described his own musical improvisation within the boundaries of the composer as "a potpourri of styles, interspersed with glittering scales in thirds and sixths, with all sorts of lollipops tossed off for high effects. It was all dazzling, provocative, vulgar, and derivative. [If you get too far away from composition as it was meant to be played] you just improvise until you get back on track.[366] (Emphasis added). In creation, there is both latitude for the sake of personal freedom, but there are also boundaries for the sake of God's intention for a created order. This is when we come to realize what I define as our "qualified autonomy" as human beings.

There is be creative improvisation in the universe and in the freedom of humanity. But the universe never given over to what is chaotic and utterly without purpose. Creation is ceaseless, even after all the injuries humanity may cause it. Created in the image of God, humanity is not static and intransigent, but is dynamic, emergent, and ever fluid with the current of human freedom to grow and learn the path toward what is of ultimate good. This phenomenon is derived from humanity's qualified autonomy in vocation as "sub-creators" with God, a purpose of being.

The Insatiable Hush: Human Solitude and God's Silence

"Be still and know I AM God." (Psalm 46:10/NASB)

"For God alone, my soul awaits in silence..." (Psalm 62:1/NIV)

"It is not possible to know him if one has not become still and purified one's mind."[367]

---

[366] Ibid.

[367] Origen, *Commentary of the Gospel of John 19.17*

In silence one may discern the harmonic voice of God. Perhaps in the stillness, one may come to the learn that even in the vast, limitless, transcendent, all-comprehensiveness of the cosmos "we have a sense of being cared for, of not being alone and stranded in the universe. God is near."[368] Just as one may be trained to distinguish good music from bad, humanity may learn to discern the voice of God through the discipline of silence.

George MacDonald wrote "The one eternal, original, infinite blessing of the human soul is when in the stillness the Father comes and says, 'My child, I am here'."[369] Even in the midst of the most chaotic of situations, humanity has the strange capacity to enter into the silent space of God's abiding presence, wherein we are not distracted by materialistic concerns— thoughts, fantasies, fears, and desires-- but instead, we are "in contact with the ultimate consciousness."[370]

In the refuge of solitude the Lord speaks to us tenderly, convicts us of our waywardness, and consoles us, "enriching us in the innermost depths of our being."[371] For the materialist, there is no reason we should be led into a devotion of silence. Noise permeates the egomaniacal culture we allow to persist today. Our current population is uncomfortably unsettled without technologically produced audio and video blaring at us 24/7.

From a religious purview, a "sabbatical" rest from the demands of our existence is distinctive from the routine of a weekly religious ritual. For those who have actualized this phenomenon, this realm of *silence* is a "place of prayerful listening."[372] Hastening to silence is a multi-sensory experience. It sensitizes us to the sights, sounds, smells, touch, and taste of the wonderful world in which we live. Finding the silent space is one of the simplest ways

---

[368] Howard Thurman *For the Inward Journey: Writings,* (Richmond, IN: Friends United Meeting, 1984), 116

[369] George MacDonald, *Alone with God in the Pulpit* (Whitethorn, CA: Johannesen, 1999), 111

[370] Sheldrake, *Ibid.,* 27

[371] Gustavo Gutierrez, *Community Out of Silence,* taken from *Essential Writings,* Ibid., 255

[372] Henri Nouwen, *Spiritual Direction: Wisdom for the Long Walk of Faith* (NY: HarperCollins, 2006), 17

to expand our "sensory and spiritual awareness,"[373] in which God reveals what is otherwise incomprehensible, even answers to fascinating questions.

Silence can be a path into "the [acquired] space in which God creates faith,"[374] wherein we discern a benevolent God through the eyes of the soul. For there is a vibrancy to silence. Wherever there is stillness here may be heard the harmonic voice of God "speaking from the whirlwind, nature's old song and dance."[375]

Thomas Merton taught that by a supernatural directive, usually in the stillness of our being, we are compelled to "drop everything find Him in the silence where He is hidden with you, [to] listen to what He has to say."[376] We can only listen to what God has to say when we are silent. When God seems distant, uncommunicative with us, we are awakened in the silence that we might pursue Him all the more—in solitude. It is in that pursuit, through the stillness of the flesh and with the listening ear of the soul, we may hear Him.

In the late 1300s, Augustinian mystic, Walter Hinton, described this solitude as "soul sighing," in solitude from "the great shouting and bestial din of fleshly desires and unclean thoughts."[377] In silence the concerns of the flesh-in-the-world wanes and the soul-in-the-Spirit soars. Silence "opens the heart to fresh breezes of new wisdom."[378] It is a "participatory act of our heart, mind, soul, and body in listening for the voice of the Beloved,"[379] actively waiting upon the Lord to mount us up with "wings as eagles." (Isaiah 40:31/ NASB). Silence is the voice of Ultimate Love.

Sometimes God is silent, patiently awaiting our return to Him. It is in the silence, "after the fire--that God speaks to us in a still small voice." (I Kings 19:11-13/NRSV). This is an articulation of an intimate love, expressed in the stilling presence of

[373] Sheldrake, Ibid., 32-33

[374] Richard Rohr, *What the Mystics Know:* (NY: Crossroad Books, 2015), 51

[375] Annie Dillard, *Teaching a Stone to Talk: Expeditions and Encounters* (NY: Harper and Row, 1982), 69-70

[376] Thomas Merton, *The Intimate Merton*, (NY: HarperOne, 2001), 4

[377] *The Scale of Perfection*, taken from the series *Classics of Western Spirituality* (NY: Paulist, 1991), 280-281

[378] Wayne E. Oates, *Nurturing Silence in a Noisy Heart* (Garden City, NY: Doubleday, 1979) 15

[379] J. Brent Bill, *Holy Silence* (Brewster, MASS: Paraclete Press, 2005) 9

compassion, grace and mercy that "never leaves nor forsakes us." (Deuteronomy 31:6; Hebrews 13:5/NRSV). Stilled in solitude, God speaks to us in ways sufficient to our apprehension, qualified by the stillness in our environment. In the silence of our moment of devotion and intimacy, when any utterance of our own is futile, God offers to us Himself in ways new and transformational.

> Because of the Lord's great love we are not consumed,
>   for his compassions never fail.
> They are new every morning;
>   great is your faithfulness. (Lamentations 3:22-23/NRSV).

Reflecting the Character and Nature of God:

Life from Life: Our Capacity for BE-Living!

More than believing in some*thing*, a religious dogma, or a scientific dictum, *BE-Living* is growing in a moment-to-moment awareness of God. In that awareness we strive to live fully our potential as humans—*being* who God has designed us to be. This *being* is our strength: our personhood, personality traits, giftedness, and talents; actualizing our intended design! To know God with an intimacy, or with the whole *heart, mind, soul and strength* is what many would define as *"holiness."* In awareness of Ultimate Love, we ascend out of a closed universe, estrangement from others, from tolerance (disguised indifference) and "spiritual apartheid," toward wholeness and holiness which, in religious language, is called "salvation."[380]

BE-Living is a metaphor for living in holistic devotion to intimacy with God. It is not to be equated with a moral code that merely regulates our behavior. It is the soul-driven momentum toward the transformation of our character; living *responsively to and responsibly before* God's holy presence. BE-Living is consciously abiding in the present as the *yet-to-be* with assurance that "God is in the midst" (Psalm 46:5/KJV) of our time, our seasons, and our eras.

---

[380] Dorothy Soelle, *Theology for Skeptics*, (Minneapolis: Fortress Press, 1995) 116

CHAPTER 4

Mystical Prompting: Biblical Documentation

God is known through intuition (fascinating questions), reasoning with empirical evidence, through revelatory experiences in the soul, and by our interaction with Him through our own spiritual personhood. Here is another fascinating question: *is there documentation of such interaction between God and those who have experienced this intimate knowledge of God in human history?*

The narratives in the Bible are a created wonder. They are intended to be more than a documentation of God's manifestation of Himself in and throughout human history. They also provide a progressive revelation of the character and nature of God Himself. Through the biblical narratives, God is progressively *revealed*, not through magic, but through mystery. God comes into focus beginning with the primitive and pre-scientific notions of a tribal community, the psalms and poetry of tendered souls, through the meditative utterances of prophetic voices, and through to the anointed presence of one who personified the *"I am God"* for the enlightenment of all humanity.

Thus, the reading of the biblical narratives is a positioning of our lives toward a vulnerability to this mysterious, progressive revelation. Meditating on the scripture brings God comes into focus within us. From a casual reading of the text or a critical assessment of its historicity, those who are transformed by the narratives are so because they meditate upon the narratives for the sake of gleaning the truth from its pages. We become subject to the whims the Text, rather than become objective critics of the text in order to conform it to our will. For this transaction to take place, one must understand how to read the text in its context and spiritually consume its content.

The Bible is a created tome of wonder, designed to offer humanity momentary glimpses of God's continuing, progressive and redemptive activity in human history. While archeological and other non-biblical sources indicate well the historicity of most biblical accounts as legitimate, there is a richness in

Scripture in passages intended to illuminate God's Presence in the present. Such inspiration is ignited by use of literary devices or **prompts:** metaphors and symbols, poetry and parable, and picturesque language. Like singing a psalm or a hymn to express the depths of one's experience, sometimes exact precise verbiage is insufficient to describe what is only mysteriously apprehended. C.S. Lewis wrote that if we are going to inquire about things which are not perceived by the senses, or empirically resolved, we are required to use language *metaphorically*; "all speech about super sensibilities is, and must be, metaphorical in the highest degree."[381]

Moreover, Lewis warned in a letter dated in 1951 that "all metaphors don't appeal equally to all imaginations."[382] The diversity of literary devices and the myriad of narratives ebb and flow to meet the moment of the respective idiosyncrasies of persons. In other words, one of the profound qualities of Scripture regards its capacity to span the length and breadth of human inquiry from generation to generation, guiding one to the "knowledge of truth." (II Timothy 3:7/NIV).

Similarly in theology, we may not all use the same metaphors in describing God. In our God-talk, we must concede to anthropomorphic images and metaphysical and theological assumptions in attempting to describe God and His activity in the world. The use of subjectively descriptive words in the articulation of our God-talk is the foundation of what J.R.R. Tolkien originated as "mythopoeia," truth that comes through the 'splintered light' of myths, metaphors, and allegory. Such devices inspire us toward the actualization or application of insight!

In the following pages, I offer various biblical narratives that use metaphors and other literary devices through which one might be discover insight for *Be-Living*. They are not sermons or homilies meant to bring the reader to my own way of thinking. They are used here as *prompts* toward a positioning or preparing the way of the Lord for the reader in his or her own context. The goal of meditating on the narratives is go ignite insight toward a deeper awareness of God's presence.

---

[381] C. S. Lewis, *Miracles* (New York: Macmillan Company, 1948), 88

[382] C. S. Lewis, *Collected Letters Vol* III (San Francisco: Harper, 2007), 146

God is ever near in the 'holy of holies' or our being. God's presence is a "given" to be discovered. Revelation into the depths and mysteries of God is a spiritual continuum, actualized in a moment-to-moment vulnerability to God's Presence. *BE-Living begins with vulnerability.* It proceeds in a simple devotional lifestyle as one grows in sensitivity to an awareness of God's presence. The profundity of this experience may be articulated by metaphors and symbols, or outlined in theological systems, but the experience of Presence is beyond any literary devise. Likewise, it is beyond the simple articulation of any one personal testimony in the biblical narratives. I can only speak for what I have experienced. Your experience with God through your devotion to the text will be uniquely your own. Frederick Buechner described his own respective experience as simply letting an empty place open inside himself, waiting for something to fill it, "and every once and so often, praise God, something does."[383]

BE-Living is simply growing moment-to-moment in the awareness of God's presence, and in deep contrition and gratitude of God's grace as sensed in His revealed goodness in all He has created. This includes growing in an awareness of His presence through the "something" to be discovered in the biblical narratives. Like the natural wonder around us, the biblical narratives can lead us to the wonder of insight within us.

> *What wonder have you sensed?*
> *What Divine works have you discerned?*
> *By Holy composition*
> *What understanding have you learned?*
> *Have you heard the mythical melody?*
> *Tasted fragrant incense in the air?*
> *Viewed the harmony in motion?*
> *Touched the compassion of God's care?*
>
> *What have you learned from scaling the summit?*
> *Or strolling softly in submission to the sea?*
> *What mindfulness have been created*
> *That transcend primal capacity?*

---

[383] *The Longing for Home: Recollections and Reflections* (NY: Harper Collins, 1996), 22-23

Wonders woo us to awareness
And to dreaded vulnerability
Through the metaphors of living: the guided Hand of Poetry
We are wondrously invited: "do not be afraid…come and see…
come and see. (Brian Shoemaker, 2016)

An ever-emerging awareness of Presence demands an ever-expanding faith, a spiritual maturity to discern the message within sometimes fleeting moments of divine manifestation. As we approach the biblical narratives, it is into the presence of God, we seek. As in the phenomenon of His presence that is yielded in the wonder of all else that God has created, a meditative rendering of the narratives may inspire such wonder as well.

Austin Farrer *was the* renowned dean of Oxford's Magdalene College during the tenure of C. S. Lewis. In his book, *A Faith of Our Own,* he wrote: to love the Lord my God with all my heart and mind and soul and strength. Let us advance step by step seeing what we can see.[384] This expression of intimacy with God, includes envisioning communion with the inspired Text, provided and preserved for our deeper apprehension.

A Momentary Pause:

The Proof is in the Presence!

"God himself is my counselor, and at night my innermost being instructs me." (Psalm 16:7/NRSV).

> Not all the intellect or metaphysics of the world could prove that there is no God, and not all the intellect in the world could prove there is a God. It is the turning of the eye to the light; it is the sending of the feet into the path that is required.[385]

---

[384] Austin Farrer, *A Faith of Our Own* (Cleveland: The World Publishing Company, 1960), 54

[385] George MacDonald, from his sermon *"Faith the Proof of the Unseen,"* preached in Brixton Congregational Church Sunday, June 1882

SECTION 1:
Biblical Prompts: Opportunistic Thresholds to Sacred Mystery

While the following biblical prompts have moved me toward a deeper awareness of God's Presence, they may not have the same significance for you. Perhaps one or two, perhaps more, perhaps none, will be significant. But the following metaphorical narratives, whether they are historically legitimate or not, may provide for you a moment of repose, reflection, or moreover, a revelation of truth.

Anglican theologian, John MacQuarrie explained that the knowledge of God comes to us as a God wills. God manifests His presence known to us, through the truth revealed by the Spirit in the scripture. The Bible never espouses humanity to figure out the mysteries of God, but to faith through our curiosities of Him-- *with* Him. There is indeed recognition of man's innate quest for God, but it is maintained that "God himself meets and satisfies the quest."[386] The Bible is an opportunistic threshold through which humanity may, through its narratives, come to a place of vulnerability and insight.

God's revelation is given respective to the vulnerablity of persons. This is NOT *relativism,* wherein one projects a god created in his or her own image. Rather, God provides for the individual an apprehensible manifestation consistent to one's degree of comprehension respective of his or her capacity for understanding. This is the multi-dimensional hue of God's activity designed for persons to apprehend Him. Glimpses of an incomprehensible God are illuminated through the diverse documentation of His peculiar activity in human history: the biblical narratives. The Bible is a created wonder documenting a progressive revelation of the character and nature of God.

In the words of Dorothy Soelle, God is no "interventionalist" who interferes by intruding, but an "intentionist" who makes the Divine will "discernible."[387] In God's tender wooing of us to Himself, we discern God's holy otherness of character with His intention for the goodness of creation. God lingers within

---

[386] *On Being a Theologian*, ed. John H. Morgan (London: SCM Press, 1999), 53
[387] Soelle, *Theology for Skeptics*, Ibid., 16

breathing distance, demure enough to ensure our freedom, yet near enough to guide, *"seek and save the lost."*

Just as humanity is often compelled toward the appreciation of the wonders of creation, so too, can the narratives in the biblical text enthrall us toward a more profound appreciation of God's intentional activity in human history. This activity is documented through diverse literary devices used by those who *interpreted* God's presence in their midst, context, and culture. Interpreting the documentation enables one to gain the insight it was meant to offer. Perhaps that is the point for which the scriptures for contemporary times has been preserved?

Perhaps this rendering of the biblical narratives includes what E. O. Wilson described as "the still teasing possibility of the supernatural?"[388] Perhaps communing with the biblical narratives as a source of wonder is still a very possible reality? Perhaps God *"teases"* or woos us with the biblical narratives rather than to stalk us with intrusive sensationalism or raw historical data? As the scripture unfolds, one comes to a deeper understanding of the progressive momentum of the Text from a perspective of God of a tribal people to the God of the prophets and psalmists and to the Abba of Jesus. There is a wooing in the veiled glimpses of God as the truth in the narratives come into focus.

The Wooing of the Moon (as the veiled light of God)

The moon is blue
 Stone-cold and foreboding from a distance
 A wonderful, compelling view
 To whom my soul bids me "come," with little resistance

Sometimes the moon is murky or missing
 Quarter, half, or full
 Taunting me into a strange submission
 To its grandiose gravitational pull

The moon is a crisp white linen –blaze
 Illumined in darkest night

---

[388] Wilson, *Consilience*, Ibid., 233

Revealing shadowlands of human haze
And a foreboding fear of its tantalizing might

The moon is red
  Deep crimson, heart- blood,
  Pulsating in dread;
  Woos us in wonder—
  an overwhelming flood. (Brian Shoemaker, 2010).

The Timbre in the Timber: **A Journal Entry**

"Sometimes the loveliness of God's presence comes in the midst of pain."[389]

September 2010:

> *I wandered away in the woods—seeking the stillness in a soft, misty morning. Against the heaviness of the traffic of my days. Alone, but for the prompting of a deeper moan indwelling me.*
>
> *I was nothing. And when I realized, "i was nothing," i began to sense the Reality of "I Am." In that Presence, i became real. It was in that breathless silence that, not unlike John Wesley, i felt myself to the core of my being, warmly embraced!*
>
> *Me: "God, I am not going to think about you right now. All I ask is that you fill my mind with YOUR thoughts."*
>
> *Presence: "Hush." (or maybe it was just the sound of a rushing breeze). Whatever the symbol, the prompting of what i sensed made me vulnerable and inclined my being toward a holistic listening mode.*
>
> *In that moment, i only heard the rustling of the leaves in a nearby birch tree. And the birds. Then the distinctive rustling of the leaves in another tree. The leaves from one tree to the other were different, but they blended. Other birds chirped—and a larger bird (a hawk*

---

[389] Madeleine L'Engle, *A Stone for a Pillow: Journeys with Jacob* (Wheaton, Illinois: Harold Shaw Publishers, 1986) 130

perhaps?) "CAWED in its own operatic aria. Somehow it became melodious.

Then there were the branches of the trees—this one and then that one. And the deep groaning of the tree trunks—truly! i heard the slight timbre of the timber. Together, it was like a jazz improvisation. Not necessary for my understanding, but somehow essential to the way things are in an ever-creative process of being. It was the timbre in the timber that soothed me to my core and enabled me to 'prepare the way of the Lord' in this moment of bliss and solitude—entering into the holy of holies of my own being.

(B. Shoemaker, Personal Journal, 2010)

"John of the Mountains:" the Wooing of God in the Pristine Innocence of Creation

John Muir, (1838-1914) was a Scottish-born American essayist and naturalist. An advocate of U.S. forest conservation, he was of great influence toward the establishment of both Sequoia National Park and Yosemite National Park. His letters, essays, and recounts of his sojourns in nature, especially in the Sierra Nevada mountains of California, have inspired millions.

In his mountaineering essays, Muir described the wonder he experienced as a devoted naturalist. Moreover, according to one biographer, "the more John Muir wandered about the woodlands, the more curious he became about man, nature, and God." Muir confirmed his intuitive belief that God was still at work, he just had to be vulnerable enough to discern Him. (Gibbs Smith from the Introduction to his edited collection of *Muir's Mountaineering Essays,* Salt Lake City: Peregrine Smith Books, 1980, p. xii)

Among the many passages from his journals, Muir affirmed his impression that more than what was visible by the eye alone was in process all about him. As he climbed from ridge to summit, through woods and meadows, he seemed to become more sensitized to a hidden, yet ever-present Reality about him. Often, he documented such occurrences:

For Muir, everything seemed consciously" peaceful, and thoughtful." Every rock, mountain, stream, plant, lake, lawn, forest, garden, bird, beast, insect seem to beckon to Muir to come and learn; to attracted him as an hospitable and "Godful wilderness." As one moves through Muir's writings, there is noted a longing within the reader to join the naturalist in his climb for greater vision and the glory in submission to the pristine (not the primitive), with the wonder of creation, a supernatural joy within the natural wonders, absorbing what Muir called, "the divine music…climbing higher, higher, as new beauty came streaming into sight."

Muir's religious experience was fueled by human capacity for consciousness, his appreciation for beauty, the natural musical compositions in creation itself, and his own strengths in word and expression to document his remarkable transformation of personhood. In the silence of it all, he sensed the Something More in his midst and within himself.

A Momentary Pause:

"And I said to myself: 'what a wonderful world'"

Perhaps the world has gone wonky because humanity has forsaken simple contentment? Original innocence and contentment in the pristine has been overwhelmed by the rabid pursuit for the mindless gratification of things primitive. Perhaps there is more to experience in the tender subtleties of a pristine and wonderful world, even God. Are we willing to make the climb to greater heights of vision, to a place where the whims of the flesh fade and the whisk of the soul emerges free?

Just as one may linger, enthralled in the wonder of creation, one may commune with unveiled mystery through the biblical narratives. In the following chapters, I hope to offer the reader a sampling of how communing with biblical narratives can be relevant to one's spiritual pilgrimage. They are various narratives that have in some way effected my own journey of faith. Some may speak to the reader, some may not. But the point of this chapter is to offer a healthier perspective in rendering the text to a meditative attitude with a vulnerability to God between the lines and its pages.

Textual Prompts: Biblical Narratives

PROMPT ONE:
The Rungs of Jacob's Ladder

> He (Jacob) came to a certain place and spent the night there...
> (Genesis 28:12/NASV)
> Slowly we climb the eternal stair, each step a virtue firm and fair"
> (Psalm 83:6/NASV)
> The voice said, 'Come up here and I will show you...' (Revelation
> 4:11/NASV)

> Who can go up to the mountain of the Lord? Or stand in his holy
> place?
> He that has clean hands and a pure heart, who does not set his
> mind on vain things. He shall receive a blessing from the Lord and
> mercy from God his Savior
> This is the generation of them that seek him, of them that seek
> the face of the
> God of Jacob. [390]

Early church father Johann Arndt taught that just as our natural life has its stages, namely childhood, manhood, and old age, so also does our spiritual and Christian life grow from repentance to revelation through "the contemplation of divine things."[391] Growing in our understanding of God and His activity in the world, includes a healthy rendering of how we meditate upon the biblical narratives in a manner holistic with our fullest capacities as human beings.

Insight from the Use of Symbols in the Bible

---

[390] Thomas Merton, *"Pure Love,"* reader ed., Thomas P. McDonnell (NY: Harcourt, Brace & World, 1962), 337
[391] Classics of Western Spirituality, (Mahwah, NJ: Paulist Press, 1978), 221

Various biblical narratives, through the use of various literary devices, prompt fascinating questions. Those questions may guide us toward reasonable investigation, and ultimately to *insight,* or the discernment of truth. In the words of Leslie Weatherhead, "I need not only sight, but insight. I pray, 'Lord, that I might receive my *insight*' (emphasis added)."[392]

The literary device of the symbol in the narratives of the biblical texts are often used to prompt higher knowledge beyond the literal or historical significance of the passage. According to Paul Tillich, a *symbol is* "a segment of finite experience to say something about God as the infinite." A psalm, a parable, or a poem *reveals* insight, not adequately explained prosaically, "unlocking dimensions of our own soul which correspond to the dimensions and elements in that reality.[393] Carl Jung is more specific in regarding "sacred" symbols as expressions of a content not yet "consciously recognized or conceptually formulated."[394]

Throughout the Bible, metaphorical language and symbols "express the inexpressible."[395] The message in the text communes with the inner core of our being, wherein that message is not only heard, it is translated into insight. The Jewish Midrash explains the connection between human history and sojourning toward a greater awareness of God *in real time.* According to these scholars, although humans cannot comprehend God's ultimate essence, we may observe "manifestations of divine *activity* in creation in the dynamics of history and society."[396] This phenomenon of experience is not to be relegated into the realm of abstract thinking or a fanciful, virtual reality. As we enter into the biblical narratives, we enter a threshold of wonder that is not only awe-inspiring but transforming of one's perspectives and personhood through the revelation of truth it provides.

The biblical perspective endeavors to articulate creative ways of articulating the Creator, Sustainer and Redeemer of the cosmos. How can mere prose or raw data adequately depict what is beyond cognitive comprehension? The

---

[392] Leslie Weatherhead, *Time for God* (NYk Abingdon Press, 1967), 89

[393] Tillich, *"The Reality of God,"* from Systematic Theology II, Ibid., 239

[394] *Essential Writings* (London: Harper/Collins, 1985), 184; 204

[395] M. Basil Pennington, *Seeking His Mind* (Brewster, MASS: Paraclete Press, 2002), 5

[396] Writings from *the Talmud* in *The Classics of Western Spirituality*, (Mahwah, NJ: Paulist Press,2009), 17

mystery of God is brought to life by "a great variety of pictures. Each picture has color, beauty, order, fascination. Different symbols and myths, images and pictures speak of God."[397]

Before his vision of a ladder from heaven to earth, Jacob "wrestled" with a mysterious presence. The "angel of the Lord" wounded him and left him vulnerable and alone in the darkness. From Jacob's view, the "ladder experience" epitomized an initiative of God's reconciliation, and subsequently prompted Jacob to an ascent toward spiritual fulfillment. This insightful ascent was documented using the symbol of one climbing a ladder to God's consummate Presence.

Symbolically speaking, spiritual depth is gained as we ascend from darkness to the light of God's initiative of divine reconciliation. The biblical narratives reveal this progressive theme of human estrangement, Divine intervention and redemption, such as in the story of Jacob's ladder.

> *By the nocturnal struggle with the divine being, by holding the 'man' fast until a blessing is obtained, Jacob passes his test. His leading God had ordered him to wander. The wanderer had to face the perilous encounter before he enjoyed the final grace of God.*[398]

Metaphorically, the Bible teaches God is ever near. *"He never sleeps nor slumbers"* (Psalm 121:4; II Timothy 2:15/NASB) but protects and provides watch care over all He loves. Consider the metaphorical lyrics of the famed Welsh lullaby, *All Through the Night*. It was composed as a parent whispering to a child. Metaphorically, so does the following lullaby reflect the symbol of a benevolent God (or "father") in watch care over humanity:

> *Sleep, my child, and peace attend thee*
> *Guardian angels God will send thee*
> *Breathes a pure and holy feeling*
> *All through the night*

---

[397] John Moses, *The Sacrifice of God*, (Hymns Ancient and Modern, 2012), 36-37
[398] Martin Buber, *Moses: The Revelation and the Covenant* (London: Horowitz Publishing, 1958), 58

Earthly dust from off thee shaken
Soul immortal shalt thou awaken
With thy last dim journey taken
Home through the night.[399]

"God Himself is my Counselor; and at night my innermost being instructs me." *(Psalm 16:7).*

In the story of Jacob, the son of Isaac, and the grandson of Abraham, we see a man who has experienced his own crucibles of existence. He fled from his father's house having deceived both his father and his brother. He finds no refuge in the house of his uncle, Laban. In fear of further reprisal, he must run for his life into the shadows of night, where he finds no rest, using a rock for a pillow. He was vulnerable enough in his *dark night of the soul* to arrive at the end of his own cunning, and so became vulnerable, *wrestling* with the God of his patriarchs. Through the struggle, God spoke to Jacob, "Remember, I am with you." Jacob responded, "if God remains with me, the Lord shall be my God." (Genesis 28:20-21/NASB).

Jacob gained insight through his own phenomenological experience with God. This revelatory moment transformed not only the bleakness of his situation but his personhood as well. He was raised with the concept of the God of Abraham and Isaac, but he had yet to experience the God of Jacob; to come to the insight of his own faith. The narrative brings a sense of God's redemptive activity into our own experience as well. Like Jacob, the attempt of persons to understand the Creator is "never static; it is constantly in motion."[400] God reaches persons in ways they can understand for themselves. That is part of the genius of God throughout the biblical narratives.

Jacob's world-gone-wonky led him to a hellish region: in darkness, alone, with "a stone for a pillow." In a self-imposed exile, he grew estranged from all things familiar, even the God of his lineage. Yet, God was not estranged from him. God drew near to him in a dream. (Genesis 31:10-11; 37:5-10/NASB). Through the visual of an ethereal ladder that stretched from heaven to earth and back again, the wayward Jacob learned that "heaven has to

---

[399] John Ceiriog Hughes (25 September 1832 – 23 April 1887)
[400] Madeleine L'Engle, *A Stone for a Pillow: Journeys with Jacob* (Wheaton, ILL: Harold Shew, 1986), 21-22

do with earth."[401] Even in the wayward journeys of one like Jacob, in one's vulnerability, God may become a presence in real time, and in the context of the one whom He silently pursues.

For Jacob this revelation was a supreme moment, from a "poignant sense of great contrition, there arose a sense of Special Presence."[402] Jacob had never rejected the notion of the God of his father and grandfather. But if he was to continue in the sojourn toward becoming his true self, *"Israel,"* he had to ascend from holding an inherited belief to the climb toward a higher and holy place wherein he himself could encounter the *I AM* God. In his vulnerability, from the darkness of a sleepless night to the light of an awakening, "God became real!"[403]

When God's presence intervenes into our vulnerability, "human reality is redefined!"[404] Like Jacob, we may encounter "a spiral that goes ever deeper and closer,"[405] our own ladder of spiritual ascent, unique to our own darkness, estrangement, or sojourn toward a holy place. In this ascension we too may be transformed by a closer reckoning of our true selves before a holy God.

The ladder event for Jacob was a "sensory perception of a manifested truth."[406] Like other biblical narratives, this story is not to be confined to an historical context. More than an historical event, it illumines our potential for the actualization of Presence of God in our lives. Like the symbol of the rungs on an ethereal ladder, we may become aware of our own estrangements and respective *stone pillows*, and our own need to ascend toward higher knowledge, and sacred communion, climbing closer to the transfixion of our souls: the holy place that woos us toward a more heavenly realm.

A Momentary Pause:

<u>**"We are climbing Jacob's Ladder…children of the Lord"**</u>

---

[401] Walter Bruggeman, *Genesis* (Atlanta: John Knox, 1982), 242-248

[402] Howard Thurman, *"God is…,"* from *Writings*, Ibid., 116

[403] Rabbi Joseph Telushkin, *Biblical Literacy: The Most Important People, Events, and Ideas of the Hebrew Bible* (NY: William Morrow and Company, 1977), 55

[404] Bruggeman, Ibid.

[405] Richard Rohr, *Yes, and…: Meditations* (Cincinnati: Franciscan, 1997), 118

[406] Martin Buber, *On the Bible*, (Syracuse: University Press, 2000), 53

As a young child, sporadically attending church, the only substantive recollection I have is the singing of the chorus, *"We are climbing Jacob's ladder...every rung goes higher, higher...Children of the Lord."* I had no idea what the story was about, or the profound significance in its simple lyric...or did I truly understand the reasons for singing hymns at all! I wasn't aware that this simple, childhood lyric could prompt insight that "each man must face the figure at the top of the ladder."[407] We all *are* climbing Jacob's ladder, and *indeed*, every rung goes higher, higher.

Still at an early age, I recall thinking the chorus must have meant something I had yet to learn. But what did a guy named Jacob and a ladder have to do with me? I just wasn't getting God out of the song. I believed in the god-notion of my upbringing but grew discontent in just accepting the belief system of my parents. My restlessness, compounded by a world-gone-wonky, left me disenchanted with religiosity. Without God in sight my young life was like "the scattered rungs of a broken ladder."[408]

Later in my life, like Jacob, I had been broken by the wonky and the wicked. Due to my own misbegotten choices and the consequences of the choices of others around me, I found myself *alone, in the dark* and in a deep despair unresolvable by the god-notion of my youth. The god of my upbringing and thinking only allowable within the logistical protocol of a denominational boundaries did nothing to move me forward toward insight. In my brokenness, after years of service in line with denominational polity and procedures, my faith wavered. My hope was rickety. I felt estranged from all things in which I had once trusted and believed.

In my own midnight hour, my notions of God imploded. Still, it was the best *worst* time of my life. In the midst of my despair, in my vulnerability, I discerned a stillness, a strange wooing, in the core of my being. While I was determined to abandon everything for which I had once put my trust, something unwavering held me fast. I realized I could not theologize a way out of this *dark place*. My true self, with all my weaknesses and maladies, was exposed! Nothing was hidden—nor could it be! I realized if I was to

---

[407] Howard Thurman, *Deep River* (Richmond, Indiana: Friends United Press, 1975), 85-86
[408] Abraham Joshua Heschel, *Man's Quest for God* (Santa Fe, NM: Aurora Press, 1998), 7

even breathe again, I had to relinquish my religious polity and holistically face the *"mysterium tremendum,"* a horrible and hopeful encounter with God's presence.

I had to re-think my inherited indoctrination. Somehow the God of my youth had become archaic, irrelevant, and lame. My life sounded like a clanging minor chord! I needed harmony in sync with the legitimate God of the cosmos. In a manner reminiscent of C. S. Lewis, I had to "I re-ascended in total surrender to the absolute leap in the dark."[409]

Then the song from my childhood began to make sense. "Climbing Jacob's ladder" meant to outgrow my elementary indoctrination, my "god-talk," for the sake of actual communion with the God of my god. In entering into a terrible vulnerability, in the reception of God's grace, the revelation came: *i must engage an ever-emerging God with an ever-expanding faith!* i had to relinquish the notion of my god and humbly arise to receive the *I AM God!* Although i cannot offer a formula or reason, "God grabbed me! God's Spirit took me up." (Ezekiel 37:1-2/NRSV).

This experience of God's presence, i could not achieve. It was an articulation of God i could only receive. i realized from that moment: *i am nothing.* But when i confessed *"i am nothing"* and professed trust in the sovereign God of the cosmos, i realized that while i am nothing, i am nevertheless, by nothing but grace, precious in God's sight. God knows me, calls me by my name, and in my vulnerability, i may hear Him. The insight from the narrative: *i too must climb Jacob's ladder!* If i was to breathe again, i had to release everything, even my learned concepts of God into the darkness, and embrace the nothingness within me: my ignorance, the delusions of my autonomy, and the notion that i was *entitled* to anything.

From his own "piece of hymnic poetry,"[410] Jacob envisioned a ladder toward a greater awareness of God. Each rung in his climb was loftier than the one preceding it. He climbed from (1) God, before whom his fathers walked, (2) to God, who guided him to this darkness, and finally (3) to the presence of

---

[409] C. S. Lewis, *Surprised by Joy,* (London: Geoffrey Bles, 1955), 213-215

[410] Gerhard Von Rad, *Old Testament Theology,* Vol I (NY: Harper and Row, 1962), 287

God who redeemed him.[411] If one dares to turn toward the God, to call to Him, Ultimate Love becomes real.

What i was seeking was a "religious experience in quality and degree"[412] to enable my *receptivity* of God; listening to hear the "voice within...the creative force of a holy revelation" of God and His grace. (Romans 5:2/NASB). In my brokenness and vulnerability, God provided for me my own ladder of ascent.

For Jacob, the ladder was a symbol for "an invitation to pilgrimage."[413] It prompted for me a symbol for a similar sojourn from a hellish experience to a heavenly revelation. The gory details of my brokenness are no longer as substantive as the glorious destination to which i arrived. i would not want to go through the hellish region again, but i would be willing if it meant reaching the insight and His grace i received.

In his classic spiritual writing to Christian ascetics, *The Soul's Journey into God*, "devout mystic" of the 13th century, Bonaventure, taught "six stages of contemplation" that brought for him a deeper awareness of God. In his teaching, alluding to the idea of a progressive revelation, he used the *symbol of a ladder*:

> *We must ascend step-by-step until we reach the height of the mountain where God of is seen in Zion (the place high and lifted up in Psalm 83:8) Since we must ascend Jacob's ladder... let us place our first step in the ascent at the bottom, presenting ourselves the whole material world as a mirror through which we may pass over to God...lest we fall into a deeper pit of darkness.*[414]

Making Sense of God through the Use of the Symbol: *Jacob's Ladder*

Symbols help our understanding of what otherwise may be incomprehensible. They help to illustrate higher knowledge by reaching the core of us as

---

[411] Ibid.

[412] Otto, *Idea of the Holy*, Ibid., 177

[413] *John Climacus*, Classics of Western Spirituality (Mahwah, NJ: Paulist Press, 1982), 8

[414] Bonaventure, *The Souls' Journey into God*, *Classics in Western Spirituality* (Mahwah, NJ: Paulist Press, 1978), 51-61

truth emerges from the narrative. The very essence of our experience of God, "springing from deep, natural impulses of the heart" are expressed in symbols and images which are imaginative and varied, addressing the contexts in which they are written. They arise as creative and poetic "responses to revelation."[415]

The symbol of Jacob's encounter with a heavenly ladder resembles for me my own quest for God. As decisively rational and spiritual beings we likewise, "move back and forth like the angels on Jacob's ladder, a symbol of relating to God at each level of our being."[416] My own pilgrimage was an ebb and flow of devotion and doubt, until I was overcome, shattered by circumstances beyond my control—of situations I could not fix. Little I had been taught in my years of formal religious education offered me much of a reason to believe there was an available ladder to ascend out of my darkness. But the children's chorus played over and over in my mind: *"we are climbing Jacob's ladder…every rung goes higher, higher… children of the Lord."*

Thomas Merton described his own symbol of the rungs of Jacob's ladder as starting from a renunciation of the world to a mystical sense of oneness with God. He described his climb as ascending:

> *from a battle with self-indulgence to a religious and literary curiosity, to the heights of obscure theologia, to the contact with God in darkness, beyond even the purest of concepts.*[417]

In very early church history, the idea of reaching to a heavenly realm was articulated in the canon of the *Apostolic Fathers. The Shepherd of Hermas* was written by a Christian living in Rome in the postapostolic period of the church. He described his *ascent* into the presence of *God* through symbols readily accessible to his congregation. The text was used as a document of instruction for a postbaptismal congregation seeking a deeper spiritual apologetic for communion with God.

---

[415] Keith Ward, *Guide*, Ibid. 252

[416] Thomas Keating, Ibid., 113

[417] Thomas Merton, *The Spirituality of Sinai: St. John of the Ladder*, from Disputed Questions (New York: Farrar, Straus, and Cudaly, 1960), 83-93

In the apocryphal work, *The Shepherd of Hermas*, Parable 9, the writer described a spiritual pilgrimage he called the ascension to "the Twelve Mountains" *toward God*. This ascension progressed from the places "sooty, lifeless, and thorny" to the gradual higher ridges of luxurious plants, where there was grazing seasonal wonders and the grazing of beasts and birds. Even higher was a place of solitude where sheep lay resting and feeding in the higher mountainside "greatly forested with fruit bearing trees."

Finally, the ascension brought the seeker to the utmost destination: where *"the mountain was completely white, and its top was cheerful; and it was the most beautiful of the mountains."* Herein, with the use of poetically symbolic language, is a description of a journey that led him to an incomprehensible, yet wholistic experience of ultimate beauty. This ascent from a hellish region of hopelessness was what i was seeking as well.

Naming the "Rungs of Jacob's Ladder:"

<u>**My Personal Steps of Spiritual Ascension**</u>

The following are symbols I use to describe a journey of spiritual ascent. For me, the biblical narrative of Jacob's Ladder has become a visual image, a symbol, reflecting a progressive revelation of God within the context of one's existence in *real time*. I don't know all the ways God reveals His presence in the expanse of the world. However, the use of symbols, metaphors, and poetic images can aid us in this awareness, to describe the journey toward a mystical experience in metaphorical terms of *a ladder: rungs, pauses and climbs.*

The biblical image for the soul's ascent to God as Jacob's ladder has been articulated metaphorically in church history as: the *'ladder to paradise'* (Johannes Climacus), the *'pilgrimage of the soul to God'* (Bonaventure), and the *'ladder to perfection'* (Walter Hilton). All describe a meticulously ordered ascetic path of purification that leads to insight and ecstasy in the realization of a mystic union with God. The climb itself is always "greater than those who speak of it."[418]

---

[418] Dorothy Soelle, *The Silent Cry: Mysticism and Resistance* (Minneapolis: Fortress Press, 2001), 77; 81

In naming the rungs of Jacob's ladder I hope others may gain a glimpse of their own sojourn toward God's presence. Sojourns are uniquely subjective to the sojourner. The following may or may not compare to your own, but the following "steps" or "rungs" are offered as a continuum of my spiritual apologetic for believing in God, and *BE-Living* in awareness of God as Ultimate Love.

The Hellish Region

"I am tormented in this flame." (Luke 16:24/NASV).

This is the place where the "Nine Satanic Statements" or the laws of animalistic preservation are held sacred. Here there is the maximization and musings of "natural selection;" a superficial existence, fanning the consuming flame of self-absorption fueled by fluff and fad. In his preface to *The Great Divorce*, C. S. Lewis remarked, "I think earth, if chosen instead of Heaven, will turn out to have been all along, only a region in Hell...an appalling zoo of lusts, a bedlam of ambitions, a nursery of fears, a hareem of fondled hatreds."[419]

This Hellish Region is earth-bound existence at the bottom of the "ladder." It is the decisive, earthbound territory of self-indulgence, ignorance, and arrogance – the deification of humanity and the idolization of human folly with a passion for the perishable. It is existing in a foreboding deadness or dormancy of the soul. John Cassian described this region as the place where "many indeed live in the body but are actually dead. They lie in hell and cannot praise God."[420]

What is this Hellish Region? It is a place of both the adipose brain and the dormant soul. It is a place of thorns and thistles, not the 'fruit of the Spirit,' where there is the scorching heat of the day, the darkness of a moonless night, and the "soul is bereft of peace." (Lamentations 3:17). Here one becomes addicted to nothingness, the "whatever" of happenstances. Thoughts for the preservation only of oneself reign supreme. The value of others is measured by how well other persons and things can be manipulated for the sake of one's own personal exclusive pleasure.

---

[419] C. S. Lewis, *Surprised by Joy,* Ibid., 213
[420] John Cassian, Conferences 1:14:3

In the Hellish Region, there no hope, there is no need for faith, for outside of their own autonomy, naturalistic urges,, there is nothing for which to ascend. This Region defines despair, an existence that "believes in nothing, cares for nothing, seeks to know nothing, interferes with nothing, enjoys nothing, hates nothing, finds purpose in nothing, and remains alive because there is nothing for which it will die."[421]

In contrast to the theological concept of a literal *hell*, an eternal place of torment, "designed for the devil and his angels" (Matthew 18:9; 25:42/ NASV), the Hellish Region is a place in real time for those who "wear fetters they forge in life." With no regard for the "common welfare; charity, mercy, forbearance and benevolence, they walk through crowds of fellow beings with their eyes turned downward."[422] The consequence of their existence is utter estrangement, a hiding away from their true selves, a community of well-wishers, and an awareness of Ultimate Love.

The hope for the one succumbed to this region lay in the fascinating questions of the psalmist: *"where can I [my true self] go from your spirit? Or where can I flee from your presence? If I ascend to heaven, you are there; if I make my bed in Hell, you are there...your hand will lead me, and your right hand shall hold me fast." (Psalm 139/NRSV).*

God can grasp the 'hand' of the one at the bottommost rung and, like Jacob, lead him to new heights on a *"ladder"* of ascent. "For the Lord can even free from Hell. Damnation has no impenetrable roof on it! For nothing is more powerful than the strong arm of God. (Ecclesiastes 18/NRSV)."[423] It was the sudden presence of God in the despair of Jacob that lifted him from the Hellish Region in which he existed, to climb the higher rungs of a heavenly ladder.

---

[421] Dorothy Sayers, *Creed or Chaos* (Manchester: Sophia Institute Press, 1949), 108
[422] Jacob Marley's admonition to Ebenezer Scrooge in Dickens' *A Christmas Carol*
[423] German Anabaptist, Hans Denek, from *Divine Order and the Work of His Creatures: To Destroy the Artificial and Hypocritical Excuses of Those Falsely and Corruptly Chosen, Giving Room for Truth to Fulfill the Eternal and Unchanging Will of God,* An Exposition of Psalm 77: *Concerning Hell, Conquered by God, Which is Correction by the Just Hand of God,* (Treatise 1527)

The Hollow Rung

"I am not what I am." (Shakespeare, *Othello I, I, 66*)

On a step above the Hellish Region is the Hollow Rung. This is a rung of enslavement to one's cultural values and popular correctness, where one is "overrun with pride, self-dependence, and security."[424] It is an existence stagnated by raw and unproductive reasoning and a lifestyle fettered by unchallenged delusions. There is no reflection or contemplation. There is no objective inquiry regarding reality outside of one's own geography. On the hollow rung, persons exist within the boundaries of familiar indoctrination or prejudice with little or no discovery of the wonders of life beyond the existence one's own self or tribe. Persons on this rung exist in chosen isolation, close-mindedness, in ignorance of any alternative or higher knowledge.

Such hollowness can be observed in both the religious and the scientific elite. Here is the practice of "sacredology," the idolatry of the "pseudoself"[425] on the one hand; and, "scientism...the enshrining of science...in the belief that science is the only reliable guide to truth"[426] on the other hand. Both offer only a block universe with a strict adherence to the preservation of one's own thinking. It is a place of *spiritual* and *theoretical homelessness*, no sense of purpose or meaning, starved for Ultimate Love. While persons lingering on the Hollow Rung outwardly appear cordial, inwardly they are empty, devoid of *enstasy*, "divine inspiration, or the enlivening of the soul."[427]

Persons who linger on the Hollow Rung are more driven than driving, in constant motion and never stopping to consider the fullness of life. They accept as they "appear to themselves [the false self] and do not care what they really are [the true self].[428] In essence, persons on this rung become what T.S. Elliott described as the "hollow men:"

---

[424] John Baille, *A Diary of Readings, Day 349* (NY: Charles Scribner's Sons, 1955)

[425] Oates, *Psychology of Religion*, Ibid., 5

[426] John Haught, *Science and Religion: From Conflict to Conversation, Annual Journal of Physics*, Volume 64, Issue 12, 1996, 1532-1533

[427] Tony Campolo, *Letters to a Young Evangelical* (NY: Perseus Books, 2006), 222-233

[428] Paul Tillich, *"The Depth of Existence,"* from *The Shaking of the Foundations* (NY: Scribner's and Sons, 1948), 55-56

Leaning together...
Headpiece filled with straw. Alas!
Shape without form, shade without color,
Paralyzed force, gesture without motion.

The Hollow Rung: Sacredology and Scientism

"I have the guts not to become the prey of superstitions." (Flannery O'Connor from *The Violent Bear It Away, 1955*)

On the hollow rung is the practice of *sacredology* or *bad religion:* irrational superstition and denominational legalism or *polity-theism*. It is also the place of *scientism* or *bad science:* myopic predictions, predetermined conclusions and study within an insistence upon a closed or *block universe*. Both extremes leave little room for the mysterious, and in their own ways, "demystify the world."[429] *Bad religion emphasizes the adipose brain, or revelation without reason. Bad science emphasizes the adipose soul, or reason without revelation.*

Bad religion reinforces superstition, irrationalism, philistinism, ignorance, disregard for the human intellect, and the perilous confluence of religion with secular power *"from inquisitions to liquidations."[430]* It idolizes rituals and rites, by-laws and traditions as if they were gods and are willing to destroy anyone who questions their validity as such. The hollowness of bad religion is most evident by the shallowness of the crusade mentality to conquer others for the sake of saving their religious systems, rather than to redeem those who are suffering and lost.

The hollowness of a lame religion can be discerned in the manner in which the phenomenon of God's presence is downsized to a list of sectarian dos and don'ts. The once flamboyant evangelist and "Chaplain of Bourbon Street," Bob Harrington pontificated, "Only by growing spiritually can you please God."[431] According to Harrington, God is "pleased" when a new convert *does* the following steps necessary to become a strong Christian:

---

[429] Campolo, *Letters*, Ibid.
[430] Gould, *Rock of Ages*, Ibid., 9
[431] *The Chaplain of Bourbon Street: An Autobiography* (Garden City, NY: Doubleday and Company, 1969), *187-191*

1. Be baptized
2. Read your Bible daily
3. Pray every day
4. Witness for Christ
5. Tithe your income
6. Attend church regularly

While these practical steps may provide some helpful hints for new church members, if one simply reduces *growing spiritually* to such regulations, one may miss the whole point that to "grow in the grace and knowledge of the Lord" *is a holistic experience of heart, mind, soul, and strength*: to love God and all that God loves. Otherwise religious assent can become routine and a way to merely appease an angry god, rather than to truly *commune with* Him. Religious legalism, as blind faith, a step on the hollow rung of *sacredology*. It promotes law and fear rather than love and fidelity. Lingering on the Hollow Rung of bad religion may also promote exclusivity toward other persons, looking at *them* as less than human, sows the seed of a crusade mentality. Mark Twain described converts to *sacredology* or bad religion: "man is the only religious animal that has the true religion—several of them. He is the only animal that loves his neighbor as himself and cuts his throat if his theology isn't straight."[432]

Moreover, bad religion can descend to the level of nothing more than escapism, retreating into delusions of wishful thinking. In contrast, legitimate or healthy religion seeks the truth about God, ourselves and others. It strengthens the good in creation, and offers all humanity a chance "to breathe the air of Heaven...the soul's greatest need."[433]

On the other hand, *scientism* reduces the phenomenon of spiritual devotion by exploiting examples of the practices of bad religion. Everything from the fanatical brutality of jihadists to the heinous behavior of predatory priests, *crude, rabble-rousing characters* are cited as the norm for religion rather than exceptions to its legitimacy. Anti-theist Richard Dawkins unfairly cites examples of bad religion as the norm for his own rhetorical purposes. He criticizes religion not from the perspective of its legitimate purpose, but

---

[432] Mark Twain, *"The Lowest Animal,"* from *Letters from the Earth* (1987)
[433] Weatherhead, Ibid., 163

through using a lens that focuses on its perversions. Those examples can be cited by Dawkins, not because they are the norm, but because they are exceptions to the norm. At best, his is a *scientistic* assessment of legitimate religious devotion.

Dawkins does not stop practicing *scientism* in his assessment of the God of the Old Testament. If the following critique is truly what God is like, I wouldn't tolerate Him either. The Oxford biologist interprets God in the Old Testament as:

> *arguably the most unpleasant character in all fiction: jealous and proud of it; a petty, unjust, unforgiving control-freak; a vindictive, bloodthirsty ethnic cleanser; a misogynistic, homophobic, racist, infanticidal, genocidal, filicidal, pestilential, megalomaniacal, sadomasochistic, capriciously malevolent bully.*[434]

Scientism proposes an unenlightened notion of God. Good science, as informed by legitimate religion, understands the God of the Old Testament as one simply filtered through the context of an early and ancient tribal people. Such primitive and early notions are superseded by the progressive revelation of God through the writings in later wisdom literature and the prophets. Dawkins does not consider those later, more progressive writings. From his *scientistic* assessment of a pre-enlightened religion, Dawkins dismisses the plausibility of God, not because of the later empirical evidence, but because of the antiquated notion of an ancient concept of god in which he has chosen to believe.

The scientist who depends solely upon an exclusively naturalistic or materialistic predisposition in his or her inquiry of a wonderful world, must understand that the discipline itself is a discipline of conjectures of varying degrees of certainty. Just as there can be bad religion, scientism can emerge from closemindedness toward the possibility of something beyond the observability of scientific inquiry alone. Moreover, an exclusive Social Darwinian approach to science could even diminish progressive experimentation, "working to create plagues and poisons for use in warfare tomorrow."[435]

---

[434] Richard Dawkins, *"The God Delusion"* (New York: Houghton Mifflin, 2006), 15

[435] Richard Feynman, *Further Adventures*, Ibid., 244-245

Steven Weinberg reminded his audience that even apart from outright errors, calculations and observations are based on "assumptions that go beyond the validity of the theory we are trying to test." In light of *this* scholarly statement, good science must be cautious not to assume that, "religion has nothing to do with factual reality and that science must serve as a corrosive to religious belief."[436] That kind of scientific mentality would certainly be outside the boundary of the intentional for legitimate scientific discovery; it would be a hollow ascent.

Modern science is intrinsically precarious. It looks upon the material world as an independent and disconnected reality, if it regards the material world as though it obeys mechanical laws independent of any First Cause or prime moving Force; matter separated from spirit, and body from soul. Mystic thinker, Bede Griffiths warned that there is a need for a radical change of consciousness "beyond the senses and beyond the mind and opens on the eternal and the infinite... in our midst.[437]

A healthy perspective regarding a higher consciousness regards stepping above both our own sacredology or scientism, away from a hollowness toward holiness, for the progress and redemption of all creation. Perhaps in that quest, we may even discover our capabilities to holistically discern more than what we have *hollowly* assume to be true.

A fair and impartial critique of both bad religion and bad science, with the angst it produces, may be an awakening. In lingering on the Hollow Rung a person grows agitated by those who differ in their thinking. They are restless, non-content, in need of higher knowledge rather than hollow conjecture, as expressed in the following lament:

> *This afternoon, let me*
> *be a sad person, Am I not*
> *permitted (like other men)*
> *to be sick of myself?*
>
> *Am I not allowed to be hollow,*

---

436 Ibid., 249

437 *Science and Wisdom*, from *Essential Writings* (Maryknoll, NY: Orbis, 2004), 102-103

Do not forbid me (once again) to be
angry, bitter, disillusioned,
wishing I could die.[438]

On the Hollow Rung, the devotee of scientism cannot well assess the heavenly-mindedness of religion. Nor can the dogmatic religionist articulate well the earthly good of science. To move from the hollowness of both scientism and sacredology one must consider the totality of the human capacity for knowledge. There is legitimacy in the scientific awareness of phenomena from a religious perspective, and religious phenomena from a scientific assessment as well. Sense experiences and perceptions, symbols, myths, and values, along with the potential for understanding their meanings with a connectedness to legitimate and factual data, are all justifiable reasons for science and religion to consider the wonder of humanity from an inclusive and complementing purview.

The Happy Rung: Giddiness and Frivolity

"When you eat a delicious chocolate cake you get short-lived feeling of pleasure spreading through your body – but it is a fleeting one nonetheless."[439]

By the very nature of existence, humanity is proffered a *given* good to sustain life and provide for happiness. This happiness is represented in the pristine garden in Genesis. Those *givens* for happiness included flowing streams of water, trees that produce fruit, light without the intensity of heat, and the protection of persons within a beloved community wherein each individual is accounted for and accountable to the God of all creation. Happiness in the biblical text includes both meaningful labor and sabbatical rest. From these essential *givens,* one may find a common happiness.

God's provides the necessities for our existence, the essentials that provide for happiness. True happiness is not dependent what we possess, but in recognition of the provision of our essential needs: air, nutrition, water, shelter, community, and vocation. Gratitude for this provision lifts humanity

---

[438] Thomas Merton, *The Strange Lands* (Abbey of Gethsemani, 1957), 11-12
[439] Itai Ivtzan, *"Why is Happiness Fleeting: Happiness and Pleasure Are Not the Same Thing"* Psychologytoday.com, March 25, 2016

to joy, an inner euphoria, a phenomenal interaction with the presence of God in Whom we live well.

Yet even with our essential provisions, there is within our human autonomy an insurgent impulse for *more*—non-essential luxuries, excessive materialism and want. This expression of unqualified autonomy convinces humanity that God's provision for happiness is not enough. We may even view God with ingratitude and obsess over collecting non-essential luxuries as a goal to happiness.

We convince ourselves we must have *more* in order to be *happier*: *"gold and silver, precious stones and pearls, fine linen and purple, silk and scarlet, every kind of wood, ivory, bronze, iron and marble, and cinnamon and incense, fragrant oil and perfume, wine, fine flour, cattle and sheep, horses and chariots and bodies and souls of persons." (Revelation 18:11-13/NRSV).* Whereas the provisions of God for human contentment may be simply for living well, many who linger on the happy rung, believe they will find more happiness in the accumulation of *more* and living wealthy.

Loitering on the Happy Rung is a place of obsessive and instant gratification, a superficial giddiness. While contentment is offered in simply living in the goodness of being, those who obsessively collect fleeting moments of self-gratification will never truly be fulfilled. This is what Martin Luther defined as that happiness which is not what it promises or seems to be "but instead of that are the occasions of innumerable cares, and fears, and sorrows, and mischiefs... vanity in the highest degree."[440]

Those who tarry on this rung, succumb to the marketing of giddiness, moving from amusement to amusement. They grapple for gratification through the lusts of the flesh, in affection with objects or by participating in the latest, fleeting fad. In grappling for mere giddiness-through-gratuitous-gratification, they lose sight of a simpler, purer happiness or joy. The potential for joy is overcome, by the whims of amusement, the drama of momentary glee or a sudden and fleeting rush of adrenaline.

---

[440] Martin Luther, *Exposition of Ecclesiastes 1:2 & 3*

When ambition for happiness translates into gratuitous self-interest, the quest for personal renown, or an addiction to things, one becomes stuck on the Happy Rung. The consequences take their toll. *"There is no end to their toil and their eyes are never satisfied with riches...the appetite is not satisfied." (Ecclesiastes 4 & 5/NRSV).*

Those who know the soft contentment in gratitude for the provisions of God learn that happiness is only a precursor to joy: "God keeps them occupied with the joy in their hearts."[441] The distinction between settling for giddiness and the happiness in the provision of God that lead to joy is illustrated in Victor Hugo's Les Miserables. Monseigneur Bienvenu was a man of religious renown, a man of contentment, humble enough to know he could never fully understand God. He pondered on the greatness and the living presence of God, "on all the infinity manifest to his eyes and to his senses, and without seeking to comprehend the incomprehensible, he contemplated these things…"[442]

A Momentary Pause:

Distinguishing Giddiness from Joy

The following account is illustrative of a man who knew happiness in the provisions of God. In Victor Hugo's masterpiece, *Les Miserables*, Monseigneur Bienvenu opened his rectory to Jean Valjean, a man imprisoned for 14 years for stealing bread for his starving family. Shunned by the world, alone and hungry, Valjean found repose in the hospitality of the man of God. He was fed well and offered a safe abode in which to spend the night.

Sometime through the night, Valjean made the decision to sojourn on from the house of the Monseigneur – stealing precious silverware from the cupboard of the pastor as he made his escape. The theft was discovered by the housekeeper, Madame Magloire, the next morning:

> *"Great, good God! It is stolen! That man who was here last night has stolen it. Monseigneur, the man is gone! The silver has been stolen!"*

---

[441] Ibid., 5:20

[442] *Les Miserables* (1909) 1.1.13.9

...there came a knock at the door.

"Come in," said the Bishop. The door opened. A singular and violent group made its appearance on the threshold. Three men were holding a fourth man by the collar. The three men were gendarmes; the other was Jean Valjean..

"Ah! here you are!" the Bishop exclaimed, looking at Jean Valjean. "I am glad to see you. Well, but how is this? I gave you the candlesticks too, which are of silver like the rest, and for which you can certainly get two hundred francs. Why did you not carry them away with your forks and spoons?"

Jean Valjean opened his eyes wide and stared at the venerable Bishop with an expression which no human tongue can render any account of.

"In that case," replied the brigadier, "we can let him go?"

"Certainly," replied the Bishop.

The gendarmes released Jean Valjean, who recoiled.

"My friend," resumed the Bishop, "before you go, here are your candlesticks. Take them."

Jean Valjean was trembling in every limb. He took the two candlesticks mechanically, and with a bewildered air.

"Now," said the Bishop, "go in peace. By the way, when you return, my friend, it is not necessary to pass through the garden. You can always enter and depart through the street door. It is never fastened with anything but a latch, either by day or by night."

Jean Valjean was like a man on the point of fainting.

"Jean Valjean, my brother, you no longer belong to evil, but to good. It is your soul that I buy from you; I withdraw it from black thoughts and the spirit of perdition, and I give it to God."[443]

Those who tarry on the happy rung would find a giddiness in their repossession of fine, polished silver. Those who know God's provision find joy in God's redemption of the thief! The joy we experience is not dependent upon outside circumstances, but an inner presence. Our simple happiness is derived from the givens in a good creation, not the giddiness from our obsession with the collecting of perishable *things* such as trophies, titles, and trivial pursuits.

In a sermon delivered at Westminster Abbey in March 1925, Anglican priest, Frederick Lewis Donaldson warned his congregation about the potential effect gratuitous giddiness has to the self and the community. In his homily, *"The 7 Deadly Social Evils,"* he delineated the results of such self-seeking, gratuitous gratification, or lingering on the Happy Rung, a place of momentary self-gratification and no redeeming purpose. Here there is an egocentric leaning toward: *science without humanity* and *worship without sacrifice.*

On the Happy Rung, there is little effort to critique one's choices in the hapless pursuit of pleasure. Obsession for gratification tends to create one's own virtual reality, fantasy and the endless quest for the fitting of one's false self into an imaginary world. Tolkien warned of this imaginary quest. He wrote that human development is best achieved as one grows, "passing from fairy to the noble and high."[444] Similarly, in a personal letter addressed to his wife, Sophia, *Leo Tolstoy* encouraged her to seek the revelation which brings us "from a region of dreams and shadows to real life."[445]

The High Rung: Intellectual Ascent and the Nobility of Learning

"...there has been an evolutionary trend in our ancestry towards increased intelligence." (Richard Dawkins, from *Science in the Soul*)

---

[443] Victor Hugo, *Les Miserables*, Book I, Chapter XII (1909)
[444] J. R. R. Tolkien, *Letters*, edited by Humphrey Carpenter, 159
[445] *Letters*, Volume II (Charles Schribner's Sons, 1991), 399

The High Rung is the climb to intellectual ascent, propositional concepts, searching for and researching theories and hypotheses, on a quest for a consensus for fact (science) and truth (religion). Scientific theory is an articulation of what is present through concentrated observation. Sacred theology is an articulation of Who is present through contemplative apprehension. Both are essential toward higher knowledge.

This is the ascent toward higher knowledge and a rational faith. Here one finds a zestful vitality in the pursuit of education and enlightenment. One might even discover a purpose for being as this "rational striving for knowledge."[446] This rung of the ladder is a place of cognitive rumination and exploration within the capacity of human acumen. It is accentuated by correct thinking over emotion or rank sentimentality. It presupposes a "theory of everything" and does not discount the possibility that such a theory may *reveal* more insight and the *God in the gasps*.

Reality is described (not proscribed) by propositions and theories through the gathering of information, and methodological testing; as well as, through mental awakening, mindfulness, and supra-rational experiences of wonder and mystery. While science is ill-equipped for the explaining of values, but beneficial in understanding of the "physical structure and operation of the world" in which we live,[447] it cannot readily answer inquiries regarding matters of spiritual phenomenon. On the high rung, *blind faith*, may cultivate an informed faith and the discipline of theology. "A religious belief has a measure of naivete about it. It is a confessional language, evoked by some powerful impression made on the believer."[448]

On the High Rung, there is formulated a structured theology based upon a personal response or what John Hick called: "a transcendent reality and consciousness.[449] The soul is not separated from the brain, nor the brain from the soul. This implies a holistic *modality* in our design, our personhood, our strength as human beings. As the flesh needs the soul, so does the soul need

---

[446] Einstein, *"Religion and Science," Ibid.*

[447] Edwin Hubble, Ibid., 1-2

[448] John Macquarrie, *Theology, Church & Ministry* (NY: Crossroad, 1986), 12

[449] John Hick, *An Interpretation of Religion: Human Responses to the Transcendent* (New Haven: Yale University Press, 1989), 172-173

the flesh. Likewise, as science needs religion to temper it, so does religion need science to refine it.

As scientific inquiry complements theological mindfulness, there emerges a wooing toward an even higher level of contemplation. Often this higher level of contemplation is prompted by narratives in sacred and profound texts, by observing the natural order of creation, or through entering into the wonder of mystery. Legitimate spirituality regards the invitation to enter into the mystery and be transformed by it as "narrative creatures living in unfolding time."[450]

Moreover, from the High Rung we are wooed to transition from a inquiry to sacred space. From theory and theology, we may step up toward a supra-rational knowledge that cannot be readily de-mythologized by either science or religion. Here one may discover "the aim of spirituality—the knowledge of God."[451] We are not only designed to be enlightened by higher knowledge, but *in-sighted* by the revelation of Ultimate Love.

Author Annie Dillard warned humanity not to try to encapsulate all things into our own pack-thinking or industrialized education. There is a greater level to understanding the fullness of reality beyond our limited wit. Intellectually we have become aware how the whole world seems "not-holy. We have drained the light from the boughs in the sacred grove and snuffed it in the high places."[452] In other words, when we reach the high rung of intellect and are satisfied with looking downward rather than upward, we have yet to experience true contentment discovered in the ascent from higher knowledge to holiness and Ultimate Love. Rationally, from the high rung, we know the un-holy, if we are to experience the Holy Other (Otto), we cannot remain on the high rung of intellectualism, but move continue the climb to the yet-to-be.

In his commentary on *Genesis 28:16: Jacob's Ladder,* Rabbi Panim Yafat addressed the fascinating question: *when can a person experience God's nearness?* He answered: only when one is "suffused by 'I don't know,'" when

---

[450] Julie Clawson, *Entering God's Story* (Sojourners Magazine, April 5, 2011)

[451] MacQuarrie, Ibid.

[452] Annie Dillard, *Teaching a Stone to Talk: Expeditions and Encounters* (NY: Harper and Row, 1982), 69

he himself knows that he does not know or pretend to know all things. It was in this place of acknowledged ignorance, when Jacob confessed his own 'not-knowing,' that God let down a *sulam*, "a ladder or stairway-- a cosmic bond between heaven and earth."[453] While reaching the level of scientific formulas and theological formulations may be invigorating, there is more to experience in the comprehensiveness of life than lingering on the High Rung of intellectual ascent.

"every rung goes higher, higher..."

As breathtaking as is the ascent toward knowledge, reasoning will take us only so far. There must be "a leap, and not a leap in the dark,"[454] but an ascent into a blinding light of absolute holiness. This holiness is beyond scientific verbiage or theological dogma. Our notions of a god cannot adequately *define* the poetic Presence we may experience in momentarily satisfying our insatiable taste for the sublime *in real time,* a place "where beauty grows."[455]

The danger of the unexamined ascent into the strictly academic disciplines of both science and theology is remarkably similar. One must be aware of one's own predispositions that could threaten an essentially objective ascent. If science is to be "truly progressive,"[456] if theology is to serve as "a lure towards greater development of positive possibilities,"[457] through which humanity is able to "postulate an ultimate spiritual environment and purpose,"[458] it follows that anyone who reaches the high rung must not be "locked into paradigms."[459] Intellect and insight must affirm the contributions of one with the other, yielding to the presence and mystery of Ultimate Love.

Perhaps the supra-rational "pull of the invisible" (Otto), "overwhelming sense that possesses and fills with ecstasy," (C.S. Lewis), "haunting scent of unseen

[453] *Commentary on the Torah*, ed. W. Gunther Plant (New York: University of Hebrew Congregation, 1981), 194-197

[454] Leslie Weatherhead, *The Christian Agnostic* (Nashville: Abingdon, 1985), 73-79

[455] Dillard, Ibid., 152

[456] Hubble, *Nebulae*, Ibid., 1

[457] Alfred North Whitehead, *Process and Reality* (New York: Social Science Publishers, 1941), 346

[458] Keith Ward, *God, Chance, & Necessity* (Oxford: Oneworld, 1996), 80

[459] Fred Hoyle, *The Nature of the Universe* (Oxford: Blackwell, 1951)

roses" (George MacDonald), or "something of the wonder and greatness of the spiritual universe is flashed upon the soul" (Leslie Weatherhead) is more likely to indicate what cannot be thoroughly theorized by science or theologized by religion. As humanity is modality of flesh and soul, so must reality be ascertained by both reason and revelation, intellect and empathy.

Distinguishing Between Haughty Intellectualism and Empathetic Insight

In the 1997 film, Will Hunting has genius-level intelligence with a prowess for memorizing facts and an intuitive ability to prove sophisticated mathematical theorems. At twenty, his intellectual aptitude is challenging to even Nobel-prize mathematicians at MIT. He is described in the preface to the Screenplay as "wildly charismatic, impossibly brilliant, and totally rebellious." Still, the young man is closed to other possibilities in his life that could raise his awareness of being far beyond his defensive and haughty intellectualism.

In a confrontation with reality via his counselor, Sean McGuire, Will is challenged with, not only his intellectual exclusivism, but also his understanding of, relatedness to, and empathy for community. Will's haughty intellectualism became a defensive wall that hindered the emergence of his true self. Rather to turn his intelligence to higher ascents of knowing, Will was stuck in a paradigm of intellectual haughtiness until he was challenged by his more empathetic counselor:

> You know what occurred to me? You've never been out of Boston. So if I asked you about art you could give me the skinny on every art book ever written...Michelangelo? But you couldn't tell me what it smells like in the Sistine Chapel. You've never stood there and looked up at that beautiful ceiling...If I asked you about war you could refer me to a bevy of fictional and nonfictional material, but you've never been in one. You've never held your best friend's head in your lap and watched him draw his last breath, looking at you for help. There's nothing you can tell me that I can't read somewhere else. Unless we talk about your life. But you won't do that. Maybe you're afraid of what you might say.[460]

---

[460] Matt Damon and Ben Affleck, Good *Will Hunting* (Screenplay, Miramax, 1997), 71-72

There is often tension or resistance in ascending the ladder from the High Rung of intellectual prowess to the next rung: a supra-rational or revelatory manifestation of the Holy. While not all intellectualism is haughty, if one is to experience the Holy, one must relinquish a dependence upon empiricism alone. In pursuit of a revelatory awareness, there must be an admission of one's intellectual limitations, a reckoning with the true self, and a surrender in vulnerability to the wooing of a holy God. This step to the next rung is arduous, but the panoramic view at its height is breathtaking and breath-giving.

Musical artist and composer, Dan Fogelberg, described this climb lyrically and insightfully:

> *The higher you climb*
> *The more that you see*
> *The less that you know*
> *The more that you yearn*
> *The further you reach*
> *The more that you touch*
> *The fuller you feel*
> *The less that you need*
>
> *The farther you reach.*[461]

The High Rung of intellectual ascent must be climbed. However, it is not the catch-all for determining the totality of all that is possible. There is another rung for which to ascend. This rung offers a coalescing of intellect with empathy. The former alone may lead to haughtiness. Coupled with the later one may find insight, or even a discernment of sacred space and Ultimate Love.

The Holy Rung: Ultimate Love in Sacred Space

> If God be far away, then He comes to us only on rare occasions and in rare situations. Of course, there is a sense in which this is the high moment...[462]

---

[461] *"The Higher You Climb,"* from the album *High Country Snows* (Dan Fogelberg, Hickory Grove Music & April Music Inc., on Full Moon and Epic Records, 1985)
[462] Howard Thurman, *Forward for the Inward Journey* (Richmond, IN: Friends United Meeting, 1984), 117

"Can you fathom the mysteries of God?" (Job 11:7/NIV.)

There are things that God reveals...even the deep things of God. (I Corinthians 2:10/NIV).

Delving into God's depths... How could it possibly be grasped or comprehended by our understanding? ...for we are melted into the depths that we know, feel, and perceives nothing but the simple, pure, unveiled One God.[463]

Ascending to the Holy Rung offers repose from the ever-tangled web of human theorizing and theologizing. This ascension addresses the deepest longings of the soul. It is, as Macquarrie wrote, "the upper limit where possibilities beyond it are disclosed.[464] Humanity has the capacity to climb from a Hellish Region, to a Hollow Rung of superficial existence, to a rung where only a shallow happiness is sustained, to a Higher Rung of intellectual acumen. But humanity also is wooed to a holiness, deeper awareness of God as Ultimate Love.

It is on this level of ascent we are redeemed from our estrangements through reconciliatory interactivity with God through "a radical grace.[465] It is our *come-uppance,* transposing our earthly existence into sacred space in real time. It is here wherein persons discover, not philosophical abstracts or theological propositions, but the spiritual phenomena of Ultimate Love; a presence that both convicts and comforts us in *ecstatic contemplation.* Here, all intellectual activities are transposed to insight. Our minds are "transformed in the presence of God."[466]

On the Holy Rung, our experience is not bound to a closed materialistic universe, but a cosmos open to repose, response and re-creation. Here one is admonished to climb to the mystery, where in "every minute, life begins

---

[463] Johannes Tauler, *The Inner Way* (1300-1361)

[464] John Macquarrie, *Principles of Christian Theology* (London: Canterbury Press, 1977), 365-366

[465] Frederick Schleiermacher, *The Christian Faith* (Philadelphia: Fortress Press, 1976), 262

[466] Bonaventure, *The Soul's Journey into God,* taken from *Classics of Western Spirituality* (Mahwah, NJ: Paulist Press, 1978), 113

all over again."[467] Chronological time is of little concern as it fades into the "aeonic time of a relative eternity," as our participation in God's creative continuum of life becomes an "inexhaustible and creative livingness."[468] Presence on the Holy Rung is a rapturously therapeutic moment of wholeness in a broken or wonky world. It may be experienced in the midst of weariness, grief, or exhaustion. When our own resources are depleted, and we release our delusions of unqualified autonomy, *we awaken:* "heaven and earth are bound together."[469]

While this spiritual phenomenon is a "given" by God to those who "actively seek Him," (Deuteronomy 4:29; Psalm14:2; 63:1; 78:34; Hebrews 11:6/ NRSV), ascent to the Holy Rung is an experience "never easy, obvious or predictable."[470] This phenomenon is given by the will and whim of an incomprehensible God! The Holy Rung is the mystery of being "grasped by a Thou."[471] It is a moment of wonder that cannot be manipulated by any scientific or theological formula. Such experiences seem both random and designed at the same time as we holistically sense God's mysterious presence. It is a supra-rational experience of Ultimate Love.

Although this *presence* is not magic, it is mystical, "the highest reality."[472] This is a vivid and descriptive symbol of what is inexpressible but not without apprehension. What C.S. Lewis called "the un-dimensioned depth of the Divine Life in a moment's consideration,"[473] Paul Tillich referred to as "essentialization," wherein we are grasped by a peace which is above reason, "above our theoretical seeking for the true."[474]

---

[467] Thomas Merton, *The Sign of Jonas* (New York: Harcourt, Brace & Company, 1953), 338ff.

[468] Jurgen Moltmann, *In the End—the Beginning: The Life of Hope* (Minneapolis: Fortress Press, 2004), 159-161

[469] Timothy Verdon, *Ecumenism of Beauty*, (Brewster, MA: Paraclete Press, 2017), XIV-XV

[470] Bruggeman, *Old Testament Theology* Ibid., *167-169*

[471] Wayne E. Oates quoting Martin Buber from *I and Thou* in *Psychology of Religion*, Ibid., 254

[472] Macquarrie, *Principles of Christian Theology* Ibid., 250-253

[473] C. S. Lewis, *Miracles*, Chapter 16: 22

[474] Paul Tillich, *"The Depth of Our Existence,"* from *The Shaking of the Foundations* (NY: Charles Scribner's Sons, 1948), 55

It is the location of soul transparency where we may seek a revelation which brings us from a "region of dreams and shadows to real life,"[475] or, biblically-stated, where we are "rescued from the power of darkness and transferred, to arise to walk in newness of life. (Colossians 1:13; 2:13/NRSV). God's presence reaches us within *our* interior Jerusalem in spiritual and mystical ecstasy."[476] God seems distant, transcendent from us, until we discover His pursuit of us in His imminence, ever near us. It is God, as Ultimate Love who woos us to the Holy Rung.

The Holy Rung is only a workable metaphor for the top of the ladder where love is clarified in "unceasing communion."[477] Lingering on the holy rung, we are freed from all temporal things to contemplate a beam of divine darkness, entering into a blinding, but *in-sighting* Light! On this level of spiritual awareness, through the insight we are given, we resolve to: (1) release personal delusions and popular mirages, (2) detach from idols and contrived gods, (3) detox from the effects of cultural or faddish behavior (4) de-complicate or simplify our lives by embracing the essential provisions of God and (5) dare to inhale the inexhaustible exhale of God's life-giving breath. More than a list of sectarian *dos and don'ts*, the climb to the Holy Rung woos humanity to BE-Live in Ultimate Love in real time.

John Moses, former Dean of St. Paul's Cathedral in London, described this climb toward union with God as one's willingness "to grow in awareness, mystery, and grace."[478] As we unconditionally receive this *radical grace*, we grow in union with God, as if we were metaphorically climbing the rungs of our own respective "Jacob's ladder." For John Donne, this perilous-yet-purposeful ascent is received with both fear and fascination:

> I dare not move my dimme eyes any way...
> That not one hour my selfe I can sustaine;
> Thy GRACE may wing me to prevent his art,
> And Thou like a magnet draw mine iron heart.[479]

---

[475] Tolstoy, *Letters*, Volume II, ed. R. F. Christian (NY: Charles Scribner's Sons, 1991), 399

[476] Bonaventure, *The Soul's Journey into God*, 7:3-5

[477] John Climacus, *The Ladder of Divine Ascent*, Preface p. xxiii

[478] John Moses, *The Sacrifice of God,* (Norwich: Canterbury Press, 1992), 183

[479] John Donne, *Holy Sonnets I*, taken from *The Complete Poetry and Selected Prose* (NY: Modern Library, 1952), 247

On this rung, scientific discovery is not a threat but a treat. It serves as a lure toward a revelation of the magnificent genius of God's creative prowess. Even those things considered *secular* (not equated with the *profane*) can be celebrated as expressions of God's *good* creation. Our own giftedness as human beings created good—athletics and the arts, academia and altruism--may become sacramental offerings in our devotion to and actualization of God. God is here. In the midst of life, breaking through the commonplace, glorifying the ordinary, God is near "in the normal ebb and flow of life as we live it."[480]

On this rung, I celebrate my life as intertwined with all of creation. I recognize I have been designed to consider the well-being of all life, present and future, not self-absorbed with my own self-interests. My being and my becoming are interconnected to the grandeur of all that is. On the Holy Rung, we do not look down, but we gaze around us with the purview of the wonder and whims of Ultimate Love.

Here the fanciful *"I"* of my existence transforms to the faithful "i" of BE-Living, responsive to and responsible before a sovereign God. When i realize i am nothing of myself, then i come to awareness of Ultimate Love and the radical grace of the *"I AM* God." In the words of Jacob, "I have seen God face-to-face and yet my life is preserved." (Genesis 32:30/NRVS). i am awe-struck with silence, conviction and comfort in the actualization that i am a minute cell in all that is being and becoming. Nouwen described this interaction as "purifying... where I can embrace my own mortality, and the inner voice reveals to me my true name."[481] (Emphasis on the small case "i" is added and intentional).

"The Heavenly Realm: *"There is a place with Himself."* (Exodus 33:21-23/NRSV)

> [From] the inner sanctuary of divine knowledge...[there is a] passing on to the tabernacle not made with hands...

---

[480] Howard Thurman, *"Barren or Fruitful,"* a message to Plymouth Congregational Church in Washington D.C. (1932), from *A Strange Freedom* (Boston: Beacon Press, 1998), 28

[481] Henri Nouwen, *Our Greatest Gift: Meditations on Dying and Caring* (NY: HarperCollins, 1991), 3

the wonderful harmony of the heavens proclaiming the wisdom which shines forth in the creation and sets forth the great glory of God.[482]

There is one final ascent we are destined to climb. It is not another "rung," but it is a passing into a realm wherein the consummate presence of God resides. John Cassian, the Egyptian monk (365-435), described this ascent, as passing through the activities of humanity where we learn to live "solely on the beauty and knowledge of God."[483] Metaphorically, I call this the Heavenly Realm for it *is* "an elevated life."[484] From the ascent on the ladder one can only envision this realm pensively, from a distance, and through insight apprehended in the soul.

"I see heaven open..." (St. Stephen at his stoning in Acts 7:56/NIV)

"As Jesus came up out of the water, he saw heaven being torn open..." (Mark 1:10/NIV)

"God offers to every man the door which leads to the knowledge of Himself, and to the knowledge of life eternal."[485]

> *I want to scale the utmost height*
> *and catch a gleam of glory bright*
> *But still I'll pray 'till heaven I've found*
> *Lord, plant my feet on higher ground.*[486]

The Heavenly Realm is certainly a place *of* an ultimate "wish fulfillment"[487] of ultimate good, with the eradication of the harsh realities of a world gone wonky. But wish fulfillment is an inadequate description in itself. This realm is not a goody-goody jaunt down some celestial yellow brick road to never-never land. The Heavenly Realm is a place of inescapable reconciliation,

---

[482] Gregory of Nyssa, *The Life of Moses*, para. 168

[483] *Conferences* 1:8

[484] Gregory of Nyssa, *Ibid.*, para. 307

[485] William Barclay, *The Revelation of John*, Volume I (Philadelphia: Westminster Press, 1959), 189

[486] Johnson Oatman, Jr., Hymn, *Higher Ground* (1892)

[487] Sigmund Freud, *Future of An Illusion* (1927)

justice and personal and community accountability. *"O God, by your mercy, you render to everyone according to his work." (Psalm 62:12/NRSV).*

One's "wish fulfillment" or imaginary projections of a *perfect haven in the clouds* would tend not to include one's own accountability for perpetuating wonky, or worse: the perpetration of evil in a lost world. This Realm is deemed more than mere "conjecture woven in the minds of humans from stories retold over and over through the centuries" (Freud). It is a transfixion of our innermost being, one that frightens the flesh, and seduces the soul. It is a place of confident expectation, an inspired hope beyond wishful thinking, and reconciliation beyond justice.

> *In the scheme of thought there will be the administration of justice tempered by grace, befitting the holy at the exclusion of the profane. A purging of evil --where God extinguishes the evil that humanity has done—with the will of those who have realized it and even perpetuated it.*[488]

A Momentary Pause:

Biblical Metaphors for the Heavenly Realm

Three distinct narratives in the Scripture describe the Heavenly Realm as a multi-sensory experience: 1) Jacob's *vision* of light atop the uttermost rung of the "ladder" (Genesis 28:2/NASB), 2) Isaiah's *feeling* of "shaking thresholds" (Isaiah 6:1-4/NASB), and 3) John's *hearing* a "voice like a trumpet saying, 'come up here!'" (Revelation 4:1/NASB). Biblical manifestations of the Heavenly Realm are revealed through light, color, movement, melody, along with the consuming Presence of God and all things *now* sacred. The responses of Jacob, Isaiah, and John to this Presence was awe and humility. In the Presence of the One who abides fully in the Heavenly Realm, there is both a sense of *justice*, the light that penetrates the darkness of human sinfulness and *grace*, the actualization of divine love that offers the way of reconciliation.

Here is where we reach the limits of poetic metaphors or even the most exquisite God-talk. For herein God is not contained spatially by human

---

[488] George MacDonald, *"Justice,"* from *Unspoken Sermons*, Series 3

imagination or verbiage. St. Augustine warned, "do not think of this [heaven] spatially, as if the birds are nearer to God than we."[489] This Heavenly Realm may not be so much a geographical location in the clouds, as it is a pristine garden in the purified dimension of the yet to be. This is the place described as life's fullest consummation, "the fuller dawning of light, once dimly seen,"[490] where God is not merely a vague presence, but fully present. Upon having their revelatory experience of the Heavenly Realm, the biblical examples mentioned above "fell into an ecstasy; in a state of spiritual exaltation; lifted up above himself and beyond themselves."[491] (I Kings 19:22; Psalm 47:8; Isaiah 6:1; Matthew 3:13; Revelation 1:17/NASB).

The Heavenly Realm is described poetically as a place where one is somehow reconciled from the bonds of fleshly existence and the soul is released into an egoless domain of a common equality. There is no need for extravagance, luxuries, or want. No one is anonymous here, for all persons are accountable and accounted for. All find shelter from the heat of the day, light that illuminates all things, and there is no foreboding darkness. A refreshed garden is well-tended and all find nourishment and are willing to share its bounty. Here there are springs of water flow endlessly, where none are thirsty. (Revelation 21/NASB).

The Heavenly Realm is the Transfixion of the Soul!

German "mystic" Johann Arndt wrote, although are designed to live in this world in our occupation and calling, our hearts are always "directed to the heavenly, eternal fatherland."[492] There is a strange transfixion of the soul toward a final, major chord of our being,--a homeland, or the Heavenly Realm! Our personhood: heart, mind, soul, and strength is truly restless, "until we find our rest in Thee,"[493] in a place of wholeness and fullest being. In his later years, biblical scholar, William Barclay whimsically hoped for the Heavenly Realm to be "a place where there will be no more stairs."[494]

---

[489] St. Augustine, *Sermon on the Mount*, 2.5.17
[490] Keith Ward, *Guide*, Ibid., p. 253
[491] Barclay, *Revelation*, Ibid., 190
[492] *True Christianity* 18:5
[493] Augustine, *Confessions*
[494] *Autobiography*, Ibid., p. 20

In his exposition of the *Sermon on the Mount,* John Wesley taught that this Heavenly Realm was an ethereal or spiritual region high and lifted up, where God's "honour particularly dwelleth."[495] Although God's influence is imminently everywhere, God's essential personhood, or transcendent Otherness, is reputed to be fully manifested in this Heavenly Realm. Here is the consummation of our "ultimate concern," the mysterious transfixion of the soul; the ascension into union with the *"I Am God",* wherein we are not only redeemed and reconciled, but welcomed *home.*

In this Heavenly Realm, all persons are united into community. All who are redeemed from the suffering and the ills of the flesh by "His" eternal grace find both recompense and refuge there. (Ephesians 1:20; 2:6; 3:10/NASB). This is the place of a "perfected humanity."[496] It is the *"most* holy and sacred space" (Hebrews 9:11,24; 6:19-20; 10:19-20/NASB), where we share in God's "inexhaustibly creative livingness."[497]

According to physicist and priest, John Polkinghorne, the Heavenly Realm is the "collective destiny" of the beloved community. It is an unfolding of creation's salvific encounter with Ultimate Love. More than "a timeless moment of beatific illumination," in this Heavenly Realm, purified hearts, minds, and souls will live in the fullness of reality, where the strengths of persons and "the exploration by finite creatures of the infinite riches of that reality will be unending."[498] Here is the destination for our unquenchable curiosity and exploration into the comprehensive awareness of life and the human quest for contentment.

This same metaphor of a climb to a heavenly realm via a *staircase or ladder,* is reflected in the early history of the Christian church. Somewhere between 202-3 C.E. was documented the martyrdom of a young, married woman, a devout Christian named Perpetua. While little detail is known about her, in the ancient work, *The Martyrdom of Perpetua,* she is described as having been a leader in the church in Carthage, offering prayers, and encouraging the courage of the saints. Before her public execution in a Roman arena, while waiting in a prison cell, she was said to have had a vision of unprecedented significance:

---

[495] Sermon XXVI: VI: vi

[496] C. S. Lewis, *Miracles,* Chapter 6. 22

[497] Jurgen Moltmann, *In the End—The Beginning: The Life of Hope* (Minneapolis: Fortress Press, 2004), 159-161

[498] Polkinghorne, Ibid., 132-133

> *While in terrible darkness, I saw a golden ladder of marvelous*
> *height, reaching up even to heaven, and very narrow. And I went*
> *up, and I saw an immense extent of garden, and in the midst of the*
> *garden a white-haired man sitting in the dress of a shepherd. And*
> *he raised his head, and looked upon me, and said to me, 'Thou*
> *art welcome, daughter.' And at the sound I was awakened, still*
> *tasting a sweetness which I cannot describe.*[499]

In the Heavenly Realm, we become more aware of our interconnectedness to a great "cloud of witnesses." (Hebrews 12:1/NIV). There is the embrace of a diversity of persons in our human community. No one is excluded, anonymous, or unaccounted for. All are reconciled with God and with those to whom God has reconciled. There is no distinction or "respect of persons" through which we may *filter* others into this Heavenly Realm.

The following are the words of Kentucky poet, James Still, who, in the waning years of his life, learned the blessing of this interconnectedness with those whom he valued and those whom he didn't. In moving closer to a vision of a Heavenly Realm, Still recognized the significance of all persons who had crossed his earthly path. In the mysterious transposition from life to Life, all are judged, or better, *reconciled* with God and others, within the Heavenly Realm. When asked about who he wanted to share this place into which he was passing, Still poetically reflected on the given goodness of his life with the envisioned grandeur of the Heavenly Realm yet-to-be:

> *First, I want my dog, Jack,*
> *Granted that Mama and Papa are there,*
> *And my nine brothers and sisters,*
> *And 'Aunt' Fanny who diapered me, comforted me, and shielded me,*
> *Aunt Enore who was too good for the world,*
> *And the grandpa who used to bite my ears,*
> *And the other one who couldn't remember my name—*
> *Who had devils dancing in his eyes,*
> *And Uncle Luther who laughed so hard in the churchyard*
> *He had to apologize to the congregation,*
> *And Uncle Joe who saved the first dollar he ever earned,*

---

[499] *Martyrdom of Perpetua*, Chapter 4

And the last one, and all those in between;
And Aunt Carrie who kept me informed:
'Too bad you're not good-looking like your daddy';
And my first sweetheart, who died at sixteen,
Before she got around to saying 'Yes';
I want my dog Jack nipping at my heels,
Who was my boon companion,
Suddenly gone when I was six;
And I want Rusty, my ginger pony,
Who took me on my first journey—
Not far, yet far enough for the time;
I want the playfellows of my youth
Who gathered bumblebees in bottles,
Erected flutter mills by streams
Flew kites nearly to heaven,
And who before me saw God.
Be with me there. (emphasis added)."[500]

I do not conceive of the Heavenly Realm as an exclusive, geo-ethereal city-of-Oz in the clouds. Rather I envision an actualization of God's intention of all creation *from ex-nihilo to creation ex materia*, in which, in some way, I may be welcome. My notion of this realm is unconcerned about any "reward" -- pearly gates, or streets of gold. It is about being with God, interwoven within a tapestry of being with all that God loves; abiding in *a timeless and inclusive community* as a continuum of God's artistry, coming home to the unfettered embrace of Ultimate Love and with others, where I too, belong and am welcomed *home*.

A Momentary Pause: A Place Where Even I am Reconciled

A Real Time Metaphor for the Heavenly Realm: The Story of Antwone "Baby Boy" Fisher

Thursday, June 2, 1959. Cleveland, Ohio. "Baby boy" was born to a single mother. His life would begin in a temporary foster home then transferred to another where, for thirteen years, he suffered abuse from his "caretakers."

---

[500] James Still, *Those I Want in Heaven with Me Should There Be Such a Place*, from the *Mountain from the Valley, New and Collected Poems*, ed. Ted Olson (Lexington: University of Kentucky Press, 2001), 150

From the refuge of a reform school, he drifted away into the nightmare of homelessness and into an existence of deprivation and hopelessness. Antwone Fisher then determinately ascended arduous steps from a wayward punk on the street to a stint in the Navy to become a corrections officer-- to an artist, poet, and storyteller, and later to a screenwriter and film producer.

Along the way, Fisher's passion was to know his true self—to whom and where he belonged. He suffered the agony of estrangement from himself and others. He remarked, *"Everything was so out of order when I was born. I wanted everything in order, a welcoming environment, a clean, loving home."*

For most of his life, Fisher had suffered from the grief of not knowing from where he came or to whom he belonged. He began a search to "unravel" his true identity. He was told by his counselor, "...you do come from somewhere...Everybody comes from somewhere." Fisher believed his counselor. "I accepted that I came from somewhere and that someday I should unravel the mystery of where that was." The estranged Antwone asked some fascinating questions:

> *After suffering and overcoming through lessons and loss, were we all destined to be mere dust in the wind? Or was there more? Was there a way to share what you've learned, a form in which to pass it on to others for them to use, from which to benefit and perhaps avoid you pain? What was the use of life, otherwise?*

Antwone Quenton Fisher grew in stature, confidence, and artistry. His autobiography became a major film. But all the while, as he ascended the ladder of personal and professional success, he obsessed over the mystery of his origin. His birth mother had given him up for adoption, and he did not know his father, nor his father's legacy. He was determined to discover his story—how he was conceived, and to where and to whom he belonged.

> *My ideas brought forth questions about every aspect of human life conceivable, including the existential issue of wondering how a person could go through so much tribulation in life and then simply die.*

While in the Navy, Antwone had discovered a glimpse of what it meant to have: "family, friendship, belonging, education, and, ultimately, purpose." At thirty years old, as he entered civilian life, he began a quest for the rest of his story. He had no next of kin that he knew of, nor did he know from where he came. He was a man estranged from his true identity. Seemingly homeless.

"Do you know who I am?"

For years he asked that fascinating question in search for his next of kin. He had never been "legally adopted," so the paper trail back to his family was often a frustrating one. He recalled his birth mother mentioning the name of a man who was reputed to be his father. This same man had been killed two months before his birth, but it would be from that man's surname that Antwone would inquire.

Undauntedly, he continued his climb toward greater awareness of his own story. Step by step, Antwone gained more and more information about his true identity, until after reading an article in the newspaper and the subsequent information about his alleged father's funeral, he "connected" to the source for the information he was seeking. He phoned the number of one who shared his father's surname who turned out to be his aunt:

> *"'Hello,' I say, nervously, 'My name is Antwone Fisher. I'm calling long distance from Los Angeles...Uh, is this Annette Elkins?'*
>
> *'Yes?' She answers in a way that tells me my name means nothing to her.*
>
> *I continue. 'I'm looking for the family of an Edward Elkins and I was wondering if you might have a relative by that name?'*
>
> *'I have a brother by that name,' she says, 'But he's been dead a long time.' She pauses, then asks, 'Who is this?'*
>
> *Softly, I say, 'I...I think I'm his son.' I pause, then say to her again, 'My name is Antwone.'*
>
> *Another stretch of silence follows which she breaks by saying, 'Well, if you are Edward's son, you have a big family.'*

Through his arduous climb, beyond the wonky of what the world threw at him, Antwone Quenton Fisher ascended to the height of discovery: his origin, his purpose, and connectedness to a community. He belonged! He found his way home. He described his trip back to Cleveland for Thanksgiving to meet his family for the first time:

> *The love and happiness I felt coming toward me and flowing out of me was like a powerful cleansing, like taking a long, long shower after being gone too long in the wilderness. It was the scene of my dream. I was the guest of honor.*[501]

Of such consummation is the Heavenly Realm. Here all persons realize their true selves in the embrace of community--our interconnectedness to the *"cloud of witnesses" (Hebrews 12:1-2/NIV)*. Like Antwone united with his family, in the Heavenly Realm, all those once estranged are welcome to a place at a table of fellowship, an honored guest, with God as our Host and the founder of our feast. The Heavenly Realm, is like the "scene of our dreams," where no one is anonymous and every is accountable for. All are welcome, for all have find their way home...after all.

PROMPT 2:
Simple Wisdom Drawn from Deeper Wells

"Then God opened her eyes and she saw..." (Genesis 21:19/NRSV)

"Deep within me, you teach me wisdom." (Psalm 51:6/NRSV)

"The purposes of a person's heart are deep waters, but one who has insight draws them out." (Proverbs 20:5/NRSV)

"If you knew the gift of God...living water..." (John 4:10/NIV)

The danger of theology is that God can be regimented to our own ruminations and concepts about Him, drawing from our own limited thought and schemes. When we become vulnerable before God, that simple interaction

---

[501] Antwone Quenton Fisher, *Finding Fish: A Memoir* (NY: Harper Collins, 2001)

between our true selves and the Presence of God allows us to "see what [we] would not notice before."[502] At times, God's presence guides humanity into a pensive silence, a silence that may, in one's respective *fullness of time* yield a glorious "glimpse of deeper belonging"[503] and a vision for living well. Such a glimpse is crucial for the acquisition of a simple and sacred wisdom more enlightening for living than is the more complicated indoctrination of dogma or complexities of a myriad of contradictory theories about the universe.

The narratives above are similar, and applicable to those who tend to downsize God to merely an outline of dogmatic convictions. For the Samaritan woman at Jacob's well, God was confined to an inherited theological hearsay that merely parroted an eschatological expectation. For the Egyptian woman, Hagar, God was a distant deity, but One who *could* save she and her son from their life-depleting horror of the desert.

Through their respective adversities, both discovered *deeper wells of wisdom* beyond their religiosity—beyond their circumstances: "it is the Lord who is the fountain of living waters." (Jeremiah 17:13/NRSV). Such *living water*, a metaphor for simple wisdom, can be discovered by all persons, not exclusively from behind the gated towers of formal academia, but even in the humble, most unpretentious of places.

The woman of Samaria discovered a simple wisdom for living raising water from Jacob's well. Hagar, a woman from Egypt found this water during a moment of crisis in a wilderness desert. This simple wisdom is availed to all of humanity by God. In the humblest locations, through the simplest of moments or, at times, the harshest of situations, within the holy of holies of our innermost being, the living water of a simple (and sacred) wisdom may be drawn.

A Momentary Pause

Wisdom is Found in Living Well in the Spirit—Not Wealthy in the Flesh

In the 1937 Pulitzer Prize winning play *You Can't Take It With You,* by Moss Hart and George F. Kaufman, Grandpa Vanderhof and his unusual family,

---

502 *Jewish Midrash* 15
503 John Moses, *The Sacrifice of God,* Ibid., 192

the Sycamores, happily lived their un-orthodox lives in their humble home by Columbia University in New York for decades. This family (and their closest friends) were considered a group of eccentrics, who had found purpose for living through their respective interests, with simple contentment and joy. Their hobbies included collecting snakes, building fireworks in the basement, writing a myriad of plays that never get published, and taking ballet lessons.

Things like stress, criticizing politicians, jobs, and worry over materialistic gain were not for them. All was well. But when Vanderhof's granddaughter, practical young Alice Sycamore becomes engaged to her company's Vice President, Tony Kirby, the Vanderhof clan must prepare to meet their more materialistic new in-laws, Mr. and Mrs. Kirby. Two paradigms for living meet as symbolized by Grandpa Vanderhof's simple wisdom and the more complex, peer-pressure driven lifestyle of the father of the groom, Mr. Kirby.

Grandpa's *simple advice* to Mr. Kirby regards the importance of living life well, uncomplicated and unfettered by the materialistic urges and egomania of the world. Through dipping from the well of Grandpa's simple wisdom, the two families find a way to communicate with each other. In a mutual appreciation for the basic essentials of life, Vanderhof and Kirby discover a sacred, less-complicated source of living water and the simplicity in living well.

From Act 3:

> Kirby: (Outraged) I beg your pardon, Mr. Vanderhof, I am a very happy man.
>
> Grandpa (Vanderhof): I don't think so. What do you think you get your indigestion from? Happiness? No, sir. You get it because most of your time is spent in doing things you don't want to do.
>
> Kirby: I have spent my entire life building up my business.
>
> Grandpa: And what's it got you? Same kind of mail every morning, same kind of deals, same kind of meetings, same dinners at night, same indigestion. Where does the fun come in? Don't you

think there ought to be something more, Mr. Kirby? You must have wanted more than that when you first started out. We haven't got too much time, you know, any of us.

Kirby: What do you expect me to do? Live the way you do? Do nothing?

Grandpa: Well, I have a lot of fun. Time enough for everything— read, talk, visit the zoo now and then, practice my darts, even have time to notice when Spring comes around. I haven't taken bicarbonate of soda for thirty-five years. What's the matter with that?

At the close of the play, Grandpa Vanderhof offers a prayer for those gathered around the family table. At the end of the prayer, he remarks, *"Well, Sir...here we are again. We want to say thanks once more for everything You've done for us. Things seem to be going along fine...and as far as anything else is concerned, we'll leave it to You. Thanks."*[504]

Very often, when we are deflated by the wonkiness of the world, there is an unquenchable thirst for wisdom. We seek *deeper wells* of applicable knowledge often after we have exhausted our own thinking and cultural demands. When we come to the limits of our own resources, when we admit that we are spiritually dehydrated, we become more likely to seek *deeper wells of wisdom*...a simple wisdom that reminds us of the sacredness of our life's *time*. We may even become more vulnerable to prayerful communion with God, and an unencumbered path to well-being.

Even physicist Richard Feynman, in a letter to an inquisitive admirer admitted, "I was as strong an atheist as [anyone] was likely to find—but I could conceive of myself praying in such a situation ...as an utterly helpless man in the face of a threatening tragedy."[505] Deeper wells are often not sought until the thirst becomes otherwise unquenchable or we are in utter despair. We may then, like Mr. Kirby, relinquish the dryness of sophisticated

---

[504] *"You Can't Take It With You,"* play by Moss Hart and George S. Kaufman copyright by Anne Kaugman Schneider and Kitty Carlisle Hart, 1937
[505] *Perfectly Reasonable Deviations from the Beaten Track*: The Letters of Richard P. Feynman, Edited by Michelle Feynman (NY: Perseus Books, 2005), 350-351

cultural fads and fashions. What we seek is simple wisdom or *"living water,"* flowing freely to us by the presence of God. Huston Smith described this as "saturating ourselves in a different reality."[506]

"Wise words are like deep waters; wisdom flows from the wise like a bubbling brook." (Proverbs 18:4/NRSV)

Biblically stated, this metaphor of *diving into the depths of divine encounter* can only be possible as we determine to "leave the elementary things…and seek maturity" (Hebrews 6:1/NASB) and to "put away childish things" (I Corinthians 13:11/NASB). The living water God provides is simple yet deep. It does not require a litany of titles or endless wading in the shallow water of degreed education. Sometimes the most complex of human equations can become, in the scheme of all things, the shallowest of endeavors toward well-being. The source of this simple wisdom, or "living water" we seek is the love of God.

God dispenses wisdom through the simple provisions of life. We may discover the sacredness of wisdom, or "living water," in just observing and inhaling the wonder of our common existence. Through the simplest of means, God offers to an observant humanity insight into being. John Haught wrote: "God is a persuading love rather than a domineering force."[507] The wisdom God offers comes to us through living the drama of life: adventure, beauty, novelty, danger, upheaval, and the wonder of living humbly and well. It is through simple wisdom that we may learn and *grow.*

"Counsel in a man's heart is deep water; but a man of understanding draws it out." (Proverbs 20:5/NIV).

Admittedly this living water may be "hard to be discovered."[508] Moments of discovery from the things taken-for-granted may come to us within the commonplace or the good "givens" of our existence. We may discern the incomprehensible in the finite, even the extraordinary in our most mundane routines. Wisdom may emerge from the simple musings of one's lifetime:

---

[506] Huston Smith, *Tales of Wonder: An Autobiography* (NY: Harper Collins, 2009), 110
[507] John F. Haught, *Science and Religion: From Conflict to Conversation* (NY: Paulist Press, 1995), 62
[508] John Wesley Commentary, from *Explanatory Notes on Proverbs 20:5*

the agonies *and* the ecstasies of our existence. If we aren't aware of such moments-from-the-musing, we tend to miss the wisdom to be gained from them.

Living water guides us in it's current toward hope and transformation. From the dust of his despair Stuart discovered, in the simplest of places, this living water! Stuart's "kingdom" is a story of the discovery of a deep well of sacred thought in the core of his own being. Through a sudden heart attack, the author described his exquisite experience of being "reborn...crossing the gate from life to Life," discerning the sacred simply within his desire to breathe. Like "water in the barren desert" (Hagar) or "water drawn from an old well" (the Samaritan woman), the novelist was guided to wisdom: a sacred space within himself, where he gleaned the simplest, yet profound wisdom: with the guidance of Ultimate Love, all will be well.

Kentucky folk author, Jesse Stuart, wrote of his own discovery of wisdom in his autobiographical novel, *The Kingdom Within*. In the story, based on his own brush with death, the main character, Shan, had a massive heart attack and was confined in a hospital for 22 days. Eleven of those days, he was bound in an Intensive Care Unit. From this vulnerability, a simple, yet profound wisdom emerged. Stuart learned a deeper awareness of the "good" God created as Life from life.

> *This was a time of exaltation! He stood as high as his universe was high. How wonderful the air was to breathe...to hear beautiful music... to see birds, leaves, and blossoms... His mind, always receptive to ideas was now filled and running over...overflowing with joy...to be home ...what a beautiful world this was...He knew here was the place of beginning and eternal ending. He knew here was the beginning of that something from within. It had been there. And it would be with him forever...It was <u>an area of rare tranquility</u>...Where the noises of what we all know as civilization are notably absent. (emphasis added).*[509]

This is an insightful story of how crisis informed a man's existence with simple wisdom. How in a moment of vulnerability, he took notice of the

---

[509] Jesse Stuart, excerpts from the novel *The Kingdom Within: A Spiritual Autobiography* (NY: McGraw-Hill, 1979)

simplest things he had previously taken for granted. He learned to become more appreciative of life in his hometown of Plum Creek Hollow, but also the insight that something of a reflection of the Heavenly Realm was mysteriously within him as well. He received in the core of his being a simple and sacred wisdom, and a deeper appreciation for a wonderful world.

PROMPT 3:
Growing and Learning: Tending the Beauty of All Creation

"come to me...do not stand still." (Genesis 45:9/NRSV).

"As for mortals, their days are like grass; they flourish like a flower in the field." (Psalm 103:15/NRSV).

"Learn from the way the wildflowers grow..." (Matthew 6:28; Luke 12:27/NAB).

In Hebrew thought, humanity is forbidden to stop growing. In rabbinical teaching, angels are called, "those who stand still." Humans are called, "those who walk about." Angels are already perfect; they cannot grow. Man, on the other hand, must never stand still, but grow and learn. "Do not be afraid, the Shechinah *[indwelling of the Spirit of God]* is here, so you will not stand still."'[510]

There is a wonder and awe in God's handiwork! That is the poetic meaning of the Psalmist: we are *"fearfully and wonderfully made." (Psalm 139:14/NRSV).* The word "fearfully" is derived from the root word, meaning to be "in wonder and awe" of an event. Consider God in awe of the emanating cosmos, of our own pulsating hearts-- our good possibilities and our capacity to grow in complement with all that is.

Perhaps humanity was not created with a *duality of natures,* flesh vs spirit, but a *modality of heart, mind, soul* and *strength*—flesh and spirit? Perhaps we were created in original innocence, with a propensity for good and only a potential for non-good? Thus, the fullness of human nature is not a duality

---

[510] Shlomo Katz, *Growing in Exile,* http://torah.org/torah-portion/hamaayan -5763-vayigash/

but a *modality*. We have a primal instinct through which we survive: to protect, defend and adapt our existence to our essential needs. At the same time, we have the longing for spiritual nurturing: to thrive, learn and adapt our being to the common good. Through primal instinct we adapt to the laws of survival. Through pristine insight we ascend to higher levels of spiritual care.

The flesh is grounded in a primal nature to survive. From the soul grows our purpose for being: to tend to the beautification of our own *garden of Eden,* our ecosystem, and to nurture our shared existence in community. Through a delicate balance and understanding of both, we may come to the reality that humanity was indeed created *BARA, or* "very good."

"Learn how the wildflowers grow" (Luke 12:27; Matthew 6:30; Genesis 11-12/NAB).

In the Greek text, *KATANSESATE TA KRINA POS AUXANE* is translated: Jesus admonished his followers to learn wisdom from observing the of the anemones, the "wildflowers."[511] Those who would live a *beautitudinal* lifestyle must perceive or come to a greater awareness of *"how they grow"* or thrive. He used this vivid word picture to describe for humanity, a purpose for being: "to flourish, to blossom in beauty, to realize our potential."[512]

The metaphor is illustrative of the wildflowers that thrive for only a moment in the Palestine of Jesus' day--scarlet anemones of the hills of Palestine. After a random summer rain shower, the mountainside would be ablaze in scarlet; "they bloomed one day and died."[513] The Psalmist observed, *"he covers the sky with clouds; he supplies the earth with rain and makes grass grow on the hills."* (Psalm 147:8/NRSV). The life of the wildflowers and grasses, although brief, are essential and purposeful. They beautify the wilderness and bring life to the desert.

Consider humanity as *the* "wildflowers," created intentionally to flourish in the garden of our existence. We are purposed to grow, to cooperate with God, tending the garden, adding beauty and goodness to our world. In our

---

[511] Translation by Nicholas King Suffolk (Mayhew Press, 2004) 29

[512] Barclay, *Spiritual Autobiography,* 56

[513] William Barclay, *Gospel of Luke,* (Philadelphia: Westminster,1956) 169

qualified autonomy, we grow to be an essential part of its splendor. From this inclination toward the pristine comes our liberation from primitive urges, addictive materialism and the vulgar mechanisms of humanity. BE-Living as "wildflowers" in this world means to grow in our awareness of purpose to create beauty and cultivate the fullness of life for all.

How do wildflowers grow?

My grandfather, Leland Norris, owned property that was plush with vegetation: orchards, gardens, and fields that every season flourished with a landscape full of color and bounteous crop: flowers of every variety, apples, cherries, and pears, strawberries, raspberries and blackberries, and vines bursting with blue grapes! It seemed that everything he sewed yielded a harvest. As a child, I was invited to help him with productive and important tasks to enable his vineyard to grow.

I asked my grandfather one day how he managed to get things to grow so well. He answered, "You need three things: fertile soil, good seed, and a healthy environment. They all have to be there if anything is to grow." Likewise, if we are to flourish as the wildflowers, unique, beautiful, fragile, and fleeting, we too must start with fertile soil (vulnerability to God' presence), the good seed of spiritual discernment, and thrive intentionally in an environment (sacred space) that regards our need for peace, intertwined within a wholesome community.

Growing in a Community of Wildflowers

A member of the Society of Friends, teacher and scholar, Elton Trueblood wrote that somewhere in the world there should be a cultural milieu consciously and deliberately devoted to the task of seeing how love can be made real or demonstrating love in practice, "centers of loving fellowship, which in turn infect the world."[514]

In his second letter to the early church, Peter admonished immature believers to *"grow in the grace and knowledge of our Lord and Savior, Jesus Christ." (II Peter 3:18/NIV)*. This *AUKSANO* or "will to grow" means to tend one's soul-- tame

---

[514] Elton Trueblood, *The Company of the Committed* (NY: Harper & Row, 1961) 113

the flesh, temper the fodder of a secular culture, and be unremittent toward realizing the beauty of creation and community.

Jesus offered a pattern toward the cultivation of personal and community growth in his *Sermon on the Mount.* In the *Beatitudes,* one begins a journey toward maturity from a sense of one's own spiritual poverty, qualified autonomy or humility before a holy God, and then to mourning the *lostness* of one's true self. From this grieve over his or her own estrangement, comes an empathy toward others, a striving toward the wholesome and good, and the practice of unconditional mercy to those who, like him (her) self, are lost and in need of mercy.

Being mature (or to grow) in God's wisdom means to live in the hope of the yet-to-be, in original innocence, purity and goodness. The crescendo of growing spiritually mature in the Beatitudes is in becoming a *peacemaker,* one who knows peace with God and promotes "just peacemaking"[515] in the world. As we consider the purpose of the wildflowers, as peacemakers, we too must become intentional for the beautification of our communities of influence, this includes our promotion of peace.

Plowing Fields for Peace:

The Admonitions of Two Wildflowers: Martin Luther King Jr. and Jimmy Carter

> Let me drink from the waters where the mountain streams flood
> let me smell of wildflowers flow free through my blood
> let me sleep in your meadows with the green grassy leaves
> *let me walk down the highway with my brother in peace.*
> (emphasis added)
> let me die in my footsteps
> before I go down under the ground. (Bob Dylan, Let Me Die in My Footsteps,
> 1963, 1965 by Warner Bros. Inc.; renewed 1991, 1993 by Special Rider Music)

---

[515] Glen Stassen, *Just Peacemaking* (Louisville: John Knox Press, 1992)

"The entire society learned from its mistakes. They learned that violence won't solve their problems, it will only make them worse. Finally, they came to believe—with good reason—that peace and political stability will enable them to enjoy unprecedented growth and prosperity. I think the Good Friday agreement will endure…the organized political violence among the deranged, the regressive, the criminal…is over for now."[516]

"We can choose to alleviate suffering. We can choose to work together for peace. We can make these changes — and we must."[517]

Peacemakers do not react to hate with hate, nor retaliate with evil for evil. They *grow* in response to the wonky of the world by first defying their own vengeance. They respond to hate with peaceful initiatives, tilling the good soil of the soul, planting the nourishing seed of wisdom, and channeling an environment of Ultimate Love to bring to fruition the most redemptive outcome. This is not an easy, instantaneous process. It is learned in cooperation with the momentum of God's creative activity in this world, striving to bring the brokenness of human reality into "a harmonious whole."[518] In the midst of what Martin Luther King Jr. called "the darkest night" in the history of civil rights movement, Montgomery, Alabama: King, the "drum major for peace,"[519] asserted, the beatitudes of Jesus prompted him to strive "to preserve, create, and restore community."[520]

One who grows to be a peacemaker attunes oneself to and honors not just the absence of violence in a community but strives toward an interdependent reconciliation. The spiritually mature peacemaker serves as a "redemptive

---

[516] Senator George Mitchell, Chairman of the International Crisis Group, a nonprofit organization dedicated to the prevention of atrocities in international affairs, in discussing the Northern Ireland Peace Accords. Taken from his book *Making Peace* (NY: Alfred A. Knopf, 1999), 186-187

[517] Jimmy Carter, Nobel Lecture (Oslo, Norway, December 10, 2002)

[518] Martin Luther King, Jr., *Stride Toward Freedom* (NY: Harper and Row, 1958), 107

[519] Coretta Scott King, *My Life with Martin Luther King, Jr.* (NY: Holt, Rinehart, and Winston, 1969), 326

[520] King, Ibid., 97; 105

force."[521] During the Civil Rights movement, the practice of "non-violent resistance" was King's methodology for social change. Those who were willing to commit themselves to "just peacemaking"[522] agreed to sign the following *"ten commandments"* of the Civil Rights Movement under King's leadership:

1. *Meditate daily on the teachings of Jesus.*
2. *Remember always that the nonviolent movement seeks justice and reconciliation—not victory.*
3. *Walk and talk in the manner of love; for God is love.*
4. *Pray daily to be used by God in order that all men might be free.*
5. *Sacrifice personal wishes that all men might be free.*
6. *Observe with both friend and foe the ordinary rules of courtesy.*
7. *Seek to perform regular service for others and the world.*
8. *Refrain from the violence of fist, tongue, and heart.*
9. *Strive to be in good spiritual and bodily health.*
10. *Follow the directions of the movement and of the captains on a demonstration.*[523]

Mature peacemakers do not claim personal divinity but are guided by an ideology that informs insight. Although there have been substantiated criticisms of Dr. King's personal behavior at times, former Executive Director of the Southern Christian Leadership Conference and United States Ambassador to the United Nations under President Jimmy Carter, *Andrew Young,* described King, the peacemaker as: "a flesh and blood human being who devoted his life to social change;" a man of flesh and soul, who believed change can only happen through "a process of continually questioning the capacity to overcome mistakes and the ability to follow a path courageously."[524]

If one is to grow to be a peacemaker, then one must learn to regard the human capacity for both instinct and insight, good works of the flesh as prompted by the guidance of the soul. We are admonished not to "return evil for evil" (I Peter 3:9; Romans 12:17/NIV), but to "do justice, love kindness, and walk humbly before our

---

[521] Ibid., 320

[522] Glen Stassen, *Just Peacemaking,* Ibid.

[523] King, Ibid., 218-219

[524] Andrew Young, *An Easy Burden: The Civil Rights Movement and the Transformation of America* (NY: Harper Collins, 1996), 474

God." (Micah 6:8/NIV). According to Andrew Young, the methodology of Martin Luther King Jr. regarded conversation, negotiation, even friendly competition as avenues to reconciliation, "essential to civilization and survival."[525]

Just peacemaking requires a spiritual ascent in recognition of God's intervention in the process of redemption and reconciliation. It does not utilize the whims of the flesh simply to overcome the powerless with another's will to power. Vessels of *peace-ware* are distinctive from weapons of warfare. The goal of the peacemaker is to strive "whenever possible" for reconciliation and the redemptive outcome to conflict. This was at the core of Dr. King's dream: a "totally inclusive community in which people love, accept, and respect one another without reservation."[526]

Peacemaking is a distinctive purpose for wildflowers. As one grows-to-flourishing in a world-gone-wonky, particularly as one recognizes the brutality and violence in our culture, growing peacemakers becomes an essential purpose for being. Those who understand the steps toward the teachings of Jesus in the Beatitudes and Dr. King's "ten commandments" of the Civil Rights movement must also apprehend the importance of *BE-Living* as peacemakers; to enable others to discover peace *with* God, the peace *of* God, peace *in community* and to tend to the well-being of all creation.

Regardless of partisan politics, former-President, Jimmy Carter, is renowned for his commitment to the teachings of Jesus in his promotion of peace in the world. His devotion to his faith is not so abstract as to be impractical. His good works through Habitat for Humanity, the many humanitarian projects of the Carter Center, his unwavering insistence for human rights around the world, and his passion for a peaceful resolution in the Middle East, are indications of a commitment to a higher calling, Carter referred to as his "best source of strength."[527]

Former National Security Advisor, Zbigniew Brzezinski, wrote of Jimmy Carter:

---

[525] Andrew Young, *A Way Out of No Way: Spiritual Memoirs* (Nashville: Thomas Nelson, 1994), 133

[526] Robert S. Graetz, Jr. A White Preacher's Message on Race and Reconciliation (Louisville: NewSouth Books, 2006), 242

[527] Jimmy Carter, *Faith* (New York: Simon and Schuster, 2018), 119

I was taken by the fact that he (Carter) said grace in a totally private fashion. I sensed in Carter a deep religiosity, which was at the same time quite private and personal...a man of genuine conviction. I pointed out that to me religion is a search, whereas he seemed to have found in religion a much more direct relationship to God... and the nature of peace.[528]

More recently, the Opinion Contributor for the New York Times, Margaret Renkl, *noted* upon visiting Carter's Sunday School Class at the Maranatha Baptist Church in Plains: "Even when is he is not teaching Sunday School, his unwavering Christian faith informs everything he says and does."[529] In her OpEd, Renkl quoted the former president: "'if we don't figure out collectively how to get along with each other and take care of each other, that might be the end of humanity...God's love [however] will prevail.'"[530]

From one of his Sunday School lessons, Carter asserted, "Jesus' teachings can help to keep us at peace with both our Creator and our neighbors."[531] Carter followed his lesson with a personal prayer: "Strengthen me to become an ambassador of peace in whatever arenas of life I find myself. In Jesus' name I pray. Amen."[532]

As an upswing of his faith, the former president and Nobel Peace Prize recipient founded the Carter Center, a nongovernmental, not-for-profit organization in 1982 in Atlanta, based on the principle that everyone on earth should be able to live in peace seeking ways to meet basic human needs—"to resolve conflict, fight hunger, disease, and human rights abuses."[533]

What then does it mean to "consider the wildflowers, how they grow?" It simply means that as we "grow in the grace and knowledge of the Lord," in the character-transforming admonitions of the Beatitudes, we

[528] Zbignew Brzeznnski, *Power and Principle: Memoirs 1977-1981* (NY: Farrar, Straus, Giroux, 1982), 9; 89

[529] *Opinion,* New York Times (April 16, 2018)

[530] Ibid.

[531] *Faith, Ibid.,* 124

[532] Ibid., 314

[533] Carter, *Talking Peace: A Vision for the Next Generation* (New York: Dutton Books, 1993), 29

SUPER-naturally mature to become "peacemakers." Our good and original innocence is rekindled and our sensitivity to reconciliation and the quelling of violence is heightened. We learn to not only love God, but ALL that God loves. Peacemaking becomes a purposeful priority.

The epitome of *BE-Living* is in flourishing as a peacemaker! One who knows the contentment of being with God, becomes what St. Francis called an "instrument of peace" within one's own concentric circles of concern and influence. Far from the superficial toiling or striving in heated political arenas, peacemaking is simply living out an awareness of God's presence and intention for all creation wherever one is planted, and growing from there. Of such is the peace that surpasses human understanding, or naturalistic instinct.

In a recent Sunday School lesson at his home church, the Maranatha Baptist Church in Plains, Georgia, Carter taught, "with the dramatic, often violent changes occurring at this time in history, it is important for all of us to learn how to best use our strengths, not only for ourselves, but for a more peaceful world."[534] Humanist, Edward O. Wilson would concur, "A civilization able to envision God and to embark on the colonization of space will surely find a way to save the integrity of this planet and the magnificent life it harbors."[535]

"I'm Just Mattie:" Mattie Stepanek, A Young Wildflower Who Honored Peace

Jimmy Carter wrote of young Mattie Stepanek as a youngster with the purity of heart, with a childlike faith and the indomitable spirit of one who has survived more physical suffering than most adults will ever know. Carter added, "Mattie convinced me that his quest for peace was not inconceivable… [Mattie was] the most remarkable person I have ever known."[536]

Born in Rockville, Maryland in 1990, Matthew Joseph Thaddeus Stepanek, known simply as Mattie, was a poet who published seven best-selling books of poetry and essays espousing peace. Before his death at thirteen in 2004, Mattie had become known as a peace advocate and motivational speaker.

---

[534] Ibid., 177

[535] *The Future of Life*, 189

[536] Jimmy Carter, from the Foreword to the book *Just Peace: A Message of Hope*

For many became he embodied the personification of hope in a conflict-riddled world.

For most of his young life, Mattie knew the hardship and suffering of a rare and eventually fatal neuromuscular disease that caused his automatic system malfunction: sometimes his brain and body would do things automatically without Mattie's control. At other times automatic things like simple breathing or the heart beating the right way, keeping a normal body temperature, the proper digestion of food, or even the correct processing of oxygen, were all affected by Mattie's disease. Mattie Stepanek wrote:

> When you hear my story, it may sound very sad. I believe that there is something bigger and better than the here and now where our essence, or spirit, lives eternally. And, I believe that I am spending my time on earth trying to do what I feel is my purpose here.

Mattie was known by thousands from his frequent appearances on talk shows such as Phil Donahue and Oprah Winfrey and appeared somewhat regularly on the annual Jerry Lewis Muscular Dystrophy Telethons. He became identified with the purpose of peacemaking. His young and brief life was devoted to the perpetuation of hope and peace, even in the midst of his own challenges. He continued in his book: "my first (and favorite) experience was teaching the second graders about God and Heaven, and love and mercy and grace…Most often, this is a message of hope and *peace*.[537]

Mattie is an example of a "wildflower," who grew in the most difficult of circumstances and locations, tending toward adding to the beauty of the world. Here is a sample of Mattie's hope for peace:

For Our World (by Mattie)

We need to stop.
Just stop.
Stop for a moment.

---

[537] Mattie J.T. Stepanek, *Just Peace: A Message of Hope* (Kansas City: Andrews McMeel Publishing, 2006), 22-28

We need to be silent.
Just silent.
Silent for a moment.

We need to notice.
Just notice.
Notice for a moment.

Stop, be silent, and notice.

We need to be.
Just be.
Be for a moment.

And now, let us pray,
for peace. (September 11, 2001)[538]

Growing as a peacemaker in a violent world is not an easy task. It requires more than adhering to a theological abstract, rather we must first pursue the insightful phenomenon of God's essential presence. We are not able by instinct alone to do what peacemaking requires of us, but we can be enabled by the insight of the soul to be the peacemakers God intends for us to become.

Another "wildflower," Mother Teresa, wrote: *"I feel sometimes afraid, for I have nothing, no brains, no learning, no qualities required for such a work, and yet I tell Him that my heart is free from everything and so it belongs completely to Him. To please Him only is the joy I seek."*[539] Perhaps God is pleased with our efforts at growing as "wildflowers"—simply growing and promoting the good and beauty of peace in a wonky world?

PROMPT 4:
Prayer: Breathing in a Sanctuary of Solitude

"Listen in silence, before Me..." (Isaiah 41:1/NIV)

---

[538] Matthew Joseph Thaddeus Stepanek *Hope Through Heartsongs*, (NY: Hyperion, 2002)

[539] *Private Writings*, 67

"'Be still and know that I AM God..." (Psalm 46:10/NIV)

"(Prayer is) a place of sweet repose..." (John Climacus, The Ladder of Divine Ascent)

> *"In the silence, O God, I adore You*
> *In the stillness of naught but my trembling heart*
> *In the soft desperation of my fainting breath—my every gasp*
> *I am in wonder, silenced—in awe*
> *O Presence of all things—and of nothing— i am here...*
> *Here in the center of what was, what is, and the yet-to-be!"*[540]

"...but he (Jesus) would withdraw to deserted places to pray." (Luke 5:16/NAB).

This "deserted" or *lonely place* 'is more than a respite in religiosity. It is an attitude of solitude wherein we prepare the way of the Lord by lowering our fleshly defenses, remove the delusions of unqualified autonomy and become vulnerable to the Ultimate Love. It is a re-envisioning of our personhood before God, where fear of God is superseded by our *awe of* Him. As in our original innocence, when humanity could stand naked before a holy Creator, in this "lonely place," our true selves emerge from the core of our being. God breathes in us the "breath of life" and we arise, a revision of our false selves. This phenomenon begins in our ascension to the *lonely place* our "holy of holies", or innermost sanctuary of prayer.

Prayer recognizes the sovereignty of God in our lives and in all of creation. In the actualization of prayer, we learn to inhale and exhale the breath of God. In prayer we inhale, breathing God's presence to the very core of our being. Through prayer we exhale, through the flesh, the articulation of God's love for others. Prayer animates our lives and activates our devotion to a wonky world in need of redemption and reconciliation.

While researching his biography of Cistercian monk Thomas Merton, journalist John Howard Griffin (*Black Like Me*) became inclined to experience the wonders of Merton's spiritual pilgrimage for himself. He decided to sojourn to the monk's Hermitage at the Abbey of Gethsemani in rural Kentucky. The abode of Merton was a simple cinder block hut in the woods

---

[540] Brian Shoemaker, Journal (2011)

outside the Abbey. Griffin was awe struck by the inviting silence, the solitude, the soft chirping of birds, and the breeze through the trees. He was also impacted by the venue that seemed to woo him to a vulnerability; a surrender to prayer and to the presence of God. In *The Hermitage Journals*, a diary of his own spiritual reckoning, Griffin described his time alone in the loneliness and solitude of Merton's humble sanctuary:

> *I felt the deepest union with Christ in the silences. The deepest silence is necessary for us to hear the deepest of all music...the music of the rain falling steadily into the deep leaf mulch of the surrounding forests. The pure gift of God.*[541]

For Merton, prayer in silent contemplation regarded being mindful of two dynamics: 1) The raising of our thinking to God, and 2) the discovery of God within, thus in the course of which one discovers one's own true self, the realization that prayer always involves an entrance into mystery—"the mystery of a God we never can name."[542]

Entering into our sanctuary of silence, the "lonely place," or our inner "holy of holies," is the moment wherein we resolve to "cut out the outer to increase the inner."[543] Henri Nouwen called this moment "resting in fullest Presence,"[544] as a moment of pause in the midst of the monstrous cacophony of one's existence. This is the deeper consecration to a higher resolve of being wherein we pray: "give me a listening ear and the eye willing to see..."[545]

The pause of prayer enables us to reflect upon what has been created, what is being created, and envision in the present what is yet-to-be. Such devotion-in-communion with God, enlivens the soul and tames or guides the flesh. Bede Griffiths described this moment as a habit of mind which "enables the

---

[541] John Howard Griffin, *The Hermitage Journals* (Kansas City: Andrews & McMeel, Inc., 1981), 87-89

[542] *Prayer*, from *The Thomas Merton Encyclopedia*, ed. Shannon, Bochen, and O'Connell (Maryknoll, NY: Orbis, 1970), 364

[543] Matthew Kelty, *The Call of Wild Geese: Monastic Homilies* (Kalamazoo, Cistercian Publications, 1996), 14

[544] Henri Nouwen, *Beloved: In Conversation,* (Grand Rapids: Eerdmans, 2007), 6-7

[545] Howard Thurman, *A Strange Freedom: Religious Experience and Public Life* (Boston: Beacon Press, 1998)

soul to keep in a state of recollection in the Presence of God whatever may be the work with which we are occupied."[546]

Silence and the Efficiency of Prayer

> Prayer is like a ladder, with contemplative prayer as the topmost rung... [it is] awfully passive because you don't DO anything in it, you're [simply] in God's presence.[547]

Holocaust survivor and novelist, Elie Wiesel wrote:

> Prayer was meant to engage man and God in eternal dialogue. Thanks to prayer, we know that God is presence, and that everything is meaningful. God descends from heaven and dwells among his creatures. Thanks to prayer, man's soul lives in its dwelling and ascends to heaven. Prayer stems from the need to go under in order to emerge again, more serene than before, atoned and purified, more than before.[548]

For famed rabbi Abraham Joshua Heschel, the opportunity we have to pray is actually an invitation to God Himself. The interaction with God in prayer is the "KAVANAH," or the yielding of the entire being to the gathering of the soul into a complete turning toward God. It is the momentary disregard of our own personal concerns, the absence of self-centered thoughts and ambitions, "to simplify the self.[549]

Prayer is the intervention of eternity-in-time. Humanity may, with humility, wonder, and awe, enter into the "holy of holies" (one's core or true self) of one's bodily "temple of the Holy Spirit" (I Corinthians 6:19/NIV), and commune with God. In reverent solitude, with the listening ear of the soul, one may pause to bask in a mutual moment of holy communion. In fact, humanity has a remarkable capacity to do this. Emphasis on stillness and quiet in prayer flows from an appreciation of this innate spiritual capacity

---

[546] Bede Griffiths, *"The Golden String"* (Springfield, Illinois: Templegate, 1980), 148

[547] Peter Kreeft, *Prayer: The Great Conversation* (San Francisco: Ignatius Press, 1991), 124-129

[548] Elie Wiesel, *Why Pray,* from *Science and Theology News* (August 16, 2008), 1-2

[549] Abraham Joshua Heschel, *Man's Quest for God*, (Santa Fe, NM: Crossroad, 1983), 15

of every human being. Thus, prayer is simply being with God, "to feel his comradeship, his concern, his caring round me and about me, and then to go out to a world warmer because I spent an hour with him."[550]

It is here that I relinquish my *unbelief*. It is here, in communion with the irrefutable presence of God, I receive grace greater than my sin. I weep with agony for my contriteness, and the joy for God's reconciliation. In this moment I am completely vulnerable ("naked") before a holy God, from Whom nothing is hidden-- yet I am loved. Dorothy Day called this interaction with God and humanity "incidents in the realm of the supernatural, *sudden insights*, in recognition of Love amidst the abyss of nothingness. It is like falling in love. (emphasis added)."[551]

In this communion, i am both gasping in awe and resuscitated by God's breath. i envision myself as a *"living sacrifice...holy and acceptable." (Romans 12:1/NASB)*. Yet at the same time, like David in his Psalm, i ponder, *"what am i that Thou art mindful of me?" (Psalm 8:4/KJV)*. In this moment of breathing to the core of my being, i both fall on my face in humility before God and at the same i am *"lifted up as on eagle's wings!" (Exodus 19, Psalm 91, Isaiah 40:28-31/ NASB)*. While i have been blinded in the flesh, yet do i receive a discerning spiritual insight. In this lonely place, in this submission, i discover without question, "prayer is ecstasy."[552] (emphasis "i" intentionally added).

A Momentary Pause:

An excerpt from *The Prayer of Thomas Merton* (from Thoughts in Solitude, 1958):

> *I have no idea where I am going.*
> *I do not see the road ahead of me.*
> *I cannot know for certain where it will end.*
> *and the fact that I think I am following Your will*
> *does not mean that I am actually doing so.*
> *But I believe that the desire to please You*
> *does in fact please You.*

---

[550] Barclay, *Autobiography*, Ibid., 47

[551] Dorothy Day, *Adventures in Prayer*, from *Selected Writings*, ed. Robert Ellsberg (New York: Alfred A. Knopf, 1983) 183

[552] Heschel, *Man's Quest for God*, Ibid., 15

PROMPT 5:
Guided to Exploration and Freedom from Delusions

"The LORD had said to Abram, 'Go from your country, your people and your father's household to the land I will show you.'" (Genesis 12:1/NIV)

"Teach me your ways, O Lord, show me Your paths..." (Psalm 25:4; 86:11/NRSV)

"'Take my yoke upon you and learn of me...'" (Matthew 11:29/NIV)

"I am only a child playing on the beach, while vast oceans of truth lie undiscovered before me".[553]

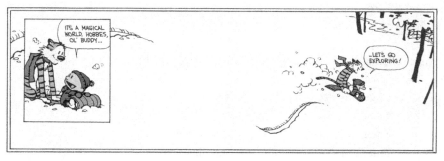

[554]

Learning is not just for the sake of gathering of facts or mechanical information, but also for our growing as mature human beings. Our innate

---

[553] Isaac Newton, *Mathematical Principles of Natural Philosophy*, 1687
[554] *Calvin and Hobbes* c.1995 Watterson. Reprinted w/permission of Andrews McMeel Syndication

curiosity and quests for truth enable humanity in the dispelling of delusions, popular mirages and religious superstition. This is a purpose for which humanity is capable: to distinguish truth from falsehood, fact from fiction. This distinction is possible and admonished in scripture: *"you shall know the truth and the truth shall make you free!" (John 8:32/NASB).*

In pursuit of what is *true*, the most devoted sojourner must be willing to consider what is intuitively, rationally, and insightfully legitimate. No information proven as factual should ever be a threat to one who is exploring for truth. Any legitimate knowledge may prove to be a source to better understand both *how* and *why* life works. While education is essential in learning the *hows* of existence, enlightenment is important in the understanding of the *whys* of life. Of such is the discipline of learning required in the dispelling of delusions.

Inaccurate thinking and belief disturbances are preludes to delusion. Superstitious rhetoric that has no positive consequence, can even be destructive if not thoroughly explored and adequately exposed. Once legitimized by the intuitive questions, rational evidence and in the light of revelation, knowing the truth can set one free from delusional thinking in the form of both scientific xenophobia and religious fanaticism and the negative wonkiness they promote.

Breaking free from delusions, or the "enchanted mist,"[555] of cleverly designed marketing ploys or commercialized cure-alls, may be painful in the moment, but essential for ascending to the comprehensiveness of both the material and the ethereal. Exploring for truth, uncontaminated by shallow, superficial, or faddish hokum is a noble exploration. Learning to dispel delusional thinking, the frenzy of fanatical religious rhetoric and the biases of scientific fallacies is a purpose for being. We must learn to discern what is realistic, healthy, informative and progressive in understanding the fullness of creation and the potentialities for humanity. Delusions can diminish the fullness, potential and purpose of our human existence: to learn and to grow.

The Beavercreek Christian Bookstore

My parents had me baptized as a baby in the Fairmont Presbyterian Church in Kettering, Ohio. Later, for some degree of compromise between them,

---

[555] Barclay, *Autobiography,* Ibid., 34

I was semi-raised into a belief in God through randomly attending David's United Church of Christ, just down the road from the Presbyterian Church. My mother's family had a history as founding members of the UCC before it united with other like-minded congregations. While in its history, David's had its roots in a German Reformed tradition, calling itself in 1934, David's Evangelical and Reformed Church, in 1957, the church joined with the Congregational Christian Churches of the United States, thus forming the United Church of Christ. This blend included historical dabbling influenced by Methodists, Congregationalists, Baptists, and Presbyterians. But as the church grew from the cultural of the 1960s and 70's, it became more and more distant from its evangelical roots, and into what the members proudly define today as a "progressive Christian community," with the motto: "Jesus didn't turn people away. Neither do we."

It was in the 1970's, as a teenager, that I began searching for my own faith. I was not inspired by the polity or the liturgy in the UCC, and began my own quest for God. It was in 1971 that I attended a youth rally for Christ at the First Baptist Church of Kettering, Ohio. The enthusiasm I saw when I entered the building was jolting, a far cry from the more reverent and dark atmosphere of the church from which I had rejected. With over 1,200 teens in attendance, more contemporary music, testimonies from my peers, and a charismatic, former-salesman as a preacher, I was immediately drawn into the venue and its message.

On that Saturday, February 13, 1971, I was "saved." At least that's what the counselor at the front of the church told me after I walked the aisle during the singing of the invitational hymn, "Just As I Am, without one plea." I walked up one aisle, while at the same time, my older brother, Rick was walking up the aisle parallel with me. Neither of us was aware that the other was in the building or even had an interest in the rally. I was told that all I had to do to be "saved," from Hell and be assured of a "home in Heaven," was to pray for forgiveness and ask Jesus into my life. My brother and I repeated the prayer as it was dictated to us by our counselor who met us at the altar. Many others walked forward for either first time salvation or to re-dedicate their lives to Christ.

The prayer we prayed was something like this: *"Dear Lord Jesus. Forgive me of my sins. And cleanse my soul of all unrighteousness. I accept you, Lord Jesus, as my only Savior, and my only hope of a home in Heaven. Thank you, Lord Jesus, for dying for me, and help me now to live for you. Amen."* And, so, according to our counselor (who was actually a neighbor who lived two doors down from our house) I was "saved," or "born again." That was all there was to it...or so I was told at this point.

After the service, we were called to stand before the Chaplain of Bourbon Street to gain more instruction regarding what we were to DO now. Bob Harrington admonished us "this step of faith will not solve all our problems overnight." Satan would now try to spoil the work that God wanted to do in our lives. He would lie to us and try to destroy us. So, we must do those things that would overcome his temptations in our lives, such as taking full part in the activities of a Gospel-preaching, Bible-believing church, supporting the minister and others in ministry with our prayers and by being generous with our money, and, most importantly, by learning how to "use God's word."

It was an exhilarating time in my young life! The enthusiasm of both my brother, Rick and I became contagious within my family and inner circle of friends. Rick and I took this experience seriously, sharing tracts and our testimonies about our conversion experience in our neighborhood and at school, with some success and by way of some persecution as well.

After being baptized together, my family formally joined the First Baptist Church and involved ourselves in the inner working of the church programs. It was at this time, that I grew hungry for knowledge about my new found faith. I also needed a Bible, a REAL Bible, not the Revised Standard Version I purchased for twenty-five cents at a garage sale in my neighborhood. I was told that Bible was a horrid mistranslation of God's word, for it either "added to" or "took away from" the original language of the Bible as articulated only by the King James Version of the text.

I was told by a deacon in the church that I could find a REAL Bible at the Christian Bookstore in Beavercreek, just twenty minutes from our home. When my grandparents heard that my brother and I both needed Bibles, they took us to choose one. While there were varied styles and designs to choose from, all were in the King James Version. I chose a small, more compact one, bound in brown leather. Later I would get some of the more influential preachers and singers I met on my revivalist trail to autograph the inside cover of my Bible for me. This included Harrington, his singer, Jack Price, Rex Humbard, pastor of the mega-Cathedral of Tomorrow in Akron, Ohio, the fiery pulpiteer of the renowned sermon, *"Pay Day, Some Day,"* R. G. Lee, country gospel quartets, and the songs of Bill Gaither.

The owners of the Beavercreek Christian Bookstore were always rather stoic and business like. Although they liked us as "Baptists" and regular customers, they themselves, were more Pentecostal and seemed to be more knowledgeable about spiritual matters, not only because we were new to the faith, but because we were not Pentecostal like them. At times, I was uncomfortable with their demeanor. Still, whenever Rick or I wanted to read something that would enable us to grow in our faith, we would go to that particular bookstore for recommended resources.

A few years after I had begun my years at Cumberland College, on leave for Christmas break, I returned to the store to return an album my mother had purchased for me there. It was a recording by Sandy Patti. Since I was more a connoisseur of country gospel music, I wanted to exchange it. When I placed the Patti album on the counter, the manager of the store actually grimaced at the sight of it.

"Sorry," he said, "but we can't take this back."

I responded, "My mom bought it here for me. I haven't opened it or played it. It's still in the plastic wrap. I just want to exchange it."

"Well, son," he began, "I'm not sure you even got this here. See, we don't sell anything by Sandy Patti anymore. We took all her music off our shelves a long time ago. So I can't take this back even if your mom DID get it here."

"Sir?" I asked, inquiring for more information.

"She's divorced!" the manager exclaimed. "She got a divorce! God hates divorce! I won't sell her music anymore nor will I keep it in my store. Sorry, but I don't really know if your mom bought it here, and even so, I wouldn't have it around my store. That's IT for Sandi Patty!"

I had not heard that Sandy Patti had gotten a divorce. Nor as a young Christian acquainted with the unmerited favor of God's grace, did I understand that because of that horrible event, she was now disqualified to sing songs of praise to Jesus. Somehow, situations like this were surreal, not at all in keeping with what I had been guided to believe—that *"old time religion makes me love everybody."*

I left with the album in my hand and the painful dispelling in my head of the delusion that all Christians are honest and loving; that somehow, God's grace does prevail in the hearts of His own people. I never returned to that bookstore. Some years later, the store went out of business and the space was sold to become an arts and crafts facility.

The challenge for many in the church is in growing mature enough to distinguish between loving behavior that is transformational toward spiritual well-being in community and what is frenzy, a raw fanaticism that disfigures the church and does not truly save anyone. The strong convictions of the later, in its own respective context, may look to a few to be a legitimate proclamation of the gospel, but that of a delusion from which those adherents themselves must be saved. I have grown to believe that such lame religion is based not upon the foundation of sacred wisdom, but on delusions ignited by selective indoctrination.

Can Science Answer the Ultimate Questions: My Brief Debate with Mr. Judd

While attending Fairmont East High School, my brother Rick and I were inclined to share our faith experience without apology or intimidation. We even carried our Bibles to class every day. Mine was stuffed with tracts addressing everything from the "4 Spiritual Laws" of how to get to Heaven, to how to read the Bible, to how to tithe one's income. Not being biblical theologians, we just shared our "born again" experience as if it was common knowledge to everyone else but us. When we discovered that others had not heard about such an experience, we shared with them our experience, not to judge anyone else, but to offer to them the same joy that we had experienced.

In 1972, the youth groups from the Greater Dayton Association of Baptists united to hold a "Purpose for Life Crusade" for the area teens. The churches rented the high school auditorium for the week long event, and together, we promoted the event through a media blitz, a parade around the city, and a "ONE WAY: JESUS" march from the First Baptist Church of Kettering to the High School. (Our march even made the front page of the Dayton Daily News.)

Contemporary music was offered and Rick preached his first sermons every night of the crusade. I served as a counselor for those peers who might come to "accept Jesus as their Savior" during the invitation or altar call. In fact, many did take advantage of this opportunity to do so, and it caused an uproar in the hallways of the high school throughout the week: "kids were coming to Christ through kids!"

Mr. Judd was a larger-than-life teacher of social studies, with a mix of sociology. He was well known for putting students on the spot in discussing politics; he himself, being quite opinionated.

Although my brother had had him for class, I never did. Still, when it came to knowing the student body by name and reputation, Mr. Judd had everyone pegged. He was an avowed atheist, holding to the notion that it would be through science and not religion that humanity would find the "theory of everything," through which all things would be made known, and so, humanity could be saved, or perfected. He had no tolerance for anything of a religious conviction.

Toward the end of the Purpose for Life Crusade, between classes, Mr. Judd met me in the hallway. "Hey. You're a Shoemaker, right?" he sounded.

"Yes, sir. I'm Brian."

"I know your brother, Rick." He responded. "He's the preacher for this Crusade thing? Are you in that stuff too?" I nodded.

"Well, I have a question for you." he said.

I remembered growing nervous, not being a theologian, I didn't feel prepared for this test. But I said, "OK."

Then came his fascinating inquiry, "What is the most profound question in the Bible?"

I thought for a moment and answered, "'What must I do to be saved?'"

Mr. Judd smiled and said, "That's a good one, but that's not the one I was thinking of. The most profound question is 'what is truth?'"

I smiled back and responded, "Sir, if you get my first question right, you might get your question answered too."

The late bell rang. We both had to get to class. Before he walked away, he remarked abruptly, "It's all about science, Brian. Religion causes war."

I was only in my mid-teens, but I knew even then, that it is a delusion to think that science can ever find an answer to Mr. Judd's first question. This is especially so, when atheistic minds refuse to consider the capacity of human beings for insight and the transformative influence of legitimate religion, or the presence of a Greater Reality in their lives.

Some very intelligent persons, like Mr. Judd, are more willing to sustain their delusions, ignited by scientifically-driven concepts in a "closed universe" than to be challenged by the evidence or possibility of deeper insight. As fact is driven by data, truth is revealed through insight! Just as religion should not cower before facts, neither should science cringe and walk away from legitimate and fascinating questions.

How can we know if one is sustaining a delusion?

A delusion can be defined as a challenge toward distinguishing between what is real and what only seems to be real, (often as the result of a disorganized process or prejudice of thought). Delusional thinking can be the unfortunate result of a lack of a full, legitimate education, confining oneself within a setting secluded from a broader worldview, or indoctrination without relevant inquiry and insight.

When in an unhealthy confrontation with each other, theists and atheists tend to raise walls of delusion to defend their views, rather than to dispel them for the sake of what is true. Neither the theist or atheist should be threatened by the fascinating questions we have as human beings. Such intuitive activity offers hope for the answers we might discover for the sake of the continuum of a good creation.

For the devoted theist, a sovereign God is not threatened by our sincerest inquiries and exploration. We are admonished to ask God questions, and may do so, without *questioning* God. *"If anyone of you lacks wisdom, let him ask God, who gives generously and without criticism, it will be given." (James 1:5/NASB).* Neither is God bound by proscriptions of scientific thought. True knowledge of God is open to, and able to stand against the harshest intellectual scrutiny. We are invited to delve into *the "depths of God"* (I Corinthians 2:10/NRSV), not only for personal edification, but also for dispelling delusions about God's proactivity in the cosmos. The prophet said, *"Come now, let us reason together." (Isaiah 1:18/NRSV/emphasis added).*

Legitimate knowledge of a consummate reality is not restricted to denominational indoctrination or pseudo-scientific instruction. From a theistic perspective, in the genius of God, exploration into scientific inquiry, social psychology, genetics, neuroscience, moral development, and educational ascents in the humanities, all have something to say about the human condition and *how life works.* Such an exploration is a purpose for humanity that includes both seeking empirical facts, or for the theist, seeking an informed faith. Sociologist Georg Simmel concluded that what makes a person religious is the particular way in which he responds to life in all its aspects or fullness. In this case, both "religiosity and science are able to perceive and interpret life in its entirety."[556]

Thus, the delusion of an intellectual prognostication being in a natural conflict with a spiritual ascent may eradicated. No legitimate *learning* should pose a threat to theism or should an informed faith ascent disturb an honest atheist. No legitimate revelation should threaten science. Exploring life through all available disciplines, for the sake of dispelling delusions, offers revealed knowledge that enables our BE-Living.

---

[556] George Simmel, *Essays on Religion,* Ibid., 5-6

Revealed knowledge should be in synchronization with legitimized education. Through an informed faith, one breaks from delusional thinking "to a training of latent faculties, a brightening of languid consciousness, an emancipation from the fetters of appearance, and a turning of attention to new levels of the world."[557] More than industrial education or sacrosanct indoctrination, humanity has the capacity to *learn* to be who we were designed to be. This insight begins with an insatiable curiosity, a zeal for truth and breaking free from the "pack thinking"[558] that would subjugate humanity to survivalist urges, faddish claims, religio-political crusades, egomania or even self-loathing. Self-loathing may stem from one's believing the marketing strategies of the media. No one can really measure up to the airbrushed appearances and perfection of the most popular celebrities of the day. What we see on film is always in some way, a delusion. From the perspective of bad religion, self-loathing is a delusion prompted by embracing an anthropomorphically-projected God—one who is angry, spiteful and vengeful. A fascinating question: is God as Ultimate Love really sinful-- to be so full of rage and vengeance?

Exploration and learning are essential for dispelling delusions and discovering truth regarding the character and nature of God and ourselves. Is God fanning the flames of hell, awaiting judgment on a depraved humanity or is God preparing an abode, constantly creating moments of reconciliation with a broken and lost community? Perhaps God is continuing to call to an estranged humanity, rather than to create ways to condemn him?

> *Adam, where are you? Come into the Light,*
> *Through judgement is near, yet the promise is bright,*
> *For hope in the darkness continues to gleam:*
> *God walks in the garden with the power to redeem.*
>
> *Adam, where are you? Come answer the call;*
> *The hope of redemption comes after the fall.*
> *The Spirit of wholeness, where chaos is rife,*
> *Is calling creation to renewal and life.*[559]

---

[557] Evelyn Underhill, *What is Mysticism?* from *Writings: Practical Mysticism: A Little Book for Normal People* (NY: Vintage, 2003), 16-17

[558] Wayne E. Oates, *The Struggle to be Free* (Louisville: Oates Institute, 2008), 52-70

[559] *Adam, Where Are You*, a Celtic Hymn composed by Michael Forster (1998)

The story of the "fall" of humanity, symbolized by the first couple succumbing to sudden estrangement from God's presence is one from which most doctrines of redemption begin. From here the story of a sinful and condemned humanity originates. Many perspectives and interpretations of a totally depraved human nature via original sin are interpreted through the second, third and fourth chapters of Genesis. Whether the story be precise history or poetic histrionics, interpretations of the narrative of Adam and Eve confronted by a crafty and articulate serpent in the garden of Eden, and the consequences of that encounter, seem to be at the core of our quandaries toward a humanity behaving both good and bad. We are ever being challenged by those significant chapters in Genesis and what they reveal about God and humanity.

In original innocence humanity was created in Hebrew *BARA, or* "very good." Humanity has innately the capacity for what is "true, honest, just, pure, lovely, virtuous, and worthy of praise." (Philippians 4:8/NRSV). Through our original innocence we strive toward the actualization of *moral imperatives*. However, in our chosen way of unqualified autonomy in a permissive promiscuous culture, we are enticed toward superficiality and megalomania: the worship of the self with the sacred icon of the *selfie*.

We actually can become delusional to believe that we can be "as gods." In other words, if left alone to our own devising, we would create God in our own image, or displace God in the cosmos with the likeness of ourselves. But we are not left to our own devising because we are not *totally* depraved, nor out of the reach of Ultimate Love. We may yet hear the still, small voice of a pursuing God.

A Momentary Pause:

<u>**Breaking Free of Delusional Notions of an Angry God**</u>

After Adam and Eve *did* whatever it was that prompted them to try to hide themselves away, God, "while walking in the garden in the cool of the day...called out to them," and asked them three questions. These questions grasp us to the core of our personhood as human beings. Perhaps if we were to *learn* the answers to these questions, we might come to a healthier perspective of our humanity—with ourselves, one another, and with God. Perhaps in answering these questions we might also dispel the delusions that keep us hiding our true selves away from the One who seeks only to redeem us.

1. **"Where are YOU?"** (Genesis 3:9/ RSV). Not <u>WHERE</u> are you—but where are <u>YOU</u>? Where is Adam? Where is Eve? Where are the persons so lovingly and intricately designed by the hand of God? In God's presence we were meant to be able to confess "Oh Lord God, here am I." But, subjected to a conniving distraction, they lost their true selves and the sense of an empathetic and loving God. He asked them to ponder, "Why are you hiding? Where is the Adam/ Eve who I created so wonderfully? And why would you hide that true self from Me?"

2. **"Who told you you were naked?"** (Genesis 3:11/ RSV). Who convinced them that they were not good enough in their vulnerability from God and one another? OR that God's provisions for their personhood were not enough for them to BE? Did they really have to alter themselves – or to re-create each other in any other Image? Note, it is was NOT God who told them that were insufficient in any way – or that the Garden was not a place from which they could meet all their needs. God's provisions for their personhood and basic needs would have offered them peace.

3. **"What have you done?"** (Genesis 3:13/ RSV). What did they do? They were educated or indoctrinated by a source that convinced them that they were *lacking good-enoughness*. They believed they had to re-create themselves, and rather than to tend the garden, they used it as a place to hide themselves away. Once they de-valued themselves and one another, they are "cast" from the garden *or their original innocence,* from which they may never return. But the message of God, is revealed in the question: "What have you done? [with the implication]: that could separate us from God's presence of His love?

Delusions are like shadows. We may even hide within them. They are, at best, facsimiles of the truth. Delusions of both self-grandeur and self-loathing cease in the articulation of God's presence. The shadows in which we try to hide our true selves dissipate with the questions, *"Where are YOU?" "Who told* you were naked?" and "What have you done that could possibly separate you from God's love?" We are wooed to come out from the shadows of our existence, our delusions, from wherever we may be hiding.

In spite of endless scientific theorizing, superstitious hokum, relio-political rhetoric, or intellectual egomania, it is still the truth that *sets us free* from our delusions-- when we come out of the *"nothing but a shadow-glory,"*[560] and walk in the brilliance of light from Light.

Breaking Free of Delusions of an Autonomous Science: "Pseudoscience"[561]

> *Although we live under the shadow of unfamiliar and potentially catastrophic hazards, there seems to be no scientific impediment to achieving a safe and secure world. We can be technological optimists, even though the balance of effort in technology needs redirection. Risks can be minimized by a culture of 'responsible innovation.'*[562]

Only decades prior to the inauguration of Woodrow Wilson as President of the United States in 1902, the scientific community had made great advances in discovery and technology. Johann Wilhelm discovered ultra-violet rays (1801), James Joule, the "first law of Thermodynamics" (1843), Hippolyte Fizeau measured the speed of light with his interferometer (1849), the Curies discovered radioactivity and Eduard Buchner discovered enzymes (1896). Charles Darwin espoused his theory of evolution in *The Origin of Species* in 1859. All of which were intended to advance human thinking and dispel delusions of both bad religion and inaccurate science.

During his inaugural address, Woodrow Wilson, a deeply religious man who "saw God's hand in the destiny of humanity and advancements in the intellect as the progress of the soul,"[563] affirmed the potential of scientific inquiry for the future of mankind. He asserted:

---

[560] *The Shadows*, taken from *The Complete Fairy Tales*, George MacDonald, 1824-1905
[561] Kurt Vonnegut, from a speech at Bennington College, 1970
[562] Martin Rees, *On the Future*, Ibid., 225
[563] Woodrow Wilson, *Essential Writings and Speeches of the Scholar-President* ed. Mario R. Dinunzio (NY: University Press,2006), 41

Science has opened a new world of learning. The influence of science has broadened and all the boundaries of knowledge are altered. An age of science has transmuted speculation into knowledge and doubled the dominion of the mind.[564]

While scientific inquiry is intended to be an expression of objective principles for the understanding of humanity and the cosmos, it is a delusion to think that all such exploration is unbiased, or with complete objectivity. While advances in medicine, technology, communication, and general investigation are intentionally good, there is also the potential for the non-good within the latitude of scientific exploration. The idea that science alone is the cure for all the maladies humanity faces can be just as delusional as rank superstition in the realm of religiosity.

Only years after Wilson's speech in 1902, the scientific community not only advanced in the development of synthetic rubber, ultrasound and radio technology, but also in the establishment and precedent of the thriving manufacture of sophisticated weapons of warfare. Due to the reality of World War I, from 1915 to 1916 alone, technological advances with the assistance of the scientific community included flamethrowers, poison gas, phosphorescent bullets and depth charges. The means for the *survival of the fittest* or a mindset of *natural selection* for national security became an all-encompassing focus for the scientific community in their quest not only for discovery, but for the sake of tribal warfare with minimal regard for the geo-political, environmental, and psychological fallout thereafter.

Science is not the cure-all for a lost humanity. It can become one of the root causes, *if* in its stoic objectivity, scientific inquiry moves, unfiltered by empathy or concern for the well-being of persons in community. Science certainly has its place in community, but it is only one path of exploration toward a fuller understanding of human beings and the cosmos.

Edward Teller, quantum theorist, astrophysicist, and the developer of thermonuclear energy--*the nuclear bomb*--warned that science must study ideas that challenge established paradigms, yet recognize what has been proven true. The task of the scientist is to fit these ideas into the larger

---

[564] Woodrow Wilson, *"On Education and Scholarship" Writings and Speeches*, Ibid.,125

framework of the cosmos. But there are other essential disciplines for knowledge, exploration and discovery as well. Politics considers what is right. Art is the development of what is beautiful—whether through words, a musical note, or architecture. Truth, morality, and beauty are somehow aligned with a spiritual sensitivity. It has been humanity's persistent hope that "these ideals should be consistent with each other. [565]

Our contemporary culture sometimes markets our lostness through overrated hype of self-importance, the hoopla of a commercialized society, and the mass hysteria of materialism. We exist in a world not only of delusions, a world of fantasy, making up our own matrix of reality. In a recent interview, poet and Nobel Peace Prize laureate, Bob Dylan warned that our technologically-driven culture, has created "a science-fiction world, a world that Disney has conquered. Disney is science fiction. Theme parks. Trendy streets. It's all science fiction. Whether we've realized it or not, it is."[566]

If humanity is to dispel delusional thinking, we must first admit that our autonomy is *qualified*. Perhaps the ultimate delusion of all is we can be as gods, without consequences to our personal and community choices. We are not *all that,* but we are an integral part of *all that is.* As we live responsive to God, and responsibly before God, we also must determine a direction in our lives toward meaningful learning and purposeful living. Meaningful learning means to explore the many dynamics of both *how* and *why* life works for the sake of understanding a comprehensive reality. Purposeful living regards the exploration for the ways and means of tending to the garden of our ecosystem (not our ego-system), to the well-being of persons, and fulfilling the epiphany of a just peace in the world. We must learn to dispel delusions for the sake of becoming the persons we are designed to be. Neither science or religion should be threatened by new thoughts or higher knowledge in the quest toward understanding the fullness of reality. The well-being of humanity demands such exploration. The inevitable discovery of such exploration is truth. In this exploration for truth, God mercifully provides for us the capacity for such an arduous journey.

---

[565] *Science and Morality, Science,* 22 May 1998 Vol. 280, Issue 5367, 1200-1201
[566] *Dylan on Dylan: Interviews and Encounters,* ed. Jeff Burger (Chicago: Review Press, 2018), 423

"You shall also love the stranger..." (Deuteronomy 10:11/NRSV).
"The steadfast love of the Lord never ceases; his mercies never come to an end"
(Lamentations 3:22-23/NRSV).
"neither do I condemn you..." (John 8:11/NRSV).
"and the grace of our Lord overflowed for me..." (I Timothy 1:12-17/NRSV).
"...grace all the more abounds..." (Romans 5:20/NIV).
"Great is the Lord beyond the borders of Israel." (Malachi 1:5/NRSV).

God's grace is the application of His *"love and tender mercies" (Psalm 103:4/ESV)* to even the *"worst of sinners."*[567] *(Timothy 1:15/ESV).* The embrace of Ultimate Love is extended and lingers near us, despite our delusions, arrogance, and apathy. God's grace pursues those who are *lost*, hiding in the shadows, or *"like sheep have wandered away, each to his own way." (Isaiah 53:6/NRSV).*

Grace is the actualization of God's tender mercy. Grace would not be "grace" if God's mercy required anything we could *do* to merit or achieve it. Such mercy is not dependent upon our achieving or conscripting to a religious formula, it is simply a threshold of opportunity to receive from God what cannot ever be earned. Barclay wrote, "grace is not a thing of narrow limitations. 'Grace needs no supplement.'"[568]

This unearned embrace is the redemptive, life-giving articulation of Ultimate Love. Grace is the insightful dynamic that gathers persons together in "awareness of its boundlessness."[569] The unmerited favor of God, which "cannot be produced but is a given,"[570] sensitizes us to God's mercy and awakens the soul a momentum toward the redemption of persons. Thus, the purpose underlying God's *judgment*, or the recompense for evil, is not condemnation, but reconciliation, *"not to condemn the world, but to save the world." (John 3:17/NIV).* Our response to grace is reciprocation. We become agents for redemption, rather than henchmen of retribution.

---

[567] John Bunyan, 1666
[568] William Barclay, *The Mind of St. Paul* (NY: Harper and Row, 1958), 63
[569] Joachim Jeremias, *New Testament Theology* (NY: Charles Scribner's Sons, 1971), 178
[570] Tillich, *Systematic Theology*, Vol III (Chicago: University Press), 211

"Blessed are the merciful" (Matthew 5:7/KJV) implies it is the person who does not *deserve* mercy, who is offered mercy and forgiveness, because of the grace offered by Ultimate Love. While grace humbles and disciplines wayward persons from the soul where transformation occurs, vengeance humiliates and punishes the flesh, where resentment remains.

No human achievement, however valuable, merits God's favor. If anything could achieve the mercy God provides, "grace would cease to be grace."[571] By grace, God proactively pursues a lost humanity as a parent unceasingly keeps watch for a wayward child to come home. Not because of the child's merits, but because of God's magnanimous love that *"does not keep account of wrongdoings." (I Corinthians 13:5/NRSV)*. God's grace is "infinitely elegant."[572]

If *"God is not willing that any should perish" (2 Peter 3:9/NAB)*, grace cannot be measured by either our legalistic dogma, stunted by the worst of human depravity, or limited to one's ignorance or lifetime. Even in the heinous crucifixion of Jesus, he himself prayed *"forgive them." (Luke 23:24/NIV)*. In this comprehensive prayer, *we all are "them."* John Polkinghorne wrote that no human being is *ever* outside the mercy of God. Grace, as defined through Ultimate Love, is not an offer for a limited period of time: "I do not think everyone's eternal destiny is fixed at death.[573] This articulation of God's love must never be limited by those who are recipients of God's grace themselves.

Fascinating questions remain: did God answer the prayer of Jesus at the cross—to forgive? Could this grace ever cease-- even after death? Does God ever give up on His redemptive purpose that *"not wanting any one to perish?" (2 Peter 3:9/ESV)*; particularly if "the mercy of God knows no limits."[574] Did God answer the prayer of Jesus in the midst of one of the worst expressions of human depravity in history? Can humanity trust God's grace as *"sufficient"* (*II Corinthians 12:9/NIV*) as an application of how He *"so loved the world?"* (*John 3:16/NIV*).

---

[571] Gustavo Gutierrez, *The God of Life*, (Maryknoll, NY: Orbis, 1991), 163

[572] *St. John of the Cross, The Ascent of Mount Carmel*, Book One, Chapter 4

[573] John Polkinghorne and Nicholas Beale, *Questions of Truth* (Louisville: John Knox, 2009), 91-94

[574] Guttierrez, *The God of Life Ibid.*, 186

The following are essential dynamics to grace, actualized through what Charles Spurgeon called God's "world-embracing love," a love that springs from Himself, because it is more than a dogma, it is His nature. *(Sermon: John 3:16)*. Grace is a dynamic to Ultimate Love that *"never fails." (I Corinthians 13:8/NIV)*.

1.   God's grace is *Imaginative*

God romantically and creatively woos all of creation into reconciliation and a redemption wherein *"all things shall be made new."* By God's grace, one may discern an imaginative way out of no way, and the liberation from our lostness. Whether it be by way of a "stone pillow," "imprisoned in the belly of whale," or "wallowing in a hog pen," God's is imaginative in how He alerts persons in crisis toward a path to His Presence.

John Newton, composer of the traditional hymn *Amazing Grace,* believed God awakens us to our lostness by His love—in allowing humanity to reach the end of their self-inflicted autonomy. Through the consequences of our choices, we may recognize that our very "desire of grace is actual grace."[575]

Newton was born in London in 1725, the son of commander of a merchant ship. In his early life, after deserting the "intolerable" conditions aboard a man-of-war vessel, he was captured, publicly flogged, and demoted from a midshipman to a common seaman.

Later he was transferred to a filthy slave ship. This ship took him aboard merchant ventures around Sierra Leone. In his book, *Out of the Depths,* Newton relayed that as the servant of a slave trader, he was often brutally abused. He eventually escaped, only thereafter after to be given command of another horrendous slave ship.

---

[575]   *Letters* (Edinburgh: Banner of Truth, 2007) 200

While his mother gave John some basic religious instruction throughout his childhood, after her untimely death, he gave up any religiosity. It was not until the crisis of a sudden and violent storm around the horn of Africa, that he experienced what he called, his "great deliverance." In documenting this terrifying experience, Newton journaled his wayward plea, "Lord, have mercy..." and from those lines came poetic lyric: *through many dangers, toils, and snares, I have already come. Tis grace hath brought me safe thus far, and grace will lead me home.*

God's *"grace is sufficient...perfected in weakness."* (II Corinthians 12:9/NASB). Even in the mishaps and blunders of human chicanery, such "interruptions turn out to be God's opportunities"[576] for humanity to learn repentance and the amazing grace of a merciful and loving God. The Franciscan monk, Bonaventure, wrote, "...the more God-like the soul becomes by grace, the more clearly it sees the truth of things." When our feelings, thoughts, and emotions are rightly ordered to God, then we start to live in a new, virtuous way of life. Bonaventure believed in an intimacy with God formed with rational thought and refined through an intimacy with God through His grace; a mystical union which cannot be explained by reason alone. God enlightens with knowledge and insight, and inspires all humanity to grow in grace! [577]

2. God's grace is *Immutable.*

Jesus reminded those with an ear to listen: *"heaven and earth may pass away, but my words shall not pass away." (Matthew 24:35/NASB).* As the *"Alpha and the Omega...the beginning and the end" (Revelation 1:8; 21:6; 22:13/NASB),* God ignited creation into existence, and moves creation-by-creation toward an end with a beginning and another ends with beginnings. In the worst-case scenario of human wonkiness, God will never allow an end without a new beginning. God oversees the perceived lost causes of human autonomy, and

---

[576] E. Glenn Hinson, *Miracle of Grace* (Macon, Georgia: Mercer University Press, 2012), 376

[577] Bonaventure, *The Soul's Journey to God,* 1260

shall continue to reveal the way to new life known, by grace, until (as quoted by English mystic Julian of Norwich), God articulates to those with a listening ear: that He will make "all things well."[578]

God is not only the God of second chances, but also the God of lost causes. The One who *"never sleeps nor slumbers" (Psalm 121:4/NRSV)* will not be silenced. *(Psalm 50:3; Isaiah 62:1).* Out of the din and the depths of human despair, someone will hear and heed "His" voice, even the wayward one who is lost. There is no noise so loud as to overcome the still, small voice of God for the one who lends an ear to listen. God never ceases to speak to humanity for the sake that someone will listen.

In the classic film *Mr. Smith Goes to Washington* (1939), freshman Senator Jefferson Smith refuses to be silenced by the power brokers in a self-serving, political system in the Capitol. He stands for hours speaking out for a redemptive purpose. But his voice seems to be muted by the clamor of his misguided and corrupted colleagues all around him. Still, because of his passion to redeem the lost cause, he would not capitulate to the clamor. The young Senator spoke for hour upon hour, believing that someone would eventually listen, even the most corrupt legislator of all, Senator Joseph Paine, who, before he became corrupted, fought for those under the label of being the "lost cause."

they are the only causes worth fighting for.. For the only reason any man fights for them. Because of one plain simple rule: Love thy neighbor. And in this world today of great hatred, a man who knows that rule has a great trust. You think I'm licked. Well I'm not licked. And I'm gonna stay right here and fight for this lost cause. Even if this room gets filled with lies ...SOMEBODY WILL LISTEN TO ME.[579]

---

[578] Julian of Norwich, *Showings*, 1373
[579] Sydney Buchanan (Screenwriter) and Lewis R. Foster (Author) *Mr. Smith Goes to Washington (Columbia Pictures, 1939)*

God's grace is immutable. He will not be "licked." Like Jefferson Smith, God is "gonna stay right her and fight for the lost cause," even the "one lost sheep who has gone astray." Why? Because "God so loved the world. (John 3:16/ NIV). In the clamorous wonky in our existence, the articulation of God's wooing is every-discernable in the message of redemption, *especially for the lost cause.* God's grace affirms there are no lost causes for whom He is not willing to pursue.

3. <u>God's grace is Immeasurable</u>

> *It is the Christian God who first extended His realm to include both those who believe in Him and those who do not. He is the God of the unfaithful as well...the divine principle allows for a diversity of paths by which to reach this one and only God.*[580]

God's very nature is redemptive. His grace is derived from an eternal love that the great preacher Charles Spurgeon described as an "eternal spring bursting forth from the very throne of grace!"[581] Or as the Apostle Paul wrote to the church in Corinth, grace is evidence of a *love that "never fails."* (I Corinthians 13:8/NAB).

The grace of God is dynamic, it is not static. There is no measure to a grace that overcomes human depravity. God's grace flows even in the swell of evil. God is imaginative in allowing the consequences of sinful behavior, "the one sows in the flesh shall from the flesh reap corruption." (Galatians 6:7/NASB). But the articulation of God's grace is also immutable, "for the grace of God has appeared that offers salvation to all people in this present age." (Titus 2:11-12/NRSV). Beyond all other concepts of God's interaction with humanity, God's "grace is sufficient" to engage every need and human mendacity, and to awaken humanity to redemption and reconciliation.

---

[580] *Simmel*, Ibid., 205
[581] Charles Spurgeon, *Exposition of John 3:16*

After more than fifty years of teaching Christian theology and spiritual formation, scholar E. Glenn Hinson of Mercer University wrote in his memoirs that the first lesson he has learned in a lifetime of devotion to his faith is that "life is grace, given to me more than planned, earned, or advanced by me. God's grace is sufficient, for God has chosen to share our vulnerability."[582]

Erudite preacher and pastor, Jeremy Taylor, wrote in 1650: "when we know Him with the eyes of holiness, and the intuition of GRACIOUS experience then we hear what we never heard and see what our eyes never saw; the mysteries of godliness shall be opened unto us, and clear for us the windows of the morning."[583]

Grace is a given from God to humanity. It is not physically earned, but is may be spiritually discerned through the awakening of insight in the soul. Igniting this insight was the message, ministry, and miracles of Jesus. Jesus who did not in any way put restrictions or limitations upon God's love, even for those who heinously put him to death. Thus, Jesus is the personification of God's imaginative, immutable, and immeasurable grace. He is the ultimate prompt toward the actualization of God's presence in the world.

---

[582] *Hinson,* Ibid., 374-375
[583] Jeremy Taylor *Works* 8:37

CHAPTER 5

Jesus: Grace Personified- and the Ultimate Prompt of God's Presence!

"Each generation has to wrestle afresh with the question of Jesus...that we should discover more and more of who Jesus was and is, precisely in order to be equipped to engage the world that he came to save."[584]

From the *"still small voice" (1 Kings 18:20-40; 19:12/NRSV)* of the Lord to the prophets, humanity has been offered glimpses of the Presence of God in the context of their history. In Jesus, we may *know* God's presence by a more direct reflection of "God with us" in word, thought, and deed. Through Jesus, humanity may grasp more definitively the God who would otherwise be only an enigmatic entity.

A Momentary Pause:

I believe in God. I BE-Live in Jesus. Through Jesus, I experience the reality that the judgment of God is intended for the purpose of reconciliation rather than revenge! New Testament scholar, William Barclay wrote: "In Jesus, there is the full revelation of the mind and heart of God."[585]

The following is in no way an exhaustive compendium of the significance and personhood of Jesus. It is intended to be a tipping point toward a deeper realization of God's Presence at a pivotal moment in history. More has been written about Jesus than could possibly be footnoted in this book. But what I will try to do is offer *intuitive questions* about Jesus, *rational evidence* for the significance of the life of Jesus in history, and a path toward the *realization* of his personhood. All of which provide one with a sense of the relevance of

---

[584] N. T. Wright, *The Challenge of Jesus* (Wheaton, ILL: Intervarsity Press, 1999), 31
[585] Barclay, *Autobiography*, 49-50

his message, mission, miracles and momentum in the world: *"to seek and to save that which was lost." (Matthew 18:11; Luke 19:10/NASB).*

Like billions of others in the world, in diverse geographical locations, and through the centuries, I am come to believe that Jesus is the ultimate prompt toward the actualization of God's presence in the world. He is the articulation of God's mindfulness and care for creation. By his words and deeds, Jesus becomes a vessel for the continuum of God's creative activity in the world. If we want to know what God is like, we look at Jesus. If we want to know what God intends to create, we look at Jesus. If we want to know what he wants from us, we look at Jesus as he fed the hungry, counseled the oppressed, walked alongside the friendless, touched the lepers and the outcasts, and offered to all humanity a path toward reconciliation with God.

In Jesus, I come to understand that God cares enough for humanity that He, Himself, enters into the human experience through the extraordinary rapport He has with, in, and through Jesus. Through Jesus, God gleans a deeper understanding and empathy *for* and *with* His creation. In some mystical way, God is exhilarated by our joys and is wounded by our pain, for, in Jesus, these transactions are actually experienced by God Himself. In Jesus, God (mystically) understands the experience of humanity. Likewise, in Jesus, humanity comes to comprehend the character and nature of God.

SECTION 1:
Did Jesus Exist?

"Jesus is a myth just like all the other saviors and gods of old..."[586]

"You know He didn't even exist. Jesus didn't exist until 325 with the Council of Nicaea..."[587]

---

[586] *The Bible and the Jesus Myth,* a tract of the American Atheist Association (Austin, Texas: April 1987), 7

[587] Madelyn Murray O'Hair to Reverend Bob Harrington Interview on the Phil Donahue Show (1970)

"Jesus most likely existed."[588]

In our contemporary culture, if Jesus existed at all, he is regarded by some, as merely a good teacher, a Messianic-wanna-be, or even a political zealot. Some project Jesus, if he existed at all, to be anyone from an intransigent judge of sinners to an egomaniacal lunatic, to a misbegotten martyr. All of which can be legitimately addressed by the narratives about Jesus in the New Testament and descriptions in extra-biblical writings of the movement of the benevolent, early church into the resistant Roman empire.

The following are later extra-biblical evidence for the existence of Jesus and the phenomenological emergence a movement called the church. This movement of those who sight to imitate the life and teachings of Jesus, give momentum to the legitimacy to the actual, historicity of Jesus of Nazareth. Such accounts from the following non-Christian sources lend credibility to, at least, the historicity of Jesus, if not his truest identity.

Josephus (A.D. 37 - c. A.D. 100)

Josephus' Antiquities (early 2nd century A.D.) refers to Jesus in two distinct passages. The common translation of the first passage, Book 18, Ch. 3, part 3:

> Now there arose at this time a source of further trouble in one Jesus, a wise man who performed surprising works, a teacher of men who gladly welcome strange things. He led away many Jews, and also many of the Gentiles. He was the so-called Christ. When Pilate, acting on information supplied by the chief men around us, condemned him to the cross, those who had attached themselves to him at first did not cease to cause trouble, and the tribe of Christians, which has taken this name from him is not extinct even today.

Tacitus (c. A.D. 55 - c. A.D. 117)

Annals, book XV:

> Christus, from whom the name had its origin, suffered the extreme penalty during the reign of Tiberius at the hands of

---

[588] Richard Dawkins, *The God Delusion* (NY: Houghton Mifflin, 2006), 122

one of our procurators, Pontius Pilatus, and a most mischievous superstition...

Julius Africanus (c. 160 - c. 240)

Chronography, XVIII refers to writings by Thallus and Phlegon concerning the time of the crucifixion of Jesus:

> *On the whole world there pressed a most fearful darkness; and the rocks were rent by an earthquake, and many places in Judea and other districts were thrown down. This darkness Thallus, in the third book of his History, calls, as appears to me without reason, an eclipse of the sun...Phlegon records that, in the time of Tiberius Caesar, at full moon, there was a full eclipse of the sun from the sixth hour to the ninth - manifestly that one of which we speak.*

Pliny the Younger (c. 62 - c. 113) to Emperor Trajan:

Letters, 10.96-97:

> *I have never participated in trials of Christians. I therefore do not know what offenses it is the practice to punish or investigate, and to what extent. They were accustomed to meet on a fixed day before dawn and sing responsively a hymn to Christ as to a god, and to bind themselves by oath. But I discovered nothing else but depraved, excessive superstition.*

A Momentary Pause:

Fascinating Questions: If Jesus did NOT exist, why is there something called the *EKKLESIA*, a gathering, or body of Christ in sundry locations in the world—rather than only Jewish synagogues? Why would the followers of Jesus in this new sect allow themselves to be persecuted and brutalized for someone who never existed?

Internationally regarded as the dean of New Testament scholars, Raymond Brown, not only affirms the historicity of Jesus, but offers a scholarly perspective of his personhood. For some the story of Jesus was made up; Jesus is some kind of Hebrew superhero from a very graphic and fictious novel. To others, Jesus was a rabbi, teacher of wisdom, or even a political zealot. But for an immeasurable number of others, including New Testament scholars like Raymond Brown, the historical account of Jesus and his personhood in the text, are factual, "Jesus himself would have supplied the kinds of material that ultimately went into the Gospels."[589] From a lifetime of exploration into the origins and tenets of religion, in his autobiography former professor of World Religions at M.I.T., Huston Smith, became convinced that Jesus reveals to humanity what God is like in human form. "Jesus points us to the direction of God."[590]

Of course, in order to make a reasonably adequate assessment of the identity of Jesus, the primary source regard the New Testament. Particularly if we want to consider the major events in the life of Jesus: His message, miracles, and the momentum of his post-crucifixion movement from Jerusalem into the Roman Empire. The writers of the both the New Testament and the first century church offer to us invaluable insight into the identity of the one in whom they believed. Most were so devoted, they did more than just die for a cause, they lived for His purpose of being. At the onset, the sect of Jesus, the Nazarene was not intended to be a new religion, but a movement of God's continuing salvation history based on love and grace.

Biblical scholar William Manson wrote:

> *The confession of the disciples, as thus given in the tradition, springs from a spiritual sympathy through which their minds, under the daily tuition of Christ. Now the confession of his disciples comes as another intimation...'flesh and blood hath not revealed it unto thee.'*[591]

The identity of Jesus is affirmed for us in a way similar to that of the early church: intuitive questions about the identity of Jesus, rational evidence that affirm the historicity of his being, and revelation from God, through our moments of meditation upon his message, miracles, and mission, and the momentum of his life. It was within the context of meditative moments-in-real-time wherein "fascinating questions" may be asked and answered. Those moments of ultimate inquiry matter in the context of one's own time and space.

---

[589] Raymond E. Brown, *An Introduction to the New Testament* (NY: Doubleday, 1997), 104-105

[590] Huston Smith, *Tales of Wonder*, Ibid., 103-106

[591] William Manson, *The Gospel of Luke* (The Moffatt NT Commentary, London: Hodder and Stoughton, 1942), 107

Who is Jesus? The answer is in the text, revealed through our vulnerability, and in God's timing. The New Testament states definitely: "He is the sole expression of the glory of God, the Light-being, the out-raying or radiance of the divine Majesty on high." (Hebrews 1:1-2/ AMPC).

The narratives in the Scripture direct the eye of the soul to answers to ultimate questions. They are answers, however incomplete, indicating that, through Jesus, God had "lit such a torch in the hearts of men as time would never put out."[592] Such answers may come in a discipline that distinguishes a casual reading from an insightful exploration. God manifests higher knowledge to those who meditate upon the narratives in an intimate moment-of-Presence -- those who "avoid the opinions of others"[593] demeaning the text as irrelevant or illegitimately inspired. In this disciplined practice, the personhood of Jesus may be revealed in a manner that no other reason may accomplish.

> *The uniqueness of Jesus is not to be confused with exclusivity. His uniqueness does not exclude other revelations of Truth, but Christian belief would see Jesus as the full self-revelation of God in human form…as well as its fullest capacity for life, consciousness, and union with God.*[594]

SECTION 2:
Jesus: the Intimate and Ultimate Revelation of God

In his book, *Jesus as They Saw Him,* William Barclay delineates how various New Testament writers offered word pictures or "living portraits" from their *respective experiences of* Jesus in real time. All through the New Testament we find individuals giving Jesus metaphorical titles which are at one and the same time "affirmations and confessions of their faith in him and summaries of what they believed him to be:"[595]

---

[592] William Barclay, *Gospel of Luke*, Ibid., 120
[593] Cyril of Alexandria, *Commentary on Luke*, Homily 49
[594] Laurence Freeman, *The Good Heart* (Boston: Wisdom Publications, 1996), 148
[595] William Barclay, *Jesus As They Saw Him* (London: Harper and Row, 1962), 9

In a biblical context, Jesus was metaphorically described as the Jewish *Son of David*, *Son of God*, *Son of Man*, *the High Priest*, *a prophet* and *Messiah*. As others experienced Jesus in the context of their own circumstances, he was described as *the Good Shepherd*, *the Divine Physician*, *the Bread of Life*, *the Light of the World*, *the Lamb of God who takes away the sin of the world*, *the Bright Morning Star*, *the Lord of Lords*, *King of Kings*, *the Word who became Flesh* and *the Resurrection and the Life*. For most who encountered Jesus, he was recognized as a messenger, if not the very image of God.

Biblical writers documented the above metaphorical titles as Jesus became known respectively through various experiences of him. But who was and IS Jesus in the context of our own contemporary culture? What information do we have of him that may enable today's population to make sense of his personhood? Can intuitive questions, reasonable evidence, and revelation serve as a prompt for the discovery of the true self of Jesus of Nazareth?

SECTION 3:
Jesus: The Man

"He asked them, 'Who do people say I am?'" (Luke 9:18/NIV).

The Apostolic Tradition of St. Hippolytus (d. 235), written about the year 215 AD, declared persons who were to be baptized (or in the case of an infant, the parents and godparents) to make their profession of faith by responding to the following three questions:

1. *Do you believe in God, the Father almighty, creator of Heaven and earth?*
2. *Do you believe in Jesus Christ, His only Son, our Lord, who was born of the Virgin Mary, was crucified, died, and was buried, rose from the dead, and is now seated at the right hand of the Father?*
3. *Do you believe in the Holy Spirit, the holy catholic Church, the communion of saints, the forgiveness of sins, the resurrection of the body, and life everlasting?*

Earlier, in the time of the Apostle, John, to know the identity of Jesus, the writer's admonition was simply to *"come and see."* (John 1:39-51; 4:29/NASB). Today, if one heeds to intuitive questions, considers the historical evidence, and pursues insight, the identity of Jesus may be *revealed*. For those who "come and see," Jesus emerges from the pages of an ancient text as more than a contrived Hebrew superhero, a rebellious zealot, a misguided Messiah, or a first century hippie.

In his *Preface to Old Testament Notes from Ecclesiastes*, John Wesley wrote that the way to understand the things of God is "meditate day and night. So shall you attain the best knowledge; even to know the one true God and Jesus Christ whom he hath sent. And this knowledge will lead you to love Him... yea, with all your heart, mind, soul, and strength." (Notes and Commentary Edinburgh: April 25, 1765, Paragraph 17).

The personhood of Jesus is revealed through

1. asking the intuitive questions,
2. exploring rational evidence, and
3. being vulnerable to the revelation of God's presence in the core of our being.

In meditating or empathetically interacting with biblical narratives, Jesus emerges as the personification of the imaginative, immutable, and immeasurable grace of God. Jesus asked the fascinating question: *Who do you say that I am?* And by the very nature of the continuing movement of his influence through the centuries to the present, that fascinating question is still relevant today. The historicity of Jesus of Nazareth is presented by the evidence of his existence in real time through the church that bears his example. But the personhood of Jesus is revealed through the insight we receive in the core of our being. William Barclay asserted, "The only real argument for Christianity is a Christian experience." This experience to which Barclay refers is a phenomenon that crosses boundaries in the human experience: geography, generation, and intellectual acumen.

The Internal Witness of the Spirit according to evangelical mystic, R. A. Torrey:

> It is only through the testimony of the Holy Spirit directly to our hearts that we ever come to a true, living knowledge of Jesus Christ (cf.1 Cor. xii.3). No amount of mere reading the written

Word (in the Bible) and no amount of listening to man's testimony will ever bring us to a living knowledge of Christ. This is the cure for both skepticism and ignorance concerning Christ. What we all most need is a clear and full vision of Jesus Christ and this comes through the testimony of the Holy Spirit.[596]

Ida "Granny" York and the Morley, Tennessee Baptist Church

William Barclay asserted, "The only real argument for Christianity is a Christian experience."[597] This experience to which Torrey and Barclay refer is a phenomenon that crosses boundaries in the human experience: geography, generation, and intellectual acumen.

As a young "preacher boy" attending a denominationally-driven, four-year college, I had the opportunity to gain experience preaching weekend revivals in various evangelical churches around the regions of Southwestern Ohio, Indiana, Kentucky, and Northeastern Tennessee. Most of the churches in which I preached were cordial and accommodating. There was little resistance to a neophyte preacher "practicing" his sermons in their pulpits. I managed to muster some confidence in my abilities for public speaking too. After all, I had taken my official "Intro to Homiletics" class and gotten a B+ on my first sermon.

Actually, I was quite nervous with the responsibility of preaching the "inspired and inerrant" Word of God. It seemed too holy for anyone to speak it as if he was an authority on what God was truly wanting to say. What could I say that someone else hadn't already said better than I?

I was appointed by the Director of Church Relations to preach a weekend revival for the Baptist Church in Morley, Tennessee. This was before the technology of GPS, so I used an ancient manuscript called a "map." It took me an hour or so to discover that Morley was barely a speck on the borderline of Kentucky and Tennessee. Still, if the Israelites could reach the promised land from wandering forty through the wilderness, I could reach Morley through a trek in the mountains of Northeastern Tennessee. I had a map.

---

[596] R. A. Torrey, *The Person and Work of the Holy Spirit* (Zondervan, 1985)
[597] Barclay, *The Gospel of John*, (Philadelphia: Westminster, 1956), 167

Interstate 75 South took me to the Jellico Exit. I followed the map, negotiating the winding, serpentine road around every bend, up the mountainous inclines, around narrow breaks where there were no guard rails to keep my car from tumbling down the mountainside, until I finally saw a dilapidated sign that fainted read, "Morley Baptist Church," with an arrow pointing DOWN! The church was at the bottom of a long, twisting and turning graveled entranceway that had been grated in the ground by the local coal company for access by their monstrous trucks to move in and out of.

When I reached the bottom of the mountain, I drove slowly into the nearly abandoned coal mining town of Morley. I passed a few shacks where former coal mining families still lived and drove on to the little, one room church in the center of town. The sight was daunting. Although, I had rehearsed our service agenda with my song leader and pianist (whom had driven separately and arrived at the location before I did), I was still not sure how I would be accepted by this humble gathering of mountain folk.

But, to insure my acceptance and ministerial success, I did what I was instructed to do by my Homiletics teacher: I chose my text, I studied my text in commentaries, I prayed over the text, and I outlined the text, using the commentaries, select illustrations, and I even had an opening joke. I had even practiced my proclamation style (gestures, inflections, pauses, etc.) with my roommate over and over again, until he finally himself threatened to repent; that is, he confessed he would turn from Christianity to atheism if I didn't stop my sermonizing!

While I was nervous about the venue, I was confident in my presentation. I knew if was worthy of at least a B+. At the end of the song service via the church's rinky-tink, out of tune piano, I arose to the pulpit and began: the joke, the text, the exposition of the text, the application to our daily lives, and the closing illustration. Suddenly, one of the members, a man in his early twenties, with a rough exterior and menacing presence, stood up, glared at me, stomped down the aisle to the door, and finally, after stepping outside, slammed the door behind him!

I was stunned. I thought I was impressive with all my prior study and scholarly notes. Not sure what to do, I just called on my team to come forward and we continued the service with the altar call by singing "Just As

I Am." As I recall, no one came forward for salvation that night. After the service, most of those who attended left without much response to me or my team. One lady came to me and asked us to stop by her house for some milk and fruit cocktail cake.

Ida York had lived in Morley all her 80-some years of life. Her husband, a coal miner had died several years before. Her children lived in other parts of the state, but she had a twenty year old grandson that lived with her. He was away most of the time, exploring the hills and hollers for what he believed to be a solid gold cannon hidden in some cave in the Appalachian mountains by the British after the Revolutionary War.

Her home was a shack. In the main room was a pot-belly stove, that warmed the whole house. There was a small kitchen with dining table, a closet-size bathroom, her bedroom (with a large, handmade feather bed), and an extra bedroom that had been built onto the rest of the house for her grandson. She welcomed us into her home with great hospitality, unashamed of her abode.

After she had pampered us with the milk and cake, she asked if she could talk with me by myself. The team had decided to leave shortly after the cake anyway, so we were alone at the table. She told me her story: her childhood in Morley, her riding on the coal trains that passed by every hour only a few feet from her house, the loss of her beloved husband, and most importantly, of her faith in Jesus. This woman LOVED Jesus! And it was that love that spoke to me that first night of our revival services in Morley.

"You feel bad about tonight?" she asked. "You know, when J.T. walked out like he did?"

I nodded.

"That's just J.T. He don't meaning nothin' by it. He does that when he gets riled when he thinks people think he's stupid, or he don't understand something. I think that was it tonight. He didn't understand what you was talking about."

Ordinarily, I would have been *self-righteously offended* by this critique, had it come from someone who didn't real care about me like this woman obviously did. I asked, "He didn't understand?"

"No, honey." She answered, "and neither did most of us. Most of us know Jesus, and we want to know more about *him*. But you said a lot of things that just…well…seemed to get in the way."

I learned much from this encounter in the little coal mining town. This woman's counsel guided me not only through the rest of the weekend, but also through my remaining college years. I visited her many times while I was a student, until to me, Ida became my adopted "Granny" York. Through Granny York, a woman of no formal education, I learned that the personhood of Jesus does not have to be articulated through the garrulity of theological discourse or philosophical abstracts. Jesus can become known even in the remotest of places to those who simply come to experience his presence in a very raw, but real way.

"You need to stop all the god-talk and just tell them about Jesus. Tell them about Jesus in the power of the Holy Spirit, with love for who you're talking to," she instructed me, "and leave the rest to God, and not all your college talk."

My Brief, but Insightful Sabbaticals at Oxford University

Admittedly, I have not always been enamored with professional scholars. My experience has been that many who promote themselves as exceptional academics tend to be…well, snobs! That's not to say that I don't appreciate scholarly research, but it is in the condescending manner of the interaction with those who do the research that at times leave me…unimpressed. But what I am about to share does not continue in that mode of thought.

In fact, I revere the intellect and inspiration I received through the guidance of many of the most brilliant minds in theology, philosophy, science, and literature. Many of whom are quoted in this book. Suffice to say here, that I was not typically a fan of celebrity-styled scholars.

I was at a time in my life—professionally and *profess*-sionally that I needed more stability in my faith. I had served on staff at a Christian college, earned my seminary degrees, pastored three evangelical churches with a modicum of success, taught in a major Christian High School for over a decade, and was a guest speaker and dramatist for events at different churches through the years. In short, I tried to do what I thought was in sync with God's will for my life. (Not that I was ever the perfect little preacher boy.)

In the summer of 2010, I began studying the old Testament books of Job and Jeremiah. Both deal with suffering and brokenness. While reading the books, I thought to myself that one day I would have to use these texts to "help someone" through the crucible of life. Little did I realize that someone would be me. In the fall of that year, my existence was shattered by a series of events that not only challenged my faith but also my will to live.

Questions of ultimate concern were raging in me, questions I could not answer. These were deep, profound questions of a nature that moved me toward even rejecting the existence of God. How could such horrible things happen to me, when I tried for decades to do what I believed God would have me do? My wife of nearly 30 years told me she didn't love me anymore and left me to marry another man, my son had graduated from high school and moved to another city to go to college. Due to the crumbling of my marriage, I was being shunned by my church tradition, my financial situation was uncertain, and I was now deemed disqualified by many to preach, teach, or serve Christ. In short, I believed my calling to ministry was done.

Everything in which I had relied upon or trusted was now insufficient to engage these horrors—even my faith in God was waning. Why did this happen to me? I learned through this emotional tsunami why indeed, "God hates divorce." (Malachi 2:16/NIV). Not so much because it is deemed the *unpardonable sin* by so many churches, but because of the agony it causes to those whom He loves. I felt isolated, abandoned, and vulnerable. I hated divorce too.

During my first desperate week, I had enough resolve to call out to those I trusted to offer me some solace and support. I called Jim Fleming, one of my former seminary professors and a pastoral counselor. He assured me that I could meet with him weekly "at not cost, you're family." While a devoted

Christian, Jim was also one of the most insightful and caring professors I had ever had. He walked alongside of me for six months without renumeration. I remember him telling me, "this is when you have to activate your faith *in Jesus.*"

It was during one of those counseling sessions that it dawned on me: "if I was pastoring someone who was going through what I was, what would I advise him to do?—and DO that!" So, I began reading: Thomas Merton, Henri Nouwen, Howard Thurman, and the classic work of St. John of the Cross, *"Dark Night of the Soul."* I drove several times to the Abbey at Gethsemani near Bardstown, Kentucky for the silence and solitude—to listen for the prompting of God's presence. At this point, I realized in spite of all my theological education and experience in ministry was not enough to enable my survival and recovery from what was happening to me. I needed something more!

My ultimate questions were many. I needed a reason to believe. I needed a spiritual experience to BE-Live! This realization prompted me to a pilgrimage to a week of seminars at Christ Church in Oxford University. I had been reading in the area of science and religion, and was deeply impressed with the writings of C. S. Lewis, Dorothy Soelle, Alistair McGrath, John Polkinghorne, and Keith Ward. In 2006 and 2007, I had attended the summer sessions at Christ Church and had taken classes with Professor Ward, but this time, I was attending not merely for the information, but also for the insight I needed.

I was quite intimated in my experience at Oxford. After all, this was Oxford University, one of the foremost and oldest universities in the world. Their ornate and stone architecture was awesome. Their graduates through the centuries impacted history. The students attending there are from all parts of the world. I came from Kentucky!

Keith Ward is a brilliant theologian and philosopher, but he never gave me the impression he was unapproachable, or holier-than-Thou. In fact, my impression of him was, and is, that he is brilliance with a heart. In every session I attended with him, I filled my legal pads, noting literally everything he said. After one of the sessions, I asked him if I could "pour my heart out" to him. He graciously agreed to offer me this time with him.

For some reason, I shared with him some of the gory details of my brokenness. With the compassion of a mentor, he simply said, "you need to discover the God of your god. You have the sovereign God of the cosmos in a sectarian box. When you discover the living God, you will discover your way again."

"How do I do that?" I asked.

"Well," he smiled that happy-go-lucky smile and said, "Jesus…it's all about him anyway, isn't it? You share what you have to say and leave the rest to God."

That encounter was a turning point in my life. Although I had studied the doctrines, did the church by-laws, served on the mission fields, and preached and taught endless sermons and lessons, and after all he had to teach me in the hours I spent with him in his classroom, all Keith Ward had to say to me was "Jesus…it's all about him anyway."

From Granny York to Professor Ward: "It's All About Jesus"

From the secluded mountain home in Morley, Tennessee, of the formally-uneducated, Ida York, to the perfect spires and stone architecture in Oxford University and Regius Professor, Keith Ward, it is all about Jesus. It is the revelation of his personhood by the wooing of God's presence that speaks to the lowly and to the lifted up, the shack in the coal mining town and the steeples in the places of higher education. His personhood is proven by his presence for all persons. We can only become prompts toward that experience. It is the spirit that reveals the identity of Jesus whether one be culturally lowly or lifted up.

SECTION 4:
Jesus in Hinduism: A Remarkable Incarnation or Avatar

Mohandas K. Gandhi believed Jesus to be one of "three greatest teachers of the world—Buddha, Jesus, and Muhammad…[who] have left unimpeachable testimony, that they found illumination through prayer and could not possibly live without it."[598] For Gandhi, Mahatma, or "great soul," Jesus taught his disciples that "man's ultimate aim is the realization of God."[599] Later, Gandhi credited Jesus as being one "among the greatest prophets,"[600] as well as an historically significant and influential teacher of illumination for the ages.

In the Forward to *The Gospel of Sri Ramakrishna,* Aldous Huxley detailed the Hindu master's perception of Jesus as "Love Incarnate." Jesus was a path leading to God-Consciousness. Throughout his life Ramakrishna believed that Christ was an incarnation of God. But Jesus, for him was not the only Incarnation; there were others—Buddha, and Krishna. For Ramakrishna, Christ was/is "'Primal Energy' as Allah, or Rama, the substance of One Deity under a different name; thus, he taught, "let each man follow his own path. If he sincerely and ardently wishes to know God, peace be unto him, he will surely realize him. [601]

Ramakrishna confessed that such an incarnation of the Presence of God, indwelled *him* as well. But unlike Jesus, the Hindu Master could not raise anyone from the dead, nor could he perform miracles like Jesus. Jesus *was* "a complete manifestation of God" rather than, like Ramakrishna, only a partial or fractional incarnation.[602]

For other Hindus, Jesus was a *sadhu,* a religious ascetic or holy man who renounced the material world to incarnate and lead others to a spiritual realm. According to Shanaka Rishi Das, Director of the Oxford Center for Hindu Studies, Jesus preached a universal message of the love of God and love for other, without respect to any particular sect or tradition. For Hindus, he was "an *empowered incarnation*" sent to fulfil God's will on earth. Humanity is not to allow sectarianism to keep humanity from following the teachings and example of such a *"great soul* as Lord Jesus Christ."[603]

---

[598] *All Men are Brothers,* Ibid., 81

[599] Ibid., 82

[600] Ibid., 220

[601] New York: Ramakrishna Vivekananda Center (1942), 35

[602] Ibid., 838

[603] http://www.bbc.co.uk/religion/religions/hinduism/beliefs/jesus_1.shtml

In the ancient work, *The Gospel of Sri Ramakrishna*, Jesus is depicted as "God's play as a human being." In order that God might be seen, Jesus displayed as the essential personhood of one supremely conscious of the love of God for all creation. The Hindu teacher, Ramakrishna, did poetically described the relation of Jesus to God, or how the Jesus--avatar revealed Brahma, the creator god in Hinduism: *We cannot quite grasp how God, Perfect Brahman that He is, can dwell in that small body (of Jesus) as a spiritual ideal. Through Jesus, one sees part of the Infinite God.*[604]

Metaphorically, imagine a field extending to the horizon and beyond. It extends without any obstruction into the beyond. We cannot see the beyond on account of a wall in front of us. In that wall is a round hole. Through that hole we see a part of an infinite field. Through that hole you can see nearly everything—an infinite meadow without any end. This is like Jesus—through him, see only a glimpse of many other contextual images of God.

SECTION 5:

Jesus in Buddhism: Bodhisattva!

The contrast of Jesus and Siddhartha Gautama, the Buddha, was illustrated by the Dalai Lama in regard to their respective capacity for compassion. In both the lives of Jesus Christ and the Buddha, it is only through hardship, dedication, and commitment that humanity learns to grow spiritually and attain spiritual liberation. As a Buddhist, the Dalai Lama taught that his perspective toward Jesus Christ is that he was either "a fully enlightened being or a bodhisattva of a very high realization: a spiritual vibration, a source of inspiration and strength.[605]

Ajahn Candasiri, senior Nun of the Amaravati Buddhist Monastery in Hertfordshire, UK, wrote that Jesus was a man of great presence, a forceful life-energy, compassion, and "significant psychic abilities." People listened

---

[604] *The Gospel of Sri Ramakrishna*, edited by Swami Nikhilanada (NY: Ramakrishna Vivekananda Center, 1992), 825-826; 839

[605] Dalai Lama, *The Good Heart: A Buddhist Perspective on the Teachings of Jesus* (Boston: Wisdom Publications, 1996), 46; 58; 83-84

to him, loved or hated what he had to say, and, in many cases, were healed or even risen from the death of despair.

Historically, Jesus is chronicled through the eyes of Buddhists as follows: Jesus died a young man. What we hear of his last hours: the trial, the agony and humiliation, being stripped naked and nailed to a cross to die, is an extraordinary account of his willingness to bear the unbearable without any sense of revenge. There is a simile used by Buddhists to demonstrate the Buddha's teaching of *metta*, (or kindness) in the experience of injustice that Jesus sufferd: *"Even if robbers were to attack you and saw off your limbs one by one, should you give way to anger, you would not be following my advice."* A tall order, but one that clearly Jesus fulfils to perfection: *"Father, forgive them for they know not what they do."*[606]

SECTION 6:
Jesus in Judaism: Rabbi? A Misguided Messiah?

Educator Clive Lawton worked for the BBC as a broadcaster, writer and one of the founders of the educational charity, Limmud in 1980. In 2016, he

---

[606] http://www.bbc.co.uk/religion/religions/buddhism/beliefs/jesusandbuddhism_1.shtml

became a lecturer at the London School of Jewish Studies. As an authority on Jewish perspectives of Jesus, Dr. Lawton wrote a special OpEd for the British Broadcasting Corporation seeking an answer to the fascinating question: *"Who was Jesus, from a Jewish point of view?"*

Lawton contended that Jesus is seen as a Pharisee, probably influenced by the Messianic fervour that was popular at the time. He was agitated by the lame nature of religion in the Jewish Temple, and Roman politics. But was neither a religious revolutionary or a political zealot. As a Jew, schooled in essential Judaism, He wanted the people live in accord with the essential teachings of the Torah, especially as it concerned loving God and others. But, according to Professor Lawton, the Messianic hope Jesus's disciples had was "devastated" in the realization that this was not the prophetic plan for which they had entrusted their lives. They had invested in a man, who had promised much, but was now dead. However, what Jesus taught about the love of God and for others, remained steadfast in their thinking and how they pursued their lives thereafter. According to the Lawton:

> *something happened back then that first Easter that persuaded those disheartened followers that what they'd been expecting and waiting for-- wasn't the point after all. It was all entirely different to the way Jews had understood the idea of the messiah for centuries... and still do.*[607]

In contrast, Jewish mystic, *Martin Buber* described Jesus as a "religious genius," of contrast or parallel to, but not greater than Moses or the prophets.[608] He explained the impact of Jesus as "the great saga" of which tended to glorify his healings, saw him walking on the sea, and turning water into wine. While those narrative stirs our hearts, Buber remarked, such stirring should not prevent us from critiquing wherever possible "the veil of legend and, as far as we can, viewing the pure form which it conceals."[609] For Buber, there was some validity to the historicity of Jesus, but he was not a Hebrew superhero or Messiah.

---

[607] http://www.bbc.co.uk/religion/religions/judaism/beliefs/eyes_1.shtml
[608] Martin Buber, *"The Words on the Tablet*: from On the Bible (Syracuse: University Press, 2000), 97
[609] Ibid., 98

Although Buber did not affirm either the Messianic fulfillment in the appearance of Jesus, nor the claim of the New Testament writers of Jesus as the "son of God," he did view positively the final days of Jesus as historical, and his teachings as "the strongest crystallization of his spirit."[610]

Buber did not believe that Jesus performed miracles, such as those which would "counter nature," like giving commands to the wind and the sea. He considered this totally unfounded scientifically and religiously. But the famed Jewish philosopher *did* believe that Jesus was the fullest extent of goodness and freedom as "a reflection of God's image…in the line of the prophets, concluding and continuing it."[611]

SECTION 7:
Jesus in Islam: A Prophet or a Political Zealot?

Traditionally for Muslims, Jesus was a prophetic teacher. By his words and deeds he pointed to the One God, Allah. This is the perspective in the Qur'an, but it is also evident in mystical Islamic poetry of *Rumi,* a thirteenth century Persian poet, Islamic theologian, and Sufi mystic. In his narrative poem, *The Masnawi* (lines 298-363), Rumi regarded the identity of Jesus as a healer:

---

[610] *Letters of Martin Buber,* February 15, 1917 (New York: Schocken, 1991), 208
[611] Ibid., October 10, 1945, 505

From all sides people gathered
around his house
Some were blind, some lame,
and some insane.
Each morning they went to his door
So that their defects could be
healed by Jesus' Breath
The people would then walk,
with no pain and trouble,
Toward the blessings and mercy
of the Divine..
They all were cured by the
prayers of Jesus.

In a 2007 film produced by the BBC entitled, "The Muslim Jesus," Palestinian historian Shaykh Zayid, Chair in Islamic and Arabic Studies at the American University of Beirut in Lebanon, explained that Islam contends that Jesus was a human being "indwelled" by the Divine Spirit. He was only one of many messengers of Allah who articulated truth. Islam does not hold to the divinity of Jesus, nor his sonship to God.

The *Qur'an 5: 116,* states that Jesus never said that people should consider him as a god beside Allah. According to the Qur'an, Jesus firmly instructed his disciples, *'I am a devotee and worshipper of God.'* (Qur'an 19:21-23). The Jesus of the Qur'an is quite distinctive from the New Testament Gospels. There is no incarnation, no ministry and no brutal crucifixion. His divinity is strenuously denied. Such a claim of divinity or being a "son of God (Allah) would be considered blasphemy. Jesus reinterpreted by the Qur'an as a prophet of very special significance, perhaps even a predecessor to God's final prophet, Mohammed.

For Muslims, at times Jesus at times he is a "fierce ascetic", at other times he is the "gentle teacher" of proper and lawful decorum. Yet other times, Jesus is the "patron of Muslim mystics, the prophet of the secrets of creation, or the healer of the wounds of nature and of man." The Islamic fascination regarding the identity of Jesus seems somewhat contradictory by varied segments of the religion. The following is a poem written by famed Arab artist, *Badr Shakir al-Sayyab.* This series of poems entitled *"Christ after the*

Crucifixion" portrays Christ as lord of nature and redeemer of "the wretched of the earth." In this account, although there is not resurrection, there is an account of the crucifixion, but without reference to an actual death.

Here, Jesus is pictured as a healer of nature and humanity as he breathes his last breath on the cross. This following poem interweaves in an apocalyptic voice, the Jesus of the Gospels with the risen Christ, and the triumphant of his message through the *emergence of a movement of believers*. While there is no acceptance of bodily resurrection of Jesus, there is a faint inference that the Muslim Jesus becomes lord over the wickedness of the earth. It is a concise gospel in itself: a vision of Jesus in suffering, but ultimately in victory:

> *After they brought me down, I heard the winds*
> *In a lengthy wail, rustling the palm trees,*
> *And steps fading away. So then, my wounds,*
> *And the Cross upon which they nailed me all afternoon and*
> *evening*
> *Did not kill me.*
> *How many lives will I live! For in every furrow of earth*
> *I have become a future, I have become a seed.*
> *I have become a race of men, in every human heart.*[612]

SECTION 8:
Jesus in a Materialistic World

Although from the perspective of other living world religions, Jesus has varied interpretations regarding his identity, there is a profound and concilatory appreciation for his teachings and the life he lived. Many in today's culture have not rejected Jesus, per se, but have yet to receive the revelation of his truest personhood. The world does not recognize him (John 1:10/NIV), and in their speculations of him and do not honor him. (Romans 1:21/ NASB).

Jesus was a devout Jew who lived and spoke out for the power of God. He owned a profound consciousness of the will of God and the whims of humanity. He did not use his consciousness of God to hold himself up

---

[612] Badr Shakir al-Sayyab, *Christ after the Crucifixion*

as a supreme being, or demand himself be served. Jesus has been seen as anything from a guru, teacher, enlightened mystic, liberator, and wounded healer. Most in the Christian tradition would agree that Jesus was a presence who lived only a short while on the earth that those who experience him could, as Dorothee Soelle contended, "see into the heart of God."

According to Huston Smith, everything that Jesus said focused on the two most important facts about life: God's overwhelming love of humanity, and the need for people to accept that love…"to let it flow through them in way water passed without obstruction through a sea anemone. This is the soul of Christianity."[613]

While many atheists and agnostics would not accept the above statements as credible or more, believable, there are those who at least accept the historicity of Jesus and would regard him as a moral teacher. Even famed evolutionary biologist and pop-culture *anti-theist*, Richard Dawkins, estimated that Jesus, was "one of the great ethical innovators of history. The Sermon on the Mount is way ahead of its time. His 'turn the other cheek' anticipated Gandhi and Martin Luther King, Jr. by two thousand years. It was not for nothing that I wrote an article called, *'Atheists for Jesus.'*"[614]

In his most recent book of essays, Dawkins concluded that Jesus was a charismatic young preacher who advocated and spread human "superniceness, [which] is just plain dumb from a Darwinian point of view."[615] The irony with Dawkins' comments is that on the one hand, he held him in esteem as a "great ethical innovator," but at the same time, disregarded his "superniceness" as incompatible or "dumb" in regard to his own anti-theistic theory of Social Darwinism.

Many outside the church recognize Jesus' phenomenal wisdom, code of ethics, as a *sign* of some visionary activity in the world, even if they do not accept the consummate identity of his personhood. For many Jesus was a divinely-inspired pathfinder, a guide to a deeper awareness of some supernatural, perhaps even a personal entity. People followed him because

[613] Huston Smith, *The Soul of Christianity* (New York: HarperCollins, 1991)

[614] Dawkins, *The God Delusion*, Ibid., 250

[615] Richard Dawkins, *"Atheist for Jesus,"* from *Science in the Soul: Selected Writings of a Passionate Rationalist* (NY: Random House, 2017), 274-277

he met them at their point of need. He reputedly performed *SEMIA or "signs and wonders"* that pointed to a Greater Reality. *He* touched and healed outcasts like lepers, persons who struggled with demonic influences. Many conclude that although Jesus was not himself, divine, he was of divine-origin and consciousness. There would have been no movement, had there been nothing about him that was extraordinary.

Jesus was one day cheered and the next day jeered. He was surrounded by foes, followers, and a few faithful friends. He was scandalized by the fickle, citizenry of his day. He was even betrayed by followers closest to him. He experienced the agony of an unjust system through a coalition and conspiracy devised between unlikely political bedfellows. And he was physically abused and brutalized without an advocate to defend him.

Is this "saga" merely a legend or myth? Or is this narrative a path toward a more profound revelation of a greater reality? Was Jesus a Jewish zealot? A liar or a lunatic? The devil in a prophet's garb? Was he self-deceived or misguided? Moreover, was Jesus a human being with divine qualities or a divine person with human qualities? Why in this new millennium do we still regard him as significant? Why is Jesus still compelling?

The most notable documents we have regarding these questions are written as close to the actual time of Jesus: the four gospels in the New Testament. There are no other known writings that disclaim or discount the otherwise biblical documented life of Jesus from that era. So, what can the writings in Matthew, Mark, Luke, and John "reveal" about Jesus?

If Jesus is more than just concocted legend from the pages of an irrelevant ancient text, then the answers to these fascinating questions (intuition) regarding his personhood must be discerned not just historically (empirical evidence), but through a revelation in the soul. Otherwise, there would be little real-time relevance to his existence. He would be just another idealist in history—a virtual-reality Don Quixote-- who exhausted his quest for an impossible dream.

SECTION 9:

Jesus in the Four Gospels

The very core of the Christian faith is that the Eternal somehow enters into time. The embodiment of Ultimate Love is manifested in the person of Jesus "as the way to eternal life."[616] Barclay asserted, in Jesus I see *revealed* and demonstrated, "the attitude of God to men; the full *revelation* of the mind and heart of God!"[617]

The value of the Gospel writers is that they hold respective and varied perspectives of this revelation of the "mind and heart of God" within their own context. Such revelation was more experiential than propositional. The four respective narratives complement one another as they center on colorful proclamations of the *EUANGELLION,* or the "good proclamation" of redemption.

There is no evidence that either Jesus, or his disciples, conspired to start a new religion or contrived for themselves a heroic zealot. Moreover the

---

[616] Keith Ward, *Re-Thinking Christianity* (Oxford: Oneworld, 2007), 50; 19
[617] Barclay, Autobiography, 50

"kingdom of God" that Jesus inaugurated was not intended to be the Empire of Israel that the Jews, or even his disciples, had expected. The entity Jesus proclaimed called for repentance, forgiveness, and a transformation of one's character in line with a new ethic based on love, rather than law, and reconciliation rather than revenge.

Had Jesus desired to incite a new Kingdom of Israel, he missed his opportunity to do so many times—such as when he entered into Jerusalem amidst the cheers of "Hosanna!" by the multitudes who thought him to be their new king. But Jesus was NOT a political zealot. He was only zealous for the souls of persons. He did not at that opportune moment call the nation to arms, but to an armistice between God and those estranged from Him. The four gospel narratives complement one another in this way. All four narratives, however, also document the person and history of Jesus via the lenses of their own idiosyncrasies. The narratives were not meant to simply offer an objective course in history, but to enable one to be subjected to its message-- to sojourn a path through which one might discover a spiritual confrontation with the kingdom of God.

The gospel writers were not "neutral historians," who wrote a factually historical account of Jesus' life as in a divine diary, they were "catalysts to evoke and inspire faith."[618] Although the central and most crucial events in their respective accounts of the life of Jesus are nearly exact, as unique individuals with diverse personalities, they obviously would not compose everything verbatim one from the other. The distinctions are revelatory as well. They were writing a theology within the context of their respective stories,

Regarding this coalescing in the perspectives of Jesus by the gospel writers, consider the essential elegance of a diamond. To truly see the fullness of a diamond, one must observe its many facets in the light, turning it from side to side. In order to define a diamond, one must bring focus on its many angles and edges, colors and hues...always in the light. Similarly, the identity of Jesus must be viewed from those "inspired" facets, the authors who became catalysts to evoke and inspire faith or the inner knowing: from intuition to empirical exploration to revelation. Each gospel writer composes

---

[618] Ward, Ibid., 19

his respective gospel with a unique perspective of the identity of Jesus as he was experienced by them.

In his book, *Re-thinking Christianity,* Keith Ward explained the variances of perspectives regarding the personhood of Jesus. Mark presents Jesus as a powerful, *"strangely secretive Messianic King."* In Matthew, Jesus is depicted as the new or greater Moses, but still *"teaching the inner truth of Torah."* Luke describes Jesus as the *"universal Savior"* for all persons: women, the poor, the non-Jews and the Jews alike. John is unique in design. Jesus is presented in symbols and abstract thinking, calling him the *"Word made flesh, the bread of life, the light of the world and the true vine,"*[619] among other inferences to his being. When seen together, Jesus emerges more dynamic in his personhood and purpose.

A Momentary Pause:

The Dynamic and Personal Attributes of Jesus According to the Gospel Writers

The gospel writers not only give an account of the events of the life of Jesus, but also interpret the personhood of Jesus within the purview of several decades after the Easter event. Those gospel writers interpreted Jesus as an invitation to hear the voice of God and respond to Him. Franciscan speaker and author, Richard Rohr, asserted that when we see of the face of Christ, we interpret this as "the face of God' and the 'face of the (true) man."[620] According to the Gospel writers, in Jesus, humanity may freely interact in dialogue with God and God, in turns, dialogues more perfectly with humanity.

The revelatory nature of the biblical narratives energizes, nourishes, and enlightens as one consumes the text *as* sometimes "sour in the stomach and sweet in the mouth." (Revelation 10:9/NIV). Similarly, the narratives of Jesus are not meant to be read casually, but with the eye of the soul. "Blessed ("contented") is the one who reads, hears, and heeds ("takes to heart") what is written." (Revelation 1:3/NIV). In this discipline, through reading the Gospels, one may come to a greater awareness of not only the historical Jesus, but Jesus in the fullest potential of his personhood.

---

[619] Keith Ward, *Re-Thinking Christianity* (Oxford: Oneworld, 2007), 19-20
[620] Richard Rohr, *The Enneagram* (NY: Crossroad Books, 2004), 232-246

Jesus: The Message

"Jesus does not only see what a man is; He also sees what a man can become. He sees not only the actualities in a man; He also sees the possibilities. Jesus is the one who sees and who can release the hidden hero in every man."[621]

In Jesus we see one who is neither consumed by the materialistic or temporal concerns of human existence, nor obsessed with otherworldliness-- a preoccupation with things distant or ethereal. His teachings reflected a love for community, a higher good: to "do justice, love kindness, and walk humbly before the Lord God." *(Micah 6:8/NRSV)*. *Jesus'* message was both prophetic and practical. His lifestyle was *beatitudinal*, a living example of how a good humanity was intended to *BE-Live!*

The Teaching of Jesus: The Beatitudes: Our Ascension to Spiritual Transformation

> *"Now when he saw the crowds, he went up on a mountainside and sat down. His disciples came to Him, and He began to teach them, saying:*
>
> *Blessed are:*
> **the poor in spirit**, *for theirs is the kingdom of heaven,.*
> **those who mourn**, *for they will be comforted,*
> **the meek**, *for they will inherit the earth,*
> **those who hunger and thirst after righteousness,**
> *for they will be filled,*
> **the merciful**, *for they shall be shown mercy.*
> **the pure in heart**, *for they will see God,*
> **the peacemakers**, *for they will be called the sons of God.*
> **those who are persecuted because of righteousness**, *for theirs*
> *is the*
> *kingdom of heaven.* (Matthew 5:1-12/NRSV).

Jesus epitomized the magnificent maturing of the *wildflower: "he grew in wisdom and stature..." (Luke 2:52/NIV)*. In the last days of his life on earth,

---

[621] Barclay, *Gospel of John*, Ibid., 74-75

his teaching became remarkably incarnational in his teaching. Following the discourse of his Beatitudes, the attributes of his own character were actualized in the Gospels, particularly in the narrative of his Gethsemane experience. Here Jesus exemplified the journey—the decision—from a prophetic voice to a peacemaker.

A Momentary Pause:

Gethsemani: The Visual Beatitudes of Jesus in the Garden

The gospel writer chronicles the step-by-step unfolding of the personhood of Jesus as he rises from the one persecuted by political correctness to emerge as the peacemaker who incites love and reconciliation rather than revolt, revenge or retribution. Note the progression of the *Beatitudinal* nature (or BE-Living) of Jesus in Gethsemane:

Blessed are the poor in spirit = Jesus went to the lonely place of Gethsemane to commune with God. Jesus' life -- his message, miracles, and momentum -- was always in conscious awareness of God's Presence. Often Jesus reminded those to whom he ministered that he could nothing without God. There were also those extraordinarily overwhelming moments in the life of Jesus when he had to break away from both the mania and the mundane of humanity in order to find solace and assurance in nothing less than the essential presence of God. This is recognizing being "poor in spirit." This is when one may find spiritual contentment.

Blessed are those who mourn = In deep supplication, Jesus prayed, "I am deeply grieved." (Mark 14:34/CEB). Jesus wept. He knew what it was like to grieve over loss and the lost-- those who exist in quiet desperation and hopelessness. His heart was aching in Gethsemane when it became obvious that those with whom he depended, those closest to him, were still unaware of the fullness of his personhood and mission. They were so unaware as to sleep through his fervent prayer of blood. They could not minister to Jesus at a time when he was most in need. He mourned for the yet unbelieving, but also for those who had yet to come to the notion of *BE-Living*, or "life abundant."

Blessed are the meek = Jesus "threw himself on the ground to pray," (Matthew 26:39/AMPC) in submission to God's presence as he took upon himself the burden of an estranged humanity. In Jesus we see the empathy for a world gone wonky. Rather than to rise up and call for retribution against his distractors, Jesus instead cries out in supplication for a way of redeeming them. Jesus instructed his disciples to forgive, even love, their enemies— to stop cycles of violence and vengeance with transforming initiatives of love. On one occasion, Jesus stepped into the circle of a mob who was condemning a woman taken in adultery. He called for their repentance in their condemnation of her. His meekness was displayed in his willingness to carry her burden for her until she was able to carry it for herself. For both, the mob and the woman, Jesus offered a new and redemptive way out of no way, without violence or revenge, or fiery condemnation.

Blessed are those who hunger and thirst for righteousness = Jesus said, "let this cup pass from me...nevertheless, not as I will, but as you will." (Matthew 26:39/KJV). The bliss we seek is not found in subjecting our minds or our flesh to the bodacious milieu of the culture. We are to walk by faith and not fad. In Gethsemane, Jesus reflected the challenge of living in the world, but not of the world. At any time, he could have chosen the way of the culture and disavowed his kingdom ethic, but his passion was for the integrity of his sacred personhood in the presence of God.

Blessed are the merciful = Jesus said to his disciples, "Put away your sword! Those who live by the sword will die by the sword." (Matthew 26:52/NIV). The mercy of Jesus was often displayed in his acts of compassion, even to those who were perceived by others as undeserving of that compassion. The effects of the principalities and powers, rulers of the darkness of the world upon the weak and lost cannot be minimized by simplistic answers or a judgmental spirit. Jesus understood the hearts of all persons. He was compassionate and merciful with all persons, even with those who would soon brutalize him on a cross.

Blessed are the pure in heart = "Nevertheless, not my will, but Thine be done." (Luke 22:42/KJV). As humans own both the primal nature and the spiritual nurture, so too is there tension between urges (or the "will to power") that are primitive or instinctive, as distinctive from promptings that are pristine and innocent. The admonition of Jesus is to incite peace within one's true self through the cultivation of God's good intention for humanity-- this pristine or original innocence in our daily lives. While secular culture may entice the former urges, the Presence of God in the core of our being woos us to be both "wise as serpents and innocent as doves." *(Matthew 10:16/KJV).*

<u>Blessed are the peacemakers</u> = When Jesus could have rallied his followers to rise up and call for the shedding of the blood of his captors, and establish himself "King of the Jews," instead, "Jesus remained silent." (Matthew 26:63/NIV). He was not coming into the world to be the King of a political, economic, or military empire, but to establish the Kingdom of Heaven—the "beloved community" for all persons to experience peace with God, the peace of God, and peaceful co-existence with one another.

Jesus suffered from the misery of judicial injustice, abandonment, and even betrayal by those who promised to never leave his side. The impression of the religious elite and the Roman officials, as well as most of his disciples, was that Jesus was going to incite a rebellion of Jews in Jerusalem against the oppression of Rome. The most opportune moment for this would have been when Jesus came riding to the center of the city to the cheers of "Hosanna!" However, he was not zealous for a political regime, but for a spiritual community. He was not trying to incite a rebellion, but to prompt insight and revelation; a peacemaker, teaching a more redemptive way of life.

The conspiracy against Jesus was both politically motivated and maniacally devised. In the duration of this injustice, inevitably, the foundations of their community shook. The elite and politicos were blinded by their own darkness. A configuration of enemies conspired together to have done with Jesus. The peacemaker had to go, for he threatened their oppressive status quo. THEY incited the citizenry with the fear of both religious and Roman reprisal and perpetuated a heinous act of brutality on a man of peace for the sake of sustaining their own will to power.

Still, in his most vulnerable moment, on the cross of crucifixion, Jesus became our visual of the process of transformation. "Father, forgive them, for they don't know what they're doing." (Luke 23:34/NASB). Jesus continued his passion as a peacemaker in seeking to be the mediator between God and humanity. For Jesus, forgiveness was the threshold to peace with God and for peaceful co-existence in community. He prayed for the redemption of his persecutors, apathetic bystanders and for those who had betrayed him. He knew the real tragedy was not in his crucifixion, but that so many had yet to discovery his personhood and receive his proposition for peace and reconciliation.

A Momentary Pause:

The transposition of all things: Jesus's Visual Metamorphose

"My God, my God, why have you forsaken me?" / *"Father, into your hands, I commend my Spirit." (Matthew 27: 46; Mark 15:34/ Luke 23:46/NASB).* Jesus grew to understand the transposition from life to Life. He personified for all humanity this struggle between the *giving up* of our earthly obsessions for the *giving in* to the spiritual life--intimacy with God, insight, contentment and the apprehension of a peace that surpasses human reason. Jesus passed the peace of God along to those who were in crisis: *"today you will be with me in paradise." (Luke 23:43/NASB).* Even in the midst of his own suffering, Jesus regarded the suffering of others. Jesus was present with the peace of Ultimate Love to share with all who were lost in a matrix of their own devising.

On one side of Jesus was a thief who disavowed any recognition of Jesus, demanding only release from his pain. On the other side of Jesus was another thief who demurred to the personhood of Jesus, and simply surrendered to a deeper awareness of God's Presence. Thus a visual of humanity in qualified autonomy: the insight of the Holy on the one hand, and the obsessions of the flesh on the other. The former offers us peaceful detachment from the realities of our mortality. The later offers us nothing but the perpetuation of our suffering in thinking we are immortal or outside the reach of the Holy.

"It is finished." (John 19:28-30/NIV). There was nothing more to say. Even at his pending death, the life of Jesus reverberated with a redemptive purpose. God had spoken to humanity through a most illustrious revelation of *the way, the truth, and the life.* Now it was—is-- humanity's choice to respond.

There is no documentation of retribution, no rage, no hatred in the final words of Jesus. Instead, the *visual* we see is Jesus the peacemaker, one who, from his childhood, *"grew, waxed strong in spirit, filled with wisdom, and the* grace of God was upon him. and stature and in favor with God and humanity." (Luke 2:40/KJV). While Jesus detached from the wonky of the world, he embraced those who were effected by its influence, offering to them the peace of God and a path toward the detoxification of sin. Jesus became the ultimate revelation of what it means, not only to believe in a religious conviction, but to *BE-Live* in a moment-to-moment awareness of God's creative, redemptive, and sustaining Presence.

BE-Living as peacemakers regards actualizing the essential demeanor of Jesus and passing along he described as *"a peace which the world cannot give." (John 14:27/NIV).* Had Jesus been a political zealot, he would not have insisted upon this resolution of peace. The legitimate peace Jesus exemplified *was* "Shalom" – the well-being of one's own mind, heart, and body, and the reconciliation or wellness of persons in community. It can exist in the midst of a war-torn world, even in the midst of unresolved human conflicts. Jesus made that peace by giving his life for his brothers and sisters. "This is no easy peace, but it is everlasting and it comes from God."[622]

Glen Stassen:

Living the Beatitudes: Practical Peacemaking in a Really Wonky World

Jesus personified a sacred humanity in his admonishment of peace. Likewise, he taught that all who followed after him would transpose this same ideal into the midst of conflict on the Earth; to imitate him in becoming peacemakers in our daily circles of influence. Glen Stassen, former professor of theological ethics and political philosophy at the Southern Baptist Theological Seminary in Louisville, is noted for his book *Just Peacemaking,* and his activism or "transforming initiatives," pro-activity in promoting peace throughout the world.

According to a fellow professor at the International Baptist Theological Seminary, Lina Andronoviene, Stassen was one who followed the example of Jesus in his sojourn of a lifestyle that reflected the Beatitudes of Jesus. He wrote of Stassen, "I have witnessed him calming down a disgruntled tourist, and have heard him recount his involvement in the fall of the Berlin

---

[622] Henri Nouwen, *Life of the Beloved:* Ibid.

wall. It did not matter how small or great the conflict was—Glen believed that the Gospel of Jesus Christ calls us to work for peace, and that peace was possible.[623]

In his book *Just Peacemaking,* Stassen re-tells the story of his involvement in the 1980s in the de-escalation of nuclear missiles in Europe; as well as, the negotiations he spearheaded behind the scenes that helped position East Germany to demolish the Berlin Wall. Both became successful *"transforming initiatives"* toward peace in the world. Stassen wrote:

> The theme of the Beatitudes is a call for us to release our efforts
> to control everything and participate in God's initiatives toward
> peacemaking, [not through] a heavy guilt trip, but by the happy
> empowerment of delivering grace.[624]

Growing in the "grace and knowledge of the Lord," essentially means that to a life filled with purpose or *BE-Living* is to "create conditions for mutual well-being."[625] We become instruments of God's peace, not simply advocates for tolerant co-existence. Biblically- informed peacemaking is critiqued in dialogue with God and with the *other*. We are convicted by a higher Authority when we are wrong, and we are affirmed through peaceful reconciliation toward the most redemptive outcome when we are right.

Thomas Merton asserted that promoting God's peace through living the Beatitudes, "demands the most heroic labor and the most difficult sacrifice, a greater fidelity to the truth and a much more perfect purity of conscience."[626] The proclamation of peace and reconciliation was at the heart of the message of Jesus. Knowing peace *with God,* the peace *of God,* and striving to actualize *peace within the community* is at the core of what it means to BE-Live in Jesus. It is not a lifestyle for the faint of heart, but it is one for the faithful in Spirit.

---

[623] Death of *Just Peacemaking* Author and Professor, Glen Stassen, EBF Press Release (April 29, 2014)

[624] Glen Stassen, *Just Peacemaking: Transforming Initiatives for Justice and Peace* (Louisville, KY: Westminster/John Knox Press, 1992), 42; 59

[625] Ibid., p. 28

[626] *Thomas Merton, On Peace* (NY: McCall Publishing Company, 1968,) 112-113

SECTION 11:
Jesus: The Miracles

"No one could do the things that you do, unless God is with him." (John 3:2/NASB).

"Truly many other signs Jesus performed in the midst of his disciples are not written in this book. But these are written so that you might believe that Jesus is the Christ, the Son of the Living God, and in believing that you might have life in his name." (John 20:31/NASB).

The following is a compendium of substantial quotes about miracles from scholarly atheists, agnostics, and theists regarding the legitimacy of such perceived phenomena. They are included in such a way as to offer the reader the spectrum of thought regarding those who dismiss the possibility of miracles, those who qualify the term with a more rational understanding of the meaning of a miracle, and those who accept a miracle as divine interactivity in human history. They begin with the most atheistic and agnostic propositions and move toward theistic interpretations of the same. Note how the concepts of miracles varies (or progresses) from the purview of the following atheists and theists, from rejection to revelation, reason to the supra-rational in the following excerpts:

Sagan, Carl: *The Varieties of Scientific Experience: A Personal View of the Search for God,* **New York: Penguin, 2006**

> *"...mere eyewitness testimony is insufficient if what is being reported is sufficiently extraordinary." (136).*

> *"Miracles speak to us of all sorts of things religious that we have powerful wishes to believe." (137).*

Hitchens, Christopher: *god is not Great: how Religion Poisons Everything* **New York: Twelve, 2007**

> *"The tawdriness of the miraculous...in this age of fraud and conjuring..." (140).*

Dawkins, Richard: *A Devil's Chaplain,* New York: Mariner, 2003

> *"...the wanton use of miracle stories...are blatant intrusions into scientific territory...religious propaganda, and very effective... with an audience of unsophisticates and children." (150).*

_____: *The God Delusion* New York: Houghlin Mufflin, 2006

> *"Miracles violate the principles of science." (p.58).*

Feynman, Richard P.: *The Meaning of It All: Thoughts of a Citizen Scientist* Reading, MASS: Perseus Books, 1998

Science must practice the *"freedom of new ideas, new possibilities and not disregard ideas simply because they might be better than anything I can do." (115).* In some cases, nobody knows what happened.

Gould, Stephen Jay: *Rock of Ages: Science and Religion in the Fullness of Life* New York: Ballantine, 1999

In explaining the thought of Sir Isaac Newton, Gould concluded that Newton held a more open view of the universe. Thus, he had a view on the possibility of miracles to scientific discourse. God could work within His own established laws. *"If God wished to suspend these laws for a moment of creative interference, then He would do exactly as He wished, and scientists would have to pursue the task of explanation as best they could." (86).*

Ruse, Michael: *Can a Darwinian Be a Christian? The Relationship Between Science and Religion* Cambridge: University Press, 2001

> *"Many if not all of the miracles happened according to law; their miraculous nature comes from their meaning or significance... turning water into wine can be explained as the enthusiasm of the moment. It is from this regeneration of spirit that Christianity stems, not from some law-defying physiological reversals..." (96).*

Barclay, William: *And He Had Compassion: The Healing Miracles of Jesus* Valley Forge: Judson Press, 1975

"A miracle is something that moves us to wonder, something which no man can perform or explain...meaningful; every [miracle] tells us something about God." (2-3).

Borchert, Gerald L.: *John 1-11 - The New American Commentary* **Nashville: Broadman and Holman, 1996**

"The meaning of 'sign' is that it points beyond the physical, concrete reality to the reality of revelation. It provides insight into who Jesus is." (262).

Lewis, C. S.: *Miracles* **NY: Harper Collins, 2009**

"Miracles thus do not pose an irreconcilable conflict for the believer who trusts in science. On the other hand, in order for the world to avoid descending into chaos, miracles must be very uncommon." (167).

"God does not shake miracles into nature at random as if from a pepper-caster." (53).

Polkinghorne, John: *Belief in God in an Age of Science* **London: Yale, 1998**

"In unprecedented circumstances, it is entirely conceivable that God will act in totally novel and unexpected ways." (73).

"Miracles are a contradiction of one's adherence to a block universe." (68-69).

_____: *Quantum Physics and Theology: An Unexpected Kinship* **London: Yale, 2007**

God is not some kind of *"show off celestial conjurer..."* (34) miracles are *"events that are windows opening up a more profound perspective into the divine reality than that which can be glimpsed in the course of everyday existence, just as superconductivity opened up a window into the behavior of electrons in metals.* (36).

Collins, Francis S.: *The Language of God: A Scientist Presents Evidence for Belief* New York: Free Press, 2007

> *"A miracle is an event that appears inexplicable by the laws of nature. Well, clearly, if one starts out with the presumption that supernatural events are impossible, then no miracles can be allowed."* (49-50).

Ward, Keith: *The Big Questions in Science and Religion* West Conshohocken, PA:

Templeton Foundation Press, 2008

> *"A miracle should occur if there were good reason for God to cause an awe-inspiring event that reveals something of spiritual importance. The context makes all the difference. They are meant to disclose the reality of God and to transform the lives of those who are open to that disclosure."* (101-102).

Tipler, Frank J.: *The Physics of Christianity* New York: Doubleday, 2007

> A miracle is more *"an improbable event whose effect is to carry out God's plan for the universe...God acting through natural law, pushing the universe in the direction He wishes to go."* (107).

Tillich, Paul: *Systematic Theology,* Volume I Chicago: University, 1963

The Greek word, *SEMION* is better translated as "sign-events," or a "revelatory experience." This is not an irrational concept, since the given event is observed within *"the structure of being in which it becomes manifest..."* and provides, through an ecstatic experience, *"inspiration to a new dimension of knowledge, the dimension of understanding in relation to our ultimate concern and to the mystery of being."* (115).

"Reason receives revelation in ecstasy and miracles; but reason is not destroyed by revelation just as revelation is not emptied by reason." (118).

Schleiermacher, Friedrich: *The Christian Faith Philadelphia: Fortress Press,* 1976

> *"Miracles are simply phenomena in the realm of nature which are supposed not to have been caused in a natural manner. Many find the purpose of miracles simply in the fact that they turn the attention to Christ. It is natural to expect miracles from Christ who is the supreme divine revelation."* (72-73).

The Supra-Rational or Revelatory Meanings in the Miracles: "Signs" of a Greater Reality?

Fascinating questions regarding miracles center around how one interprets the possible activity of God in creation. In summary of the above compendium, for a theist, miracles or "signs" may denote the following possibilities:

1. The evidence of a Higher Mindfulness acting in human history or ecosystem through the diversion of the ordinary or naturally occurring events.

2. A supra-rational awareness of a previously unforeseen "way out of no way."

3. A "sign" or "wonder" is merely an illustrative word picture or event that reveals truth.

4. Sudden insight apprehended through wonder, in recognition of an open cosmos—full of possibilities never before imagined.

5. The historical evidence of the truest identity of Jesus as a *"mediator between God and humanity"* through his affirmative action within the human experience.

6. Divine activity suddenly "revealed" through a momentary pause of contemplation within the continuum of God's creative activity.

7. A holistic experience of phenomena unconfined by the predictable, common or routine that points to a supernatural *Manifestation*

within, yet from outside of our natural existence, not explainable by trivial magic, or trifling sensationalism.

If one believes in the continuing and creative activity of God, there is a justifiable belief in "signs and wonders," or purposeful *manifestations* of God's presence. Divine manifestations are designed for a creative purpose. Thus, from a biblical perspective, "signs" (or "miracles') are neither pious prestidigitation, nor are they random and unexplainable events performed merely to exploit the power of a wizard. These moments of eternity-in-real-time may confound the most erudite thinker, for they are not magical but *mystical,* manifesting the presence of a Greater Reality, revealing purpose and meaning to an observant and vulnerable humanity.

Miracles are not commercialized acts performed by some magical slight-of-hand, or a formalized incantation pronounced by a commercialized soothsayer. They do not esteem the sensationalistic notion of "my wish is God's command." Neither do they demure to the close-minded who will not allow themselves to be challenged by possibilities outside the confines of their own anatomized universe. If God is a mindful Creator, then miracles would be neither magic tricks or the *jumping through hoops* of academia to prove His existence to those who would require such non-sense in order to believe in something.

Legitimate miracles are a means through which God *continues to create* and consequently manifest Himself to humanity. In the biblical narratives, a miracle is a timely prompt toward insight. Such a momentous event exceptionally noticed by observation with an underlying meaning discerned by insight. The miracle event awakens a transfixion of the soul toward a mysterious moment of revelation, perhaps a manifestation of God's presence.

A Momentary Pause

The Meaning of a Miracle in the Gospel of John: The Transformation of Water into Wine

"But as it is written, 'eye has not seen, nor ear heard, neither have entered into the heart of man, the things which God has prepared for them that love him.'" (I Corinthians 2:9/NIV).

"...for we cannot stop speaking about what we have seen and heard." (Acts 4:20/NIV).

In John's poetic composition, miracles are defined by the Greek work, *SEMIA* or "sign." The seven "signs" in John's gospel are not performed by Jesus indiscriminately, but in the context of creating the community into which they are articulated. There is meaning underlying each "sign" perceivable by those who notice them and become enlightened to interpret them, those given to insight! Consider one example from the numerical word picture below in the "sign" of Jesus from the transformation of water into wine in John 2:1-12/NASB. There are poetic meanings to the respective dynamics to the miracle of turning water into wine that offer a threshold to insight.

Verse Six: the **"six stone water pots"** may signify the way in which the scripture describes humanity:

"**6** "= the Hebrew number of incompleteness or indefiniteness. It is contrast to the number "7," which is the most sacred number, the number of creation, the annual year of Jubilee, and the number of altars and lamps in the Temple. Thus, six is the number for humanity, created in God's image, but not divine.

Stone = ornately and intricated created in a unique design by a master artist; highly valuable; not easily contracting uncleanness, for they are derived from stone, not clay.

water pots = for religious purposes such as purification ceremonies, the washing of hands before a meal and the cleansing of other religious vessels used in rituals of worship.

<u>*Insight from the text:*</u> What is the meaning underlying the "sign?" *We are like* "the six stone water pots!" We are incomplete (not divine), of high value-- precious to our Creator, and we share a common quest for "religious" fulfillment through ceremonial practices. But ceremonial religiosity, ritual without substance, is insufficient for the transformation toward our true selves.

Verse 11: **"water into wine"** signifies the gradual giving way of antiquated religious rituals with the jubilate intimacy with God. The water of religious ritual must be transformed into the wine of celebration that only Jesus

can provide. The fermentation of a vintage wine takes years—as does the intimacy of one's soul in sync with God's presence. For such intimacy to occur, we must "grow in the grace and in the knowledge of our Lord." (2 Peter 3:18/NASB).

In context, the wedding supper itself may connect to the Old Testament idea of the jubilant relationship between God and His people. The nation of Israel celebrated their Passover through their Seder meal. The church celebrated a fellowship meal. All owned a sense of intimacy of God as their *Bridegroom*. For John, this symbol of a wedding was not only evidence of an intimacy with God in the past and in the present, but also as a foreshadowing of the *Marriage Supper of the Lamb* yet to be. (Revelation John 19:6-9/NASB). At this feast, John noticed those invited as "a great multitude that no one could count, from every nation, tribe, people and language, standing before the throne and before the Lamb." (Revelation 7:9/NASB).

The biblical accounts of the miracles of Jesus are more than God's intruding into natural law or interfering with human autonomy. They are meant to be interpreted for the visual meaning underlying the "sign." In summary of the *sign* of transforming water into wine, the following dynamics may be learned and thus, actualized with the creation of a new humanity:

1. Our old religious notions which leave us empty are now to be replaced with the joy of the Kingdom of God. A new creation is emerging through our relationship with Jesus. Jesus replaces empty rituals with the essential presence of God, in a relationship that is intimate and transformative.

2. Only those who participated and co-operated with the instructions of Jesus in the moment were able to experience the revelation in the miracle. In the turning of the water into wine, the servants who followed Jesus' instruction to fill the water pots to the brim actually "saw" the miracle unfold. They served the community through the miracle in which they participated.

If one only critiques the miracles of Jesus as simply a bystander, then the meaning of the event for the purpose of revelation is muddled. *Miracles are a picturesque language of God*. The miracles of Jesus were word pictures, articulated visuals of God's continuing creativity in the lives of persons, in community, and in an open cosmos of possibilities.

With each of the seven miracles in the Gospel of John, a meaning undergirding them is meant to be discerned. The accounts of the miracles were not preserved as a tabloid account of Jesus as a master magician or illusionist. Miracles or "signs" in the biblical narratives document the articulation of the ongoing creation of God in the context of human history-- initiatives through the momentous life, teaching, and ministry of Jesus, for the redemption of a new humanity.

SECTION 12:
Jesus: The Mediator: Dialogue between God and Humanity

"Between God and man stands no one—not God-man, not angel, not advocate. Nor is intercession or intervention required. As nothing comes between soul and body, father and child, potter and vessel, so nothing separates man from God, soul of his soul, his Father and Fashioner."[627]

Then Abraham pressed his request further. "Suppose there are only forty?"

And the Lord replied, "I will not destroy it for the sake of the forty." (Abraham in the role of a "mediator" in Genesis 18:21/NRSV)

Accordingly, He designed and devised me, and He prepared me before the foundation of the world, that I should be the mediator of His covenant." (Moses in the role of a "mediator" in the Assumption of Moses 1:14; 3: 29)

Then the LORD said to Moses, 'Go in to Pharaoh and say to him, 'Thus says the LORD, the God of the Hebrews, 'Let my people go, that they may serve me.' (Moses in the role of a "mediator" in Exodus 9:1/NRSV)

---

[627] Milton Steinberg, *Basic Judaism* (NY: Harvest Book, Harcourt, Brace & World, 1947) 57-58

In the account of Abraham above, the patriarch of the nation of Israel mediates with God for the sake of any "righteous persons" in Sodom and Gomorrah. In the later accounts of Moses, the founder of Judaism, described himself as a *"mediator of the covenant"* negotiating a message from God to the Pharaoh of Egypt for the liberation of Israel from slavery. Thus, there IS a precedent in religious history of mediation between the Holy and the heathen through individuals noted for their intimacy with God. Jewish mystic, Martin Buber wrote that the story of the Burning Bush represented an early "prophetic spirit" as God spoke through Moses, using a "stammering mouth" to bring "the voice of Heaven to Earth.[628]

Jesus said, "I am the way, the truth, and the life. No one comes to the Father, but through me."(John 14:6/NIV).

> *God being love, needs man. Man being weak and sinful and helpless, needs God. And Jesus is the mediator [the MESITES, or the 'middleman' in Job 9:33/NIV]; the one standing in the midst who draws man and God together again.[629]*

In Jesus God is speaking to humanity as God never spoke before. Humanity is capable of seeing the personification of the message and mind of God expressed our own context of history and in flesh. In the redemptive activity of Jesus, not only is there displayed a deep consciousness of God, but also a conscientiousness of how God's love is yet articulated even in a wonderful world *gone wonky.* If we want to understand the character and nature, even the suffering of God, we look at Jesus. To understand the character and nature, even the suffering of humanity, God (in a way perhaps beyond our comprehension) *experienced* the life of Jesus. Through Jesus, God suffered the travails and tragedies of humanity *with* humanity. Whereas God was once transcendent and sympathetic to the evil consequences of an unqualified human autonomy, in Jesus, God is revealed as imminent and empathetic with the dilemmas and suffering of our human existence. Jesus is our mediating presence in dialogue between God and humanity._*"God was reconciling the*

---

[628] Martin Buber, *Moses: The Revelation and the Covenant* (London: Horowitz Publishing, 1958) 57, 59

[629] Barclay, *Jesus as They Saw Him*, Ibid., 338; 427

world to himself in Christ, not counting people's sins against them." (II Corinthians 5:19/NIV).

In Jesus, God "rejoices and weeps" with humanity in a way not experienced by God *before* the passion of Jesus. Jesus is thus, the *"one mediator between God and the human race." (I Timothy 2:5/NAB)*. Jesus as mediator *clarifies* the experience of humanity with God, and God with humanity, in a way that is unprecedented, profound, and transforming. Through Jesus, humanity may apprehend a clearer notion of the incomprehensible God. Jesus said, *"he who has seen me has seen the Father."* (John 14:9/NASB). In turn, through Jesus, God may now empathetically, *grieve and groan with* all creation in the misery of its estrangement. (Romans 8:22/NAB).

In his consciousness of God, Jesus, BE-Lived the qualified autonomy of humanity in the midst of the *un*-qualified autonomy in human existence. Through this consciousness of Jesus, God enters into the situations of humanity in real time; *"we have an advocate with the Father." (I John 2:1/NRSV)*. In awareness of the attitude, purpose and mind of Jesus (Philippians 2:5/ AMP), humanity may explore our curiosities about God. Nineteenth century Scottish novelist and pulpiteer, George MacDonald wrote: "in order that we should know God and see how loveable he is, we must first of all know and understand Jesus."[630]

As a mediator, Jesus tempers the judgment *of* God with reconciliation. Before Jesus, humanity could only fear God, through shadowy images and projections of His terrifying royalty. In Jesus, "the shadows and the mist of the dark are gone,"[631] humanity sees God as Ultimate Love, a love that *"puts fear out of our hearts." (I John 4:18/NLV)*. We fall before God, but now in submission and reverence, no longer suffering from the threat of a vengeful God who would make us cower before Him—or like Adam and Eve, hide ourselves away. Jesus clarifies our vision of God, and refines God's empathy for and with a lost and broken humanity.

---

[630] *Letters*, August 3, 1869, edited by Glenn Edward Sadler (Grand Rapids: William B. Eerdmans, 1994), 170

[631] Barclay, *The Gospel of John*, Volume 1, Ibid., 34

SECTION 13:
<u>Jesus: A Visual of Sacred Humanity</u>

*"And when they came to a place called Golgotha, which means Place of a Skull."
(Matthew 27:33/NAB).*

*"Then they brought Him to the place Golgotha, which is translated, Place of a Skull."
(Mark 15:22/NRSV).*

*"When they came to the place called The Skull, there they crucified Him and the
criminals, one on the right and the other on the left." (Luke 23:33/NIV).*

*"They took Jesus, therefore, and He went out, bearing His own cross, to the place
called the Place of a Skull, which is called in Hebrew, Golgotha." (John 19:17/NASB).*

> The only son of God Almighty
> The holy one called Jesus Christ
> Healed the lame and fed the hungry
> And for his love they took his life

The accounts of the final days of Jesus on the earth have been so dogmatically theologized almost to the point of obscurity and irrelevance. Have we lost the essential meaning of the cross event for our lives through our systematized interpretations of the cross? Does the simple *visual* itself of Jesus at Gethsemani and on Golgatha supersede any foray of theological opinions masterfully crafted and articulated through generations of thought? The most popular theologies of *the cross event* through the centuries include the following:

A. **The Ransom of Christ**. A slave could be "redeemed" by another— one who could pay the purchase price of a slave in order to "set him free." (*Ruth 4:4-9; Mark 10:45; Eph 1:3-7/NIV*). Jesus *paid the price* of human sin and the suffering it causes. His sacrifice frees us from its bondage. In other words, by this theological interpretation, Jesus surrendered his life as a "ransom" to appease an angry God or as a payment to the devil for the lost souls of humanity. (See: The writings of *Gregory of Nyssa, 376-378 AD*).

B. **Satisfaction**. Because of sin, we owe God what we cannot repay— His honor. God became human to offer Himself for *the demand of justice* that is required. Jesus' perfect obedience, even in His death, is offered on our behalf to meet God's justice: "the demand for punishment for injustice is satisfied." (See: *St. Anselm, Archbishop of Canterbury, 1093-1109*).

C. **God as an Ultimate Example of Love and Morality**. Divine love is at work on the cross as the historic act of God's participation in human suffering. The cross is an objective act of God that actually brings about human salvation as we follow the example of Jesus to die to self and to sin. We are *"changed"* when we are confronted by the self-sacrifice and suffering of God by the injustice of human devising. (See: The writings of *Peter Abelard, 1125 AD*).

---

[632] *"They Killed Him"* Lyrics by Kris Kristofferson (1986)

D. John Calvin's idea of **Penal Substitution**. Christ took upon himself the curse of our sin. He made satisfaction of our separation from God upon himself through the shedding of His blood as the "perfect sacrifice" for forgiveness of sin. Since humanity is "totally depraved – Christ was put in the place of evil doers—to bear the punishment that ought to be ours." (See: The Writings of *John Calvin, 1536-1541*).

E. *Liberal Theology:* **Gaining a Higher Consciousness** because of the cross event. The innocence of Jesus and his "slaughter" spark us to think about the nature and needs of humanity to be liberated from our bad ways and behave more like Jesus. Through the unjust brutality of the cross, *we are awakened* and must repent from our own unjust and sinful practices. (See: The Writings of *Frederick Schleiermacher, 1821-1822*).

F. "**CHRISTUS VICTOR:**" A supernatural conflict between the divine power of God versus the evil powers of the cosmos was raged to its climax at the cross. Through the injustice perpetrated upon Jesus, a "domination system" *of evil* was exposed when it killed Jesus. But, God won the battle of good over evil. For Jesus died, but conquered even death with the greater hope of the resurrection. Humanity was awakened to what evil can do and can choose salvation: *eternal victory over sin, death, the devil, and even the wrath of God.* (See: The Writings of *Gustav Aulen, Bishop in the Church of Sweden, 1931-1948*).

G. **Liberation Theology**. Through the visual of the cross, God identifies with the oppressed, the outcasts, the poor, and the dying. When one looks at Jesus on the cross, the image ignites a *spiritual awakening to the injustices* perpetrated upon the "underlings" in our world. We renounce the madness of materialism and care for the destitute. We must identify with the man on the cross and relinquish a materialistic culture if we are to be truly "saved." (See: the writings of *Gustavo Gutierrez, Leonardo Boff, Juan Luis Segundo, and/or Jon Sobrino, Late 1900s*).

All the above have in some way infiltrated various and respective sectarian dogmas through the centuries. While there may be some credibility to their theology for the time and context of those respective theologians, one must be cautious to consider the perspectives of those at the time of Jesus's final days with them. What can we see simply in viewing the cross through the lens of the narratives themselves? How did those closest to Jesus interpret what was happening?

In the cross event, Jesus epitomized *a sacredness of life*—the intentional design of God for humanity. The cross event is the true "transvaluation of all values, to die to the standards and values of the 'world'."[633] There are values worth dying for and there are causes worth living for. Both of which are seen as the crucifixion of Jesus. Leslie Weatherhead, pastor of the City Temple in London during the Nazi attacks of World War II, wrote that Jesus imparts "the highest kind of life to us. God's power invaded the earthly scene."[634]

At Gethsemani and Golgotha, Jesus actualized a *sacred humanity*. In living responsively to God's presence, he matured into the fullness of his personhood as designed by God. He lived fully God's purpose for humanity, even in his devotion to a purpose-driven death. By his Be-Living to the fullest extent of his existence, Jesus articulates the "qualitatively unsurpassable and irreversible approach of God,"[635] he was one-with-God.

At the cross event, Jesus displayed the perfect love of God, raised up, with open arms, gasping for breath, whispering words of forgiveness, and bleeding for the sake of the "lost causes" in a world gone wonky. Both the agony of the brokenness of humanity and the empathy of God are revealed in the suffering of Jesus. Through the cross event, Jesus exposed the unjust religious, political, and cultural systems of the world! But he did more than that. Jesus revealed God's redemptive grace with the potential for a lost humanity to find the way to truth and life! An ever-transcendent deity, from a distance, could hardly speak to humanity, but "a God who shared their suffering to utmost might be heard."[636] The cross spoke boldly of an imaginative, immutable, and immeasurable grace—the perfect love of God.

---

[633] John Macquarrie, *Jesus Christ in Modern Thought* (London: SCM Press, 1990), 84

[634] *"The Resurrection and the Life Over His Own Signature"* (NY: Abingdon Press, 1955,) 123; 133

[635] Karl Rahner, *The Practice of Faith: A Handbook of Contemporary Spirituality* (NY: Crossroad, 1986), 8

[636] John Macquarrie. *Two Worlds Are Ours* (Mineapolis: Fortress Press, 2004), 148

A Momentary Pause:

Revelation at the Cross: What Did the Disciples See?

In the seventh grade at Indian Riffle Junior High School, I had a crush on Sandy Shaver. She had straight brown hair that blew in the wind, a really nice smile, and her hand didn't sweat with I held it. I always managed to sit beside her at lunch, and sometimes she would share her mom's homemade snickerdoodles with me. As subtle as it was, to me, that was a sign that "she liked me." I liked her too. But unlike others who flaunted themselves in front of those they liked, I was not so bold. I wanted to woo her—but not stalk her. So, when it came time for the upcoming Junior High Valentines Dance, I sent her a note during English, asking her if she planned to go. I didn't ask her to go, I simply asked her if she "planned to go." I was subtle. However, at the end of the note, when I signed my name, I didn't DOT the "I" in "Brian," I put a very light, little heart over the letter. I didn't want to frighten her away.

When she wrote back, she wrote that she was planning to go, with the "hope" that I would be there too. It was rather formal, but encouraging. We showed up at the dance, overcame our adolescent fears, and actually danced together—sort of. It was awkward, but we were awkward together, so it really didn't matter. From this gradual growing together, we learned to care for each other. It started with the simple signs of awareness that grew to a deeper understanding of one another. (At the end of the year, Sandy wrote in my yearbook, "I'm yours 'til the sidewalk walks." Later that year, she moved away and I never heard from her again.)

But the point of the matter is that the person of Jesus, his humanity, message, mediation, and the cross event are signs of God's wooing of persons to himself, not stalking humanity for the sake of divine retribution. As God searched for Adam and Eve in the garden, so does God pursue humanity, now, through Jesus, with an empathy and understanding of our brokenness and fragility.

No one can hide from the sign of the cross of Jesus. In preparation for the cross, Jesus confronted the brutality of humanity through the perfect love of God that enabled him. In turn, Jesus epitomized the love of God, fearlessly submitting himself to the worst of human depravity, without hatred or malice, climaxing with words of grace and mercy to the merciless: "Father, forgive them, they don't know what they are doing." (Luke 23:34/NIV).

From the sign of the cross, we discover insight: *there is nothing in all the world that humanity can do that will stop God from loving humanity with a perfect love,* not even the "powers of hell." (Romans 8:38/NLT). Jesus reveals to humanity the unconquerable and quintessentially-infinite love of God. The crucifixion of Jesus lifted up boldly before humanity, "the perfect love of God." Through the cross event, humanity need no longer be fearful or estranged from God; instead we can be "at home with God without fear— as a child with his father." [637]

In Jesus we see a sacred humanity, or a person who transfixed the core of his being toward Ultimate Love. Within this context we measure the meaning of the cross event. The legitimate question might be how the witnesses to the crucifixion subjectively experienced and interpreted Jesus on the cross, rather than how it became objectively interpreted or theologized centuries later. Even with all the theology throughout ecclesiastical history that has tried to explain the cross event, the quintessence of the cross, above all, is the articulation of a loving God through the sacred humanity of Jesus.

> 'What wondrous love is this.' It is the kind of repetition that sounds trite when spoken, yet gains strength and power through singing. These are not the carefully crafted words of a theologian, but utterances directly from the heart or, even more profoundly, from the soul."[638]

> *What wondrous love is this, O my soul, O my soul!*
> *What wondrous love is this that caused the Lord of bliss*
> *To bear the dreadful curse for my soul, for my soul.*

Jesus was the ultimate expression of a sacrificial love. For some this devotion is baffling, irrational in the flesh. But for many through the centuries since the event, this revelation of love awakens the soul to insight. This love

---

[637] Barclay, *Autobiography*, Ibid., 54

[638] C. Michael Haun, *A History of Hymns* (Perkins School of United Methodist Theology. A traditional southern Spiritual, of unknown origin, c. 1811)

moved those closest to him to consider a message to humanity: *"do your worst, yet still God will love you."* What wondrous love is this---indeed!

Sometimes the magnitude of a message of redemption can *only* reach the core of us through the alarming visual of the *unjustified suffering* or bloodshed of the innocent. In his *Memoirs,* peace activist, Robert McAfee Brown relates a story from his own pilgrimage toward his own revelatory understanding of the cross of Jesus. He relates that in the cross event, the love of the creator of the cosmos is present, participating in that transaction. *"This is not the crude image of God sacrificing Jesus instead of taking the rap himself, it is God at the center of a sacrificial act of love the heart of the universe, showing us a place where brokenness would be healed and love would finally triumph.*[639]

In this transaction, God more than sympathizes, God visually empathizes with the brokenness of humanity. Likewise, in this same transaction, humanity comes to the actualization of *grace and mercy,* the "highest good" or the "perfect love" of God exemplified by Jesus. Through his faithfulness in revealing the love of God, "Jesus accepted a miserable death."[640]

The cross event exposes the tension within the modality of the body and the soul. Like Jesus, we suffer from the consequences of our mortal selves and ask of God, in the flesh, *"Why hast Thou forsaken me?" (Matthew 27: 45-50/KJV).* But also like Jesus, the *"me"* in the flesh learns to transpose my being to the *"Thee"* experience of the soul, in absolute surrender: *"into Thy hands I commend my spirit." (Luke 23:46/KJV).* On the cross, Jesus revealed to humanity the transposition of our earth-bound autonomy to a perfect absolution, spiritual repose, and to our place in God's consummate and empathetic presence.

---

[639] Robert McAfee Brown, *Memoirs,* Ibid., *42*
[640] John B. Cobb, *Jr., Jesus' Abba: The God Who has not Failed* (Minneapolis: Fortress Press, 2015), 17-22

SECTION 14:

Jesus: The Momentum of BE-Living

"...that I might know Him in the fellowship of His suffering and in the power of His resurrection..." (Philippians 3:10/NAB).

"The resurrection in itself, Christ's resurrection...even after, it was still a mystery, beyond the compass of reason."[641]

Often the existential tension in our culture is somewhere in the mix of a post-Enlightenment mentality, the church's confessions of faith and the hazy opinions of the uncertain populace. In our high-technological age, our world of science fiction, the idea of a resurrection from death is difficult to accept as an historic fact—"outside of a faith in the supernatural."[642] Perhaps many today would rather believe that Jesus was an alien, who like Mr. Spock on *Star Trek,* beamed up to the USS Enterprise, rather than to succumb to believe in such a thing as a resurrection.

---

[641] John Donne Sermons VII.3.212-14

[642] John MacQuarrie, *Jesus Christ in Modern Thought* (London: SCM, 1990) 4

The resurrection of Jesus from the dead and his subsequent appearances to both a select and random community is the essential dynamic in the development of the Christian faith. <u>Something happened</u> through this event that distinguished Jesus from any and all other religious leaders in history. Could it actually be that God manifested his healing power through the person of Jesus, and that the resurrection can be intelligibly seen as a disclosure of the ultimate spiritual destiny of all humans, or even the phenomenon of *"the primacy of spiritual over physical reality?"* [643]

Legitimate scholars must come to terms with the evidence that <u>something happened</u> in the account of the life of Jesus of Nazareth at the end of his life from which emerged not a new religion, but an ecstatic movement of persons. This movement rippled unencumbered from "Jerusalem, in Judea, in Samaria, and into Rome, the uttermost parts of the world." The early sect of Jesus based on "grace" and BE-Living as "peacemakers," overcame the obstacles in its confrontations with the religious, political, economic, and military powers of the Rome through a world-transforming momentum that continues to this day in the innermost hearts of persons.

Scholars John B. Cobb and David Ray Griffin believed that the contemporary church needs to continue to tell and re-tell the narrative of the resurrection. Not that it can be ever be historically "proven," but that it is of "revelatory significance." The BE-Living of Jesus was a momentous moment in history, "and its repeated enactment and remembrance has strengthened its field of force"[644] in the lives of persons, communities and regions throughout the world.

The Resurrection: God's "Field of Force" in the Continuum of Creation

Sceptics continue to offer their rationales against the resurrection event: to discredit the creative transformation of those who experienced it and the subsequent and unquenchable "field of force" it created. Disclaimers of the resurrection of Jesus include:

---

[643] Keith Ward, *Rethinking Christianity* (Oxford Oneworld, 2007) 144

[644] John B. Cobb, Jr. and David Ray Griffin *Process Theology: An Introductory Exposition,* (Philadelphia: Westminster, 1976) 102-103

1. A resurrection would defy the laws of nature.
2. Just because there may have been an empty tomb, does not mean a resurrection happened. The body could have been stolen, or, Jesus was not really dead when taken from the cross. He was resuscitated while in the tomb.
3. If something "supernatural" did occur, it may have been because Jesus was an extra-terrestrial being, an alien who either could not be killed or beamed up to another dimension, or to a mother-spaceship.
4. The resurrection was either a hoax or mass hallucination. Either the disciples wanted to overthrow the Roman empire with a new religio-political revolution or they all just projected their delusions of grandeur into the formation of covert operation they called the "church."
5. Those who visited the gravesite on the day after the crucifixion were actually so emotionally wrought that they only saw who they so desperately wanted to see, or they simply went to the wrong tomb.

However, there are reasonable responses to the above suppositions that may assume some empirical legitimacy—especially for possibility of the supra-rational:

1. Laws of nature are descriptive of what is observable. They do not prohibit what is either not observable, possible, or yet to be experienced in a mindfully driven cosmos.
2. There would have been no reason to have stolen the body of Jesus. Moreover, a resuscitated Jesus would not have ignited the same following as a resurrected one. The devoted disciples who were so brutalized and tortured in the aftermath of the crucifixion did so because they believed in the resurrection of Jesus.
3. There was a Roman census and Jewish record of physical births. No one was unaccounted for—especially had there been the unusual behavior of an alien or a foreigner in their midst.
4. Hallucinations are not a community phenomenon. They usually happen to one person. A hoax does not linger for long without a disclaimer. There are no disclaimers concerning any hoax about the resurrection of Jesus as the movement of the event began to emerge in the Roman empire.

5. The crucifixion of Jesus incited public attention. Because his followers WERE grieving a significant loss, they certainly would have known where Jesus had been settled.

Could there be another reason for the sacrificial devotion of the disciples in their insistence upon sharing the resurrection of Jesus throughout a dangerous world? What other than believing so fervently in the resurrection event itself have motivated the early disciples to risk horrible torture and death rather than to renounce what they knew to be true? Did something of *supra-rational* significance happen?

Sometimes the most reputedly rational retorts can reach absurdity. In a debate with Christian apologist William Lane Craig, noted Professor of Chemistry at Oxford University, *Peter Atkins,* contested the resurrection by arguing that those disciples who saw their beloved leader were simple-minded people so desperate to believe, "they made up the resurrection story". They wanted so badly to be in the notoriety of miraculous events at the time, *"they simply made it up. They were bored. There wasn't much to do in Palestine at the time."*[645]

Atkin's highly biased statement is an irrational and inconsistent with his inclination toward the evolutionary dictum of the survival of the fittest. It was an event by which terrified men and women, hiding in fear of religio-political reprisal, were transformed into a devoted and courageous community, transformed into vessels of peace and redemption—by wielding the words of Jesus, and not by the edge a sword. What else but the magnitude of the resurrection event could echo throughout human history for over two thousand years and continue to ignite wonder and hope for humanity?

A Momentary Pause:

"The resurrection is pivotal for Christian belief."[646]

"Jesus is Alive!"

---

[645] *Debating the Resurrection of Jesus, William Lane Craig vs Peter Atkins,* hosted by William F. Buckley, 1998 (https://www.youtube.com/watch?v=fhNHuRkWEhs)
[646] John Polkinghorne, *God of Hope,* Ibid., 68

"He is alive, indeed!"

Although profound, the teachings of Jesus alone were not the unquenchable force that gave birth to the church. It was the belief in the resurrection that set Jesus apart from other good teachers or miracle workers. It distinguished his sect of followers from other cults. It was an exceptionally creative event with the magnitude and momentum befitting a comprehensive, all-embracing transformation of persons in community.

> *If the Lord's message is universal, if it acknowledges no boundaries,*
> *it is because the starting point is the conquest of death, which is*
> *the greatest limitation set on human beings. The resurrection*
> *is thus an affirmation and promise of life for all human beings*
> *without exception.*[647]

If Jesus was the *"the radiance of God's glory and the exact representation of his being" (Hebrews 1:3/NIV)* in human history, then he would have been a resilience in the afterglow of his life; an energy that could not have been extinguished by his death. If Ultimate Love was present in Jesus, there would have been a crescendo, a climactic moment, a definitive revelation of his Being—*perhaps a resurrection?*

The BE-Living of Jesus could neither be confined in a tomb or extinguished in history. There was nothing ordinary about his transformative influences on those to whom he made himself known. Jesus BE-Lived an inspired way of life before death. The momentum of his life before his death, could not be quenched by his crucifixion; "only because of this God-in-him were they unable to kill him."[648] Those who were truly *in-sighted* through Jesus' life *before death* experienced Jesus's *life after death*. They themselves arose through the "field of force" of Jesus's life within them and were transformed.

The church or the *EKKLESIA* is a community *risen* from the hellish and the hollow to the high and holy purview of the resurrection, grew to pass the peace of God into the world through the exhilaration of Jesus' resurrection.

---

[647] Gustavo Gutierrez, *The God of Life* Ibid., 109
[648] Soelle, *Theology for Skeptics*, Ibid., 107

Through the telling and retelling of this "good news," we "recover the same sense of his presence:"[649] *Jesus is risen! He has risen, indeed!*

According to New Testament historian and scholar, Glen B. Siniscalchi, the most compelling evidence for the resurrection of Jesus regards the shift in the worship practices in the early church from Judaism. The change that took place from various ceremonial meals in Judaism to the specifically Christian understanding of the Eucharist.

It is significant that the Eucharist was celebrated on a weekly basis on Sundays, and the symbolic liturgical actions that accompanied the earliest Christian assemblies are empirical evidence of a paradigm shift significant in the history of Judaism. "Jewish and Greco-Roman religious influences seem incapable of accounting for these relatively undisputed practices. By contrast, I argue that Jesus' resurrection best resonates with them.[650]

From the profundity in telling his story, the presence of Jesus emerges above the confines of our skeptical or mechanistic culture and ignites the soul in revelation and hope for the redemption of humanity. This is an experience of transcendence that moves humanity toward the sense of a more complete sense of being. It is not a momentary sensation, but an actualization of ultimacy, intimacy and interpretive movement.

This experience—is interpreted by countless persons crossing generational and geographical lines as a legitimate, supra-rational encounter with God that "liberates the devotee into a reality larger than himself, to the life of moral striving and a sense of being called to service in the world."[651] By no other means proffered to humanity, receiving the resurrection of Jesus transforms us with the momentum and fortitude to be like Jesus, to BE-Live as *peacemakers* in a wonderful world gone wonky and sometimes wicked. Through our intentional imitation of the teachings of Jesus in the Beatitudes, and with insight of his resurrection, we ourselves, may become vessels of revelation. In our *BE-Living*, we are enabled by God to bewilder and engage injustice, challenge tyrannies of power in high places that exploit the poor

---

[649] John B. Cobb, Jr. Ibid., 24

[650] "*Eucharistic Origins as Evidence for Jesus' Resurrection" Journal of the International Society of Christian Apologetics*, Volume 4, Number 1 (2011), 83-95

[651] John MacQuarrie, *Theology, Church, and Ministry* (NY: Crossroad, 1986), 71-76

and innocent and offer the hope and potential for a sacred humanity to emerge toward creating a more wonderful world.

SECTION 15:
Jesus: Hope for a Dimension of Consummate Being

"Jesus said, 'I go to prepare a place for you...'" (John 14:2b/KJV).

"The domain of God is certainly beyond our finite thinking...God's domain has plenty of room."[652]

"Death...thou shalt die."[653]

Jesus is called by the early church the *"Alpha and the Omega...the first and the last, the beginning and the end." (Revelation 22:13/NRSV)*. The life of Jesus as filtered through the gospels reminds us that if our finite demise should occur by our death or if humanity were to instigate a catastrophic event of

---

[652] Gerald L. Borchert, *John 12-21 The New American Commentary* (Nashville: Broadman & Holman, 2002), 104

[653] Excerpt from *Death be not Proud* by John Donne, Holy Sonnet 10, 1609

apocalyptic proportions, God will continue to provide a place for humanity to *be*.

If God is *eternally present*, the beginning and the end, and the new beginning and its corresponding end, old things pass (as in the crucifixion) and new things emerge (as in the resurrection). God abides steadily in a domain respective of His Being, yet influential in the momentum on earth toward the consummation of all things. In God, there is a hope that with the end of an era, there will emerge the beginning of another, until there is (perhaps) the realization of a garden of Eden—*revisited through the redemption of Ultimate Love.*

There is an end to our finite *AION* or "age," or "cycle of time" that will give way to the future eras, culminating in the end of days and the beginning of whatever providence God will provide. This is what the Archbishop of Constantinople, John Chrysostom, referred to as "the consummation of all things. So let us not fear and shudder."[654] Like others before it, our *AION* will pass, only to be transposed into the era yet-to-be. As the "Alpha and the Omega," God is sovereign over the beginning and the end of our cycles of time as the momentum of His creation continues progressively forward in the momentum of God's continuum of creation.

By the very nature of *BE-living*, there is a trust in the ever-abiding nature of God. Our intuitive questions, rational thought, and insight indicate there is a longevity of life beyond the temporal existence for which we become all-too accustom. Intimacy with God, "heart, mind, soul, and strength," prompt for us not only wishful thinking, but an intuitive hope that life *somehow* continues from Ultimate Love. John Polkinghorne asserted this "intuition of hope" as a universal dynamic in what it means to be human. Human beings possess a significant intuitive knowledge that in the end, *"all shall be well.*[655]

Jesus assured his disciples: *"I go to prepare a place for you."* After all he had experienced with Jesus, his disciple, Thomas boldly asserted, *"Lord, we do not know where you are going." (John 14:1-5/NASB).* Like Thomas, truly, no one literally knows to where Jesus ascended at the end of the first chapter of the book of Acts. Nor does anyone know literally what that place is like.

---

[654] Gospel of Matthew, Homily 90.2

[655] Polkinghorne, *God of Hope,* Ibid., 30-31

All we have are images, symbols, metaphors and poetry to enable our hope of a "prepared place" in which to abide in the consummative presence of Ultimate Love. By his life, death and exultation Jesus made it possible for this place to be made known, to be hopeful for our lives to be transposed into the fullness of its wonder, but also "to be there *with him*."[656]

A Momentary Pause:

Metaphors and Symbols of Our Prepared Place from the Book of Revelation

"Hope is tenacious. It goes on living and working when science has dealt it what should be a death blow." [657]

God "supplies all with a suitable dwelling place…this is the couch on which the guests shall recline, having been invited to the wedding."[658]

Words are insufficient to describe *the prepared place*, of which Jesus taught. Still, humanity has the capacity to discern an ascent into the consummate of God. This is the ascent to a "heavenly realm," that can only be described by symbols and metaphors, poetry and psalms. Here is God's ultimate provision for the life of humanity, where there is no shadow of death. It is inhabited by a diverse community for whom all needs are provided. Some call this place, *eternity*, others call it is an expanse called *Heaven*, but to the hopeful it is merely called *home*.

1. *It is a place of personal belonging.* From the foreshadows of the wedding feast in the gospel of *John, in chapter 2* emerges the "Marriage Supper of the Lamb" (Revelation 19:7-9/NASB), a joyful and intimate celebration in a place of ethereal "wedlock" between God and all whom God loves.

2. *It is a place of justice: divine reconciliation.* The heinous sinfulness of earthly "principalities, powers, rulers of the darkness of the work,

---

[656] G. R. Beasley-Murray, *John* Word Bible Commentary (Nashville: Thomas Nelson, 1999), 249

[657] Paul Laurence Dunbar, *The Faith Cure Man* (1986)

[658] Irenaeus, *Against Heresies* 5.36.2

and spiritual wickedness in high places" (Ephesians 6:12/KJV) are extinguished and reconciled by justice by the very Word of God. (Revelation 18:9-20; 20: 11-14; 21:8/KJV).

3. *It is a holy place.* God will be with those whom He loves and, in the fullness of His presence heal them from the travail of their earthly existence. (Revelation 21:3-4; 22:2/KJV).

4. *It is a place wherein all essential needs are met.* No one will hunger or thirst. *(See: Revelation 21:6; 22:2). No one will fear the darkness of night nor suffer from the heat of the day.* (Revelation 21:23-25; 22:5; 22:17/KJV).

5. *It is a place of community.* No one is autonomous, anonymous, or unaccountable. All of creation is safe within an exquisite sanctuary of interconnectedness. (Revelation 21: 9-21/KJV).

6. *We are guided into this place by God's consummate Presence.* God's bids us "Come!" by the guidance of a "Bright and Morning Star." (Revelation 22:16-17/KJV). This is a visual of a cosmic occurrence that navigates our passage through the darkness of night to the herald of dawn. It is distinguishable from all other sources of light.

7. *It is a place of infinite mercy, grace, and peace that, even in our present existence, infiltrates the soul of humanity.* This is the transfixion of our being, complete. In the meanwhile, we reside in the yet-to-be, in the grace and hope of abiding in God's prepared place. (Revelation 22:21/KJV).

EPILOGUE

Spiritual Modulation: The Story of Micah, Psalm 46 and the Hymns of Andrea Crouch

I first saw Micah while Christmas shopping at the Mall in Fairborn, Ohio. The twenty-some young man was playing the grand piano near the food court. The music resembled "Silent Night," but it had been arranged in rather gothic-sounding minor chords. It was haunting and drew me closer.

Micah's appearance was bizarre as well—especially for the Christmas season. He looked more like someone promoting Halloween: clad in a black cape-like rain coat that he draped over the back of the piano bench, his head was shaven, his skin almost looked to be bleached, and his hands boney, almost skeletal, as he waved them up and down the keyboard. And he seemed to be totally alone, huddled over the piano like the Phantom of the Opera. After a few disconcerting minutes, I moved on. This music was not in sync with what I looked forward to hearing in a more traditional celebration of Christ's birth.

Several weeks later, I was approached by one of my parishioners. She asked me to visit her son, who had been admitted to Miami Valley Hospital for experimental treatment for terminal cancer. Of course, I agreed. She further explained that during his Junior year in high school, her son had run away to California. Although he had once believed in God, he had grown disillusioned with the church and hypocritical believers and desired to live "real" in the "real world."

While he was in California, he was diagnosed with cancer. With no money and no health insurance, he returned home. Although he did not personify the role of the repentant prodigal son, he was alarmed by this sudden downward spiral of sickness in his life. The prognosis was dismal. There was an urgency to her request for a pastoral visit.

The next day, I dressed in my preacher-go-on-visitation suit and tie, and with Bible in hand, I went to visit her son, Micah. As I stepped into his private room, I was jolted to see that this was the pianist I had seen at the Mall!

He was sitting up, obviously with some discomfort, gliding his fingers on the keys of a small keyboard he balanced on his lap. As I stepped into the room he glared at me suddenly. I'm not sure if it was because I interrupted his composing, or because I was not a part of his more gothic worldview. He grimaced at me, "You're a preacher, right?" I responded with a shaky grin, "Does it show?"

"You look like a preacher." He replied. Then he proceeded to severely cuss me—quite creatively, before returning to his keyboard. After a moment or two, to regain my religious equilibrium, I asked him to tell me about what he was playing. "It sounds really dark to me. What is that?"

"The music I'm feeling." he said.

After a few minutes of superficial conversation that made us both feel awkward and uneasy, I left, but promised to return with a better entrance than I had made that day. I did return, several times. But I didn't wear the preacherly apparel, and I just depended upon carrying the Scripture, not in my hand, but in my heart. I learned to love Micah. He was REAL, broken, and lost, but honest.

He shared with me many things about his life, his music, and his deepest thoughts about his condition that was continuing to worsen. The last time I communed with Micah was shorty after a bone marrow transplant, a procedure that, along with chemo and radiation, belayed him in intense pain. Sores and blisters even coated the roof of his mouth and down his throat. He could barely swallow and could only talk with me above a whisper.

I wore protective garb to prevent any germs I might have from effecting Micah's health any worse than what it already was. I moved a chair for myself near his bed and held his hand. "What can I do for you, Micah?"

He groaned above a whisper, "Just pray, just pray, just pray." There was melodious moment of modulation in his words.

I prayed, then closed with an *"Amen."* Micah squeezed my hand, and said, "pray some more." I prayed again, and after a second "amen," he repeated, "pray more, pray more." I had run out of words to pray with. Then it came to me: Micah was a musician! So, I decided to pray the Psalms, all that I could remember—then when I exhausted all of those, I would make up my own. My prayers became melodic and he seemed to calm himself.

Then abruptly, he spoke. "I want you to do my funeral."

"I will." There was a moment of silence between us, then I asked him, "What do you want me to say?"

"Tell them about Jesus." He replied. "My friends…tell them about Jesus—not about the church or church stuff, just tell them about Jesus."

Only hours later, Micah died. I was strong for those who were grieving him at the hospital, but when I was alone, I cried. I learned to love Micah—his honesty, compassion for others, intellect and artistry were amazing. He also had a great devotion to Jesus and his teachings about love and grace. He depended on Jesus! In spite of all he endured during his illness, in his last hours, he exhibited a hope that all would be well--eventually.

I asked several of Micah's friends to help me plan his funeral which was to be held in the small, conservative Baptist church for which I was the pastor. Micah had told his friends that even though I was a pastor, I was "ok" and could be trusted. The day of the funeral that little church was filled with a menagerie of persons pierced and tattooed, with spiked hair, and a sundry of bizarre jewelry and designed tee shirts. Not at all a typical Sunday morning service.

We played Micah's music over the PA system, his best friend played a ten minute solo on his bass guitar, and I offered an open mic for those attending to share their final thoughts about Micah. One girl stood up and shared how he had composed a poem about love that he shared with her once. She had memorized the poem. The poem she shared was actually from I Corinthians 13.

I closed the service by telling them about Jesus. There was not a sound in the sanctuary. With the mention of the name of Jesus, there was a curious reverence in the room, a hope, and sense of Something more in our midst. One could almost feel the gathering being transposed from their vulnerability in the gloom and despair of Micah's death, to the hope and upswing of a revelatory moment. It was all about Jesus.

This experience ignited intuitive or ultimate questions that reason alone could not answer. Reason could offer medical and bio-chemical explanations for Micah's death, but it could not offer substantive responses to the fascinating questions that only a spiritual ascent could offer. Such responses required a change in the tonality of one's life or spiritual modulation.

Modulation: Ultimate BE-Living!

In musical theory, *modulation* or change in color-tonality is properly defined as "the transformation of feeling...the metamorphosis of different rhythmic treatment of a succession of notes...moving from one key to another."[659]

In his classic work, *Harmony,* music theorist, Walter Piston, suggests that modulation in a composition is essential for the fullest auditory experience of the piece. He wrote that composers most often are consistent in not remaining in one key throughout any piece of music. Most would agree that staying within one key is most "aesthetically undesirable." Thus, the process of modulation, or change in key is one of the most important resources of variety in music. A change of key means a "change of tonal center, which all the other tones are to be related."[660] While this can be an intentional technique in musical composition, it may also be a metaphor in describing the progressive deepening of one's awareness of the Presence of God. As one grows in the grace and knowledge of the Lord, there is a "change of tonal center," *sacred modulation, as if climbing Jacob's ladder!*

This modulation transposes us from believing in something to BE-Living in awareness of God's presence. We learn or grow to love *(or know intimately)* God more holistically: through *"heart (intuition), mind (reason), soul (revelation), and strength (personhood)."*

[659] Aaron Copland, *What to Listen for In Music* (NY: McGraw-Hill, 1957), 24-25; 53
[660] Walter Piston, *Harmony* (NY: W. W. Norton & Company, 1969) 139

A Momentary Pause

<u>The Modulation in Psalm 46 (NRSV) and In the Lyrics of Andrea Crouch</u>

1

God is our refuge and strength,
  a very present help in trouble.

2

Therefore we will not fear though the earth gives way,
  though the mountains be moved into the heart of the sea,

3

though its waters roar and foam,
  though the mountains tremble at its swelling. **Selah**

    I've had many tears and sorrows,
    But in every situation,
    God gave me blessed consolation,
    that my trials come to only make me strong.

    Through it all,
    I've learned to trust in Jesus,
    I've learned to trust in God. *(Andrae Crouch, "Through It All," Universal Music Publishing Group, 1971).*

4

There is a river whose streams make glad the city of God,
  the holy habitation of the Most High.

5

God is in the midst of her; she shall not be moved;
  God will help her when morning dawns.

6

The nations rage, the kingdoms totter;
  he utters his voice, the earth melts.

7

The Lord of hosts is with us;
    the God of Jacob is our fortress. **Selah**

    When trouble is in my way
    I can't tell the night from day
    When I'm tossed from side to side
    Like a ship on a raging tide
    I don't worry, I don't fret,
    My God has never failed me yet,
    I've got confidence,
    God is going to see me through. *(Andrae Crouch, "I've Got Confidence,"*
    Capital Christian Music Group, Raleigh Music Publishing, 1971).

8

    Come, behold the works of the Lord,
how he has brought desolations on the earth.

9

He makes wars cease to the end of the earth;
    he breaks the bow and shatters the spear;
    he burns the chariots with fire.

10

"Be still, and know that I am God.
    I will be exalted among the nations,
    I will be exalted in the earth!"

11

The Lord of hosts is with us;
    the God of Jacob is our fortress." **Selah**

    How can I say thanks for the things He has done for me?
    Things so undeserved, yet He gave to prove His love for me?
    All that I am or ever hope to be,
    I owe it all to Thee
    To God be the glory
    For the things He has done. *(Andrae Crouch, "My Tribute: to God be the*

Glory," Bud John Songs, Inc., Admin. by EMI Christian Music Publishing, 1971).

"Boy, it's called 'MODULATION:'" My Memorable Faith Lesson From Andrae Crouch

Andraé Edward Crouch was an award-winning gospel musician, recording artist, songwriter, arranger, and producer. Born July 1, 1942 in Los Angeles, California, he was a key figure in the Christian Music movement of the 1960s, 1970s and into the early 80's.

> *Crouch who is credited with revolutionizing the sound of contemporary gospel music, was one of the first black gospel artists to crossover to mainstream contemporary Christian music, and his songs have become staples and popular hymns in churches all around the world.[661]*

Crouch died in January 2015 of a heart attack. He was 72 years old.

During my latter years as a student at Cumberland College in Williamsburg, Kentucky, I had the chance to meet and share a significant conversation with Andrae Crouch. At the time, his music moved me spiritually more than any sermon I had ever heard. His songs, "The Blood Will Never Lose Its Power," "My Tribute: To God Be the Glory," "I've Got Confidence," and "Through It All" were uplifting to a young man moving away for the first time from a sheltered suburban upbringing.

At the time of my attendance, Cumberland College, located in the wilds of Whitley County in Southeast Kentucky, was dominantly and conservatively Caucasian, even in its choice of church music. While more contemporary spiritual artists were up and coming, such as Larry Norman, Randy Stonehill, Petra, and Nancy Honeytree.

At that time (the late 70s), the rock beat and the folksy style of spiritual music was coming into vogue. Many churches still did not accept such styles—they hinted of rock and roll. Some even, equated drums with the evil influence of Satan. This was much to the dismay of Christian "rockers" like Larry

---

[661] *"The Journey,"* biography of Andrea Crouch from AndraeCrouch.com

Norman who asked the musical question, "Why should the devil have all the good music?"

It was a revolutionary time as church music was transitioning from the traditional hymns and country gospel to contemporary sounds for a new generation. From this groundswell of change entered Andrae Crouch into my pilgrimage, with his own unique blend of black gospel, R&B, pop rock and soul. The emphasis for me was on the word and experience of "soul."

Cumberland College was not only a predominantly white school, it might have been called "lily white." Williamsburg, Kentucky was not what anyone could call integrated. The school was known for its outreach to lower income families in the foothills of Appalachia. It became known for its focus on its nursing program and its emphasis on Christian education. Although it was a four-year liberal arts institution, most of its graduates at that time were moving into careers in nursing or "full time Christian service" in the Southern Baptist Convention.

Into this setting came Andrae Crouch and the Disciples to do an evening concert. The Gatliff Gymnasium was packed. The bleachers were filled with probably one of the whitest audiences Andrea had ever seen. That night, Andrea ignited the audience into a soulful extravaganza for over two and a half hours! Students were on their feet, raising their hands in the air, singing at the top of their voices, and clapping their hands. Although I had discovered Andrea's music soon after my conversion in a Baptist church and was always moved by it myself, most of my peers on campus were not so Andrea-savvy, preferring less "soulful" rhythms and rhyme. This was my first Crouch concert and I was amazed by how the man was able to move the crowd by his non-negotiable performance.

After the concert, I had the pleasure of meeting Andrea. When the crowd fanned out of the gym, he strolled out from backstage. His roadies were tearing down the lights and sound. He sat on the bleachers in a tee shirt and jeans and just "exhaled." I hurried and sat down beside him. I found him to be jovial and conversational with me. No celebrity pretense; he put me quite at ease.

"Andrea?" I asked. "How did you do that?"

"Do what?" Andrea responded.

"Get this crowd on its feet? Do you know just how to work a crowd?"

Andrea Crouch smiled and chuckled a bit. "Boy!, it's not about performance, it's about presence. It's called 'modulation!' [a change in musical tonality]. I can compose it into a song, but only the Holy Spirit of God can breathe it into the soul!"

"Many of the songs I've written speak to me as far as telling me the process of how to get through things. 'Through It All' in particular, lets me know you have a lot of experiences in life and you must learn to trust in God through Jesus."[662]

SELAH: A Change in Spiritual Tonality!

"We are (still) climbing Jacob's Ladder, children of the Lord."

"Jesus said to love/know God, with all your heart (intuitive, fascinating questions), with all your mind (observing the empirical evidence of His being), with all your soul (the revelatory experience of the inner "holy of holies" in the core of our being, and your strength (in the BE-Living of the persons God has designed us to be).

There is spiritual modulation in Psalm 46. The Psalmist described experiencing the challenges of life, as "like the earth changing…the mountains shaking… the roaring and foaming of the sea…" (Psalm 46:1-3/NRSV). The writer is aware of the wonky of the world! God does not prevent tribulation, but he is at hand when it comes, "providing greater encouragement from the assistance, than the pain from the tribulations."[663] Through it all, we may have confidence to learn and grow—to God be the glory!

Selah!

---

[662] Interview with Andrae Crouch (https://www.crosswalk.com/culture/music/andrae-crouch-through-it-all-540114.html)
[663] Chrysostom, *Commentary of the Psalms 46:1*

There follows in verses 4-7 a confession of faith. The writer professes a greater hope: "There is a river," a place of solitude where God is ever-present. No matter how long the darkness may linger, God will help when "the morning dawns!" God is with us "in our soul by the rising of spiritual light, the darkness that comes from ignorance and wickedness is destroyed."[664]

Finally, the Psalmist not only hopes for the Presence of God, but even in the midst of a wonderful world gone wonky he experiences insight: "Come and behold the works of the LORD!" God reveals "Himself" to humanity as the peacemaker: in the core of our being. "He causes wars to cease. He breaks the bow, shatters the spear, burns the chariots with fire…He makes wars to cease…" *(v. 8-9/NRSV)*. He "makes wars to cease" within the soul of the Psalmist, and conflict to cease in me!

SELAH. The Hebrew: סֶלָה, *selāh* is a word used seventy-four times in the Old Testament. It is noted seventy-one times in the *Psalms* and three times in *Habakkuk (3:1, 3, and 13/KJV)*. The meaning of the word is not easily interpreted. It is probably either a "liturgical-musical mark" or an interlude on the reading of the text: "rest, silence, listen." It can also be a sign of preparation for the sake of the impact of the following text.

Four times in this Psalm, *SELAH is* used as an extension of the passages. The musical command launches the passage from the Psalmist's view of earthly *chaos* to a "confession of faith: 'There is a holy place'" that lends ascension of the Psalmist to the awareness of God as Ultimate Love. Thus, the word, "selah!" resonates with the ascent to "modulation;" a spiritual "change in tonality."

At the closing of Psalm 46, God's voice is heard: "Be still and know I AM God." (Psalm 46:10/NRSV). The crescendo of this sojourn of the Psalmist is the Presence of God: the *"I AM"* GOD, who has led the likes of Jacob to the higher rungs of a phenomenal "ladder;" to envision a holy place and a heavenly realm! Likewise, "The Lord of hosts is *with us*; the God of Jacob is *our* refuge." (Psalm 46: 11/NRSV).

SELAH!

---

[664] Basil, *Homilies on the Psalms 18.5*

BENEDICTION

BE-Living: Modulating to a New Invocation

God of all and everything good,

Illumined by the life, teachings, death, and raising up of the Body of Christ,

i am humbled by Your grace and mercy;

i am awed in Your Holy Presence, your provisions, and protection;

i am hope-filled in Your promise of a prepared place for me...

That in the appointed time, i may not fear,

For "when i awake, i will be content beholding your face" (Psalm 17:15/ NRSV) ..._after all;_

In the interlude of my being, may I learn to apprehend your Presence,

Feast at the table of fellowship with others,

Love all that You love

In the fullness of creation,

And _BE-Live_ as the person you designed me to be...

Amen

BIBLIOGRAPHY

CLASSICS cited:

Thomas Aquinas "Summa Theologica"

Aristotle "Metaphysics"

Arndt, Johann "True Christianity"

Augustine "Confessions"

Avicenna "On Theology"

Basil, the Great "Homilies on the Psalms"

Bonaventure "The Soul's Journey into God"

John Cassian "Conferences"

Cervantes "Don Quixote"

John Climacus "The Ladder of Divine Ascent"

Chrysostom "Homilies"

Cyril of Alexandria "Commentary on Luke, Homily 49"

Charles Darwin "Autobiography: 1809-1882"

_____ "The Descent of Man"

Angela DeFoligno "Book of Divine Consolation"

Charles Dickens "A Christmas Carol"

Dionysius "Mystical Theology, Volume I"

Hans Derek "Treatise 1527"

Meister Eckhart "Sermons"

Gregory of Nyssa "The Life of Moses"

Walter Hilton "The Soul of Perfection"

St. John of the Cross "The Ascent of Mt. Carmel"

Julian of Norwich "Showings"

Abraham Isaac Kook "The Pangs of Cleansing"

Gottfried Leibniz "Monadology"

Maimonides "Guide for the Perplexed"

Martin Luther "Exposition of Ecclesiastes"

Madam Guyon "Union with God"

Mechthild of Magdeburg "The Flowing of Light from the Godhead, Book VI"

John Newton "Letters" / "Out of the Depths"

Origen "Homily XXVIII

William Paley, "Natural Theology"

Theresa of Avila "Little Flower"

Terese of Lisieux "The Story of a Soul"

Johannes Tauler "The Inner Way"

Jeremy Taylor "Works of"

John Wesley Ecclesiastes: Notes and Commentary Edinburgh: April 25, 1765

_____ "Exposition of the Sermon on the Mount"

SELECTED TITLES: _Researched and/or Cited:_

Allen, Steve But Seriously Amhurst, NJ: Prometheus, 1996

Baillie, John Readings NY: Charles Scribner's Sons, 1955

_____ The Idea of Revelation in Recent Thought NY: Columbia University Press, 1956

Barclay, William A Spiritual Autobiography Eerdmans, 1975

_____ Acts of the Apostles Edinburgh: St. Andrews, 1953

_____ Corinthians Philadelphia: Westminster, 1956

_____ Jesus as They Saw Him London: Harper and Row, 1962

_____ Revelation of John, Volume I Philadelphia: Westminster, 1959

_____ The Gospel of John Volume 1 Philadelphia: Westminster, 1956

Beasley-Murray, G.R. John Word Biblical Commentary Nashville: Thomas Nelson, 1999

Berry, Wendell Conversations Jackson, Mississippi: University, 2007

_____ Life is a Miracle Washington DC: Counterpoint, 2000

Begbie, Jeremy Music, Modernity and God: Essays in Listening Oxford: University Press, 2013

Buechner, Frederick The Longing for Home: Recollections and Reflections New York: HarperCollins, 1996

Bill, J. Brent Holy Silence Brewster, MASS: Paraclete, 2005

Brown, Robert McAfee Reflections On the Long Haul: a Memoir Louisville: Westminster/John Knox, 2005

Bruggemann, Walter Awed to Heaven, Rooted in Earth Minneapolis: Fortress Press, 2003

_____ Genesis Atlanta: John Knox, 1982

_____ Theology of the Old Testament Minneapolis: Abingdon, 1997

Brunner, Emil Revelation and Reason Wake Forest: Chanticleer, 1946

Brzezinski, Zbigniew Power and Principle: Memoirs 1977-1981 NY: Farrar, Straus, Giroux, 1982

Buber, Martin Between Man and Man England: McMillan, 1947

_____ I and Thou NY: Simon and Schuster, 1970

_____ Letters of Martin Buber NY: Schacken Books. 1991

_____ Moses: The Revelation and the Covenant London: Horowitz, 1958

Burger, Jeff (editor) Dylan on Dylan: Interviews and Encounters Chicago: Review Press, 2018

Campolo, Tony Letters to a Young Evangelical NY: Perseus, 2006

Carter, Jimmy Faith NY: Simon and Schuster, 2018

_____ Talking Peace: A Vision for the Next Generation NY: Dutton, 1993

Chaplin, Charles My Autobiography NY: Simon and Schuster, 1964

Clapton, Eric Autobiography NY: Broadway, 2007

Cobb, John Jesus' Abba: The God Who has not Failed Minneapolis: Fortress Press, 2015

Comte-Sponville, Andrea The Little Book of Atheist Spirituality NY: Viking, 2007

Copland, Aaron What to Listen for in Music New York: McGraw-Hill Company, 1957

Davies, Paul The Mind of God: The Scientific Basis for a Rational World NY: Simon and Schuster, 1993

Dawkins, Richard The God Delusion NY: Houghton Mifflin, 2006

_____ Science in the Soul: Selective Writings of a Passionate Rationalist NY: Random House, 2017

_____ The Selfish Gene Oxford: University, 1976

Day, Dorothy Selected Writings NY: Alfred A. Knopf, 1983

DeChardin, Pierrre Theilhard Hymn of the Universe NY: Harper and Row, 1961

Dillard, Annie Reader and Selected Work NY: HarperCollins, 1994

_____ Teaching a Stone to Talk: Expeditions and Encounters NY: Harper and Row, 1982

Donne, John Complete Poetry and Prose NY: Modern Library, 1952

Dubal, David Evenings with Horowitz NY: Birch Lane Press, 1991

Einstein, Albert The Ultimate Quotable Einstein Princeton: University Press, 1951, 1930, 1934

Elliott, T. S. Collected Poems: 1909-1962 Harcourt Brace Jovanovich, 1991

Farrar, Austin A Faith of Our Own Cleveland: World, 1960

Flew, Antony Atheistic Humanism Buffalo, NY: Prometheus Books, 1993

Feynman, Michele (ed) Letters of Richard Feynman NY: Perseus, 2005

Feynman, Richard The Meaning of It All: Thoughts of a Citizen Scientist Reading, MASS: Perseus, 1998

_____ The Pleasure of Finding Things Out Cambridge: Perseus Books, 1999

_____ What Do You Care What Other People Think? Further Adventures of A Curious Character New York: W. W. Norton and Company, 1988

Foster, Russell G. & Leon Kreitzan Rhythms of Life New Haven: Yale University Press, 2004

Gandhi, Mohanndas K. All Men are Brothers Narajivan Press, 1960

George, Timothy Galatians Nashville: Broadman and Holman, 1994

Glenn, John A Memoir NY: Bantam, 1999

Gould, Stephen Jay Rock of Ages: Science and Religion in the Fullness of Life NY: Ballantine, 2002

_____ An Urchin in the Storm: Essays and Books and Ideas London: WW Norton, 1987

_____ The Richness of Life: Essential Writings edited by Steven Rose New York: W. W. Norton and Company, 2006

Graetz, Robert S., Jr. A White Preacher's Message on Race and Reconciliation: Based on His Experiences Beginning with the Montgomery Bus Boycott Louisville: NewSouth Books, 2006

Greene, Brian The Elegant Universe: Superstrings, Hidden Dimensions, and the Quest for the Ultimate Theory New York: W. W. Norton, 1999

Griffin, John Howard The Hermitage Journals Kansas City: Andrews and McMeel, 1981

Griffiths, Bede The Golden String Springfield, ILL: Templegate, 1980

Guiterrez, Gustavo Essential Writings (ed. James B. Nickoloff) Maryknoll, NY: Orbis, 1996

_____ The God of Life Maryknoll, NY: Orbis, 1991

_____ On Job: God-Talk and the Suffering of the Innocent Maryknoll, NY: Orbis, 1985

Harrington, Bob The Chaplain of Bourbon Street Garden City, NJ: Doubleday and Company, 1969

Harris, Sam Waking Up: Searching for Spirituality Without Religion NY: Simon & Schuster, 2014

Hart, Moss and George S. Kaufman You Can't Take It With You A play in three acts, 1937

Patrick Hart (ed) The Legacy of Thomas Merton Kalamazoo, MI: Cistercian, 1986

Haught, John Annual Journal of Physics Volume 64, Issue 12, 1996

_____ God and the New Atheism Louisville: Westminster/John Knox, 2008

_____ Science and Religion: From Conflict to Conversation NY: Paulist Press, 1995

_____ What is God? How to Think about the Divine NY: Paulist Press, 1986

Hawking, Stephen W. A Brief History of Time Bantem Dell, 1988

_____ The Theory of Everything: The Origin and Fate of the Universe Beverly Hills: New Millennium Press, 2002

Herschel, Abraham Joshua I Asked for Wonder NY: Crossroad, 1983

_____ Man's Quest for God: Studies in Prayer and Symbolism Santa Fe, NM: Aurora Press, 1954

Hick, John An Interpretation of Religion New Haven: Yale, 1988

_____ Death and Eternal Life Louisville: Westminster/John Knox Press, 1976

_____ The Fifth Dimension: An Exploration of the Spiritual Realm Oxford: Oneworld, 1999

Hirshfeld, Alan The Electric Life of Michael Faraday New York: Walker and Company, 2006

Hitchens, Christopher god is not Great: How Religion Poisons Everything NY: Twelve, 2007

Hoyle, Fred The Anthropic Cosmological Principle Oxford: Clarendon Press, 1988

Hubble, Edwin The Realm of the Nebulae New Haven: Yale, 2013

Janzen, J. Gerald Job Atlanta: John Knox, 1985

Johnson, Timothy Luke Acts of the Apostles Collegeville, MN: Liturgical Press, 1992

Jung, Carl Interviews and Encounters Princeton: University, 1977

_____ Memories, Dreams, and Reflections NY: Vintage Press, 1989

_____ The Spirit in Man, Art, and Literature Princeton: University, 1966

Kandinsky, Wassily Concerning the Spiritual in Art and Painting in Particular NY: Wittenborn and Schultz, 1947

Kanigel, Robert The Man Who Knew Infinity London: Washington Square Press, 1991

Kant, Immanuel Critique of Practical Reason Create Space, 2010

Keating, Thomas Fruits and Gifts of the Spirit NY: Lantern Books, 2007

Keller, Helen Light in My Darkness Westchester, PA: Chrysalis, 1998

Kelly, Matthew The Call of Wild Geese: Monastic Homilies Kalamazoo, MI: Cistercian, 1996

King, Coretta Scott My Life with Martin Luther King, Jr. NY: Holt, Rinehart, and Winston, 1969

King, Martin Luther Jr. A Knock at Midnight: Sermons (edited by Carson Claybourne) NY: Time Warner, 1998

_____ Papers, Volume Seven "To Save the Soul of America" University of California, 2014

_____ Stride Toward Freedom NY: Harper and Row, 1958

_____ Thou Dear God: Prayers that Open Hearts and Spirits (edited by Lewis V. Baldwin) Boston: Beacon Press, 2012

Kreeft, Peter Prayer: The Great Conversation San Francisco: Ignatius Press, 1991

Lackner, Stephan Peaceable Nature: An Optimistic View of Life on Earth San Francisco: Harper & Row, 1984

Langer, Laurence L. (ed.) Art from the Ashes: A Holocaust Anthology Oxford: University, 1995

L'Engle, Madeleine A Stone for a Pillow: Journeys with Jacob Wheaton, ILL: Harold Shew Publishers, 1986

Lewis, C. S. Collected Letters, Vol III San Francisco: Harper, 2007

_____ God in the Dock Grand Rapids: Eerdmans, 1970

_____ Mere Christianity San Francisco: HarperOne, 2015

_____ Miracles NY: MacMillan, 1948

_____ Surprised by Joy London: Geoffrey Bles, 1955

MacDonald, George In the Pulpit Whitethorn, CA: Johannesen, 1999

_____ Letters edited by Glenn Edward Sadler Grand Rapids: William B. Eerdmans, 1994

Macquarrie, John In Search of Diety: The Gifford Lectures, 1983-84 London: SCM Press, 1984

_____ Jesus Christ in Modern Thought London: SCM Press, 1990

_____ On Being a Theologian London: SCM Press, 1999

_____ Principles of Christian Theology London: Canterbury Press, 1977

_____ Theology, Church, and Ministry NY: Crossroad, 1986

_____ Two Worlds Are Ours Minneapolis: Fortress Press, 2004

Manson, William The Gospel of Luke London: Hodder and Stoughton, 1942

Marsalis, Wynton On Music NY: W.W. Norton Company, 1995

Marx, Arthur Red Skelton: An Unauthorized Biography NY: EP Dutton, 1979

Marx, Harpo Harpo Speaks! New Jersey: Limelight Books, 2008

Maslow, Abraham Motivation and Personality NY: Harper, 1954

McGrath, Alister The Journey: A Pilgrim in the Lands of the Spirits NY: Doubleday, 1999

Merton, Thomas The Ascent to Truth London: Burnst and Oates, 1951

_____ Collected Poems NY: New Directions, 1977

_____ Disputed Questions NY: Farrar, Straus, and Cudaly, 1960

_____ New Seeds of Contemplation Abbey at Gethsemani, 1961

_____ No Man is an Island Boston: Shambala, 2005

_____ On Peace New York: McCall Publishing, 1968

_____ Selected Essays Maryknoll, NY: Orbis, 2013

_____ The Seven Story Mountain NY: Harcourt, Brace, and Company, 1948

_____ The Strange Lands Abbey of Gethsemani, 1957

Mitchell, Ed The Way of Apollo: An Apollo Astronaut's Journey Through the Material and Mystical Worlds NY: Putnams, 1996

Mitchell, George J. Making Peace: The Story of the Ireland Peace Accords NY: Alfred A. Knopf, 1999

Moltmann, Jurgen In the End—the Beginning: The Life of Hope Minneapolis: Fortress Press, 2004

Moses, John The Sacrifice of God: A Wholistic Approach to Atonement Hymns Ancient and Modern, Ltd., 2012

_____ One Equal Light: Anthology of John Donne Norwich: Canterbury, 2003

Mother Teresa The Private Writings of the Saint of Calcutta edited by Brian Kolodiejchuk, M.C. New York: Doubleday, 2007

Muir, John Mountaineering Essays edited by Gibbs Smith Salt Lake City: Peregrine Smith Books, 1980

Myers, Conrad The Spirituality of Comedy: Comic Heroism in a Tragic World London: Transaction, 1996

Nelson, Kevin The Spiritual Doorway in the Brain: A Neurologists Search for the God Experience New York: Dutton, 2011

Newell, J. Phillip Christ of the Celts: The Healing of Creation Glasgow: Wild Goose Publishing, 2008

Niebuhr, Reinhold Essential Writings New Haven: Yale, 1986

Nouwen, Henri Our Greatest Gift: Meditations on Dying and Caring NY: Harper Collins, 1991

_____ Reader NY: Doubleday, 1997

_____ Spiritual Direction NY: Harper Collins, 2006

_____ Spiritual Formation NY: Harper Collins, 2010

Oates, Wayne E. Nurturing Silence in a Noisy Heart Garden City, NY: Doubleday, 1979

_____ The Psychology of Religion Waco, TX: Word, 1973

Otto, Rudolf The Idea of the Holy Oxford: University, 1958

Peacocke, Arthur Paths from Science Towards God: The End of All Our Exploring Oxford: Oneworld, 2001

Pennington, M. Basil Seeking His Mind Brewster, MASS: Paraclete Press, 2002

Piston, Walter Harmony NY: W. W. Norton & Company, 1969

Plant, W. Gunther Genesis: Commentary on the Torah NY: Union of American Hebrew Congregations, 1981

Polhill, John The Acts of the Apostles Nashville: Broadman, 1992

Polkinghorne, John The God of Hope and the End of the World London: Society for Promoting Christian Knowledge, 2002

_____ and Nicolas Beale Questions of Truth Louisville: Westminster/ John Knox, 2009

Rahner Karl The Practice of Faith: A Handbook of Contemporary Spirituality NY: Crossroad, 2015

Rashdall, Hastings The Theory of Good and Evil, Volume II Oxford: Clarendon Press, 1907

Rees, Martin On the Future: Prospects for Humanity Princeton: University Press, 2018

Rice, Anne Called Out of Darkness: a spiritual confession New York: Alfred A. Knopf, 2008

Rohr, Richard and Andreas Ebert The Enneagram: A Christian Perspective NY: Crossroad, 2004

_____ What the Mystics Know NY: Crossroad, 2015

Ruse, Michael Can a Darwinian Be a Christian: The Relationship Between Science and Religion Cambridge: University Press, 2001

Rust, Eric C. Religion, Revelation, & Reason Macon, GA: Mercer University, 1981

Sagan, Carl The Varieties of Scientific Experience: A Personal View of the Search for God NY: Penguin Books, 2006

Sayers, Dorothy Creed or Chaos Manchester: Sophia Institute Press, 1949

_____ Letters to a Diminished Church Nashville: Thomas Nelson, 2004

_____ The Mind of the Maker London: Continuum Books, 2004

_____ Spiritual Writings London: Society for Promoting Christian Knowledge, 1993

Schleiermacher, Frederick On Religion: Speeches to it's Contemporary Despisers Cambridge, 1988

_____ The Christian Faith Philadelphia: Fortress Press, 1976

Schultz, Mona Lisa Awakening Intuition: Using Your Mind-Body Network for Instinct and Healing New York: Harmony Books, 1998

Schweitzer, Albert Out of My Life and Thought NY: Holt, Rinehart, and Winston Inc., 1933

Sheldrake, Rupert Science and Spiritual Practices: Transformative Experiences and Their Effects on Our Bodies, Brains, and Health Berkeley, California: Counterpoint, 2017

Shoemaker, Rick Dissecting the Serpent: Exposing Twenty-One of the Devil's Most Destructive Devices Bloomington, IN: CrossBooks, 2012

Simmel, Georg Essays on Religion New Haven: Yale University Press, 1997

Smith, Huston The Soul of Christianity NY: Harper Collins, 1991

_____ Tales of Wonder: Adventures Chasing the Divine NY: Harper Collins, 2009

Soelle, Dorothy Theology for Skeptics Minneapolis: Fortress Press, 1995

_____ The Silent Cry: Mysticism and Resistance Minneapolis: Fortress Press, 2001

Solzhenitsyn, Alexander Reader Wilmington, DE: ISI, 2016

Stephanek, Mattie J. T. Hope Through Heartsongs NY: Hyperion, 2002

_____ Just Peace: A Message of Hope Kansas City: Andrews McNeel, 2006

Stassen, Glen Just Peacemaking: Transforming Initiatives for Justice and Peace Louisville: Westminster/John Knox, 1992

Stern, Isaac My First 79 Years NY: Alfred A. Knopf, 1999

Stuart, Jesse The Kingdom Within: A Spiritual Autobiography NY: McGraw Hill, 1979

_____ The World of Jesse Stuart: Selected Poems NY: McGraw Hill, 1975

Suter, John Wallace Prayers of the Spirit New York: Harper and Brothers, 1943

Swinburne, Richard Is There a God? Oxford: University, 1996

Talbot, John Michael The Music of Creation NY: Jeremy P. Tarcher/Putnam, 1999

Teluskin, Joseph Biblical Literacy NY: William Morrow and Company, 1977

Thurman, Howard A Strange Freedom Boston: Beacon, 1998

_____ Deep River Richmond, Indiana: Friends United, 1975

_____ For the Inward Journey: The Writings of Howard Thurman selected by Anne Spencer Thurman Richmond, Indiana: Friends United Meeting, 1984

_____ Meditations of the Heart Boston: Beacon, 1981

Tipler, Francis J. The Physics of Christianity NY: Doubleday, 2007

Tillich, Paul The Shaking of the Foundations NY: Charles Scribner's Sons, 1948

_____ Systematic Theology Volumes I and II Chicago: University, 1963

Tolkien, J. R. R. Letters Humphrey Carpenter (ed.) Boston: Houghton Mifflin, 1981

Torrey, R. A. The Person and Work of the Holy Spirit Grand Rapids: Zondervan, 1985

Tolstoy, Leo The Lion and the Honeycomb: The Religious Writings San Francisco: Harper and Row, 1987

_____ Living Thoughts London: Cassell and Company, 1948

_____ Letters (edited by R. F. Christian) Charles Scribner's Sons, 1991

Trueblood, Elton The Company of the Committed NY: Harper & Row, 1961

Twain, Mark Collected Tales, Sketches, Speeches and Essays: 1852-1890 Library of America Series

Underhill, Evelyn Mysticism Scarborough, Ontario: Meridian, 1974

_____ Practical Mysticism Columbus, OH: Ariel Press, 1986

_____ The Ways of the Spirit NY: Crossroad, 1996

Van Dyke, Dick My Lucky Life In and Out of Show Business: A Memoir New York: Crown, 2011

Van Rad, Gerhard The Old Testament, Volume I NY: Harper and Row, 1962

Victorinus, Marius Homily on Philippians Bibliotheca Scriptorium Leipzip: Teubner, 1824

Vonnegut, Kurt Cat's Cradle (1963) New York: The Library of America, 2011

Ward, Keith Are Faith and Reason Incompatible? London: Darton, Longman, and Todd, 2012

_____ Divine Action: Examining God's Role in an Open and Emergent Universe London: Templeton Foundation Press, 1990

_____ The Evidence for God: The Case for the Existence of the Spiritual Dimension London: Darton, Longman, and Todd, 2014

_____ God: A Guide for the Perplexed Oxford: Oneworld, 1986

_____ God, Chance, and Necessity Oxford: Oneworld, 2001

_____ Morality, Autonomy, and God London: Oneworld, 2013

_____ Re-thinking Christianity Oxford: Oneworld, 2007

_____ The Mystery of Christ: meditations and prayers London: spck, 2018

Watts, John D. W. (ed.) How I Changed My Mind: Essays by Retired Professors of the Southern Baptist Theological Seminary Louisville: Review and Expositor, 1993

Weatherhead, Leslie The Christian Agnostic Nashville: Abingdon, 1985

_____ Over His Own Signature NY: Abingdon, 1955

_____ Time for God NY: Abingdon, 1967

Steven Weinberg Dreams of a Final Theory New York: Pantheon Books, 1992

_____ The First Three Minutes New York: Bantam Bools, 1979

Welborn, Laurence First Epistle of Clement Anchor Bible: Paulist Press, 1946

Whitehead, Alfred North Science and the Modern World: Lectures Pelican Mentor Books, 1925

Wicks, Robert J. and Richard D. Parsons Clinical Handbook of Pastoral Counseling NY: Integration, 1993

Wiesel, Elie Memoirs: All Rivers Run to the Sea NY: Alfred A. Knopf, 1995

_____ Memoirs: And the Sea is Never Full NY: Alfred A. Knopf, 1999

Wilde, Larry The Great Comedians Talk Comedy NY: Citadel Press, 1968

Wilson, Edward O. Consilience: The Unity of Knowledge NY: Alfred A. Knopf, 1998

_____ The Future of Life NY: Alfred A. Knopf, 2002

Wilson, Woodrow Essential Writings and Speeches of the Scholar-President edited by Mario R. Dinunzio New York University Press, 2006

Wink, Walter The Powers that Be NY: Doubleday, 1998

Williams, Charles The Descent of the Dove: A Short History of the Holy Spirit Vancouver: Regent College, 1939

Winters, Jonathan Winter's Tales: Stories and Observations of the Unusual NY: Random House, 1987

Wright, N. T. The Challenge of Jesus Wheaton, ILL: Intervarsity Press, 1999

Young, Andrew A Way Out of No Way: Spiritual Memoirs Nashville: Thomas Nelson, 1994

_____ An Easy Burden: The Civil Rights Movement and the Transformation of America

New York: HarperCollins, 1996

BIOGRAPHICAL INFORMATION

Brian Shoemaker graduated from Fairmont East High School in Kettering, Ohio. He received his Bachelor of Arts Degree from Cumberland College in Williamsburg, Kentucky, and both his Master of Divinity and Doctor of Ministry degrees from the Southern Baptist Theological Seminary in Louisville, Kentucky. His continuing education includes studies in Christian Spirituality and Science & Religion at both Bellarmine University in Louisville and University of Oxford in the United Kingdom.

Dr. Shoemaker has been the pastor of three churches, and has served in many mission ventures in various locations in the United States, the UK, and India. He was designated a "Master Teacher" by the Association of Christian Schools International, having taught biblical and religious studies for nearly two decades at a major secondary school. He continues to teach in various church venues.

Among his merits include the following awards and honors: High School Senior Superlatives: "Funniest Senior" & "Most Likely to Become a Minister" (1974), Who's Who Among Students in American Colleges & Universities (1979), T.J.Roberts Cumberland College Campus Leadership Award (1979), Outstanding Young Men of America (1979), Personalities of the South (1984), D.A.R.E. "Friend of the Year" (Scott County, KY) (1989), Who's Who Among American Teachers (2002, 2005, 2006 & 2007), Outstanding American Teachers Honor Roll (2005, 2006, & 2007), Christian Academy of Louisville Yearbook Dedication(2008), and Who's Who Among American Professionals (2011, 2017). Shoemaker also holds a "Lifetime Teaching Certification" and a "Master Teacher" designation from the Association of Christian Schools International.

Brian Shoemaker has been, or is presently, involved in the following civic and religious activity: the American Association of Christian Counselors, the Association for Applied and Therapeutic Humor, the Honorable Order of Kentucky Colonels, Kentuckians for the Commonwealth, the Louisville & Jefferson County Human Relations Council, ("Race Relations Conference"), the Cumberland Regional Lyric Theatre, the National Forensic League, Friends of the Jimmy Carter Center, the Red Skelton Museum, the Wendell Berry Center, and the University of the Cumberlands Alumni Board of Directors.

The title of Dr. Shoemaker's doctoral dissertation is: *Establishing a Pastoral Care Network for Persons with AIDS in the Miami Valley, Ohio" (1996)*. Along with this book, several articles and OpEds have been published in magazines and newspapers. He has written several plays that have been produced on the high school stage. *Beyond Believing* is his first major work encompassing over fifty years of spiritual devotion and ministerial practice.

He is the father of one son, Andrew James-Vincent, a graduate of both Asbury University and the Louisville Presbyterian Seminary. He considers Andrew a motivating influence in the completion of this project and an example of perseverance of meeting the challenges of life with an abiding faith.

Dr. Shoemaker is a prolific speaker, teacher, pastoral caregiver, and humorist. He and his wife, Rhonda, offer a ministry of music and comedy for churches, civic groups, schools, and comedy clubs. One of the highlights of such performances was when they were booked to share their life-together story at the Red Skelton Performing Arts Center in Vincennes, Indiana.

Permissions Granted

Works by Albert Einstein from THE ULTIMATE QUOTABLE EINSTEIN provided by a License Agreement with Princeton University Press and Copyright Clearance Center.

CALVIN & HOBBES provided by a License Agreement copyright with 1995 Watterson. Reprinted with permission of ANDREWS MCMEEL SYNDICATION.

Excerpts from "The Kingdom Within" by Jesse Stuart used with permission from the Jesse Stuart Foundation, 4440 13th Street, Ashland, KY 41102.

Poem, "Those I Want in Heaven with Me Should There Be Such a Place" from the anthology, FROM THE MOUNTAIN, FROM THE VALLEY by James Still, permission to reproduce and distribute by University Press of Kentucky.

THE COLLECTED POEMS OF THOMAS MERTON permission to use by New Direction Publishing Corporation, 80 Eighth Avenue New York, NY. 10011.

Permission to use speech by Paul Davies, from Beyond Center for Fundamental Concepts in Science, Office of Professor Paul Davies, Arizona State University, Tempe, Arizona 85287. Email dated October 9, 2019.

Permission to use the poem, "For Our World" by Mattie J. T. Stepanek. Granted by Laura J. Bauer, Executive Director, and Dr. Jenni Stepanek, Founder, of the Mattie J. T. Stepanek Foundation P.O. Box 111 402 King Farm Blvd., #125 Rockville, MD 20850. Message dated, October 19, 2019.

Permission to use the song, "Singing Lessons," words by Judy Collins. Produced by Universal Music Group/The Wildflower Company (ASCAP).

CPSIA information can be obtained
at www.ICGtesting.com
Printed in the USA
FSHW020752030920
73537FS